DIVINE FAITH

This is an important book on the topic of the rational grounding of Christian faith, that everyone involved in the field should read. It opens new pathways in the history of its topic, and in the consideration of the philosophical and theological questions that are crucial to it.

Romanus Cessario, O.P. Professor of Theology,
Saint John's Seminary, Brighton, Massachusetts

Using philosophical and theological reflection, this book explores the rational grounding for Christian faith, inquiring into the basis for believing the Christian revelation, and using the answers to give an account of Christian faith itself. Setting the discussion in the context of the history of views on revelation, *Divine Faith* makes an original contribution to historiography and draws out hitherto unnoticed affinities between Catholic and Protestant thought. Re-examining the question from the beginning by asking how it is that the Christian revelation is made, Lamont then looks at the fundamental philosophical issues concerning the nature of knowledge and the reasonableness of belief in testimony that are crucial to an understanding of Christian belief. Through theological considerations on the relations of grace and the church, and new advances in the philosophy of belief in testimony and how God speaks to communicate the Christian religion, this book offers an original and powerful account of the nature of Christian belief.

ASHGATE NEW CRITICAL THINKING IN RELIGION, THEOLOGY AND BIBLICAL STUDIES

The *Ashgate New Critical Thinking in Religion, Theology and Biblical Studies* series brings high quality research monograph publishing back into focus for authors, international libraries, and student, academic and research readers. Headed by an international editorial advisory board of acclaimed scholars spanning the breadth of religious studies, theology and biblical studies, this open-ended monograph series presents cutting-edge research from both established and new authors in the field. With specialist focus yet clear contextual presentation of contemporary research, books in the series take research into important new directions and open the field to new critical debate within the discipline, in areas of related study, and in key areas for contemporary society.

Other Titles in the Series:

John's Gospel as Witness
The Development of the Early Christian Language of Faith
Alexander S. Jensen

The Ecclesiology of Stanley Hauerwas
A Christian Theology of Liberation
John B. Thomson

Divine Faith

JOHN R.T. LAMONT
University of St Andrews, UK

ASHGATE

Published by
Ashgate Publishing Limited
Gower House
Croft Road
Aldershot
Hampshire GU11 3HR
England

Ashgate Publishing Company
Suite 420
101 Cherry Street
Burlington, VT 05401-4405
USA

Ashgate website: http://www.ashgate.com

British Library Cataloguing in Publication Data
Lamont, John R.T.
   Divine faith. – (Ashgate new critical thinking in religion,
   theology and biblical studies)
   I. Theology, Doctrinal 2. Faith
   I. Title
   230

Library of Congress Cataloging-in-Publication Data
Lamont, John R.T., 1964–
   Divine faith / John R.T. Lamont.
      p.cm. – (Ashgate new critical thinking in religion, theology and biblical
   studies)
   Includes bibliographical references and index.
   ISBN 0-7546-3709-3 (alk. paper)
      1. Christianity–Philosophy. 2. Philosophy and religion. I. Title. II. Series.

   BR100.L265 2003
   230'042–dc21

                                                              2003048196

ISBN 0 7546 3709 3

Printed and bound in Great Britain by MPG Books Ltd, Bodmin, Cornwall

Contents

Acknowledgements

I have contracted many debts of gratitude in the course of writing this book. The most important intellectual debt is to Professor Richard Swinburne, who supervised the D. Phil. thesis from which the book emerged. This debt is to his own ideas, as well as to the scrupulous care with which he performed his work as a supervisor, and the valuable insights he provided into the subjects I discuss. My D. Phil. examiners, Dr Richard Cross and Dr Martin Stone, were most helpful in their discussion of my thesis, and made suggestions that were crucial in remedying its shortcomings. Fr Fergus Kerr OP also kindly read the thesis, and made useful suggestions. Dr Mark Edwards, Dr John Hyman and Dr Joseph Shaw offered their help with sections of the book. Dr Angus Bowie provided assistance with translations from the Greek. Any theological merits that the book might have will be largely due to the late Fr Jean-Marie Tillard OP, who was my mentor as a theologian. I am grateful to the editor of *New Blackfriars* for permission to reprint material from my article 'The nature of revelation' (July/August 1991) on pp. 9–10, and to the editor of *The Thomist* for permission to reprint material from my article 'Plantinga on Belief' (October 2001) on pp. 119–20, 160–5, and 211–12. All Scriptural quotations in this book are from the Revised Standard Version.

I owe a great deal to my family for their practical support, especially to my mother, to whom I dedicate this book.

John Lamont

Chapter 1

Fundamental Assumptions

To be a Christian means having faith. This is because there is a Christian gospel, a message, that originates in God, and being a Christian involves accepting this message. This acceptance includes not just believing the contents of the message to be true, but also holding that the message comes from God, and accepting it on account of its coming from God. This book will attempt the task of answering the question: what is the rational motivation that leads Christians to accept the Christian gospel? If it is successful in this attempt, it will turn out to have also furnished an answer to the question: what is the nature of Christian faith?

Some people will not accept the assumptions behind the first question, denying that Christianity involves accepting a message, the gospel, because it in some way originates in God. The attitude taken to this objection – that of assuming its falsity at the outset – reflects the nature of this book. It is an exercise in philosophical theology, and the theology in question is Christian theology; not only that, it is Christian theology of a particular sort (as all Christian theology must be). The practice of Christian theology involves accepting certain starting points on faith. There may be something to be said in defence of these starting points, as there is for the assumption made in the paragraph above, but if one begins to make a defence of something one takes to be a datum of faith, one is no longer engaging in theology: one is engaging in apologetics instead. That is not my purpose.[1]

This theological standpoint is not dictated simply by my own beliefs, or by the beliefs of the audience towards which this book is directed, but by the nature of the task in hand. When recent philosophers have talked about the rational motivation for religious faith, what they have generally understood by religious faith is belief in the existence of God. For an investigation of this sort of faith, a purely philosophical method can and perhaps ought to be used. But when religious faith is understood in its more ordinary meaning, that of belief in and adherence to a particular religion, a purely philosophical method is no longer always appropriate.

---

[1] This is not to say that the theological account of faith arrived at need not be helpful for apologetics. It is clearly important from an apologetic standpoint that one's theological account of faith be such as to present faith as theoretically and practically rational. But this is necessary from a theological standpoint as well; and this theological standpoint, which is the one taken here, is prior to the apologetic one, since we have to decide what it is that we believe before we begin to defend it. Admittedly some theologians would deny this priority on the grounds that the reason for which we believe and the reasons we give to unbelievers to defend the rationality of our belief must be one and the same. The argument of this book will show why I do not think that these must be the same.

That is because certain religions contain teachings about why it is that they should be believed, and the form of Christianity that I will be considering is one of them. A rational motivation for believing this form of Christianity must conform to these teachings, or else it will fail to be rational. Were it not to so conform, it would be undermining itself, by endorsing a set of teachings that condemns it as mistaken.

Of course, this line of argument is not needed to justify the taking of a theological approach, since it would be quite legitimate to simply adopt such an approach because one is engaging in Christian theology. It is, rather, concerned to point out the necessity of such an approach in tackling the question at issue.

The sort of Christian theology that I will engage in is a broadly Catholic one. ('Broadly Catholic' is a term chosen to distinguish my approach from a specifically Roman Catholic one, a distinction made for reasons that will be discussed below.) It will not argue for the truth of the teachings of the Christian faith, but rather assume that they are true; and it will take a certain position on what these teachings are. I will assume that the Christian faith is what the Christian Church says it is, and that the teaching of the Christian Church is to be found in the teaching of visible bodies of Christians. Rather than assuming that a particular Christian body is or speaks for the Church, I will offer criteria for determining what the Christian Church teaches that will be true on any plausible view that maintains that a particular visible Christian body (or bodies) is or speaks for the Church of Christ. I take the message of the Scriptures to be the Christian faith that the Church teaches. I take it that what is asserted by the councils held by both the Roman Catholic Church and the Orthodox Church to be ecumenical is Church teaching. (It is of course true that in order to understand what these councils taught, we must take into account their aims, context and reception.) I hold the principal liturgies of the Eastern and Western Churches, and the sacramental practice and theology of these Churches, to be evidence for what is taught by the Church. I hold the views of the Fathers of the Church to be evidence for what is taught by the Church. The Fathers were those Christian saints and theologians of the first Christian millennium whose wisdom and holiness were widely recognized, and whose views on Christian doctrine were widely held to have authority.[2] Some of these saints have been taken to have more authority than others; particularly influential ones that should be mentioned are St. Ambrose and St. Augustine in the West, and St. Athanasius, St. John Chrysostom and the Cappadocian Fathers in the East. Acceptance of a view by the Fathers gives better evidence for that view's being a teaching of the Christian Church when it is more widely held, and when the Fathers who hold it are more diverse in theological, cultural, geographical and temporal terms. Finally, I will assume that the teachings discoverable by these criteria form a coherent whole, any part of which may be used to interpret any other part.

This starting point encompasses a deep and wide tradition. It is not possible to enumerate here all the beliefs that are contained in it. Nor even is it possible to describe all the parts of it that this book will assume, because the tradition is not divisible into independent theses whose truth can be established individually. The

---

[2] For an account of the evolution of the concept of a Father of the Church, see E. Schillebeeckx, *Revelation and Theology*, vol. I, 1967.

assumptions underlying the arguments I will make should however be familiar to those who are acquainted with this tradition. And although a complete account of these assumptions cannot be given here, I can indicate the ones that form the main foundation for this book. As well as the conception of theological method that has been given, I assume certain doctrinal positions that form part of Catholic tradition. The principal ones assumed are the following: there is one God, all-powerful, all-knowing, and perfectly good, creator of everything that exists aside from himself. This one God is three persons, Father, Son and Holy Spirit. The human race that God has created is fallen and estranged from him. This fall and estrangement means that humans are on their own incapable of living good and just lives, and of being in friendship with God. It is only divine grace that can enable them to be good people and to be in a state of friendship with God. Divine grace consists in God's conferring some good upon humans, when this good is something that cannot be acquired other than through God's direct and immediate action, and whose conferral is a free gift from God that cannot be compelled or deserved in justice. God has chosen to redeem humanity through the incarnation of the Son, the Second Person of the Trinity, as Jesus Christ, who is the Second Person, true God and true man. All divine grace given to fallen humanity comes through this incarnation and the events involved in it, and chiefly through the death and resurrection of Christ. This grace includes the gift of a message, the Christian gospel, and the gift of belief in this message. Grace is also given through the sacraments of the Church. I will not give a list of these sacraments, but only state that they include baptism and the Eucharist.

This conception of theological method would be accepted by Roman Catholics, Orthodox and many other Oriental Christians, some Anglicans, and some non-Anglican Protestants.[3] I call it 'broadly Catholic' to bring out the fact that it is not specifically Roman Catholic. Not that I think there is anything wrong with a Roman Catholic theological approach. I am a Roman Catholic myself, and accept all the teachings of my church. But aside from the fact that adopting a Roman Catholic rather than a broadly Catholic theological message would not actually make much difference to the arguments I offer, I have an ecumenical purpose in mind in this book. I want to arrive at an account of Christian faith that will be acceptable to Christians of different communions, and will bring home to them what they already hold in common. The similarities between Catholic, Protestant and Orthodox accounts of faith that will come to light in the historical chapters that follow – specifically, the similarities between the view of St. Thomas Aquinas and that of the Puritan theologian John Owen, and the affinities between the Thomist view of faith and that of Eastern Fathers like St. John Chrysostom – offer hope that this aspiration can be realized. (Many of the conclusions arrived at in this book will

---

[3] An example of a theological approach of this sort can be found in the ARCIC Final Report's document on Authority in the Church: 'In its mission to proclaim and safeguard the Gospel the Church has the obligation and the competence to make declarations in matters of faith ... In both our traditions the appeal to Scripture, to the creeds, to the Fathers, and to the definitions of the councils of the early Church is regarded as basic and normative'. *ARCIC: The Final Report*, 1982, p. 61.

follow from a narrower base of assumptions than the one proposed here. For example, the positions arrived at on the existence of divine speaking and the nature of divine faith should be acceptable to Protestants who accept only the Scriptures as a norm for Christian belief.)

Something else should be said about the method pursued in this book. It differs from many works of contemporary philosophical theology in giving a fairly extensive historical overview of past thought on the subject it discusses. This overview can be justified at the lowest level by the fact that it provides information that will be of interest to the reader (very likely of more interest than my own reflections), and that is not readily available elsewhere. But there is a more important reason that has motivated its inclusion, which is that it is essential for a proper discussion of the topic that is being addressed. This is not just because a historical survey will make available the resources of past thought on the question in hand. It is because the concepts in the question itself – those of faith, rationality, belief – are not straightforward and immediately accessible ones. They have developed in the course of a long history, during which they have taken significantly different forms, and they cannot be properly understood without looking at that history. This plea of necessity is indeed the only thing that could justify the attempt to give a historical overview, however modest, of a topic that has been one of the great concerns of Western civilization. I am aware of the inadequacy of my knowledge and abilities for this task, and can only hope that they will suffice for the production of work that has at least some value.

This book, as a consequence of its subject matter, addresses questions in both philosophy and theology, and its intended audience includes both philosophers and theologians. This has the unfortunate consequence that both sorts of readers will find parts of the discussion to be a recapitulation of what to them is elementary, and other parts to be concerned with issues that are quite unfamiliar to them, according to whether the subject discussed does or does not belong to their particular specialization. I have done my best to minimize this disadvantage, but am aware that I will not always have succeeded, and can only beg the reader's understanding for this shortcoming.

Before proceeding, I will make a brief apologetical aside. Some scholars might object to the contention that there is such a thing as the Christian tradition as described above, and claim that the views of Christians past and present are too heterogenous for anyone to claim that such a tradition exists or has existed. Since the existence of this tradition is a fundamental assumption of this book, I am not going to attempt to disprove this objection. I will only note that this book itself provides evidence against it, because it describes a history of thought and debate about its subject, and makes a contribution to that debate. A coherent debate of this kind would not be possible if it were not founded in a continuous tradition, because in the absence of such a tradition there would be no foundation for discussion and mutual comprehension.

Chapter 2

The Existence of Divine Speaking

Consideration of what leads Christians to believe the gospel must begin with the question of whether or not God speaks to humanity. Traditional Christian thought has taken it for granted that God has spoken to humanity, and that the Christian message originates in this speech. More recent theologians have, however, largely abandoned this view because they have rejected the idea that revelation is propositional. This rejection must therefore be discussed in any consideration of divine speaking. But such a discussion should not be conceived of as intended to offer a general account of revelation. Revelation is a broader concept than divine speaking. This can be seen in accounts of revelation like the following, which is that of the nineteenth-century theologian Matthias Scheeben (as described by René Latourelle):

> In the broad sense, God reveals Himself to man through the works of creation which reflect his power and perfections, and also through the communication of the inner light of reason, which makes us capable of knowing the works of God and God Himself in his works. This activity deserves the title of divine message; still, it does not give rise to faith, but only to an imperfect and indirect knowledge of God.
> 'In a more restricted and elevated sense, we speak of revelation as the act through which one mind presents to another mind the object of his own knowledge, and enables him, without seeing the object himself, to make the contents of that knowledge his own, basing himself upon the lights of the one who reveals to him. The vehicle of this revelation is the word properly so-called (*locutio formalis* ...). Corresponding to this word, there is, on the part of him who receives the revelation, that form of knowledge which we call faith.' (M. J. Scheeben, *Handbuch der Katholischen Dogmatik* (Freiburg, 1948), 1:10.)
> '... In a still more restricted and more elevated sense, we speak of divine revelation as a manifestation through which God makes our knowledge in complete conformity with his own, such that we know him as he knows himself; this is vision face to face.'(Ibid.)[1]

---

[1] Quoted in René Latourelle *Théologie de la révélation*, 2nd edn, 1966, pp. 200–201. In his *Tractatibus de fide*, de Lugo distinguishes between divine revelation in its most general sense and divine speaking: 'dicimus tamen communiter revelationem esse objectum formale fidei, qui loquimur de revelatione, non in tota sua latitudine, sed prout convertitur cum testificatione'. ('However, we say generally that revelation is the formal object of faith when speaking of revelation, not in its fullest extent, but insofar as it is interchangeable with testimony.') de Lugo, *Disputationes scholasticae et morales*, vol. 1, new edn, 1891, pp. 101–2.

A conception of revelation of this sort has much to recommend it, but it will not be argued for here; I am only concerned to argue for the existence of one of the kinds of revelation that it postulates, that of divine speaking.

Concepts, Propositions and Speech Acts

In order to address the question of whether God speaks, we need to consider the nature of speech and of the content of speech. Such a consideration should begin with an examination of propositions, which form the content of much of both language and thought. Propositions are truth-bearers; that is, they are, or can be, true or false. (They do not make up *all* the contents of language or thought, since not all such content is or can be true or false. Also, they are not the only things that can be true or false, since sentences are true or false, and propositions are not the same as sentences.) It is helpful to begin by distinguishing between sentence tokens and sentence types, in order to indicate what the content of language consists in, and what the difference between sentences and propositions is. A sentence token is a concrete thing, a particular sequence of sounds uttered on a particular occasion by a speaker or a particular series of marks. These two expressions:

Birds have feathers   Birds have feathers

are two sentence tokens that are instances of the same type. We distinguish between sentence tokens and types on the one hand, and what they express on the other, because it is possible for the same thing to be expressed by different tokens that belong to different types. If I say 'Snow is white', and a French speaker says 'La neige est blanche', we both say the same thing, although the tokens that we utter are different, and the types to which these tokens belong are different. These two sentences have the same content, and since this content has a truth-value, the content that we both express in these utterances is a proposition.[2] As remarked above, not all parts or uses of language, or even all sentence types, have propositional content. Propositions are, or can be, true or false, and some meaningful sentence types cannot be true or false. An example would be a sentence

---

[2] For a full statement of an argument from the fact that we express the same things in different utterances to the conclusion that there are propositions that are expressed by these utterances but are not identical with them, see R. Cartwright, 'Propositions', in *Analytical Philosophy*, ed. R. J. Butler, 1962. Cartwright's argument, which I accept, goes into some necessary complications that I will not reproduce here. The meaning I give to the term 'proposition' follows that given by E. J. Lemmon in 'Sentences, statements and propositions', in *British Analytic Philosophy*, ed. B. Williams, A. Montefiore, 1966; two sentences express the same proposition, in Lemmon's view, when they have the same sense, and the sense of a sentence is what it has in common with its translation into another language.

type like 'It is raining', which does not specify where or when it is raining, and thus cannot have a truth-value.

In saying that propositions exist, no metaphysical account of the nature of propositions (as for example saying that they are abstract objects) is being proposed. It is only asserted that they exist and have the properties described. Postulation of the existence of propositions does not commit us to acceptance of any particular metaphysical theory about the nature of propositions, just as believing that there are human minds does not commit us to acceptance of a particular metaphysical theory about the nature of human minds.

The fact that propositions form the content of much language means that they also form the content of much thought. This is so because we can think what we say. One can have the thought that all whales are mammals, and express that very thought in uttering the English sentence 'All whales are mammals'. The thought and the sentence have exactly the same content, which is the proposition that all whales are mammals. Another person can understand the sentence uttered, and think that all whales are mammals in turn. In that case both thoughts will have exactly the same content, which is again the proposition that all whales are mammals. Propositions are thus the content, not only of sentences, but also of thoughts that are or can be true or false. This in a way provides them with a wider scope than does the fact that they are the contents of sentences. It is debatable whether or not we can think propositions that we are *unable* to express in language, but it is certain that we frequently think propositions that as a matter of fact we never do express in language.

The content of propositions is evidently complex. For example, the proposition that all whales are mammals contains the concept of whales and the concept of mammals. Contents of thought that are not themselves propositions, because they are not capable of truth or falsity, but make up the content of propositions, are termed concepts in standard philosophical use. Concepts extend as far as thought does, because concepts just are the contents of thought, which when combined or operated on form propositions.[3]

This characterization of propositions and concepts is of importance for our discussion, because many theologians seem to feel that propositional knowledge is something different from direct knowledge of realities, and that there are forms of knowledge of reality that are non-propositional or non-conceptual, and even superior in some respects to propositional knowledge. This view is a mistaken one. Since propositions are the contents of any thought that can be true or false, it is through (or in) propositions that our minds grasp the world, and that we relate to the world in a personal way. We can relate to the world in an impersonal way,

---

[3] It should perhaps be noted that not all philosophers would agree with this. Most philosophical accounts of non-conceptual thought have no merit, but Gareth Evans in *The varieties of reference*, 1982, offers an account of non-conceptual thought that has some philosophical weight. I do not accept his account, but even if it were true, the existence of non-conceptual thought of the kind he has in mind would not be relevant to a discussion of revelation, because the contents of the Christian revelation could not be expressed in the non-conceptual thoughts that he proposes.

without propositions entering in to it; when a doctor gives us an injection, or when we inhale oxygen and exhale carbon dioxide, the effect on us and our effect on our surroundings is independent of what we think about it. But our relating to the world as persons involves our entertaining propositions about it – that is, it involves our thinking about it. It is not as if propositions, *instead of* realities, are the objects of propositional attitudes like knowing, believing, hoping, fearing, and so on: rather, it is in having propositional attitudes that we know realities, fear realities, and so on. We can only identify things if we know something about what they are, and such knowledge involves believing them to have a certain character. Our desires, aversions and volitions are all based on how we think of the things we desire or loathe or choose. Loving something (or someone) involves thinking it to be in some way good and lovable: hating something involves thinking it to be in some way evil. And not only is holding a thing to have some characteristic a matter of thinking some proposition to be true of it; more fundamentally, thinking of a thing is propositional or at least conceptual, just because it is thinking. It may of course be the case that someone has thoughts that he is unable to formulate or express to himself, or even be conscious of, but that does not make these thoughts any the less propositional.

Having given an account of propositions, we can go on to consider propositional communication. Such communication is speech; propositional communication happens when we do speech acts. Some primitive speech acts, like saying 'Ouch!', do not have sense or propositional content, but speech acts of this sort are too rudimentary to be able to disclose anything about God and his plans, so they need not be considered in a discussion of revelation. Common types of speech acts are assertions, commands, promises, threats, questions, requests, offers and expressions of desire. It is important to realize that all these kinds of acts, not just assertions, have propositional content. Propositions are what are asserted, but they are not the same as assertions; assertions are rather a particular use of propositions. This can be seen in conditional statements like 'If James is a smoker his insurance premiums will be high.' This statement contains the proposition 'James is a smoker', but does not assert it. Imperatives and expressions of desire also express propositions, although they do not assert them. John Searle, in his book *Speech Acts*, illustrates this with four examples:

1. Sam smokes habitually.
2. Does Sam smoke habitually?
3. Sam, smoke habitually!
4. Would that Sam smoked habitually.[4]

These are speech acts of different kinds that all express the same proposition, 'Sam smokes habitually'. Using Frege's terminology, I will speak of the proposition

---

[4] John Searle, *Speech Acts*, 1969, p. 21.

expressed by a speech act as the sense of that act, and the kind of act – assertoric, imperative, interrogatory, and so on – as the force of the act.[5]

As the above example of someone's saying 'Ouch!' illustrates, some communicative acts do not have propositional content. Another example would be someone shaking his fist at me; this would be a threat, and hence a communicative act, but would not have any propositional content. A test for determining whether a communicative act has propositional content is whether it can be described by a 'that ...' locution, as in 'He said that ...', 'He exclaimed that ...', 'He promised that ...', 'He threatened that ...'. Shaking a fist obviously does not fit into one of these locutions, because we cannot specify what it is that someone threatens when they shake a fist; it is just an expression of hostile intent of a general kind, and has no propositional content. But communicative acts that tell us what it is that is promised, asserted or threatened will fit into this locution, and thus will have propositional content.

Before looking at the strength of the case that can made for non-propositional views of revelation and against the existence of divine speech, it should be pointed out that certain positions on this issue are based on misconceptions of the nature of propositions. This is true of the objections raised by Fr. (now Cardinal) Avery Dulles in his article 'The Symbolic Structure of Revelation'.[6] Cardinal Dulles defines 'propositional speech' as 'conceptual language that is amenable to syllogistic logic'.[7] He then goes on to contrast a propositional theory of revelation with a symbolic theory, which maintains that divine revelation is given in symbolic form. Propositions and symbolic expressions are thus seen as different and mutually exclusive. Here Cardinal Dulles is adopting a position he put forward in 1964, when he wrote: 'The mutual discourse of persons is normally accomplished more through symbolism than through propositional speech'.[8]

Having thus described propositions, he argues against a propositional view of revelation in this way. Revelation is contained in Holy Scripture; much of Holy Scripture is expressed symbolically and is not amenable to syllogistic reasoning; therefore, much of revelation is not propositional.

Cardinal Dulles's characterization of propositions is mistaken. A propositional assertion is not the same thing as an assertion that uses words literally. Symbolic and metaphorical words and expressions can be used in assertions that are true or false, that can convey information, and that can be the objects of cognitive attitudes. This is true, whether or not it is always possible for the propositional content of assertions that contain symbolic or metaphorical words or expressions to be put in literal terms. Nor should we suppose that propositions must be amenable

---

[5] See Gottlob Frege 'Thoughts', in *Propositions and Attitudes*, ed. Nathan Salmon and Scott Soames, 1988, p. 33. It could be debated whether this use of 'sense' corresponds to Frege's, but I will not go into the question of whether it does, and will simply stipulate that I will take the sense of a sentence to be the proposition it expresses, whether or not that is what Frege meant by it.

[6] Avery Dulles SJ, 'The Symbolic Structure of Revelation', *Theological Studies* 41, 1980.

[7] Dulles 1980, p. 52.

[8] Avery Dulles SJ, 'The Theology of Revelation', *Theological Studies* 25, 1964, p. 57.

to syllogistic logic. There are many perfectly good inferences from one proposition to another that cannot be described using syllogistic methods.

Another misconception about propositions is found in the objection that a propositional account of revelation must be mistaken, because what is revealed is not something abstract or static or unhistorical. It is clear that 'what is revealed' is meant, in this objection, to refer to the things that revelation is about – the things that we learn about through revelation. But we need not hold that if revelation is propositional then the things that revelation is about must be abstract or static or unhistorical. The understanding and description of change, or of the concrete and particular, is just as propositional as the understanding and description of what does not change or of the general or abstract.[9] Beliefs, hopes, desires and statements about particular concrete things are just as propositional as ones that are about general or abstract things, and our grasp of historical reality is just as propositional as our grasp of things that do not exist in history.[10]

Having cleared away these misconceptions, we can set forth the arguments that can be made for and against the existence of divine speech.

Arguments for the Existence of Divine Speaking

An important argument for divine speech is that such speech is in principle necessary in order to make known to mankind the contents of the Christian gospel. In order to see why this should be so, we need to consider how on a non-propositional view of revelation this gospel can be made known. Revelation, on such a view, will happen through divine acts that are not communicative acts. There are several sorts of act that could be held to constitute revelation:

1. God's ordinary action in creation. Through reflecting on the existence on the universe, we can be led to conclude that there is a God who created it, and the greatness and beauty of the universe can give us a hint of the greatness and beauty of its creator. There is thus a sense in which God's creating the universe can be called a revelation.
2. Particular, publicly observable miraculous acts of God that are not speech acts.
3. Divine illumination or enhancement of our cognitive capacities, that are not communicative acts, but that enable us to know more about God and his purposes through reflecting on acts belonging to (1) and (2) than we would otherwise be able to do.[11]

---

[9] Description of change is not necessarily non-abstract; consider the differential calculus.
[10] James Barr and Paul Helm have pointed out that these objections to propositional revelation are misconceived; see Barr, *The Bible in the Modern World*, 1973, p. 123, and Helm, 'Revealed Propositions and Timeless Truth', *Religious Studies* 8, 1972, pp. 127–136.
[11] For a non-propositional view of revelation that contains these elements, see William Temple, *Nature, Man and God*, 1934, lecture XII, 'Revelation and its Mode'.

A believer in divine communication can argue that none of these forms of revelation can make known certain central features of the Christian faith. Some of the contents of this faith, like the existence of God and the basic principles of morality, can be known by humans on their own without divine assistance.[12] (Even for these parts of the faith it is possible to argue, as Aquinas does, that the difficulty of knowing them through unaided human reason is so great that for most people a divine revelation is necessary in order for them to be known.) But other parts of the faith cannot be known by humans using only their own intellectual powers, and can hence only be known by God's telling us that they are true. Knowledge that can only be acquired through divine assertion includes some essential knowledge about the divine nature, knowledge about God's intentions, and knowledge about the nature of some of God's salvific actions; without such assertions, none of these things would be revealed to us.[13]

There are strict limits on how much we can know in principle about the divine nature through our own intellectual capacities, and the limits that exist for most people in practice are stricter still. I would maintain that the Trinitarian nature of God, the ultimate salvific reality, is not at all discoverable by even the most exalted human capacities. But even if there is a theoretical possibility of arriving at this doctrine through reason alone, this theoretical possibility can only exist for a few outstandingly brilliant and knowledgeable individuals, and it is a remote possibility that has not in fact been realized, since the only people who have ever actually believed this doctrine are those who have accepted it on the basis of Christian revelation. It is thus true that practically speaking, if we are to know that God is triune, it can only be through God's telling us about it. The same point applies to God's intentions for humanity and the universe. We have no way of knowing what intentions for the future are in God's mind, so we can only know about God's intentions for us and the universe through God's telling us about them.[14] If God

---

[12] Some theologians, rejecting the idea of natural theology, might claim that none of the contents of the Christian faith can be known to us independently of God's telling us about them. If true, this would strengthen the argument.

[13] This was asserted by the First Vatican Council in its constitution *Dei Filius*, ch. 4: '1. The perpetual agreement of the Catholic Church has maintained and maintains this too: that there is a twofold order of knowledge, distinct not only as regards its source, but also as regards its object. 2. With regard to the source, we know at one level by natural reason, at the other level by divine faith. 3. With regard to the object, besides those things to which natural reason can attain, there are proposed for our belief mysteries hidden in God which, unless they are divinely revealed, are incapable of being known.' The council cites 1 Cor. 2:7–10, in support of this assertion. It issues this canon on the subject: '1. If anyone says that in divine revelation there are contained no true mysteries properly so-called, but that all the dogmas of the faith can be understood and demonstrated by properly trained reason from natural principles: let him be anathema.' Norman Tanner and Giuseppe Alberigo eds., *Decrees of the Ecumenical Councils*, 1990, vol. 2, p. 808.

[14] Cf. 1 Cor. 2:9–11: 'But, as it is written, "What no eye has seen, nor ear heard, nor the heart of man conceived, what God has prepared for those who love him", God has revealed to us through the Spirit. For the Spirit searches everything, even the depths of God. For what

'has made known to us in all wisdom and insight the mystery of his will, according to his purpose which he set forth in Christ as a plan for the fullness of time, to unite all things in him' (Eph. 1:10), it can only be through God's telling us about this purpose, not through our surmising it ourselves. The Scriptures clearly assert that God intends in the future to bring all sin and evil to an end. There is no necessity for him to do this, and there is nothing in the course of human history that warrants us in believing that he will – he has obviously been content to let sin and evil abound from the beginning of recorded history until the present – so we can only know that this will happen if he tells us so. This is all the more true for the particular steps he will take to bring sin and evil to an end – the second coming of Christ, the resurrection of the dead, and the future happiness of the saved. The Christian hope requires divine assertion to ground it.

We need to be clear that this problem cannot be solved through an appeal to divine enhancement of human cognitive capacities in inspiration. No enhancement of cognitive capacities can enable them to go beyond what the evidence available to them can warrant them in believing; if a change to our cognitive capacities were to do this, it would not be an enhancement but a corruption of them. If our cognitive capacities lead us to accept conclusions that go beyond the evidence available to them, they are malfunctioning, and our exercise of them is irrational. The only experience that could enable cognitive capacities of any sort to arrive at knowledge of the trinitarian nature of God, or knowledge of the free decisions that God has made before those decisions are realized, would be a direct experience of God's nature and God's mind. But the conferring of such experience on a prophet or apostle would be a far stronger form of divine revelation than divine communication of propositions, since it would be a direct encounter with a reality that can only be inadequately conveyed by propositions. It would be hard to provide a rationale for denying the existence of divine communication, while accepting that there is revelation of this stronger sort.

It might be said that revelation included not just a divine enhancement of cognitive capacities, but also the actual suggestion of thoughts and ideas to its recipients, so that God would have caused the idea that Christ was divine as well as human to occur to the first Christians. But God's revealing himself through actually placing thoughts into someone's mind would amount to a kind of propositional communication. A divine action must be recognized as such, if it is to constitute part of divine revelation. If God were to reveal himself through suggesting thoughts to people, the recipients of such thoughts would have to recognize the thoughts as having been placed in their minds by God with the intention that they should come to know them, and with the intention that they should recognize these thoughts as coming from him and as intended to give them knowledge. If they did not do so they would not recognize the thoughts as being divinely revealed. In consequence, they could not be justified in passing on the contents of the thoughts as divine revelation, and they would not be warranted in

---

person knows a man's thoughts except the spirit of the man which is in him? So also none comprehends the thoughts of God except the Spirit of God.'

believing the thoughts (unless they had independent evidence for the truth of what is contained in the thoughts, a possibility that has already been ruled out in the cases under discussion). But, as will be argued in Chapter 6, for God to act in this way would be for him to communicate a proposition.

These considerations about the necessity for divine assertion bring home the deficiency in the position that 'what is offered to man's apprehension in any specific revelation is not truth concerning God but the living God Himself',[15] and that in the New Testament 'revelation is likewise understood, not in the sense of a communication of supranatural knowledge, but in the sense of a self-disclosure of God'.[16] We do not have a self-disclosure of God in revelation *instead of* a communication of knowledge. Rather it is in part through a communication of knowledge that God's self-disclosure takes place.

In addition to the necessity of divine assertions for the revelation of the Christian message, we should consider the fact that the doctrine of the Incarnation entails that divine assertions were actually made to humans. The man Jesus Christ is the Second Person of the Trinity, a divine person. Thus, whatever was asserted by the man Jesus was asserted by the Second Person of the Trinity. Some of what Christ said no doubt did not reveal anything about God, as for example when he asked what was for dinner, but his teaching about God and the way to God was a teaching about God asserted by God himself, belief in which is an exercise of Christian faith. It might be objected that Christ was human as well as divine, that his human knowledge suffered from limitations as all human knowledge does, and thus that some of his assertions were one-sided, misleading or false. Although this may have been the case for some of Christ's assertions, I would not accept that it was true of his preaching on religious subjects. But even if it was true of his preaching, this only implies (given the doctrine of the Incarnation) that a divine being made one-sided, misleading or false assertions; it does not follow that the assertions are not those of a divine being. (There are, of course, difficulties in supposing that a divine being can make assertions of this sort, but the objection given presupposes that this state of affairs can obtain, since it accepts that Christ is divine as well as claiming that some of his assertions were misleading or false.)

Divine assertions are thus a necessary part of the Christian revelation. But it should not be forgotten that other forms of communication besides assertion are also essential to Christianity.[17] Divine commands, promises, threats, offers and forgiveness are essential parts of the Christian message, and are at the centre of salvation history. These communicative acts are of course propositional; the propositions they express describe what it is that is commanded, offered, promised or threatened. It is no good saying that descriptions of these acts in the Scriptures are metaphors for other, non-propositional acts. It is an essential part of the

---

[15] Temple 1934, p. 322.

[16] Albrecht Oepke, 'καλύπτω', tr. Geoffrey W. Bromiley, in Gerhard Kittel ed., *Theological Dictionary of the New Testament* vol. III (Θ – K), 1965, p. 586.

[17] Ronald Thiemann, who makes this point in *Revelation and Theology*, 1985, is unusual both in his grasp of the nature of speech acts and their propositional content, and in his emphasis on speech acts other than assertion.

Christian message that such acts literally happened. If there are no divine commands there is no revealed Law, and if there are no literal divine offers, promises and threats there is no divine covenant with humanity, because law and covenant depend on the literal occurrence of communicative acts.

This objection is not usually addressed by theologians who hold a non-propositional view of revelation. Such theologians have generally attacked the idea of divine assertion, without giving much consideration to other forms of divine communication. But if we accept that God utters commands, promises, threats and so on, as the scriptural evidence induces us to do, it would not seem reasonable to deny that he makes assertions. It is unreasonable to suppose that divine communication consists entirely in God's making assertions, but one ought not to confuse the claim that God makes assertions with the claim that such assertions are the whole of revelation.

This brings us to what I think is the deepest objection to entirely non-propositional views of revelation. Such a view of revelation denies the existence of divine communication to humanity. But without communication, there can be no such thing as a personal relationship. If someone never speaks to you, you cannot have a personal relationship with them. More than that; if someone does not speak to you, although you are present to them (as we are all present to God), it is as if you are not a person to them. And the speech in question here is not something that can only be metaphorically described as speech, but is literal communication; it is such communication that is needed for a personal relationship. The connection between speech and personal relationship is brought out in the book of Genesis. God brings the works of the first four days into existence by his word. But when he gets to living things on the fourth day, he not only creates them but blesses them, telling them to be fruitful and multiply. And when he gets to the man and the woman on the sixth day, he not only blesses them but speaks to them, telling them that he has given them plants and fruit for food. This difference marks the fact that the man and the woman are persons, with whom God enters into a personal relationship. The existence of a personal relationship between God and Israel, and between Christ and the Church, is a fundamental part of the biblical message. The Christian faith thus requires us to hold that God communicates with man.

Since communication is necessary for personal relationships, it is also necessary for a society. In order to be members of one society, people must be able to communicate. This is implicit in the story of the tower of Babel. When the Lord confuses the language of the builders of the tower, so that they cannot communicate with one another, their society is destroyed, and they are scattered over the face of the earth. The gift of tongues at Pentecost is meant by Luke to be understood as a reversal of this process, by which the apostles are made able to bring all the peoples of the earth into one society through communicating with them. But redemption in Christ involves making us Christ's friends, and making us members of a society of which God is the chief member. Since common membership of a society requires communication between the members, God's being a member of a society to which we belong requires that he communicate with us.

That is why John Baillie is mistaken in saying that 'the deepest difficulty felt about the equation of revelation with communicated truths is that it offers us something less than personal encounter and personal communion'.[18] To see his mistake, we need to draw a distinction between the truths that are communicated in revelation, and the act of communicating those truths. If revelation were simply equated with the truths that are communicated in revelation, then there might be something to his assertion that such an understanding of revelation offers less than personal encounter and communication. But the traditional accounts of revelation that he is attacking do not make this equation. Rather, they identify revelation as primarily the act of communicating truths, and they extend this primary sense of 'revelation' to a secondary one, by giving the name 'revelation' to the truths that are revealed, as well as to the act of revealing them. Baillie's criticism, through suppressing this primary sense of revelation, thus merely sets up a straw man to knock down.

It is worth considering the difficulties involved in reconciling a non-propositional view of revelation with the Scriptures. Such a view of revelation will see the Scriptures as being the sole, or at least the principal, witness to the non-communicative divine acts that constitute revelation proper. But this view is not compatible with the actual contents of the Bible. As James Barr has pointed out, divine communication is an inseparable part of the events of salvation history as they are presented in the Bible. Barr makes this point in response to the school of 'biblical theology', which argued that the Bible itself presented revelation as consisting in divine non-communicative acts in history. Barr writes:

> If you treat this [biblical] record as revelation through history, you commonly speak as if the basis were the doing of certain divine acts (what, exactly, they were is difficult to determine), while the present form of the tradition in its detail and circumstantiality is 'interpretation' of these acts, or 'meditation' upon them, or theological reflection prompted by them ... This is not how the texts represent the Exodus event. Far from representing the divine acts as the basis of all knowledge of God and all communication with him, they represent God as communicating freely with men, and particularly with Moses, before, during and after these events. Far from the incident of the burning bush being an 'interpretation' of the divine acts, it is a direct communication from God to Moses of his purposes and intentions. This conversation, instead of being represented as an interpretation of the divine act, is a precondition of it. If God had not told Moses what he did, the Israelites would not have demanded their escape from Egypt, and the deliverance at the Sea of Reeds would not have taken place ... We cannot attribute to history a revelatory character, in a sense having a substantial priority over the particular divine, spoken communications with particular men, without doing violence to the way in which the biblical texts in fact speak ...[19] Such direct communication [between God and particular men on particular occasions] is, I believe, an inescapable fact of the Bible and the Old Testament in particular. God can speak specific verbal messages, when he wills, to the men of his choice. But for this, if we follow the way in which the Old Testament represents the incidents, there would have been no call of Abraham, no

---

[18] John Baillie, *The Idea of Revelation in Recent Thought*, 1956, p. 39.
[19] James Barr, 'Revelation through History in the Old Testament and in Modern Theology', *Interpretation* 17, 1963, p. 197.

Exodus, no prophecy. Direct communication from God to man has fully as much claim to be called the core of the tradition as has revelation through events in history. If we persist in saying that this direct, specific communication must be subsumed under revelation through events in history and taken as subsidiary interpretation of the latter, I shall say that we are abandoning the Bible's own representation of the matter for another which is apologetically more comfortable.[20]

As Barr indicates, divine communication is presented by the Bible not only as part of the significant happenings in salvation history, but as what initiates those happenings. It is a divine communication that begins God's relationship with Abraham and causes Abraham to leave Ur of the Chaldees, and that causes Abraham to offer up Isaac. Moses begins his relationship with God by hearing him speak from the burning bush, where he is told to take the people of Israel out of Egypt. Samuel is called by the Lord, and anoints Saul and later David because he is told to. The career of the prophets begins with a call, after which they prophesy as the Lord tells them to, and so on. And the content of these communications is a contingent choice of God's about a specific course of action that he wishes people to take, or that he himself intends to take. The whole history of God's relations with Israel, and later with humanity in general through Christ, is a history of such contingent choices, since God could have arranged his plan of salvation quite differently or never have undertaken such a plan at all. An actual communication from God is the only way that we can come to know about divine choices of this sort. Since we are not able to look into the mind of God, the only way to know that God wishes us to take one specific course of action out of many that he might have wished us to take is through God's communicating it to us.

Barr's concern was to argue that the 'biblical theology' school was mistaken in asserting that the Bible's conception of revelation was a non-propositional one.[21] His reasoning can be extended to argue that non-propositional accounts of Christian revelation present the Bible as being a witness to revelation, but that if one denies that God ever communicates with man it is most implausible to assert that the Bible is such a witness. The Bible would have thoroughly misrepresented what God's revelatory acts actually were, by presenting them as essentially involving acts of divine communication that never took place. It would give us little idea of what these real acts were, because its whole account of God's action in history is couched in terms of these fictitious divine communicative acts. A non-

---

[20] Barr 1963, p. 201.

[21] The 'biblical theology' movement was a diverse grouping, whose members often disagreed with one another (on this movement see Henning Graf Reventlow, *Problems of Old Testament Theology in the 20th Century*, 1985. In the description of the 'biblical theology' position that I quote, Barr seems to me to exaggerate (perhaps for polemical purposes) the importance of a non-propositional view of revelation to this movement. Non-propositional views are certainly expressed by thinkers of this sort, but many of their central themes and insights can be separated from these views. Since divine communications, if they happen, will be historical events, it is clearly possible to postulate such communications while also holding that 'history is the absolutely supreme milieu of God's revelation' (Barr 1963, p. 193).

propositional account of revelation thus implies that the Bible is not a witness to revelation, but rather gives a thoroughly misleading account of it, a position that is incompatible with Christianity.

A further Biblical objection to a non-propositional view of revelation that should be mentioned is the fact that Scriptural texts are frequently described in Scripture itself as having been uttered by God (see Chapter 8). One might of course say that since the Bible is not itself revealed we do not have to believe these biblical assertions, but that does not on its own solve the problem that these assertions pose for a non-propositional view of revelation. The non-propositional view will still want to accept the basic message of the Bible, and must face the question of whether this propositional conception is a part of this basic message. The evidence suggests that it was so taken by the Apostles, who continually used it in their preaching. The point is not only that they accepted that the Scriptures (or the parts of them that were written in their time) were spoken by God, as every believing Jew did, but also that this position had an essential role in their preaching. Of course one can say that they were wrong, but that is to no longer take Christianity seriously.

In reply to this it might be said that many of the divine communications reported in the Bible must be admitted to be fictitious by believers in propositional revelation, so such believers are not in a position to object to the non-propositional account's denial of the reality of divine communication. Examples of fictitious communications would be God's commands to Noah and Jonah. Since the stories of Noah and Jonah are not historical, these communications never happened.

This reply is not a sufficient one, because the divine communications described in the Bible are not limited to stories that have no historical basis: they also occur in those parts of Scripture that describe history. Divine communications are an essential part of the history of Israel as presented by the Bible, and if they never really happened the account of the history of Israel that the Bible gives is fundamentally mistaken. We must therefore accept that some of the divine communications reported in the Bible were historical events and not myths or fictions, if we do not wish to conclude that the Bible's account of the central events that it is concerned with is fundamentally mistaken, and hence that it cannot be described as a witness to the saving acts of God that constitute revelation. Accepting that divine communication occurred does not, however, require us to accept that all the divine communications described in the Bible were historical events. It is quite possible to believe in divine communication, and to believe that the Bible is communicated by God, while recognizing many of the stories in the Bible for what they obviously are, mythical or fictional accounts rather than historical descriptions.

The point made above about personal relationship involving communication is made by Barr in reference to the Scriptural text:

> In so far as it is good to use the term 'revelation' at all, it is entirely as true to say that in the Old Testament revelation is by verbal communication as to say that it is by acts in history ... When we speak of the highly 'personal' nature of the Old Testament God, it is very largely upon this verbal character of his communication with man that we are

relying. The acts of God are meaningful because they are set within this frame of verbal communication. God tells what he is doing, or tells what he is going to do. He does nothing, unless he tells his servants the prophets (Amos 3:7). A God who acted in history would be a mysterious and supra-personal fate if this action was not linked with this verbal conversation.[22]

Arguments against Divine Speaking

The case for the existence of divine speech is thus a strong one. To determine whether this case should convince us, it is necessary to balance it against the arguments that can be made against revelation involving divine communication.

Barth's Argument

One argument that can be considered is that offered by Karl Barth. Barth rejects the view that Holy Scripture, Church tradition or the living apostolate of the Church could themselves be the reality of divine revelation, on the grounds that an identification of a statement in any of these sources with divine revelation would be an unacceptable constraint on God. Such an identification would mean 'that the essence of the Church, Jesus Christ, no longer the free Lord of their existence, but bound up with the existence of the Church, is finally limited and conditioned by definite concrete formulations of man's understanding of His revelation and the faith that grasps it'.[23] Barth asserts that it is theologically impossible for there to be such a thing as 'truths of revelation', if revelation has its truth – as it does – in the free decision of God.[24]

Barth's view is open to question, on the grounds that it is hard to see how uttering propositions would limit God's freedom. If God does reveal propositions, he will freely decide whether or not to reveal, what it is that he will reveal, the persons to whom he will reveal, and the way in which he will reveal. There will be no limitations of his freedom with respect to any of these factors. It may be, though, that Barth also had in mind the view that any propositions that make positive assertions about God, or at least any such propositions that humans are able to grasp, would limit God in some way. He might have thought that because God's nature surpasses any propositional description, such descriptions must necessarily constrain God in an unacceptable way; any such descriptions must be provisional, inadequate, and open to correction, which could not be the case if they were asserted by God himself.

I do not accept this objection, since I hold that it is possible to make positive analogical statements about God that are entirely true and are not misleading. However, even if it were true it would not support a rejection of propositional revelation. It is obviously possible for negative statements about God (for example,

---

[22] Barr 1963, pp. 77–78.

[23] Karl Barth, *Church Dogmatics* vol. 1, 1936, p. 43.

[24] Barth 1936, p. 16.

'God did not have a beginning in time') to be entirely accurate and literally true, and thus possible for God to make such statements with complete truth and accuracy. It is also possible for God to reveal propositions that are not about himself as such, but about the world he has created; and there is nothing to prevent these propositions from being entirely accurate. We might ask as well: what if some of the sayings attributed to Christ by the gospels were literally said by Christ, as seems probable? Since Christ is divine, as Barth confesses, these sayings would be divinely uttered propositions. So if we think Christ said them, and believe them on this account, we would be believing divine speaking.

Barth's positive view of revelation is an illustration of the difficulties involved in consistently holding a non-propositional view of revelation. He asserts that divine revelation happens when proclamation is real proclamation. But what is it that makes proclamation real? Barth's answer is that proclamation is real when it is God speaking.

> Proclamation is human language in and through which God Himself speaks, like a king through the mouth of his herald, which moreover is meant to be heard and apprehended as language in and through which God Himself speaks, and so heard and apprehended in faith as the divine decision upon life and death, as the divine judgement and the divine acquittal, the eternal law and the eternal gospel both together.[25] ... But as Christ is not only true man, it [proclamation] is not only the volition and execution of the man performing. It is also and it is primarily and decisively the divine volition and execution.[26]

The trouble with this answer is that speaking, as we have seen, is itself a propositional notion. Propositions are what we speak. If God literally speaks to us in divine revelation, then he communicates propositions to us in that revelation. It may be that Barth uses 'speak' metaphorically, not literally, but in that case the question arises of what 'speak' is a metaphor for. A metaphorical use of 'speak' does not on its own give us much insight into what divine revelation actually consists in. Barth's description of revelation as God's self-revelation, as God's making himself known, is not helpful in explaining this, because the question at issue is how it is that God makes himself known in proclamation; if it is not literally through speaking, how does it happen? And in any case, Barth often writes as if 'speak' in 'God speaks' is meant to be taken literally, not metaphorically; as if God literally does speech acts that command, promise or inform us. He thus reintroduces notions that belong to a propositional understanding of revelation, after denying that such an understanding is correct.

Pannenberg's Argument

Another argument for a non-propositional view has been given by Wolfhart Pannenberg:

---

[25] Barth 1936, p. 57.
[26] Barth 1936, p. 105.

Until the Enlightenment, Christian theology was doubtless a theology of revelation in this sense, appealing to revelation as a supernatural authority. The authoritative revelation was found in the 'Word of God', i.e., in the inspired word of the Bible. As the product of the divine Spirit, this word was regarded in a strongly literal sense as the 'Word of God'. In the twentieth century the neo-orthodox theology of the Word no longer sought the 'Word of God' primarily in the Bible ... In both cases the authoritarian character of the appeal to revelation remained untouched. But for men who live in the sphere in which the Enlightenment has become effective, authoritarian claims are no longer acceptable, in intellectual as little as in political life. All authoritarian claims are on principle subject to the suspicion that they clothe human thoughts and institutions with the splendour of the divine majesty. Thus they are defenseless against the reproach of interchanging the divine and the human, and to the accusation of absolutizing what in truth is finite in content, with the result of subjugating all other men to those who represent this authority.[27]

Pannenberg does not deny that there are elements of what he calls an 'authoritarian' view in the Scriptures themselves, but he asserts that these elements should be rejected:

... It is certainly undeniable that authoritarian forms of tradition play a significant role in the Old and New Testaments ... It also belongs to the authoritarian features that the foundations of law and ethics were stylized and passed on traditionally as words of God, that the prophets received and presented their words directly as words of God, and that the early Christian apostles, such as Paul, proclaimed their message as the 'Word of God', certainly in a more differentiated sense, but nonetheless with the claim to represent the authority of God himself to their hearers and readers ... Before any 'demythologizing' is undertaken, it would seem reasonable for Christian theology to strip away the authoritarian forms of the premodern Christian tradition.[28]

This view of course raises the doubts expressed by Barr, as to whether such a 'stripping away' does not in fact amount to abandoning the Bible's own representation of revelation.[29] But it is a weak position quite independently of this difficulty. To evaluate it, we need first to consider the relevant senses in which 'authority' can be understood. One sense is that found in statements like 'Dr. Jones is an authority on heart disease'. This means that Dr. Jones is a trustworthy source of information on heart disease. Other senses are found in statements like 'Officers in the army have authority over their men'. This can be taken to mean that officers

---

[27] Wolfhart Pannenberg, 'Response to the Discussion', in *New Frontiers in Theology,* vol. III, 1967, p. 226.

[28] Pannenberg 1967, pp. 227–8.

[29] It is notable that when Pannenberg explicitly responds to Barr's criticisms in later writings, he seems to tone down his position considerably. In his *Systematic Theology* vol. I, 1991, he denies that divine communication can be said to be the only sort of revelation found in the Bible (see pp. 195, 198, 204, 233). He does not, however, dispute Barr's claim that a rejection of divine communication is an abandonment of the self-understanding of the Bible, and in some passages seems to admit that such communication actually takes place (pp. 202, 207).

have a legal or moral right to be obeyed by their men, or that officers have the power to compel their men to do what they command. The authority that consists in being a trustworthy source of information is obviously attributed to the Bible by those who hold it to be the Word of God. It is absurd to say that to men who live in the sphere of the Enlightenment claims to authority of this sort are not longer acceptable. Obviously, men during and after the Enlightenment have accepted that doctors, geographers, scientists, and specialists of various other kinds are reliable sources of information, and have been reasonable in doing so; one of the influential projects of the Enlightenment was the construction of an Encyclopedia, which set out to be just such a source. It is obviously possible for claims to authority of this sort to be false. But it is not reasonable to simply reject such claims, as Pannenberg does in the case of the Bible, on the grounds that all claims of this sort are false or unworthy of belief. Rather, we ought to evaluate them in order to determine whether they are well-founded, and if we reasonably judge that they are well-founded we ought to accept them. The questions of how we can reasonably accept a claim to knowledge as trustworthy, and how we can reasonably accept that Christian claims to be providing knowledge are trustworthy, will be directly addressed in Chapters 6 and 8; they are the central questions of this book.

There are differences between these two sorts of authority that are relevant to Pannenberg's criticism. People with the right and power to command can decide what it is that they will command, but people who are trustworthy sources of information cannot decide what is true. The claim to the latter kind of authority is not, as the former is, a claim to the right to direct others according to one's will; it is merely a claim to be knowledgeable and trustworthy concerning the subject matter of which one speaks. In consequence, someone with the right to command can order one thing at one time, and then withdraw the order at another, or order something else, even something directly contrary to the original order, but this does not work with a claim to authoritative knowledge. If you withdraw or contradict an assertion that you claimed to have made with authority, it means that you are denying your claim to authority. A claim to teach with authority binds the person making the claim to his assertions, in a way that a claim to the right to command does not.[30]

---

[30] St. Gregory the Great addresses concerns like those of Pannenberg's, in his commentary on the book of Job (book 23, 23–4): 'When Paul says to Titus, "Command these things, teach them with all authority", he is not recommending the domination of power but the force of the disciple's life. A man teaches with authority what he first practises himself before preaching to others, for when conscience is an obstacle to speech, what is taught is more difficult to accept. So then Paul is not recommending the power of haughty words but the trustworthiness which comes from good conduct. Our Lord too, we are told, taught as one who had authority, and not as the scribes and the Pharisees. He alone spoke with a unique authority because he had committed no sin from weakness. It was from the power of his divinity that he possessed that which he bestowed on us through the sinlessness of his humanity.' (*The Divine Office* (1974), vol. 3, pp. 147–8.) The relation of trustworthiness to authority, the grounding of faith in the trustworthiness of Christ, and the relation between faith in Christ's authority and faith in the Bible will be discussed in Chapters 6 to 8.

The authority that consists in being a trustworthy source of information is not the only kind of authority that has been claimed for the Bible. The Bible contains many commands that purport to be uttered by God. The existence of a purported divine command in the Bible obviously does not compel people to obey it, but the view that the Bible is the word of God will imply a moral obligation to obey these commands, since we have a moral obligation to obey God. It will thus claim for the Bible authority in the sense of a moral right to be obeyed. Claims to this sort of authority are a more suitable target for Pannenberg's objections than claims to the authority that consists in being a trustworthy source of information. Pannenberg makes two assertions to support his contention that what he calls authoritarian claims are not acceptable. The first is that 'authoritarian claims are on principle subject to the suspicion that they clothe human thoughts and institutions with the splendour of the divine majesty', and the second is that such claims are 'defenseless against the reproach of interchanging the divine and the human, and to the accusation of absolutizing what in truth is finite in content, with the result of subjugating all other men to those who represent this authority.'

It is worth pointing out that the authors of the Scriptures, and people with teaching authority in the Church, do not claim to *themselves* possess divine authority, but only to be conveying commands from God that have divine authority. Claims of the latter sort have obviously been made falsely, and hence abusively, in the past. It may therefore be right that they should be *in principle* 'subject to the suspicion that they clothe human thoughts and institutions with the splendour of the divine majesty'. But even if they are in principle subject to suspicion, it does not follow that this suspicion is not defeasible. It is possible to defeat the suspicion that a purported divine command is actually meant to subjugate people and establish the power of those who announce it, if for example it turns out that the messengers who announced this command did so despite knowing that their announcing it would bring disaster on their heads, or that following this command would have a liberating rather than a subjugating effect. Pannenberg's second assertion, that claims to divine authority are 'defenseless against the reproach of interchanging the divine and the human', is thus false. It is quite possible to offer defences against this reproach. What needs to be done, in the case of a claim to be conveying divine commands, is to investigate these defences and see whether they stand up.

It could be that what Pannenberg means here is that a claim by humans to be uttering a divine communication must by its very nature constitute 'interchanging the divine and the human', and 'absolutizing what in truth is finite in content', and that these are necessarily objectionable. By 'absolutizing what is finite in content' he may have something like Barth's criticism in mind, to the effect that human utterances must be finite in some respect, and thus incapable of expressing what is in the divine mind. But, as remarked above, there is no reason why God should not adjust his communications to the finiteness of our capacities. As for an 'interchange of the divine and the human', this is surely what happens in the Incarnation, and thus not something that a Christian theologian can object to as such.

Criticisms of the Bible as Propositional Revelation

There is a widely accepted group of arguments for a non-propositional view of revelation that rests on the common (usually unspoken) premise that if we are going to identify any propositions as divinely revealed, we will hold that the propositions asserted by the Bible are divinely revealed. These arguments all take the form of maintaining that it is impossible for the Bible to be made up of divinely revealed propositions, and therefore that revelation cannot be propositional. I will not criticize these arguments by raising doubts about this premise, whose truth will be considered in the discussion of direct and deistic views of revelation given in Chapter 7: instead, I will consider whether these arguments can succeed if the premise is granted.

An argument of this sort has been expressed by William Temple, who states:

> The traditional doctrine [of Christendom] has rather been that the Book itself is the revelation than that it contains the record of it ... Now this traditional doctrine of revelation implies, first, that God has so far overridden and superseded the normal human faculties of those through whom the revelation was given as to save their utterance by voice or pen from all error in its communication. That God is able to do this we need not be concerned to deny; the question is whether it is consonant with what we otherwise know of His dealings with men that He should wish to do so, and also whether this view of the general nature of revelation is consistent with the actual content of the revelation supposed to be so given ... it is ... indispensable to faith and to morality to hold that God empowers men to do His will through the enlightenment of their natural faculties and the kindling of their natural affections, and not by any supersession of these. But to provide, by some process of suggestion, oracles directly expressive of divine truth ... would be to repudiate this principle alike as regards the prophet and as regards the hearers.[31]

Temple claims that the Bible's being a divine oracle, and its being believed for that reason, would involve the supersession of the natural faculties of both its human authors and the people who receive it as divinely spoken; such supersession he claims to be unacceptable.

However, Temple provides no reason for believing that the inspiration of the Bible must involve such supersession. When it comes to the faculties of its human authors, the postulation of supersession contradicts the traditional view of inspiration, which, although (as Temple says) stating that God spoke through these authors, denied that inspiration involved the suspension of their minds and wills. Augustine, for example, held that the Scriptures had God himself as their author:

> ... He who sent the prophets before His own descent also despatched the apostles after His ascension. Moreover, in virtue of the man assumed by Him, He stands to all His disciples in the relation of the head to the members of His body. Therefore, when those disciples have written matters which He declared and spake to them, it ought not by any means to be said that He has written nothing himself; since the truth is, that His

---

[31] Temple 1934, pp. 308–9.

members have accomplished only what they became acquainted with by the repeated statements of the Head. For all that He was minded to give for our perusal on the subject of His own doings and sayings, He commanded to be written by those disciples, whom He used as if they were His own hands. Whoever apprehends this correspondence of unity and this concordant service of the members, all in harmony in the discharge of diverse offices under the Head, will receive the account which he gets in the gospel through the narrative constructed by the disciples, in the same kind of spirit in which he might look upon the actual hand of the Lord Himself, which He bore in the body which He made His own, were he to see it engaged in the act of writing.[32]

But he also held that the minds and wills of the evangelists were involved in their teaching. He states that John the Evangelist 'had in view that true divinity of the Lord in which He is His Father's equal, and directed his efforts above all to the setting forth of the divine nature in his Gospel in such a way as he believed adequate to men's needs and notions ... in him you perceive one who has passed beyond the cloud in which the whole earth is wrapped, and who has reached the liquid heaven from which, with clearest and steadiest mental eye, he is able to look upon God the Word ...'[33] St. Athanasius condemned the view that the prophets had their intellects suspended when they were inspired, describing it as '... the trespass of the Phrygians, who say that the Prophets and the other ministers of the Word know neither what they do nor concerning what they announce.'[34] In his *Contra Celsum*, Origen attacks the claim that the Pythian priestess is inspired by Apollo by saying:

> Furthermore, it is not the work of a divine spirit to lead the alleged prophetess into a state of ecstasy and frenzy so that she loses possession of her consciousness. The person inspired by the divine spirit ought to have derived from it far more benefit than anyone who may be instructed by the oracles to do that which helps towards living a life which is moderate and according to nature, or towards that which is of advantage or which is expedient. And for that reason he ought to possess the clearest vision at the very time when the deity is in communion with him.
>
> 4. From this ground, by collecting evidence from the sacred scriptures, we prove that the prophets among the Jews, being illuminated by the divine Spirit in so far as it was beneficial to them as they prophesied, were the first to enjoy the visitation of the superior Spirit to them. Because of the touch, so to speak, of what is called the Holy Spirit upon their soul, they possessed clear mental vision and became more radiant in their soul ...[35]

---

[32] St. Augustine, *The Harmony of the Gospels*, in *Library of the Nicene and Post-Nicene Fathers*, first series, vol. VI, 1956a, p. 101.

[33] St. Augustine, 1956a, p. 79.

[34] St. Athanasius, *Third Discourse Against the Arians*, in *Library of the Nicene and Post-Nicene Fathers*, second series, vol. IV, 1978, p. 419.

[35] Origen, *Contra Celsum* 1965, book VII, pp. 396–7. Henry Chadwick remarks in a footnote to this passage that 'According to the Platonic view divine inspiration clarifies rather than confuses the mind.'

It is hard to see why a believer in the divine inspiration of the Bible should accept Temple's view of inspiration rather than a view like the ones of Origen or Augustine. There is no apparent contradiction in supposing that God speaks directly through people without suspending their minds and wills. Temple's position reveals itself as improbable, when we consider parallels taken even from purely human affairs. If an ambassador conveys an ultimatum on the part of his government, it is the government itself that delivers the ultimatum, even though the ambassador is acting freely. (The account of how God can speak through humans that is offered in Chapter 7 will enable us to see how such divine speech is compatible with human freedom.)

When it comes to the hearers who believe the Bible as divinely inspired, it is difficult to see how Temple could have thought that such belief involved the supersession of their natural faculties. Perhaps his idea was that if we believe that something is spoken by God we will have no choice but to believe it. But even this will result from an exercise of one of our faculties, our reason, rather than its supersession, and it does not rule out the possibility of our having a choice about whether or not to believe that something is spoken by God. Traditional theology held that we do have such a choice, and that this choice involves our will and affections. It is true that the traditional view held that in faith we surpass the capabilities of our natural faculties, but that is not the same as their being superseded. It is rather a case of their being enhanced, and such enhancement is not contrary to what we otherwise know of God's dealings with humanity, or to what the Christian revelation tells us about these dealings.

The argument given by Temple indicates a difficulty that arises in discussing non-propositional views of revelation. These views became dominant in academic Protestant circles in the nineteenth century, and since then they have been for the theologians who accept them more of an inherited assumption than a position that is examined and argued for. With some, they have become a basic part of their understanding of Christianity, and hence are effectively an aspect of the faith they profess rather than a theological deduction from that faith. It is thus hard to garner arguments from such theologians that can make a good case for their views. If they bother to give arguments, they usually pass on the ones that occurred in eighteenth- and nineteenth-century debates, which may tell against the specific forms of propositional views of revelation that were prevalent in those times, but do not help in deciding the general question of whether revelation involves the communication of propositions by God. The shortcomings of such arguments may have something to do with the polemical context in which they often originated (and continue to be used). Theologians like Temple and his predecessors were not engaged in pure academic investigation when they discussed the nature of revelation. They were also concerned to oppose theological views which they found objectionable for more reasons than an espousal of propositional revelation; they intended to criticize fundamentalism, conservative evangelicalism, and perhaps orthodox

Calvinism and Roman Catholicism.[36] Such polemical contexts are not conducive to doing justice to one's opponents' arguments.

One influential argument against propositional revelation has been clearly stated by Dodd. He assumes that a propositional view of revelation is equivalent to the view that the Bible is divinely revealed, and argues that the Scriptures contain quite a lot of falsehood, contradiction and moral error. Divine assertions cannot have these features, so the Scriptures cannot be communicated by God, and since they are not communicated by God revelation is not propositional. Dodd states:

> Historic Christianity has been a religion of revelation. This has been held to mean that the ultimate truths of religion are not discoverable by the unaided faculties of the human mind, but must have been directly communicated by God in a 'supernatural' way, and that the Bible is the 'Word of God' in this unique sense[37]... It long ago became clear that in claiming for the Bible accuracy in matters of science and history its apologists had chosen a hopeless position to defend. Much more important is the fact that in matters of faith and morals an unprejudiced mind must needs recognize many things in the Bible which could not possibly be accepted by Christian people in anything approaching their clear and natural meaning.[38]

Dodd cites the precept 'an eye for an eye and a tooth for a tooth' and the imprecatory psalms as examples of immoral biblical statements. The scientific discovery to which he refers presumably includes the findings of nineteenth-century geology and Darwin's theory of evolution, which revealed that the earth is millions of years old, that there was no world-wide flood, and that animal species came into being by evolution instead of being directly created by God over a period of several days.

Dodd's objection is a good one, if the Scriptures do in fact make the false statements that he refers to. It is indeed the best argument against the postulation of divinely revealed propositions, and the only one that identifies a real difficulty for this view. It is obviously not possible here to go into the question of what statements are made by the Bible, and whether any of them are false. I can only say that Dodd's argument does not establish his conclusion, because he just assumes that it is obvious that the false statements he has in mind are asserted by the biblical text, and this assumption is not obvious; it needs to be based on proof that he does not offer. (It is also open to question whether all the statements that he would take to be false, especially those that pertain to faith and morals, actually are false, but I will not go into this issue. Some of the statements that he takes to occur in Scripture certainly are false, and I will only consider these ones.) He does not see that in holding that, for example, the Scriptures state that the universe was created in six days, with plants being created on the third day, fish and birds on the

---

[36] In view of the weakness of the case against propositional revelation, I would venture a guess that this theological antagonism, rather than difficulties with the idea of revelation having a propositional character, was the principal motivation for non-propositional views of revelation.

[37] C. H. Dodd *The Authority of the Bible* , 1928, p. 8.

[38] Dodd, 1928, p. 13.

fifth, and so on – a statement that science has shown to be false – he is assuming a particular interpretation of the biblical text that is not obviously correct, and that has been rejected by many important Christian thinkers. It is well known that Jerome and Augustine, for example, did not interpret the beginning of the book of Genesis in this way.

It is likely that underlying Dodd's argument is the assumption that the 'clear and natural' meaning of the Scriptures is the meaning that its parts had when they were originally written down by their human authors. This assumption has been effectively criticized by Richard Swinburne in the valuable discussion of the principles that should be used in interpreting the Bible that he gives in his book *Revelation*.[39] Swinburne addresses the accusations Dodd makes against the Bible, and shows how they rely on this doubtful assumption. I will not recapitulate Swinburne's arguments, which he makes better than I could. I will only remark that what Dodd needs to make his accusations plausible is a view of biblical inspiration that sees it as occurring through the Holy Spirit's inspiring the individual authors of the texts that were assembled to make up the Scriptures, in their composition of these texts; the formation of the Bible as a whole then consisting simply in these texts being assembled together in a single cover. This may well have been the view of biblical inspiration that Dodd found to be generally accepted, but, as the discussion of inspiration in Chapter 7 will bring out, it is neither the only nor the most plausible view of how the Bible could have God as its author.

This discussion enables us to reach the conclusion that God speaks, and that the Christian message originates in God's speaking. The answer to the question of how Christians come to believe this message is thus to be found in a description of how we come to believe what God says.

---

[39] Richard Swinburne *Revelation*, 1992. I have defended Swinburne's position against criticism, and offered some anticipation of the ideas of the present book, in John Lamont, 'Stump and Swinburne on revelation', *Religious Studies*, 1996a.

Chapter 3

History of Christian Views on the Basis of Belief I: Patristic Themes

Since there is such a thing as divine speaking, and Christian faith includes believing God when he speaks, we can ask the question, 'What is it that leads us to believe God?'

It should be noted that on some views of faith, an explanation of what leads us to believe will not include rational grounds for belief. Such views hold that it is of the essence of Christian faith that it need not or even must not have rational grounds, or even that it be held in the face of rational grounds for not believing. The rational grounds in question here are ones that make belief theoretically reasonable, rather than ones that make belief practically reasonable, and they are not understood in the narrow sense of evidence from which a conclusion is inferred, but the broader sense of a good reason for believing. Theoretical reasonableness is an attribute of beliefs; it means that a belief is a reasonable thing to have. Practical reasonableness on the other hand is an attribute of actions; it means that an action is a good thing to do. The classic illustration of the difference between these two is that of the man being chased by wolves, who sees a crevasse in front of him barring his only route of escape. He may realize that he will have a better chance of jumping over the crevasse if he persuades himself that he is able to jump over it. In this case, his persuading himself that he is able to jump over the crevasse will be a good thing to do, and will thus be practically reasonable. The resulting belief that he can jump the crevasse may however not be theoretically reasonable, because the evidence available to him indicates that he is very unlikely to succeed. As far as I know, no Christian thinker has maintained that Christian faith is not practically reasonable. Some of them, however, have maintained that it is practically but not theoretically reasonable. Views of this kind are, however, late appearances in the history of Christian thought. They do not agree with the vastly preponderant view in Christian tradition, which is that Christian faith is eminently reasonable. They do not consort well with the apostle's injunction to be able to give a reason for the hope that is in you (1 Peter 3:15). I will assume that such views are false, and that faith is indeed theoretically reasonable.

In order to attempt a satisfactory answer to a question like this, one must have an idea of how it has developed historically. This is necessary to make available the resources of past thought on the subject, thus guarding against the dangers of reinventing the wheel or falling into already exposed blunders, and to grasp the nature of the question itself. It is also necessary because an answer to this question is an exercise in Christian theology, and as such must root itself in Christian tradition and the reflection of the Church on this subject. At the very least, any solutions or reflections on the question must at least cohere with past Christian thought on the subject in order to have a chance of being correct; in order to be probable, it must have elements of continuity with a main strand in Christian tradition.

A complete history would be an enormous task that is beyond my powers, but I will attempt to describe what seem to me to be the most important points in the evolution of thought on this question. Before embarking on this description, however, it is necessary to take note of the fact that not everyone would agree that past thought on a theological question can provide us with insights that will be helpful in our own efforts to solve it. Some scholars hold that thinkers who are remote from us in time and culture differ from us so greatly, in their presuppositions, interests and modes of thinking, that we cannot hope to share their beliefs or be convinced by their arguments. I do not accept this position. It incorporates a true insight, which is that we cannot think like the prophet Isaiah, Aristotle, Aquinas or Locke. They all lived in cultural worlds radically different from each other's and from our own. These cultural worlds conditioned the way they thought, and we cannot make ourselves into inhabitants of those worlds. Their worlds are gone beyond recall, and even if they still existed we could not leave behind our own cultural world in order to enter in to theirs.

But the fact that we cannot think in the same way as they did, and must necessarily differ from them in important ways, does not imply that we cannot be convinced by their arguments or share their beliefs. To take a clear example, it is quite possible for a contemporary person to be convinced by Aristotle's dissolution of some of Zeno's paradoxes.[1] That is because the unavoidable differences between the way we think and the way people thought in the past do not amount to complete unlikeness. And, in fact, they cannot amount to complete unlikeness, because we and the people who have gone before us live in the same universe, and both we and they have the capacity to arrive at knowledge of the world we live in. That means that when people in the present and the past arrive at knowledge of some universal feature of the world or of human existence, they will know and think the same things. Human knowledge and Christian faith are things that existed in the times of everyone who will be considered in our historical survey, as well as in the present, so we can hope to learn from what our predecessors thought.

In introducing an account of the history of views on this question, it is worth anticipating a crucial finding that will emerge from it. Discussion of what it is that leads us to believe gave rise to, and then to some extent centred itself around, a problem posed by three affirmations about Christian faith. Christian tradition has made three important affirmations about Christian faith. These affirmations are;

---

[1] This is an unquestionable but rather trite example; a more substantial one would be Aristotle's asking whether by 'democratic behaviour' we mean the kind of behaviour that is good for democracies, or the kind of behaviour that democracies like to indulge in. This is a point that we can find valuable and illuminating, even though the sort of democracy that Aristotle had in mind was wildly different from our own democracies.

1. Faith requires divine grace. It is not possible for the unaided human mind and will.

2. Faith is voluntary; we choose whether or not to have it.

3. Faith is theoretically reasonable.

For those who believe these affirmations – and I do – any acceptable description of faith must conform to them. But they have given rise to a problem that theologians have wrestled with for centuries.[2] The problem arises from conciliating these three affirmations. If faith is reasonable, because the believer is in possession of solid grounds for believing, how can he be able to choose whether or not to do so? Moreover, if such grounds are available, why is grace necessary in order to believe? If faith depends on free choice acting through grace, where is the role or need for rational grounds for belief?

This problem gives insight into how the question of what it is that leads us to believe bears upon the narrower issue of what it is about faith that makes it reasonable. Insistence on the voluntary character of faith, for example, might lead us to hold that the rational grounds for faith cannot be of a sort that would compel belief. Insistence on the necessity of grace for faith might lead us to hold that the rational basis for faith cannot be something available to sinners and the righteous alike. The problem also connects the question of what it is that leads us to believe to the wider issue of what Christian faith is, because it links the motivation for belief to God's action of grace in believers, and to the turning of the believer's will to God. It thus leads us to anticipate that an answer to the narrow question of what it is about faith that makes it rational, may involve an account of the nature of Christian faith itself. This anticipation will prove to be confirmed by the discussion in this book.

The problem also gives a guide to the scope of the historical examination that will be undertaken. The affirmations that give rise to it are in the fact the three main answers that have been given to the question 'What is it that leads us to believe?', namely, our choosing to believe, God's grace leading us to believe, and there being a good rational basis for belief. The history of these affirmations, and of the efforts made to conciliate them, will be a main theme of our investigation.

Patristic views on the grounds of faith

It would not be possible to give a complete account of patristic views on what it is that leads us to believe. Instead, what will be attempted is an account of the views of important figures who devoted a substantial amount of work to consideration of this question, and who between them made almost all the points of importance connected with the question that were made by anyone during the patristic period.

---

[2] On this problem see the standard work by Roger Aubert, *Le problème de l'acte de foi*, 2nd edn, 1950.

There are, as far as I can discover, four Fathers who satisfy this description: Clement of Alexandria, Origen, St. John Chrysostom, and Augustine. These four have the advantage of representing different schools of thought. Augustine was the most important of the Latin fathers, and the others are Greeks. Among the Greeks, St. John Chrysostom belonged to the school of Antioch, and Clement and Origen belonged to the school of Alexandria.

Clement of Alexandria

Clement's *Stromateis* contain the first substantial reflection on the reasonableness of faith in the history of Christian thought. Clement was aided in his task of reflection by the fact that he was well-educated and had a good grasp of the philosophy of his day, which he looked on favourably when it agreed with Christian teaching. His epistemological outlook is an eclectic and sometimes confused mixture of Stoic, Aristotelian and Platonic elements.

Clement's discussion of faith (πίστις) has in mind both Gnostic dismissals of faith as inferior to reason, and pagan criticisms of it as irrational. Galen criticized both Christ and Moses for insisting that their followers accept their teachings on faith alone. A surviving fragment of one of his works says, 'They compare those who practice medicine without any scientific knowledge of it to Moses, who framed laws for the tribe of the Jews, since it is his way to write his books without demonstration, saying "God commanded, God spoke."'[3] In his *De pulsuum differentiis* (ch. 4), he criticizes Archigenes for putting forward undemonstrated and unexplained laws, like Moses or Christ. Celsus was more harshly critical, accusing Jews and Christians of gullibility and superstition, and comparing them to people who believe soothsayers, mountebanks or conmen (see Origen's *Contra Celsum* I, 9; III, 75).[4]

Three principal meanings for the term πίστις can be found in Clement.[5] One of them is borrowed from the Stoic logicians of his time, who argued that every demonstration must eventually be traced back to some undemonstrated belief, and gave the name πίστις to belief in the undemonstrated first principles of demonstration (Clement uses this meaning in *Stromateis* (henceforth *Strom.*) *VIII*, 6, 7–7.2, a passage that he may have simply copied from a contemporary logic text). Another meaning is firm conviction in something known by scientific demonstration. The third is the religious belief that the New Testament terms πίστις. Clement describes this belief as belief in a teacher, Christ. Christ is the only

---

[3] Richard Walzer, *Galen on Jews and Christians*, 1949, p. 18.

[4] This continued to be a theme of pagan criticism of Christianity. Porphyry seems to have made it in his *Against the Christians* (cf. Eusebius, *Praeparatio Evangelica*, 1, 1). Julian the Apostate, as described by St. Gregory Nazianzen in his fourth oration (*Contra Julianum*), claimed: Ours are the reasoned arguments (οἱ λόγοι) and the pagan tradition (τὸ ἑλληΐζειν) which comprehend at the same time due worship of the gods; yours are want of reason and rusticity, and all your wisdom can be summed up in the imperative "Believe"' (translated by Walzer, 1949), p. 54).

[5] See on this question the discussion by Salvatore Lilla, *Clement of Alexandria*, 1971.

teacher for the Christian (*Strom. IV*, 25), and is the principle of teaching (*Strom. VII*, 16). He says, 'Because our soul was too weak to grasp the true realities, we had need of a divine teacher (διδάσκαλος): and our Saviour is sent here below, as a teacher who teaches how to acquire the good and who gives the means of doing so' (*Strom. V*, 1, my translation). This belief in a teacher gives rise to love (*Strom. V*, 13). We should hear the word of truth purely and without malice, like the children who obey us; it is in this way that Clement understands the statement in Matthew 18:3, to the effect that those who do not become like children will never enter the kingdom of heaven (*Strom. V*, 13).

Clement opposed the Gnostic views of Basilides and the Valentinians, who claimed that faith is not freely chosen; in this he is characteristic of all the Fathers. He argued that faith must be voluntary, since if it were not, unbelief could not be justly punished or faith rewarded (*Strom. II*, 3). Obedience to God requires us to have faith. Not only is faith required by good will and charity, rightness of will and charity are needed for faith. He compares charity to fertility in the earth, which is needed for the seed of teaching to take root in faith (*Strom. II*, 6). The decision to have faith involves divine assistance; a change so great as that from incredulity to belief must be something divine (*Strom. II*, 6).

In defending the reasonableness of faith, Clement assimilates faith in the third sense to faith in the first sense. Faith in Christ's teaching is for him a first principle, that, like the first principles of demonstration, is certain, and itself requires no demonstration. Clement holds Christian belief to be an infallible guide (*Strom. II*, 4). This is so because it is faith in the Logos, who is truth itself; such faith does not depend on demonstration, and is superior to it:

> Now the disciples of the philosophers define knowledge as a state which cannot be overturned by reasoning. But does there exist elsewhere a situation as stable with respect to the truth as in a religion that has the Logos for her sole teacher? I do not think so … Therefore, he who has believed in the divine Scriptures, with a firm judgement, receives as an irrefutable demonstration the voice of God who gave us those Scriptures. So faith is no longer something that is confirmed by demonstration. 'Blessed then are they that have not seen, and yet have believed' [John 20:29].[6]

Clement considers it absurd that the followers of Pythagoras should content themselves with the assertion that 'the master himself said so' when asked for the demonstration of a problem, but that people should refuse to trust a master who is worthy of faith, God the only Saviour, and ask him for proofs of what he said (*Strom. II*, 5). The fact that Christians are believing God is a sufficient refutation of the criticisms of non-Christians:

> We give to our adversaries this irrefutable argument; it is God who speaks and who, for each one of the points into which I am inquiring, offers answers in the Scriptures. Who would be an atheist to the point of not believing God and requiring proofs from him, as one does from men? (*Strom. V*, 1, my translation.)

---

[6] Clement of Alexandria, *Stromate II*, 2, 9, 1953, p. 39. I owe this translation to the help of Dr. Angus Bowie.

In a very important passage, he denies that Christian faith is based on signs (σημεῖον, a term that he probably takes from the Gospel of John). In *Strom. II*, 6, he writes: 'If "Abraham was believed and it was counted unto him for righteousness" [Rom. 4:3], and we are the seed of Abraham from what we have heard, we too must believe. For we are the children of Israel who obey not because of signs but because of what they heard.'[7] He thus explicitly denies that signs, such as those worked by Christ, are the reason why Christians believe; they believe simply on account of the spoken word of God. This is a striking anticipation of the Thomist view of the rational motivation for faith, discussed in the next chapter, which holds that God's speaking is the sole formal object (i.e. the sole theoretically rational motivation) for faith.

Clement places this view of faith into the framework of Hellenistic thought by describing it as a preconception, a πρόληψις. The notion of a preconception was proposed by the Epicureans, and adopted by the Stoics as well. They were understood to be general concepts, rather than propositions, that are formed without reflection through the operation of an innate rational capacity. Examples that were offered were the conception of God as a blessed and imperishable animal (described by Epicurus), or the conception of the good as something profitable and to be chosen (offered by Epictetus). The early Stoics thought of these preconceptions as arising from (although not inferred from) our sense experience, but later Platonizing Stoics held them to be innate ideas (cf. Epictetus, *Discourses*, book II, ch. 11). Although they were held to be concepts rather than propositions, they had propositional implications; from the concept of God as imperishable, for example, we can infer the proposition that God will never die. They enable us to draw conclusions about what exists; both Stoics and Epicureans appealed to preconceptions to show that God existed. They serve as criteria of truth, and anything that conflicts with them is to be rejected. Their status as criteria was justified by these arguments:

1. If we do not accept them as a starting point for reasoning, we will end up with an infinite regress; this argument was given by Epicurus, and quoted with approval by Clement in *Strom. II*, 4.

2. They have a certain clarity and obviousness that serve as a guarantee of their truth.

3. There is a common consensus in favour of them, and such a consensus ought to be accepted. Balbus, in Cicero's *De natura deorum II*, 5, makes this point; 'The years obliterate the inventions of opinion, but confirm the judgements of nature.'[8]

---

[7] Clement of Alexandria (1953), p. 56; this passage was kindly translated for me by Dr. Angus Bowie.

[8] Quoted in Malcolm Schofield, 'Preconceptions, Argument and God', in *Doubt and Dogmatism*, 1980, p. 298.

4. They come to us naturally, and because nature is ordered by God towards a providential end they are therefore trustworthy. (This was a Stoic argument that was not accepted by the Epicureans, who denied the existence of providence.)

Clement explicitly accepts Epicurus's definition of 'πρόληψις', with its claim that no judgements can be made without being based on them (*Strom. II*, 16, 3). He also asserts, along with the Stoics and Epicureans, that we know God to exist through preconceptions (*Strom. V*, 133). And, crucially, he describes faith in Christ as a πρόληψις,[9] thus giving a philosophical rationale for his description of it as infallible and not requiring evidence.

Clement's view that faith is an autonomous source of knowledge on a par with demonstration, and not merely a source of true belief, is a radical departure. However, it should be noted that he did not go so far as to claim that faith in testimony generally could provide knowledge that was on a par with that provided by other basic principles of demonstration; as the passage cited above makes clear, he thought that it was only God's testimony that could provide such knowledge.

Clement's position with respect to Gnostic criticism of faith was that although faith is an initial and (on its own) a second-best state for the Christian, it is nonetheless indispensable as the base for Christian life. He believed that the goal of the Christian life should be to obtain gnosis, a state of virtue and perfection where the divine mysteries are experienced and understood through contemplation. Clement was influenced in this by the Gnostics against whom he struggled, hoping to oppose a true gnosis to their false gnosis, although some mention of gnosis can be found in the Scriptures and the Apostolic Fathers.[10] Many of the Fathers held this idea of a divinely bestowed knowledge that surpasses faith, and that comes from something like experience of the realities believed in rather than from simply accepting what one is told about these realities. In the Latin Church this knowledge has come to be codified under the heading of the Gifts of the Holy Spirit.[11] Clement, like later tradition, did not think of this knowledge as replacing faith, but rather as presupposing it. Although faith was only a starting point for gnosis, it was necessary for it (*Strom. II*, 6, 31), and could never be abandoned by the gnostic. Faith is never left behind by the Christian, who is always in the position of a child trusting his father (*Strom. IV*, 25). It is as necessary for the gnostic as respiration for life; without faith there is no gnosis. We can draw a parallel between the relation of faith and gnosis and the relation of natural knowledge to the other preconceptions. Just as Clement holds, following Epicurus, that natural knowledge must be constructed on the basis of natural preconceptions, so he holds that gnosis must be constructed on the basis of faith.

---

[9] On this see Michel Spanneut, *Le Stoïcisme des pères de l'Église,* 1957, p. 280.

[10] See John 8:32, Phil.1:9, Col. 2:2, 2:3, and the Epistle of Barnabas 2.2, Ignatius to the Ephesians 17.2, Didache 9.3, 10.3.

[11] The Gifts that pertain to this knowledge are those of wisdom, knowledge and understanding.

Behind Clement's unsystematic presentation there can thus be found a powerful and important conception of faith. He thought of Christian faith as being:

- an autonomous source of knowledge, rather than of true opinion, that does not rest on anything else for its justification;
- based solely on belief in God's testimony, and not on the evidence of signs;
- superior in certitude to all other forms of knowledge;
- owing its superior certitude to the unsurpassable authority of the teaching of Christ, the Logos.

This is a striking and important conception of faith. It anticipates in a startling way many of the essentials of the view that was to be taken by St. Thomas Aquinas eleven hundred years later. Its importance is not merely historical; in it, Clement takes a position that remains one of the fundamental options for Christian accounts of faith.

Origen

Origen was the first person among the Fathers of the Church who could be described as an original genius. His work contains extensive and valuable consideration of what it is that leads us to believe. Origen and Clement stand on opposite sides of a watershed in ancient philosophy. This is the eclipse of the Hellenistic schools of philosophy, which were still active in Clement's time, and their replacement by adapted forms of Platonism, that attempted to incorporate Aristotle's logic and some elements of his metaphysics into a general Platonic framework. The chief importance of this change for thought about faith is that the Stoics and Epicureans held that sense experience could provide us with knowledge, and hence that we could have knowledge of particular contingent happenings. Platonism and Aristotelianism, however, denied that particular contingent events that occur in the physical universe could be the object of knowledge. Since many of the articles of faith concern such events, this change of philosophical outlook provided a motivation for holding that faith had to be seen as belonging to a different epistemic category than knowledge. For those Fathers who were Platonists (the vast majority), this motivation was usually overridden by their identification of Christ as the ultimate source of all knowledge, due to his being the Logos of God. When Aristotelian views of knowledge became preponderant in the Middle Ages, however, the fact that the subject matter of theology deals partly with contingent events was to raise difficulties with the ideas that theology is a science or that faith is a form of knowledge.

Like Clement, Origen thinks of faith as something inferior to and preparatory of a higher state, divine wisdom:

> Divine wisdom, which is not the same thing as faith, is first of what are called the spiritual gifts of God; the second place after it, for those who have accurate understanding of these matters, is called knowledge; and faith stands in the third place,

since salvation must also be available for the simple folk who advance in religion as far as they can comprehend.[12] (*Contra Celsum* (henceforth *C.C.*), VI, 13).

This faith consists in simply believing Christ:

> ... anyone who constructs a Christian philosophy will need to argue the truth of his doctrines with proofs of all kinds, taken both from the divine scriptures and from rational arguments. The simple-minded masses, however, who cannot comprehend the complex theology of the wisdom of God, must trust themselves to God and to the Saviour of our race, and be content simply with the *ipse dixit* of Jesus rather than with anything beyond this. (*C.C.* IV, 9)[13]

Origen, an intellectualist, has a low opinion of the simple believers and their faith. Nevertheless, he defends the reasonableness of their belief by appealing to the rationality and necessity of faith:

> Why is it not more reasonable, seeing that all human life depends on faith, to believe in God rather than in them [the teachers of philosophical schools]? Who goes on a voyage, or marries, or begets children, or casts seeds into the ground, unless he believes that things will turn out for the better, although it is possible that the opposite may happen – as it sometimes does? But nevertheless the faith that things will turn out for the better and as they wish makes all men take risks, even when the result is not certain...Now if it is the hope and the faith that the future will be better which maintain life in every action where the result is uncertain, why may not this faith be accepted by a believer in God more reasonably than by a man who sails the sea, or sows seed in the earth, or undertakes any other human activity? For he puts his faith in the God who created all these things ...(*C.C.* I, 11)[14]

Origen is clear that there is evidence that can conclusively establish that one ought to believe. He thinks it possible that the doctrines of Christianity can be mightily proved to be true by his defence (*C.C.* VIII, 1), and holds that there are many reasons to incite one to believe (*In Ioan.* II, 202).[15]

The strongest reason for belief, in his view, is the fulfilment in Jesus of the prophecies of Moses and the other prophets (*C.C.* I, 49). 'The proclamation of future events is the mark of a divinity, since they are not foretold by a natural human faculty ...' (*C.C.* VI, 10).[16] The same thing can be said about the fulfilment of Jesus's prophecies that his gospel would be preached in all the world, and that

---

[12] Origen 1953, VI, 13, p. 327.

[13] Origen 1953, pp. 189–90. Origen, like Clement, compares the faith of simple believers to that of the Pythagoreans who accepted what they were taught on the grounds that Pythagoras said so; see *C.C.* I, 7.

[14] Origen 1953, p. 14. Chadwick remarks in a footnote to this passage: 'Origen's four examples ... are commonplace, and go back to Clitomachus, leader of the New Academy. Cf. Cicero, *Lucullus*, 109.' Origen seems to be understanding πίστις here in its broader sense as true opinion, and not just as belief in testimony.

[15] Origen, *Commentaire sur St. Jean, tome IV* , 1982, II, §202, p. 347.

[16] Origen 1953, p. 324.

his disciples would be persecuted by rulers for no other reason than their espousal of his teaching (*C.C.* II, 42).

The miracles of Jesus are another reason for believing. Origen is quite sensitive to the difficulties involved in arguing from them: '... we must say that an attempt to substantiate almost any story as historical fact, even if it is true, and to produce complete certainty about it, is one of the most difficult tasks and in some cases is impossible.'[17] (*C.C.* I, 42). The miracles were capable of attracting to faith those who lived in the time of Christ, but with the passage of time their persuasive force has diminished, and many take them for myths (*In Ioan.* II, 202). His task was complicated by the fact that Celsus and other pagan critics of Christianity were willing to accept the existence of at least some of Christ's miracles, but to attribute them to sorcery rather than to divine intervention. Origen's reply to this is that Christ's life shows that he was not a sorcerer: '... no sorceror uses his tricks to call men to moral reformation; nor does he educate by the fear of God people who were astounded by what they saw, nor does he attempt to persuade the onlookers to live as men who will be judged by God.' (*C.C.* I, 68).[18] He defends the trustworthiness of the witness of the apostles. 'How could Jesus's disciples have received such great patience and determination to the point of death if they had been prepared to invent fictitious stories about their master? To people with an open mind it is quite clear that they were convinced of the truth of what they recorded from the fact that they endured such persecutions for the sake of him who they believed to be Son of God.' (*C.C.* II, 10).[19] The honest purpose of the apostles is shown by the fact that they recorded discreditable things about themselves (*C.C.* I, 63). They were eyewitness to the events they described (*C.C.* III, 24). Christians can show the prior probability of Christ's miracles: 'when we tell the stories about Jesus, we give a powerful defence to show why they happened. We argue that God wanted to establish the doctrine spoken by Jesus which brought salvation to men ...' (*C.C.* III, 28).[20] Moreover, miracles worked by Christians persist to this day, although not as abundantly as in apostolic times. 'Some display evidence of having received miraculous power because of this faith, shown in the people they cure ... By these we also have seen many delivered from serious ailments, and from mental distraction and madness, and countless other diseases, which neither men nor daemons had cured.' (*C.C.* III, 24).[21]

The Church is another great evidence for the truth of Christianity. 'If [Jesus] was a mere man, I do not know how he ventured to spread his religion and teaching in all the world, and was able to do what he desired without God's help and to rise above all the people opposing the spread of his teaching – kings, governors, the Roman Senate, rulers everywhere, and the common people.' (*C.C.* II, 79).[22]

---

[17] Origen 1953, p. 39.
[18] Origen 1953, p. 63.
[19] Origen 1953, pp. 75–6.
[20] Origen 1953, p. 145.
[21] Origen 1953, p. 142.
[22] Origen 1953, p. 127.

Origen cites the transformation in the lives of Christians as proof of the trustworthiness of the Christian message. 'But if any man were able to deliver souls from the flood of evil and from licentiousness and wrongdoing and despising God, and were to give as a proof of this work one hundred reformed characters (supposing this to be the number for the purposes of argument), could one reasonably say that it was without divine help that this man had implanted in the hundred men a doctrine capable of delivering them from evils of this magnitude?'[23] We can see how many converts, formerly plunged in a depth of licentiousness, injustice and covetousness, have become reverent, reasonable and stable after accepting the word. (*C.C.* I, 26).

The credibility of Christian teaching is defended by Origen through appealing to the agreement of these teachings with the moral principles known through the universal notions, κοιναὶ ἔννοιαί, that, following the Stoics, Origen thought were implanted by nature in all human minds. (*C.C.* II, 40).[24] He remarks of the Christian attitude to idolatry that 'in respect of this doctrine also, the knowledge of what is right conduct was written by God in the hearts of men.' (*C.C.* I, 5).[25]

In Origen we find the best and most complete patristic account of the evidence in favour of Christian belief. Virtually all the arguments for believing that are adduced by the Fathers are to be found in him. The major themes of patristic apologetics are prophecy, miracles, the extension and holiness of the Church, the transformative power of the Christian message and the independently establishable goodness and truth of Christian teaching. The description of Origen's views given above is enough for our purposes to serve as a representative account of patristic views on this subject.

Origen is confident that he can offer evidence to unbelievers that will show them that they ought to believe. He is equally clear, however, that such evidence is quite unnecessary for the faith of a Christian. The arguments he offers against Celsus will be unnecessary for anyone with real Christian faith. '... I have no sympathy with anyone who had faith in Christ such that it could be shaken by Celsus ... or by any plausibility of argument. I do not know in what category I ought to reckon one who needs written arguments in books to confirm and restore his faith after it has been shaken by the accusations of Celsus against the Christians.' (*C.C.* I, 4).[26]

If the reasons that Origen adduces against Celsus are not needed by believers, what is it that leads them to believe? He does not, in describing how people are actually led to believe, explicitly draw a distinction between the role of the kind of arguments he offers against Celsus and other factors. But in his account of how people are led to believe, he places the most stress, not on the evidence he uses in his apologetics, but on a certain divine power in the preaching of the gospel that causes people to believe:

---

[23] Origen 1953, pp. 26–7.
[24] For these notions see e.g. Cicero, *De Legibus*, I, 6, 18: Philo, *Quod Omnis Prob.* 46.
[25] Origen 1953, p. 9.
[26] Origen 1953, p. 5.

But when we consider that the doctrines which Celsus calls vulgar have been filled with power as though they were spells, and when we see that the words turn multitudes all at once from being licentious to living the most righteous life....are we not justified in admiring the power in the message? For the word of those who proclaimed these doctrines at the beginning and laboured to establish Churches of God, and their preaching also, did not possess a persuasion such as that of those who profess the wisdom of Plato or of one of the philosophers, who were but men and had nothing beyond human nature about them. The demonstration in Jesus' apostles was given by God and convinced men by spirit and power [cf. 1 Cor. 2:4]. For this reason their word ran very quickly and sharply, or rather God's Word which was working through them to change many of those who sin by nature and habit. Those whom a man could not change even by punishment, the Word transformed, shaping and moulding them according to his will. (*C.C.* III, 68).[27]

As this passage makes clear, Origen thinks that this power:

- surpasses the power of human nature;
- is the power of the Word, so that its action is the action of the Word;
- transforms its hearers and frees them from sin.

One might claim that the last of these features contradicts what he says elsewhere, when he asserts that rejection of sin is needed for faith.[28] But Origen's idea in making this assertion seems simply to be that faith and sin are not mutually compatible, not that the rejection of sin is something independent of and prior to reception of the Word.

The divine power of the Word preached is accompanied by divine action of the Word in the spirit of the hearer. 'But when the Logos of God says that "No man has known the Father except the Son, and the man to whom the Son may reveal him", he indicates that God is known by a certain divine grace, which does not come about in the soul without God's action, but with a sort of inspiration.' (*C.C.* VII, 44).[29] This divine power is what gives divine wisdom, and this divine wisdom is what enables believers to grasp the spiritual sense of the Scriptures, a sense that is completely inaccessible to unbelievers.[30]

Origen does not say any more than this about what this divine power is, or how it works. His Platonism may help to explain why he did not do so. This philosophy, which in a Christianized form he shared with most of the Fathers, made him think of all knowledge of truth and all good action as somehow being the work of the

---

[27] Origen 1953, pp. 173–4.

[28] See Origen, *Homélies sur le Lévitique*, vol. II (homélies VIII–XVI), 1981, book XIII, 2, pp. 203–205. This is the Latin translation of Rufinus, who on his own admission took considerable liberties with Origen's text. However, his alterations had the purpose of removing assertions that contradicted later orthodoxy, and in passages such as this one, which does not relate to any of the views for which Origen was later criticised, his translations still have value as evidence for Origen's positions.

[29] Origen 1953, p. 432.

[30] See Origen, *Homélies sur la Génèse*, 2nd edn, 1985), hom. VII, 6.

Logos. 'For nothing good has happened among men without the divine Logos who
has visited the souls of those who are able, even if but for a short time, to receive
the operations of the divine Logos.' (*C.C.* VI, 79).[31] This view obviously makes
distinctions between divine and human roles in faith and preaching difficult to
draw, and to some extent removes any motivation for drawing them. With Origen,
as with the other Platonist Fathers, precision about these distinctions is not to be
looked for. The Platonic assimilation of evil in human character to ignorance, and
of goodness to knowledge, was also an influence in Origen's thinking of our
coming to know the truth and our becoming good in character as more or less the
same thing. It is not that he was necessarily mistaken in closely associating these
two things. The New Testament often presents them as linked, or even as two
aspects of the same reality. We are, however, inclined to think that the explanation
for our coming to know and the explanation for our coming to be good must be in
some respect distinct, and to ask what that distinction consists in. The Platonism of
Origen, and of the Fathers in general, meant that they did not concern themselves
much with this question, and hence that they did not offer considered answers to it.

St. John Chrysostom

Chrysostom did not address the question of faith in any systematic way. His
writings nonetheless contain a substantial amount of reflection about faith, and set
forth a distinctive position on the subject.[32]

Unlike Clement and Origen, he does not present faith as a second-class citizen
of the spiritual world, inferior to a higher wisdom. His account of the evidences for
belief does not add anything to Origen's; he sees these evidences as consisting
principally in miracles and prophecy, although he makes some mention of the
Church as a miracle.

The object of faith, in Chrysostom's view, is the spoken word of God. In
believing the Scriptures, we are believing God's direct assertions, because he is
their author (*in Gen.* 5, 1–2; *in 2a Tim.* 3, 15). He makes it clear that the only
reason we believe God's message is that God says it. We should not ask proofs of
veracity from God as we should from a man (*in 1a Cor.* 2, 5). It is right to weigh
the veracity of human assertions, but with divine ones we must simply revere and
obey (*in 1 Tim.* 1, 4). The miracles and signs that accompany God's message do
indeed show that we should believe, and that is why God brings them about, but
they are a condescension to those weak in faith and character. We ought to believe
simply because of the preaching of the word, and not because of signs that
accompany it. The preaching of God's word is in fact something greater than any
sign.

Our motive for believing is simply that God's word is worthy of faith (*in 1a
Cor.* 6, 14; *in 2a Cor.* 4, 18). God's word is more worthy of belief than is sight,
because sight sometimes errs, but God's word never does (*in Jo.* 3, 5). What is true

---

[31] Origen 1953, p. 392; cf. Justin Martyr, *Apol.* I, 46.
[32] In this account of Chrysostom's views on faith I follow Ephrem Boularand, *La venue de
l'homme à la foi d'après S. Jean Chrysostôme*, 1939.

of sight is true of reasoning in general. Reasoning never gives full certainty (*contra Anomaeos*, 11), but faith does (*in Hebr.* 13, 16; *in 1a Cor.* 3, 20). In fact, what before the time of Christ was known by reason, like the existence of God, ought now to be accepted solely on the more sure basis of faith (*in Hebr.* 11, 6; *in 1a Cor.* 1, 29).

Faith completely excludes doubt, and the existence of any doubt means that there is no faith. As sight is to visible things, so faith is to invisible ones. Faith is a vision of the invisible, that brings the same full certitude as sight. It is not possible to have faith if one is not more undoubtingly assured of what we do not see, than we are of what we do see (*in Heb.* 11, 1).

This does not mean that there is any conflict between faith and reason. It is unreasonable to try and discover through reason what can only be known by faith. Chrysostom compares attempting to know divine mysteries through reason with attempting to pull a red-hot iron out of the fire with one's fingers, instead of with tongs (*in 1a Cor.* 1, 26). God gave us our reason so that it could learn and receive what he teaches it, not so that it could think itself to be self-sufficient (*in 1a Cor.* 2, 14). Unbelief is foolish and criminal, and belongs to intelligences that are weak and small and miserable.

Given this view of the role of reason, it is natural for Chrysostom to see the main obstacle to faith as being pride, which leads to our reason not being willing to recognise its proper limits (*in Gen.* 11, 2; *in Jo.* 3, 4; *in Rom.* 1, 21-23), although other bad passions also serve as obstacles. Chrysostom is insistent that faith is freely chosen. His explanation for the diminution in the number of miracles since the Apostles' times is that miracles reduce our freedom to believe, and thus take away its merit. When Christ comes in glory with all his angels, the Greek will believe in him, but this belief will not be faith, and will not be meritorious, because it will be necessary. It will be compelled by the evidence, and thus not the effect of a free choice (*in 1a Cor.* 2, 5).

Chrysostom's views on the relation of grace to faith have been the subject of controversy. In some texts, he describes the beginning of faith as being our work, and God as waiting to see if we freely respond to him and after our positive response giving us the grace we need to go on (*in Hebr.* 7, 10; *De verbis Apostoli, Habentes eundem Spiritum*, I; P.G. 51, 276). This has led some scholars to describe his views as akin to Semi-Pelagianism.[33] But this is a mistaken and anachronistic reading of his views. Chrysostom describes grace as a gift of God that is not due to our merits (*in 1a Cor.* 1, 4). So understood, it is obviously capable of extremely wide application, and he does indeed use it to designate such diverse things as creation, the natural law, and the gift of the Holy Spirit at baptism. The view that our acceptance of faith is not due to grace, and that grace is only provided in God's response to this acceptance, does not fit well with Chrysostom's broad conception of grace. Moreover, his assertions about our initiative in choosing to believe are made in order to reject the view that God removes our free will in bringing us to faith. They are part of his insistence on the voluntary nature of faith, an insistence

---

[33] For instance, J. Turmel, *Histoire des Dogmes*, vol. 5, 1936, pp. 22–4.

that was partly a reaction to the denial of this freedom on the part of the Manichees. But the contention that our choosing to believe is not caused by God in a way that overrides our free will, is not the same as an espousal of Semi-Pelagianism. The opponents of Semi-Pelagianism held that our choice to believe requires grace, and is impossible without it, but denied that this grace excludes freedom in our choosing to believe. They thought instead that grace was necessary in order to enable us to freely choose to believe. Chrysostom in fact thought that all our good actions require divine grace. All our bad actions are done solely by our own will, while our good actions are done by both our will and God's impulsion (*in 2a Tim.* 3, 15). All our efforts to do good will be fruitless without this help (*in Gen.* 33, 17). From the text 'What have you that you have not received?' (1 Cor. 4:7), he concludes that our good actions are not our own, but from the grace of God (*in 1a Cor.* 4, 7). Since the choice to believe is a good action, it must on his view require the grace of God.

The most interesting feature of Chrysostom's views is also the one that leaves us with the most questions. This feature is his claim that God's testimony is the sole ground we have for faith, and that this testimony is the strongest kind of rational ground that it is possible to have for any belief. The reaction one is likely to offer is that this position is a strong one, provided it is granted that we can identify God's speaking. Chrysostom just assumes that we do this; he does not explain how it happens.

St. Augustine

The study of Augustine's views on faith is a huge and difficult field. It often requires one to confront difficulties on central questions for which there is as yet no agreed solution (an example would be the nature of his theory of intellectual illumination). This being so, a comprehensive account of his ideas on faith cannot be attempted here. Instead, what will be offered is an account of the highlights of those features of his thought that are important for our investigation.

Augustine, like Chrysostom, awards the highest degree of certainty to faith. In his early work the *Contra Academicos*, he situates this position within a discussion of the history of philosophical thought up to his time. Zeno had associated knowledge with perception of truth (in Greek κατάληψις), and had claimed 'that nothing could be perceived unless it was so manifestly true that it could be distinguished from what was not true through a dissimilarity in indications, and that the wise man could not admit an opinion'.[34] The Academics had claimed that such perception was impossible, and thus that we should suspend judgement on the truth or falsity of assertions. When attacked on the grounds that suspension of judgement would make action impossible, they replied that we should act according to what is truth-like. Augustine accepts Zeno's definition, and claims

---

[34] St. Augustine *Contra Academicos*, 1951, pp. 79–80. Cf. Cicero, *Acad.* 2.59.

that the authority of Christ gives knowledge. 'I, however, am resolved in nothing whatever to depart from the authority of Christ – for I do not find a stronger.'[35]

Why is it that Christ's authority gives certainty? We should be careful about assuming that Augustine's answer to this question is to be found in the defence he offers for believing. He cites the usual evidences of miracles, prophecy and the Church as proofs of the truth of Christian claims, and improves on some other apologetic reasonings of this sort by bringing out the fact that these happenings are not independent signs, but rather aspects of a single salvation history which is the fundamental evidence for Christianity (see his Letter 137[36]). He also argues in favour of the rationality of belief in testimony;

> I omit to mention in how many things they, who find fault with us because we believe what we see not, believe report or history; or concerning places where they have not themselves been; and say not, we believe not, because we have not seen. Since if they say this, they are obliged to confess that their own parents are not surely known to them: because on this point also they have believed the accounts of others telling of it, who yet are unable to show it, because it is a thing already past; retaining themselves no sense of that time, and yet yielding assent without any doubting to others speaking of that time: and unless this be done, there must of necessity be incurred a faithless impiety towards parents...Since therefore, if we believe not those things which we cannot see, human society itself, through concord perishing, will not stand; how much more is faith to be applied to divine things, although they be not seen; failing the application of which, it is not the friendship of some men or other, but the very chiefest bond of piety that is violated, so as for the chiefest misery to follow.[37]

He distinguishes between human authority and divine authority, and states that while human authority often fails, divine authority is true, solid and supreme.[38]

If we were to ask Augustine why it is that faith is certain, it is unlikely that he would mention any of the signs that he enumerates in his Letter 137. They occur in his writings only when he is replying to the objections of unbelievers. Rather, the answer that he would give would simply be that faith is in Truth itself, which has taken flesh. This Truth, for him as for Origen, is the source of all human knowledge whatsoever, and when we arrive at this Truth our search for knowledge reaches its goal. The question 'Why have faith in Christ?' literally means for Augustine 'Why believe the truth?', and it is not a question that he could think of as genuinely in need of an answer.

Augustine's views on the necessity of grace for faith represent an advance in precision on previous patristic views on this question. He specifies the sense of faith that he has in mind when he discusses whether faith requires grace; faith is believing someone, and believing is consenting to the truth of what is said (*De spiritu et littera*, ch. 54, 1993b). In the course of his controversy with Pelagius, he

---

[35] St. Augustine 1951, p. 150; *De ordine*, 1948, p. 200.
[36] St. Augustine, *S. Augustini epistulae*, 1895.
[37] St. Augustine *De fide rerum quae non videntur*, 1993a, p. 339. See also *Confessions*, 1991a, book 6, ch. 5, v. 7.
[38] St. Augustine 1948, p. 410.

also specifies what he means by grace. Pelagius had distinguished between the capacity for action, the willing to do an action, and the action itself. Pelagius maintained that the capacity to act well is bestowed by God, and is thus rightly described as grace, but the other two belong to men. It is because the capacity for action is needed for all good action that we can say that good action depends on grace (*De gratia Christi*, chs. 4, 5).

Augustine states that this account of grace cannot be right, because the capacity to act belongs to all men whether sinners or righteous, but grace does not (*De gratia et libero arbitrio*, ch. 18, 1993c). Like Chrysostom, he holds that grace is a gift of God that is not due to our merits (*De natura et gratia*, ch. 4). He is more precise than Chrysostom, however, in that he states that the grace of Christ that brings about our salvation is not part of our nature, or even of our nature as it was before being damaged by the Fall, and does not pertain to the constitution of our nature. Rather, it is that which assists our frail and corrupted nature (*De natura et gratia*, ch. 12; *De gestis Pelagii*, ch. 20). In all our good actions, it is not only our capacity, but our willing and action as well, that are owing to the grace of God. Without grace, man can do nothing good, in thought, will, affection or action (*De correptione et gratia*, ch. 3). This does not mean that grace takes away our free will. Rather, it is grace that makes it possible for us to freely choose to do good (*De correptione et gratia*, ch. 2). The children of God are acted upon so that they may act, not so that they may do nothing (*De correptione et gratia*, ch. 4).

This general view on the necessity of grace for good action is explicitly applied by Augustine to faith. He says that the capacity to have faith and to love belongs to our nature, but actually having faith and love belongs to grace (*De predestinatione sanctorum*, ch. 8). When the gospel is preached, some believe and others do not. The difference between the two sorts of people is that those who believe hear the Father within. 'To be drawn to Christ by the Father, and to hear and learn of the Father in order to come to Christ, is nothing else than to receive from the Father the gift by which to believe in Christ. For it was not the hearers of the gospel that were distinguished from those who did not hear, but the believers from those who did not believe, by Him who said, "No man cometh to me except it were given him of my Father."'[39] Augustine describes the grace within as more important than the preaching from without in bringing men to faith:

> What do men that proclaim tidings from without? What am I doing even now while I speak? I am pouring a clatter of words into your ears. What is that that I say or that I speak, unless He that is within reveal it? Without is the planter of the tree, within is the tree's Creator. He that planteth and he that watereth work from without: this is what we do. But 'neither he that planteth is anything, nor he that watereth; but God giveth the increase.' (1 Cor. 3:7).[40]

---

[39] St. Augustine, *On the Predestination of the Saints*, 1993d, p. 506.

[40] St. Augustine, *Tractates on the Gospel of John*, tractate XXVI, 7, 1993e, p. 170.

In disputing with the Semi-Pelagians, Augustine admits to having been mistaken on the necessity of grace for the acquisition of faith.[41] Before becoming a bishop, he had thought that the beginning of faith was our own work, whereas its increase was due to God. He changed his mind on this question while studying Paul's letter to the Romans, in the course of writing a letter to Simplicianus, Ambrose's successor as Bishop of Milan. He asserts that the text 'What have you that you have not received?' (1 Cor. 4:7) does not allow any believer to say that he has faith which he has not received (*De predestinatione sanctorum*, ch. 8, 1993d). He points out that in 1 Thessalonians 2:13 Paul thanks God for the belief of the Thessalonians ('And we also thank God constantly for this, that when you received the word of God which you heard from us, you accepted it not as the word of men but as what it really is, the word of God, which is at work in you believers'), and asks why Paul should have offered thanks if this belief were not God's work (*De predestinatione sanctorum*, ch. 39, 1993d).

It is important to distinguish between Augustine's views on the necessity of grace for good action in general and faith in particular, and his views on predestination. He thought that only those people predestined by God to salvation received the grace necessary for good action and for faith, and hence that those who hear the gospel but do not believe because they are not taught by the Father, are not taught because the Father has not predestined them to receive grace and be saved. But his position on predestination is independent of his position on the necessity of grace for faith and good action. If we reject his views on predestination, as many are inclined to do, that does not mean that we ought to reject his views on the necessity of grace for faith.

One of the most valuable features of Augustine's thought on faith is the connection that he makes between it and his Trinitarian theology. An adequate theological understanding of our believing God must relate this act of believing to the Holy Trinity. Augustine holds that everything done to elicit faith is either produced by the mission or is the mission of the Son (*De trinitate*, book 4, ch. 5, v 25). The Word is sent by the Father to someone, when the Son is known and perceived by that person. The Word's sending is not his being sent into the world, but his being known by someone in time (*De trinitate*, book 4, ch. 5, v. 28). As mentioned above, it is the Father that draws us to believe in the Son:

> But what is this, 'Whom the Father shall draw', when Christ Himself draws? ... the Father draws to the Son those who believe on the Son, because they consider that God is His Father. For God begat the Son equal to himself, so that he who ponders, and in his faith feels and muses that he on whom he has believed is equal to the Father, this same is drawn of the Father to the Son. Arius believed the Son to be creature: the Father drew not him; for he that believes not the Son to be equal to the Father, considers not the Father. This revealing is itself the drawing. Thou holdest out a green twig to a sheep, and thou drawest it ... does not Christ, revealed by the Father, draw? For what does the

---

[41] For a classic account of the evolution of Augustine's thought on faith, grace and reason, see André Mandouze, *Saint Augustin, l'aventure de la raison et de la grâce*, 1968.

soul more strongly desire than the truth? For what ought it to have a greedy appetite ...
unless it be to eat and drink wisdom, righteousness, truth, eternity?[42]

Augustine relates the Holy Spirit to the love that must vivify faith if faith is to avail
for salvation (*De trinitate* XV, 32).

The patristic materials on faith are far less extensive than the medieval ones.
This reflects the fact that the great concerns of the patristic era were the doctrines
connected with the Trinity, the Incarnation, and the person of Christ. In a natural
ordering of thought, the content of the chief articles of faith was addressed before
the way in which we come to know these articles was considered in depth.
However, our examination of patristic thinkers has revealed definite common
views. These views are developments of the more general view, held by all the
Fathers, that the Scriptures are an autonomous source of knowledge, that does not
depend on philosophy, and that judges philosophy rather than being judged by it.
This general view is significant in itself, because it rules out the possibility of
Christian faith being based on natural human reasoning. What we find in Clement,
Origen, Chrysostom and Augustine are reflections on why faith and the Scriptures
are thus autonomous. As we have seen, these reflections agree on certain important
points. All of them react to pagan criticism of the irrationality of Christian belief
by flatly contradicting it. They claim that it is rational; and the reason they give for
its rationality is the fact that it is believing God, who has the highest possible
degree of authority. This authority gives faith a certainty that is equal to, or greater
than, that of any other kind of knowledge. This certainty is not conferred by the
signs or evidence for God's having spoken, although these signs suffice to make
the fact of his having spoken beyond reasonable doubt. Faith is not based on these
signs, it is based simply on God's spoken word. When it comes to the question of
how this word is recognized if not through signs, however, these Fathers are not
very clear. They agree that such recognition involves and requires the intervention
of divine grace, but, aside from Origen's assertion about a divine power inherent in
the word, they do not give an account of how this grace operates to bring about
recognition. The absence of such an account left an opening for medieval debates
on this subject, and may have contributed to the scholastic departure from their
views.

---

[42] St. Augustine (1993e), pp. 169–70.

Chapter 4

History of Christian Views on the Basis of Belief II: Medieval and Modern Options

The Fathers of the Church offer reflections on what it is that leads us to hold that Christianity is divinely revealed, but they do not make this question into a distinct subject of investigation. It is in the Middle Ages that the question is first addressed independently and explicitly, and that different answers to it are debated. This means that the medieval and modern periods are extremely rich in resources for the consideration of this question, far too rich for it to be possible to give a complete account of them within the confines of this book. What will be attempted here is not such an account, but rather a focussing in on one question, whose answer will be seen to be the key to an understanding of the rationality of Christian faith. This issue is the role of the motives of credibility in faith. 'Motives of credibility' is the term that theologians have coined to refer to the publicly available evidence, accessible to believer and unbeliever alike, that can be used to support the contention that the Christian message is communicated by God. The fact that these motives are accessible to both believers and unbelievers means that they cannot include evidence whose acceptance would presuppose faith. Thus, for example, the claim that the Christian message is true because God has spoken it could not form part of the motives of credibility, because its acceptance presupposes faith (although it could be a conclusion established by these motives). By 'Christian faith' I mean the virtue of Christian believers by which they believe the Christian gospel, the virtue that is an essential part of the Christian life, that is pleasing and acceptable to God, and that is conducive to (or actually brings about) one's salvation. This specification is necessary because it can be maintained that there are different sorts of faith in divine speaking. The devils, for example, are said to believe and tremble. Their belief, as we shall see, has been thought by many theologians to be different from the virtue of faith possessed by Christian believers. If it is different, its relation to the motives of credibility will not be a final goal of our investigation; what we want to know about is the connection between the motives of credibility and the faith of Christian believers.

This consideration of views on the motives of credibility will have two parts. The first will be an account of how the discussion of the role of these motives first emerged. The second will be an account, not of the history of thought on this question (something that would be too great an undertaking), but rather of the three different sorts of answer that have been given to it.

The role of motives of credibility: beginning of the discussion

The history of explicit discussion of the role of motives of credibility begins with
Peter Abelard. Abelard is important because he is the first major Christian
theologian to attack the rationality of accepting Christian teachings solely on the
basis of God's testimony.

In his *Theologia 'Scholarium'* Abelard asks what we should think of those
people who claim that faith is not to be established or defended through reasoning.[1]
The establishment and defence in question is not concerned with the rationality of
accepting that the Christian faith is divinely revealed; it is rather the establishment
and defence of the articles of faith. He raises this question because he holds that
these articles can be established by reason alone, independently of divine
revelation. This view leads him to oppose theologians who maintain that our belief
in the articles of faith is founded solely on God's telling us that they are true.

He argues against such theologians by asserting that if we put our trust solely in
authority, we are committed to acquiescing equally in false as in true preaching. He
considers an objection to this argument that appeals to a text from a sermon of
Gregory the Great, a text that becomes a standard reference point for subsequent
discussion of this issue: 'Sciendum nobis est quod diuina operatio, si ratione
comprehenditur, non est admirabilis, nec fides habet meritum, cui humana ratio
prebet experimentum' ('It is known to us that the divine beneficence is not worthy
of wonder if it is grasped by reason, nor does that faith have merit, for which
human reason provides proof').[2] He asks if this text does not imply that nothing
connected with the mysteries of the Catholic faith should be investigated by
reason, but rather that everything connected with them should be accepted at once
on the basis of authority, no matter how remote from human reason they are. He
replies that if Gregory were really to be understood as meaning this, he would be
contradicting his own practice and that of the many other holy doctors who use
reason to defend the truthfulness of the articles of faith. This position would make
it impossible to prove false the faith of any people whatsoever, even if they were so
sunk in blindness as to declare any idol to be the God who created heaven and
earth. In fact, Abelard maintains, Gregory is not saying that faith is not to be
reasoned about or investigated, but rather that belief which is based on human
reason alone is not meritorious. However, the fact that the beginning of faith,
which is based on human reason, does not have merit, does not imply that this
beginning is useless when charity is added to it and provides the merit that it lacks.
Abelard quotes the text of Ecclesiasticus, 'Qui cito credit, levis corde est et
minorabitur' ('One who trusts others too quickly is lightminded', Eccles. 19:4), to
argue that it is wrong to believe without rationally assessing what it is that you are

---

[1] Peter Abelard, *Theologia 'Scholarium'*, 1987. In his earlier works Abelard takes a more
positive view of the rational value of believing on the basis of authority, and does not claim
that the contents of the faith can be established by reason alone.

[2] St. Gregory the Great, Hom. 26, 1 (P.L. 76, 1197C).

believing. He claims that those who believe easily will also turn away from belief easily.[3] Abelard turns a standard patristic apologetic move on its head by quoting in support of his position a text from Jerome that praises St. Marcella for not accepting the 'ipse dixit' of her teacher as the Pythagoreans do, or accepting authority unsupported by the verdict of reason.[4] The patristic move, as we have seen, was to say that if the Pythagoreans were not thought unreasonable in offering 'The master said so' as a ground for their assertions, much less should Christians be thought unreasonable in doing so when they have a divine master instead of a human one.

Abelard does not deny that faith involves believing on divine authority; he just wants to maintain that divine authority cannot on its own provide rational grounds for faith. His positive account of faith does not have the interest and the widespread influence of his sceptical arguments about the rationality of believing on the basis of authority. His contemporaries were not inclined to accept his views on the possibility of proving the articles of faith on the basis of human reason unaided by revelation, a view that in any event was condemned by the Church along with several of his other positions (publication of the *Theologia 'Scholarium'* led to Abelard's excommunication by Innocent II). They were, however, led by his arguments to explicitly raise the question of whether Christian faith is reasonable, and explain why they thought it was.

Abelard's contemporary Hugh of St. Victor, reacting to some extent to Abelard's views, maintained that faith is essentially located in the will. He describes faith as consisting in two things: cognition and affection. Cognition is understanding of what it is that is proposed to us for belief; affection is constancy and firmness in believing. This constancy and firmness, a property of the will, is the substance of faith, and the things believed are the material of faith.[5] This constancy is what gives merit to believing. In order for this constancy to be meritorious, the things believed cannot be manifestly true, because if they were there would be no place for unbelief. Nor can they be entirely hidden, for if they were faith would be impossible.[6] Faith is thus placed by Hugh between knowledge and opinion, in a definition that is subsequently very influential:

> ... if any one wishes to note a full and general definition of faith, he can say that faith is a kind of certainty of the mind in things absent, established beyond opinion (*opinio*) and short of knowledge (*scientia*). For there are some who straightway repel with the mind what is heard and contradict those things which are said, and these are deniers. Others in those things which they hear select any one side whatever for consideration but they do not approve for affirmation. For although they believe one of the two as the more

---

[3] 'Vix enim qui levitur credit, firmus in fide permanserit. Nec quod levitate geritur, stabilitate firmabitur.'Abelard 1987, p. 431.

[4] St. Jerome, *Commentariorum in Epistolam ad Galatas*, P.L. 26, book 1. The text does not support Abelard's argument, because Jerome is praising Marcella for inquiring about what it is that the Scriptures are saying, not for inquiring about whether what the Scriptures say is true or not.

[5] Hugh of St. Victor, *On the sacraments*, 1951, book 1, part 10, ch. 3.

[6] Hugh of St. Victor, 1951, book 1, part 3, ch. 2.

probable, yet they do not presume to assert whether it itself is still true. These are the conjecturers (*opinantes*). Others thus approve the other side, so that they assume its approbation even unto assertion. These are the believers (*credentes*). After these kinds of cognition that more perfect kind follows when the thing is made known not from hearing alone but through its presence...These are the knowers (*scientes*).[7]

Richard of St. Victor confronted Abelard's view more directly by asserting that the miracles that accompanied the preaching of the gospel were so great that it is certain that the Christian faith comes from God, so certain that we can say that if there is any error in this faith it is God himself who has deceived us.[8]

It is with William of Auxerre that the idea of whether or not faith is based on the motives of credibility is first raised and discussed. This occurs when William asks whether the same things can be both known and believed. In his answer, he distinguishes between three kinds of accidental knowledge of God. By 'accidental' he means knowledge that is acquired, as opposed to innate. These three kinds are the knowledge acquired by natural reasoning, of the sort possessed by philosophers; the knowledge acquired from miracles and the testimony of the Scriptures, which he calls formless faith (*fides informis*); and the knowledge that is given by grace and brought about through divine illumination, which does not rest on natural reason, but rather assents to first truth for its own sake. When people who have the first two sorts of knowledge acquire the third sort, the first two kinds cease to exist, just as the light of the stars is extinguished when the light of the sun appears. The reasons that give rise to the first two sorts are not forgotten when divine faith is acquired, but divine faith does not rest on them. Rather, these reasons serve to confirm and increase faith.[9]

In the *Summa Theologica* of the Franciscan theologian Alexander of Hales the issue of whether faith is acquired through reasoning or persuasion reaches the stage of being discussed as a separate question. (This *Summa* was begun by Alexander, but completed by members of his school, so the authorship of this question is uncertain.) The arguments considered in this question are worth considering in some detail.

The arguments given against the conclusion that faith is acquired through reasoning include the following:

- Just as it is one thing to love someone because of their good qualities and another thing to love someone who lacks good qualities purely out of virtue and grace, so it is one thing to believe because of probability and evidence and another thing to believe because of the virtue of believing. Just as the virtue of charity lies in loving those who are evil, so the virtue of believing lies in believing what is improbable. If therefore from charity

---

[7] Hugh of St. Victor, 1951, book 1, part 10, ch. 2, p. 168.
[8] Richard of St. Victor, *De Trinitate*, 1958.
[9] See William of Auxerre (also known as Guillelmus Altissidorensis), *Summa aurea*, liber tercius, tomus I, cap. IV, 1986, p. 206.

we love those who are evil, so through saving faith we believe without proof or persuasive reasons that which is improbable.[10]

- It is only liars who are not believed in the absence of suitable proofs for what they say. Those therefore who only believe God when they possess sufficient and certain proofs hold him in open contempt, and therefore saving faith believes God without proofs.

- Just as the rational will owes a due love to the highest good, so the reason owes belief to the highest truth. Thus, as a love of God that seeks him only on the grounds of the goods that may be received from him is unworthy, so also a rational belief that believes First Truth because of proofs is unworthy of God.

- The intellect's believing only when it possesses proof can be compared to a merchant's paying only when he has received pledges or guarantees. The demand for a guarantee results from a lack of belief; even so the intellect's demand for proof springs from its lack of belief. If therefore the intellect cannot please God through unbelief, neither can a faith that is acquired from proofs please God.

On the other hand, these arguments are given in favour of the position that faith is acquired through reasoning;

- Augustine states[11] that we believe what is not present to our senses when we possess suitable testimony through which it can be believed. Therefore that which is believed although not seen is established through testimony.

- We believe the testimony of the Apostles (Acts 1:8), and we believe the testimony of creatures that God is all-powerful and the Creator (Rom. 1:20, Wisd. 13:5). But if the faith by which we believe these things is necessary to salvation, saving faith consists in believing on account of the proof of testimony.

- According to Bernard of Clairvaux,[12] faith rests on authority. If it rests on authority, it can be proved through authority.

The solution to the question states that saving faith is not acquired through reasoning or persuasion. It reaches this conclusion through distinguishing between two kinds of faith: one kind is acquired through hearing and the testimony of the Scriptures, and another is a grace that is infused by God to the end of assenting to First Truth for its own sake. The first kind of faith is gathered from testimony and reasons, and is not sufficient for faith. The second is infused through a supernatural illumination, and is a gift of grace that suffices for salvation.[13] The faith described

---

[10] This argument is taken from William of Auvergne, in tract. *De fide*, c. 1.

[11] St. Augustine, 1895, epist. 147, c. 2.

[12] St. Bernard of Clairvaux, *De consideratione*, V, c. 3, n. 5, in *Sancti Bernardi opera*, vol. 3, 1963.

[13] Alexander of Hales *Summa theologica*, vol. 4, 1948, pp. 1066–67.

by St. Augustine is said to be the first kind of faith, faith *ex auditu* or acquired faith. This acquired faith, so called because it is acquired through human effort, is something that can be achieved through our unaided natural powers. Although it is not sufficient for salvation, it is a sort of preparation for infused faith. It disposes the soul to receive the light by which it can assent to First Truth for its own sake, just as a bristle is used to introduce a thread. (The analogy is to using a bristle to thread a needle.) Infused faith is not attainable by any natural power, and is not the result of human actions. Rather, it is directly caused in the soul by God's action. As to the argument about believing the Apostles, it is one thing to believe on account of testimony, and another thing to believe what is testified to. Acquired faith believes on account of the testimony given by men; infused faith believes the content of what is asserted in this human testimony, but it does not believe it on account of human testimony. Rather, it believes on account of the testimony of God alone.[14] Faith does not rest on authority as on a proof, but as on something that confirms and strengthens it.

This distinction between infused and acquired faith led to a change in the understanding of formless faith. This faith, which is defined as the faith possessed by bad Christians who do not have charity, is no longer equated with faith that comes from testimony or with the faith of the demons, as it is in William of Auxerre and Peter Lombard.[15] It is rather seen as a gift of grace, which can be said to remain with the advent of charity; charity does not remove the faith that exists in formless faith, but completes it and makes it salvific.[16]

With this question, the discussion of the role of motives of credibility in faith can be said to have properly got under way. The issue is raised, a range of arguments for and against are considered, and a clear solution is proposed.

Positions on the role of motives of credibility in faith

It is not possible within the scope of this book to do justice to the history of the discussion of the role of the motives of credibility in faith. Instead, what will be attempted is an examination of three different positions that make up the alternatives available for answering it. These three positions are:

1. Christian faith in divine speaking is not rationally grounded on the motives of credibility.
2. Christian faith in divine speaking is partially, but not entirely, based on the motives of credibility.
3. Christian faith in divine speaking is entirely based on the motives of credibility.

---

[14] Alexander of Hales, vol. 4, 1948, p. 1067.
[15] See Peter Lombard, *In IV Sent.*, book III, dist. 23, cap. 4, in Peter Lombard, *Magistri Petri Lombardi Parisiensis episcopi Sententiae in IV libris distinctae*, 3rd edn, 1971–81.
[16] See Alexander of Hales, vol. 4, 1948, pp. 1032–33, 1040–41.

We will examine a selection of theologians and philosophers who have elaborated versions of these positions. This examination will look at the stronger arguments that have been made in the past for and against these positions on the role of the motives of credibility, and bring out the connections between these positions and broader views of the nature of faith, grace and knowledge.

Christian faith is not rationally grounded on the motives of credibility

This view on the relation of faith and the motives of credibility can be found in St. Thomas Aquinas and in the Puritan theologian John Owen, a strangely ill-assorted pair.

St. Thomas Aquinas Aquinas's conception of faith is worth examining as a whole. His views on the nature of faith and its relation to knowledge are of importance both in connection with his views on the motives of credibility and as influencing later discussions on this topic.

Two crucial aspects of his thought need to be set out in order to provide the background for his conception of faith.

The first is his Aristotelian conception of the mind's activity. He held mental activity to be the actualization of a power of the soul. Human knowledge thus results from the actualization of a human power. He distinguishes between two ways in which something can pre-exist in potency in natural things.[17] One way is as an active and completed potency, which has the power to realize a perfect act; an example would be healing, where a sick person is restored to health by the natural power within him. The other way is as a passive potency, which does not have sufficient power to act; an example would be the power to burn in something that can only burn if set on fire by another thing. The power to know is a power in the active sense. This power is implanted in us by God as a likeness of uncreated truth; divine truth speaks in us by the impression of its likeness.

This conception of knowledge is radically different from the Christian Platonist understanding of knowledge as resulting from divine illumination that is found in Augustine and most of the other Fathers. For them, the Logos himself, rather than a power created by God in the human mind, was thought of as the source of the divine illumination that gives rise to knowledge. As we have seen, the fact that these Fathers thought of all knowledge as resulting from an illumination of the mind by the Logos meant that they did not see any difficulty in classifying faith as knowledge, since faith is also an illumination produced by the Logos, and that they did not consider arriving at knowledge through faith as fundamentally different from other ways of acquiring knowledge. The adoption of an Aristotelian conception of knowledge means that the question of what makes faith rational arises much more clearly and sharply than it did for the Platonist Fathers.

The second aspect of Aquinas's thought that needs to be considered is his understanding of grace. Medieval theologians had arrived at a more precise

---

[17] St. Thomas Aquinas, *Quaestiones disputatae de veritate,* 1972, q. 11 a. 1.

conception of grace than that found in their patristic predecessors. This conception was developed in the course of trying to describe what distinguishes grace from nature. All agreed that grace was a free and undeserved gift of God. But since our creation is a free and undeserved gift of God, what is there to distinguish grace from the other gifts of God, and give it a definite character that would prevent it from simply being God's act of creation in general? Augustine had already gone part of the way towards answering this question, by saying that grace confers a gift that surpasses the powers of even unfallen human nature. Medieval theologians brought a further precision to his answer by defining grace as a free undeserved gift of some good that surpasses not only human nature but all (actual or possible) created nature. Such gifts were termed 'supernatural'. (Gifts that surpass human nature but not all created nature are merely 'preternatural'.) This understanding of the supernatural character of grace provided an explanation of the claims in the New Testament and patristic tradition that sanctification conferred a certain participation in the divine nature. Aquinas held this view of grace as a conferring of supernatural gifts.

The different kinds of grace fall into one of two categories, that of *gratia gratis data* and *gratia gratum faciens*. *Gratia gratum faciens* is grace that is given for the sanctification of the person who receives it; *gratia gratis data* is grace that does not as such sanctify the person who receives it, but is rather given for the sanctification of others besides him (an example would be the gift of prophecy).[18] Aquinas's classification of the various aspects of sanctifying grace is shaped by the Aristotelian character of his anthropology. The most fundamental aspect of sanctifying grace is a change in the nature of the soul that is brought about by God. From this change in the nature of the soul spring the infused virtues. These include both the infused theological virtues of faith, hope and charity, and the infused moral virtues. In addition to the infused virtues, there are the gifts of the Holy Spirit. These are not active powers that enable people to act on their own, but rather capabilities that give the power to be moved to act by the Holy Spirit. (Compare a guitar that has strings to one that does not. If a guitar has strings, it can produce a musical note when they are plucked; if it does not have them, it cannot produce such a note. But even if it has them, it cannot produce a note on its own. It can only do so if someone plucks it. The gifts of the Holy Spirit in St. Thomas's view are analogous to the strings on a guitar: the notes are analogous to good actions produced by the exercise of the gifts; and the plucking is analogous to the action of the Holy Spirit on the person.) All these graces are properties that cannot belong to the nature of any created being, and cannot be caused by any created being.

The main sources for Aquinas's conception of faith are his *Commentary on the Sentences of Peter Lombard* (henceforth *Sent.*), the *Quaestiones disputatae de veritate* (henceforth *D. V.*), and the *Summa theologiae*, although useful material

---

[18] Aquinas does not always give these meanings to the terms *gratia gratis data* and *gratia gratum faciens*, but I use them with these meanings because of the usefulness of doing so, and because these are the meanings that the terms took on in later theology.

can be found in many other works.[19] There are some differences between his earlier and later works, but no substantial changes. Instead of earlier and later positions on what it is that leads us to have faith, we can discern two rather different accounts of faith that exist side by side in both his earlier and later works, and that are not entirely reconcilable one with another.[20]

The first account considers faith from the standpoint of what it is that is believed, the propositions that Aquinas calls the material object of faith. It describes faith in revealed propositions as an act of the intellect, commanded by the will, that lies between knowledge (*scientia*) and opinion (*opinio*).[21] This follows Hugh of St. Victor in holding faith to be between knowledge and opinion, but rejects Hugh's contention that faith is substantially in the will as opposed to in the intellect (cf. *D. V.* 14, 4). Some account of what is meant by 'knowledge' and 'opinion' needs to be given here; the concepts that St. Thomas has in mind here are not well translated by the English words used for them.

There is no one term used by Aquinas that expresses the meaning of the English word 'knowledge'. The modern philosophical conception of knowledge – or rather of propositional knowledge – would include two different words used by St. Thomas that describe two different cognitive acts. The first sort of act, *intellectus*, is the grasp of self-evident principles whose truth is known as soon as the meaning of the terms that make them up is known. The second sort of act, *scientia*, is the knowledge of propositions that are known to be true through being deduced from principles that are known through *intellectus*. In both *intellectus* and *scientia*, there is no choice about whether to believe; the object – the proposition – grasped in these acts compels the mind to assent, leaving no possibility of doubt concerning it, and puts an end to questioning. *Scientia*, unlike *intellectus*, involves discursive thought, but the role of discursive thought is to bring about *scientia* through deduction. Once *scientia* is arrived at, the discursive thought that brought it into being comes to an end (cf. *D. V.* q.14, a.1).

Opinio does not mean what is meant by the English word 'opinion'. *Opinio*, according to Aquinas (*D. V.* q.14, a.1), happens when the intellect accepts one of two contradictory universal propositions, but is not fully determined to it, and still has some fear of the other's being true. Its counterpart for propositions about

---

[19] For a discussion of Aquinas's views on faith that considers virtually all the relevant passages in his works, see the excellent monograph by Benoît Duroux, *La psychologie de la foi chez St. Thomas d'Aquin*, 1963.

[20] The first position is more explicitly set out in his earlier works, the *Commentary on the Sentences* and the *De veritate*, than it is in the *Summa theologiae*, where the second position is more prominent. There is however nothing in the *Summa* that is incompatible with the earlier position, so we cannot talk about a change of mind concerning it. As far as I can discover, this contention that Aquinas gave two different accounts of faith has not been asserted by previous scholars. This is why I cite a number of Latin texts in the footnotes to the discussion; when advancing a new thesis in such an important and well-trodden field, direct reference to the documentary evidence is necessary. The essential meaning of the Latin is always given in the English discussion.

[21] See e.g. *D. V.* q. 14 a. 2, and *In Heb.* c. 11, l. 1, in *Super epistolas S. Pauli lectura*, 1953a.

particulars is *suspicio*.[22] The fear involved in opinion may be weak enough to admit of a kind of certitude. In discussing the degree of evidence needed by a court, St. Thomas states that when it comes to singular contingent things we cannot achieve the certainty of a demonstration, and should be content with 'probable certitude', *probabilis certitudo*.[23] The probable evidence that grounds opinion is however not sufficient to compel belief, and opinion does not bring to an end discursive thought on the proposition believed.

Faith lies between *scientia* and *opinio* because it has the assent (*assensus*) that belongs to *scientia*, but it has the lack of evident truth in its object that belongs to *opinio*. By 'assent' is meant a firmness of belief in the truth of a proposition that rules out any fear of its not being true. Such assent is brought about either by the proposition that is the object of belief, or by the will. The object of belief brings about assent through being evident, either through *intellectus* or *scientia*. The propositions that are the object of faith are not evident. (Some revealed propositions, like the existence of God, can be known by *scientia* and thus become evident, but the person who comes to know them in this way ceases to have faith in them; see e.g. *2a2ae* 1, 4). Since they are not evident, faith does not bring about an end to discursive thought concerning their truth, as *scientia* does. What causes the assent of faith is the choice of the will, a choice that is motivated by the fact that we are promised eternal life as the reward for believing.[24] The desire for eternal life that motivates this choice need not be charity (which is the love of God, considered as he is in himself rather than as the creator of the universe, above all created things); if this desire had to be charity, it would be impossible to have faith and to sin, because sin banishes charity. Charity is a love, and love is an enjoyment of what is already possessed, but a desire is a movement of the appetite seeking a promised good that need not actually be possessed (*D. V.* 14, 2 ad 10). A desire for eternal life is compatible with a rejection of it through sin, which is what makes it possible for people to have formless faith, and for people to be converted and choose to believe before they have charity. However, in formed faith, the faith that merits and justifies, the motive for the choice to believe is charity. That is why

---

[22] *In VII Ethicorum*, l. 3; '... virtutes intellectuales sunt habitus, quibus anima dicit verum ... Ab horum autem numero excludit suspicionem, quae per aliquas coniecturas habetur de aliquibus particularibus factis; et opinionem quae per aliquas coniecturas habetur de aliquibus universalis. Quamvis enim per ista duo quandoque verum dicatur tamen contingit quod eis quandoque dicitur falsum, quod est malum intellectus, sicut verum est bonum intellectus. Est autem contra rationem virtutis, ut sit principium mali actus. Et sic patet quod suspicio et opinio non possunt dici intellectuales virtutes.' St. Thomas Aquinas, *In decem libros Ethicorum Aristotelis ad Nicomachum expositio*, 1949, pp. 314–5.

[23] *2a2ae*, 70, 2; 'Respondeo dicendum quod secundum Philosophum in I Eth., "certitudo non est similiter quaerenda in omnia materia". In actibus enim humanis, super quibus constituuntur iudicia et exiguntur testimonia, non potest habere certitudo demonstrativa, eo quod sunt circa contingentia et variabilia. Et ideo sufficit probabilis certitudo, quae ut in pluribus veritatem attingat, et sic in paucioribus a veritate deficiat.' St. Thomas Aquinas, *Summa theologiae*, 1953b, vol. 3, p. 1789.

[24] *D. V.* 14, 1; 'Et sic etiam movemur ad credendum dictis Dei in quantum nobis repromittitur, si credideremus, praemium aeternae vitae.' Aquinas, 1972, p. 437.

charity is said to be the form of faith. Voluntary acts get their nature from their end, which is the object of the will, the state of affairs the will seeks to realize in acting; this end is like the form of natural things ('form' here is the essential nature of a thing). The object of the will in a perfected act of faith is the divine good which is loved with charity (*2a2ae* 4, 3). In justifying faith, which brings salvation, this love is what moves the will to believe.[25] The action of believing God, then, will also be an action of loving God, and it will be on account of the latter feature of the action that the believer will choose to do it. The natural order of the action that leads to faith is that first we have an understanding of God, which pertains to the knowledge that precedes faith; then we wish to reach him; then we wish to love him.[26]

Faith is not a moral or intellectual virtue, but a theological virtue (*D. V.* 14, 3). It is a theological virtue because it has God as its immediate object and because it merits eternal life. It cannot be a moral virtue because it has the intellect, not the will, as its subject, and because it does not, as moral virtues do, have as its object a good that is achievable through natural human powers. The intellect is the subject of faith because it is the intellect that actually does the act of believing, although it does so at the command of the will. Aquinas's most extensive discussion of why faith is not an intellectual virtue occurs in his early work, the *Commentary on the Sentences*. He considers the following arguments for faith's being an intellectual virtue (*3 Sent.* d. 23, q. 11. a. 3, qla. 3);

1. An intellectual virtue has the intellect as its subject. But faith has the intellect as its subject; so it is an intellectual virtue. [Presumably this argument assumes the premise that faith is a virtue.]
2. The articles of faith that faith is concerned with are like the principles of other sciences. But grasp of principles is an intellectual virtue; so faith is an intellectual virtue.
3. An intellectual virtue, as Aristotle says, is a virtue through which one always makes true judgements. But faith cannot embrace falsehood; so faith is an intellectual virtue.

His reason for denying that faith is an intellectual virtue is that it belongs to the nature of a virtue that it reach its final goal not only with respect to its action, but also with respect to its mode of action. The good and final goal of the intellect is truth. It does not suffice for faith to be an intellectual virtue that we know the truth through it; the act of faith through which we arrive at truth would also have to perfect the intellect with respect to its mode of action. The goodness of the mode of action of the intellect is not achieved through its operation being commanded by a

---

[25] This is concisely put in *3 Sent.* d. 23 q. 2 sol. 2 ad 4: 'amando credere est actus fide per caritate motae ad actum suum.' St. Thomas Aquinas, *Scriptum super sententiis Magistri Petri Lombardi*, 1933, vol. 3, p. 728.
[26] *3 Sent.* d. 23 q. 2 a. 5 ad 5: 'Unde iste est naturalis ordo actuum, quod prius apprehenditur Deus – quod pertinet ad cognitionem praecedentem fidem – deinde aliquis vult ad eum pervenire, deinde amare vult, et sic deinceps...' Aquinas, 1933, vol. 3, p. 740.

good will, as happens in faith. Rather, St. Thomas – following Aristotle – holds that it consists in the intellect's grasping its object as true, either by grasping it as true in itself – self-evidently true – or by analyzing it into something that it grasps as true in itself. Faith causes the intellect to reach its final goal through making it assent to First Truth, but it does not cause it to reach its goal through the mode of action that is proper to the intellect; it does not cause the articles of faith to be seen as true in themselves (which is why believing the articles of faith is not like grasping the principles of a science). Thus, it is not an intellectual virtue. (*3 Sent.* d. 23, q. 1, a. 3, sol. 3.)

Aquinas seems to have felt the difficulty in saying that although faith is in the intellect, and is not an intellectual virtue, it is nonetheless a virtue. He responds to this difficulty by saying that when two powers are ordered to one another, the perfection of the lower power lies in its being subject to the higher one. Thus, for example, the virtue of the concupiscible appetite lies in its being subject to reason. Faith can be said to be a virtue in the intellect, because it subjects the intellect to the will when the will commands it to achieve the good of eternal life through believing, and the good of the intellect lies in its being subject to the will adhering to God.[27] One might ask: why is it that in this case the will is the higher power, and the intellect is the lower? The answer, in Aquinas's scheme of things, is that the purpose of human virtues is to enable humans to reach their ultimate good. Indeed, what makes a *habitus* in the soul a virtue is its being directed towards a human good. (A *habitus* is a dispositional power and propensity to act; the term has no adequate English equivalent.) One virtue is higher than another when its action is more directly related to the achievement of the ultimate human good, which is salvation. The theological virtues, which have the ultimate good of salvation as their object, are thus higher than the moral and intellectual virtues, which have as objects things different from this end, in so far as they are lead to this end.[28] Since the action of the will in directing the intellect to believe is motivated by the desire for salvation, the will's disposition to act in this way is a higher power than the intellect, and the intellect is acting well in obeying it. Thus he asserts;

> ... since it belongs to virtue to cause good activity, its operation can be said to be good either formally, insomuch as it proceeds from a potency that is moved towards a good because it is good, or materially, insomuch as it is congruent with and connatural to that potency. The act of faith is good in both these ways: because it is both suited to the intellect, insofar as it is concerned with that which is true; and proceeds from the

---

[27] *D. V.* 14, 3 ad 8: '... in quibuslibet duobus ordinatis ad invicem perfectio inferioris est ut subdatur superiori, sicut concupiscibilis quod subdatur rationi; unde habitus virtutis non dicitur expedire concupiscibilem ad actum ut faciat eam libere effluere in concupiscibilia, sed quia facit eam perfecte subiectam rationi. Similiter etiam bonum ipsius intellectus est ut subdatur voluntati adhaerenti Deo: unde fides dicitur intellectum expedire in quantum sub tali volunte ipsum captivat.' Aquinas, 1972, p. 447.

[28] *D. V.* 14, 3 ad 9: '... fides neque est virtus intellectualis neque moralis sed est virtus theologicus; virtutes autem theologicae, quamvis conveniant subiecto cum intellectualibus vel moralibus, differunt tamen obiecto: obiectum enim virtutum theologicarum est ipse finis ultimus, obiectum vero aliarum ea quae sunt ad finem.' Aquinas, 1972, pp. 447–8.

command of the will, which is moved to the good as its object. However, on the side of the intellect, although it has goodness with respect to the object of reasoning, the act of faith lacks perfection, because, as was said above, he who lacks the vision of the truth to which he adheres fails in the mode of perfection of intellectual activity ... It is apparent that faith is a virtue; not an intellectual one, but a virtue in the sense commonly used, that is, something that produces an act that is good and that proceeds from a good will. [29]

One might object that there is a circularity in Aquinas's description of the motive of the choice to believe. This motive is supposed to be the desire for eternal life. But does not the intention of gaining eternal life by choosing to have faith itself presuppose beliefs that have to be accepted through faith? The claim that one must believe the Christian revelation in order to be saved is itself a part of that revelation, and not knowable independently of it. St. Thomas does not consider this objection, but an answer to it is suggested by the answer he gives to a similar difficulty. In *D. V.* 14, 9, where he discusses the question of whether something accepted by faith can also be known, he considers the objection that one of the things that must be believed through faith is that God exists. But we cannot believe this because it is a teaching received from God, since no-one can believe that something is received from God unless he first believes that there is a God from whom it is received. Thus the judgement by which God is believed to exist precedes the judgement by which anything is thought to be received from God, and cannot be caused by it. His answer is that someone can begin to believe what previously he did not believe, but very weakly supposed to be true. Thus it is possible that someone before believing God could suppose (i.e. believe it to be somewhat probable) that there is a God and that God would be pleased by one's believing him, and on this basis believe God, and hence believe that there is a God, since God's existence is presupposed by the articles of faith that we believe when believing God. (*D. V.* 14, 9 ad 9.)[30]

This picture of the resemblances and differences between faith, knowledge and opinion enables St. Thomas to give an admirably clear account of the nature of the certainty of faith. Certainty, he says, can mean two things; it can mean firmness of

---

[29] *3 Sent.* d. 23 q. 2 a. 4: '... cum virtutis sit reddere opus bonum, operatio potest dici bona vel formaliter, in quantum procedit ex potentia quae movetur in bonum secundum rationem boni; vel materialiter, secundum quod est congrua et connaturalis potentiae. Et utroque modo actus fidei est bonus; quia et congruit intellectui inquantum est verorum; et iterum procedit a voluntate imperante, quae movetur in bonum quasi in objectum. Ex parte autem intellectus, quamvis habeat bonitatem ratione objecti, non tamen habet perfectionem, quia deficit modus, ut dictum est, eo quod non habet conspicuam veritatem cui adhaeret ... Unde patet quod fides est virtus, non quidem intellectualis, sed eo modo quo communiter loquimur de virtute quae producit actum bonum ex bonitate voluntatis procedentem.' Aquinas, 1933, vol. 3, p. 736 (the translation is mine).

[30] *D. V.* 14, 9 ad 9: '... aliquis potest incipere credere illud quod prius non credebat sed debilius extimabat; unde possibile est quod aliquis antequam credat Deum, extimaverit Deum esse et hoc esse ei placitum quod credatur eum esse. Et sic aliquis potest credere Deum esse eo quod sit placitum Deo, quamvis etiam hoc non sit articulus, sed antecedens articulum quia demonstrative probatur.' Aquinas, 1972, p. 464.

adherence to a proposition, or the evidentness of a proposition.[31] In the first sense, the certainty of faith is greater than that of knowledge (of *intellectus* or *scientia*). In the second sense, faith is not certain at all. This means that the question of the theoretical reasonableness of the certainty of faith does not arise, because that is not the sort of reasonableness that such certainty requires or can have. It is practical reasonableness that can and should be demanded from the firmness with which the will commands the reason to assent to faith.

However, the reason he gives for this firmness of assent detracts somewhat from the coherence of his position. He says that the assent of faith is firmer than that of *intellectus* or *scientia* because First Truth, which is the cause of the assent of faith, is a stronger cause than the light of reason which causes the assent of *intellectus* and *scientia*. Elsewhere (in his commentary on Boethius's *De Trinitate*) he explains this contention by saying that the light of faith is more capable of inducing assent than demonstration (which produces *scientia*) because although demonstration cannot reach false conclusions, men are often deceived concerning it through taking something to be a demonstration when it is not. The light of faith is more capable than *intellectus* of inducing assent because the light by which we assent to first principles can be impeded by bodily infirmity. The light of faith, on the other hand, which is like the seal of first truth in our mind, cannot fail, just as God can neither be deceived nor lie.[32] But this explanation of the firmness of assent of faith – the impossibility of God's lying or being deceived, and the consequent impossibility of the light of faith that he implants ever causing assent to a falsehood – describes something that would prevent the light of faith from ever arriving at a falsehood. Aquinas does not explain why the impossibility of faith's

---

[31] *3 Sent.* d. 23 q. 2 a. 2 sol. 3: 'In intellectu enim principiorum causatur determinatio ex hoc quod aliquid per lumen intellectus sufficienter inspici per ipsum potest. In scientia vero conclusionum causatur determinatio ex hoc quod conclusio secundum actum rationis in principia per se visa resolvitur. In fide vero ex hoc quod voluntas intellectui imperat. Sed quia voluntas hoc modo non determinat intellectum ut faciat inspici quae creduntur, sicut inspiciuntur principia per se nota vel quae in ipsa resolvuntur, sed hoc modo ut intellectus firmiter uni adhaerat; ideo certitudo quae est in scientia et intellectu, est ex ipsa evidentia eorum quae certa esse dicuntur; certitudo autem fidei est ex firma adhaesione ad id quod creditur ... (Ad 1um); Certitudo enim scientiae consistit in duobus, scilicet in evidentia, et firmitate adhaesionis. Certitudo vero fidei consistit in uno tantum, scilicet in firmitate adhaesionis ... Quamvis certitudo fidei de qua loquimur, quantum ad illud unum sit vehementior quam certitudo fidei quantum ad illa duo.' Aquinas 1933, vol. 3, pp. 728–9.

3 Sent. d. 23 q. 2 a. 3 sol. 1 ad 2: 'scientia et intellectus habent certitudinem per id quod ad cognitionem pertinet, scilicet evidentiam ejus cui assentitur. Fides autem habet certitudinem ab eo quod est extra genus cognitionis, in genere affectionis existens ...' Aquinas 1933, vol. 3, p. 732.

D. V. 14, 1 ad 7: '... certitudo duo potest importare, scilicet firmitatem adhaesionis, et quantum ad hoc fides est certior etiam omni intellectu et scientia quia prima veritatis quae causat fidei assensum est fortior causa quam lumen rationis quae causat assensum intellectus vel scientiae; importat etiam evidentiam eius cui assentitur, et sic fides non habet certitudinem sed scientia et intellectus ...' Aquinas 1972, p. 438.

[32] St. Thomas Aquinas, *Super Boetium de trinitate*, 1992, q. 3 a. 1 ad 4, p. 109.

ever being mistaken should move the will to firmness of assent. This impossibility is suited to move the reason to assent, because it gives grounds for believing the articles of faith to be true and excluding all doubt. But it is not suited to move the will, which, as St. Thomas goes on to say right after offering this explanation, is what causes the assent of faith rather than the reason. What moves the will is a good to be sought. The only good that would arise directly from the impossibility of faith's being in error would be the good of always arriving at the truth in believing; and if this were the good sought in faith, the motive of belief would be primarily an intellectual one,[33] which Aquinas denies. (The impossibility of faith's being in error would be an advantage from the point of view of the will when considered together with the information that faith claims to impart, which is about how to achieve perfect and eternal happiness, since it would remove any doubt about how we can achieve this happiness. But this advantage does not attach to the infallibility of faith considered in itself.) This motive does not harmonize with his claim that it is a good thing for the intellect to be subject in the act of faith to the will adhering to God. There is no subjection in the intellect's believing when its motive for belief is the impossibility of being in error. Nor does it harmonize with his assertion that the will chooses to believe in order to attain salvation. My being saved is a different motive for action than the impossibility of God's deceiving me. It would be more in keeping with Aquinas's first account of faith if he were to say that what causes the firmness of assent of faith is the surpassing goodness of the good that is sought in assenting, viz., eternal life.

This incoherence is due to the intrusion of the second account of faith that is to be found in Aquinas. The first account, as we have seen, looks at faith from the standpoint of *what* is believed, the propositions that are its material object; the second account looks at faith from the standpoint of *who* it is that is believed in faith, which is its formal object. Aquinas holds that the person believed in faith is God. Where God speaks is in Holy Scripture and the doctrine of the Church, or, more precisely, in Holy Scripture rightly understood according to the teaching of the Church.[34] This means that a heretic who rejects some of the teachings of the Church is not believing God even when he believes other Church teachings, and does not have the *habitus* of faith.[35] In believing, the faithful believe God rather

---

[33] He holds that truth is the good of the intellect, not of any appetitive virtue (*2a2ae* 1, 3 ad 1): 'verum est bonum intellectus, non autem est bonum appetitivae virtus ...' Aquinas 1953b, vol. 3, p. 1403b.

[34] Aquinas slides between describing *sacra scriptura*, Holy Scripture, and *sacra doctrina*, sacred teaching, as containing the divine message that is to be believed with faith. This imprecision expresses his realization of the unity of the Scriptural message and Church teaching, but it does not yield a worked-out theory of the nature of that unity.

[35] *2a2ae* 5, 3: 'Formale autem obiectum fidei est veritas prima secundum quod manifestatur in Scripturis Sacris et doctrina Ecclesiae quae procedit ex veritate prima. Unde quicumque non inhaeret, sicut infallibili et divinae regulae, doctrina Ecclesiae, quae procedit ex veritate prima in Scripturis Sacris manifestata, ille non habet habitum fidei, sed ea quae sunt fidei alio modo tenet quam per fidem ... (ad 2um;) ... omnibus articulis fidei inhaeret fides propter unum medium, scilicet propter veritatem primam propositam nobis in Scripturis secundum doctrinam Ecclesiae intelligentis sane'. Aquinas, 1953b, vol. 3, pp. 1438a, b.

than the men through whom he speaks.[36] Faith cannot consist in believing the testimony of men as such, because this testimony is fallible; it can only be belief in the testimony of God who can neither deceive nor be deceived.[37] No-one is so unbelieving as to think that God would not tell the truth. Unbelief does not consist in thinking that God is lying when he speaks, but in not believing him when he is speaking through men.

Aquinas expresses the contention that in faith God is the person we believe, and on account of whom we believe, by saying that the formal object of faith is First Truth.[38] Any cognitive *habitus* has two objects: the material object, that which is known, and the formal object, that by which the material object is known. The formal object is what defines the nature of the *habitus*. We can grasp the difference between these two sorts of object by considering that it is possible to believe propositions that God has asserted (e.g. that one ought not to steal) for a reason other than his having asserted them. In this case the material objects will be the same as in faith, but the formal object will be different. In faith, the material object is the propositions that are said by God, and the formal object is his having said them. Faith assents to something only because it is said by God. God is not only truthful, he is First Truth itself, the uncreated truth that all other truth participates in; faith rests upon this divine truth. Thus Aquinas asserts that 'if someone believes God to exist on account of certain human reasoning and natural signs, he is not yet

---

[36] In *3 Sent*. d. 23 a. 2 sol. 2 qla. 2, Aquinas considers this objection to the position that faith is believing God: 'Praeterea, in actu fidei discernitur fidelis ab infideli. Sed nullus est ita infidelis quin credat quod Deus non loquitur nisi verum. Ergo credere vera esse quae Deus loquitur, non est actus fidei, sed magis vera esse quae nuntius Dei loquitur. Et sic credere homini magis est actus fidei quam credere Deo.' Aquinas, 1933, vol. 3, p. 723. The answer given to this objection (ad 3) is '... fidelis credit homini non quia homo, sed inquantum Deus in eo loquitur: quod ex certis experimentis colligere potest. Infidelis autem non credit Deo in homine loquenti.' Aquinas (1933), vol. 3, p. 728.

In *In Ioan*. c. 5 l.4 no. 5, Aquinas asserts: 'Innititur autem fides non verbo hominis sed ipsi Deo...Sic nos introducit per verbum hominis ad credendum, non ipsi homini qui loquitur, sed Deo cuius verbo loquitur; 1 Thess. II, 15: "Cum accepissetis a nobis verbum auditus Dei, accepistis illud non sicut verbum hominem, sed, sicut vere est, verbum Dei."' St. Thomas Aquinas, *Super evangelium S. Ioannis lectura*, 1952, p. 146.

Aquinas even goes so far as to say that teachers in the Church are gods with respect to those they teach, in *3 Sent* d.25 q. 2 a. 1 sol. 4: '... illi quibus incumbit officium docendi fidem, sunt medii inter Deum et homines; unde respectu Dei sunt homines, et respectu hominum sunt dii, inquantum divinae cognitionis participes sunt per scientiam Scripturarum vel per revelationem, ut dicitur Ioan. X,35: "Illos dixit deos ad quos sermo Dei factus est." Et ideo oportet quod minores qui ab eis de fide doceri debent, habeant fidem implicitam in fide illorum, non inquantum homines, sed inquantum sunt participatione dii.' Aquinas, 1933, vol. 3, p. 799.

[37] *In Heb*. c. 6 l. 1: 'Proprium autem fidei est, quod credat homo et assentiat non visis a se, sed testimonio alterius. Hoc autem testimonium vel est hominis tantum: et istud non facit virtutem fidei, quia homo et fallere et falli potest. Vel istud testimonium est ex iudicio divino; et istud verissimum et firmissimum est, quia est ab ipsa veritate, quae nec fallere, nec falli potest.' Aquinas,.1953a, p. 398.

[38] See *3 Sent*. d. 24 a. 1 qla. 1 and sol. 1: *D. V*. 14, 8; *2a2ae* 1, 1.

said to have the faith of which we speak, but only when he believes for the reason that God says it (ex hac ratione credit quod est a Deo dictum).'[39]

We could put this view by saying that God's having said certain things is the reason why we believe them in faith, but it is important not be misled by such a way of expressing Aquinas's position. We might be willing to say that the reason we believed a statement in the past was because God said it, even when we now realize that as a matter of fact he did not say it. What we would mean by this is that we thought that God said it, and hence believed the statement in question. This is not what Aquinas means when he says that First Truth is the formal object of faith. Rather, he means that God's *actually having said something* is the reason for our believing it. This is clear from his saying that nothing falls under any *habitus* except in virtue of the formal object of that *habitus*, and since the formal object of faith is First Truth, which excludes all falsehood, it follows that nothing false can fall under faith. This line of reasoning presupposes that it is God's actually saying something that is the formal object of faith, since it is such actual speech that is incompatible with falsehood. This means that when we believe something on account of God's having said it, and God actually has said it, we are believing for a *different reason* than we would have if we believed something because we thought God said it, but God had not in fact said it. The rationale for saying that these reasons are different will be given at the end of chapter 6.

First Truth's being the formal object of faith means that faith is an instance of belief in testimony. We believe God concerning things we do not see, as one would believe a good man concerning things which one does not see but which he does see.[40] Aquinas gives an account of the nature of belief in human testimony. The need for such testimony comes from the fact that some things, like singular and contingent states of affairs, can be known to one man but not to another. Because in human society it is necessary that men be able to use the goods of other men as if they were their own, when it comes to pass that their own goods are not sufficient, it is therefore necessary to hold to what others know as if we knew it ourselves. Hence it follows that faith, by which one man believes what another asserts, is necessary in the social intercourse of men, and is the foundation of justice, as Cicero says in his *Offices*.[41] That is why lying cannot be without sin, since every lie derogates from the faith so necessary to human society.[42] There are two reasons for refusing to believe someone; because he is or is imputed to be ignorant, or because he is or is imputed to be a liar.[43] Belief in someone's testimony is voluntary. No-one believes unless he chooses to do so.[44]

---

[39] *In Rom.* cap. 4 lect. 1, in Aquinas, 1953a, my translation.

[40] *3 Sent.* d. 23 q. 2 a. 2 sol. 2: '... Ratio enim quare voluntas inclinatur ad assentiendum his quae non videt, est quia Deus ea dicit: sicut homo in his quae non videt, credit testimonio alicujus boni viri qui videt quae ipse non videt.' Aquinas (1933), vol. 3, p. 727.

[41] Cicero, *De officiis*, 1994, I c. 7 n. 23.

[42] Aquinas, 1992, 3, 1.

[43] St. Thomas Aquinas, *In librum Beati Dionysii de divinis nominibus expositio*, 1950, c. 1, l. 1, p. 8.

[44] *3 Sent.* d. 23 q. 2 a. 1 ad 7: 'nullus credit nisi volens'. Aquinas, 1933, vol. 3, p. 721.

Aquinas holds belief in testimony to be an essential part of learning from a teacher. His description of what a teacher attempts to do in teaching does not seem to leave a role for belief in testimony; he says that a teacher communicates knowledge to his student by communicating to the student the principles that he, the teacher, knows, and the deductions that he has made from those principles. Such communication, when understood, gives the student *intellectus* of the principles and *scientia* of the conclusions, and thus confers on the student a knowledge that is independent of the teacher's assertions. (*D.V.* 14, 1.) But although the knowledge that is the goal of teaching does not involve any reliance on belief in the teacher's word, such belief is an essential part of the acquisition of such knowledge. Aquinas argues for this necessity as follows;

> In the beginning man is imperfect in knowledge; to him who is to obtain the perfection of *scientia*, a teacher is needed, who can lead him to this perfection. Such a teacher cannot do this, unless he himself has the perfection of *scientia*, insomuch as he grasps the reasons of those things which fall under a science. But the teacher does not at the beginning of his instruction at once hand on the reasons for the more subtle things concerning which he intends to teach; because then the student would have to have at the very beginning a perfect *scientia* of what he is to be taught. Rather, he teaches the student things whose reasons the student cannot grasp when he is beginning to learn, but that the student will know afterwards when he is perfect in science. Hence it is said that it is necessary for the learner to believe (*oportet addiscentem credere*); the learner cannot attain the perfection of *scientia* otherwise than through accepting as true that which is first taught to him, the reasons for which he cannot then understand. The ultimate perfection to which man is ordered, however, is the knowledge of God; which no-one can attain save through the activity and teaching of God, who is the perfect knower of himself. But man in the beginning is not capable of this perfect knowledge, so it is necessary that he accept, through believing, things by which he is led to reach perfect knowledge. Some of these things are of such a nature that it is impossible for us to have perfect knowledge of them in this life, because they totally exceed the power of human reason. These it is necessary for us to believe while we are pilgrims in this life; we will have perfect knowledge of them in our heavenly fatherland. Others can be known perfectly even in this life, as those things concerning God which can be given a demonstrative proof; but even with these things it is necessary to believe in the beginning. [45]

The necessity of learners' believing is thus given as a reason for the necessity of faith. We must begin by believing (not knowing) as principles the articles of faith that God reveals to us, so that later we can be led by God to the knowledge to which these principles lead, the knowledge of his essence. Aquinas attributes to

---

[45] *D. V.* 14, 10 (the translation is my own). 'Perfect knowledge' of God is meant to be opposed to imperfect or defective knowledge; the perfect knowledge referred to would not be imperfect or defective, because it would be a grasp of God's essence. It does not mean a complete and comprehensive knowledge of God that would leave nothing else to be grasped, since Aquinas holds that such knowledge is impossible for created intellects.

Aristotle the view that learners must believe,[46] but this position is not clearly to be found in Aristotle's text; it seems rather to have originated in Alexander of Aphrodisias's commentary on the beginning of the *Posterior Analytics*. This position on the necessity of learners believing has implications for the status of testimony as a source of belief that Aquinas did not explore. It means that belief in testimony need not be based on other sorts of belief, since the learners in question will not have the opportunity to determine whether or not the teachers they are believing know what they are talking about; if they were able to know this, they would not be learners. (If they were to accept that the teachers were knowledgeable on the basis of other people's assertions, they would have to know that the others possessed the knowledge that would enable them to tell that the teachers knew what they were talking about, which would again require them to not be learners; and so on.) Alexander of Aphrodisias's commentary did lead some thinkers to draw this conclusion, and was influential in persuading Jewish and Muslim philosophers that traditions require no proof.

Faith in divine testimony is not however the same as faith in human testimony. The chief difference between the two comes from the fact, alluded to above, that although human testimony is fallible, the testimony of God,[47] who can neither deceive nor be deceived, is not. This means that it is impossible to be credulous in believing God. Credulity is excess in belief, but it is impossible to exceed in believing God.[48] As stated above, since divine faith always attains the object of the intellect, which is truth, its act is always good, and hence it can be a virtue. Belief in human testimony does not always attain the truth, because men can deceive or be deceived, so it is not a virtue (cf. *3 Sent.* d. 23 q. 2 a. 4 sol. 1 ad 2; *D. V.* 14, 8; *2a2ae* 4, 5). Aquinas considers the objection to the rightness of faith raised by Abelard, that appeals to Ecclesiasticus 19:4 ('Qui cito credit levis est corde, one who trusts others too quickly is lightminded') to argue that believing what you can

---

[46] Aquinas asserts the necessity of learners believing when he comments on the text of the Letter to the Hebrews that states that faith is the substance of things hoped for: *In Heb.* c. 11 l. 1: 'Ipsa ergo plena visio Dei est essentia beatudininis. Hoc autem videmus in scientiis liberalibus, quod si quis aliquam velit addiscere, oportet eum primo accipere principia ipsius, quae oportet credere cum sibi tradentur a magistro. Oportet enim credere eum qui discit, ut habetur 1 Poster. Et in illis principiis quodammodo continetur tota scientia, sicut conclusiones in praemissis, et effectus in causa. Qui ergo habet principia illius scientiae, habet substantiam eius, puta geometriae. Et si geometria esset essentia beatudinis, qui haberent principia geometriae, haberent quodammodo substantiam beatudinis. Fides autem nostra est, ut credamus quod beati videbunt et fruentur Deo. Et ideo si volumus ad hoc pervenire, oportet ut credamus principia istius cognitionis. Et haec sunt articula fidei qui continent totam summam hujus scientiae, quia beatos nos facit visio Dei trini et unus.' Aquinas 1953a, p. 458. The view that learners must believe is also stated in *Super Boet. de Tr.* 2, 2. The text from Aristotle that Aquinas seems chiefly to have in mind is *De sophisticiis elenchis* c. 2, 165b3.

[47] Cf. *In Heb.* c. 6 l. 1, cited above, and *3 Sent.* d. 23 q. 2 a. 4 sol. 1 ad 2.

[48] *D. V.* 14, 10 ad 6: '... esse credulum in vitium sonat quia designat superfluitatem in credendo, sicut esse bibulum superfluitatem in bibendo; ille autem qui credit Deo non excedit modum in credendo quia ei non potest nimis credi ...' Aquinas, 1972, p. 468.

in no way see is excessively light-minded. He answers that to believe a man in the absence of probable reasons is excessively light-minded, because the understanding of one man is not naturally ordered to the cognition of another man as its rule. But human cognition is thus ordered to first truth.[49] Divine faith gives a real participation in the divine knowledge.[50]

Aquinas's position on objections to the truth of the propositions we believe through faith is significant. He does not say that First Truth speaking gives a better reason for accepting a proposition than any reasons that could be found for rejecting it. Rather, he holds that the fact that a proposition is known through faith means that there cannot be such a thing as a good reason for not believing it. The propositions given to us in faith cannot be contrary to what is discovered by the light of reason implanted in us by nature, because if they were God would be the author of falsehood, which is impossible. If, therefore, something is found in the assertions of philosophers that is contrary to the faith, it is not philosophy, but rather an abuse of philosophy that springs from a defect in the reason.[51] The inspired teachings of the prophets and the Apostles contain nothing that is contrary to what natural reason teaches, but they do contain things that surpass natural reason. That is why these teachings seem to be contrary to reason, although they are not; just as it seems to a peasant that it is contrary to reason that the sun is larger than the earth, or that the diagonal is incommensurable with the side, although the wise see that these things are reasonable (*D. V.* 14, 10 ad 7). This means that there is nothing like a rational obligation for the believer to provide answers to objections against the faith, or even to take such objections seriously. Indeed, it would be unreasonable to take them seriously, just as it would be unreasonable to take the peasant's views on the relative size of the earth and the sun seriously.

To present-day inquirers, this dismissive stance might seem overconfident and unwarranted. Those who are inclined to criticize Aquinas's position in this way need, however, to take into account the fact that his conception of knowledge and reasonable belief differs in important respects from the conceptions that are dominant today. Knowledge, as he understood it, did not include anything like what is presently described as justification, where justification is thought of as something that can be present in both knowledge and false belief. As we have seen,

---

[49] *3 Sent.* d. 24 a. 3 sol. 2 ad 1: 'credere hominum absque ratione probabili est nimis cito credere; quia cognitio unius hominis non est naturaliter ordinata ad cognitionem alterius, ut per ipsam reguletur. Sed hoc modo est ordinata ad veritatem primam.' Aquinas, 1933, vol. 3, pp. 775–6.

[50] *Super Boet. de Tr.* 2, 2: 'de diuinis duplex scientia habetur: una secundum modum nostrum, qui sensibilium principia accipit ad notificandum diuina ... Alia secundum modum ipsorum diuinorum, ut ipsa diuina secundum se ipse capiantur, que quidem perfecte in statu uie nobis est impossibilis, set fit nobis in statu uie quedam illius cognitionis participatio et assimilatio ad cognitionem diuinam, in quantum per fidem nobis infusam inheremus ipsi prime ueritati propter se ipsam.' Aquinas, 1992, p. 95.

[51] *Super Boet. de Tr.* 2, 3:'Si quid autem in dictis philosophorum inuenitur contrarium fidei, hoc non est philosophie, set magis philosophie abusus ex defectu rationis.' Aquinas, 1992, p. 99.

Aquinas held that the powers of our reason that give us knowledge are intellectual virtues, whose purpose is to give us true beliefs, and whose operation consists in arriving at true beliefs. What confers the status of knowledge upon a belief is its being arrived at through the exercise of an intellectual virtue. If a proposition that we believe is false, that means that it is not arrived at through the action of an intellectual virtue, and thus that we do not have reasons of a sort that could form a basis for knowledge. When we have reasons for both a proposition and its negation, therefore, it is impossible for both these sets of reasons to be good ones. Since one of the two propositions must be false, one of the sets of reasons must be a bad one. In the sphere of *opinio*, as opposed to that of knowledge, Aquinas would admit the existence of something that could be called justification and that could apply to both true and false beliefs; it would simply be the existence of probable reasons for a proposition. But evidence that makes a proposition probable does not belong to the same epistemic category as the reasons that enable you to know a proposition.[52] And such probable evidence is not what underlies the propositions accepted in faith, because faith is not a kind of *opinio*. If it were, it would not be a virtue. Since it is a virtue, it provides good reasons for believing the propositions it assents to, and thus there cannot be good reasons against these propositions; objections to them can only be an abuse of philosophy.

Whether Aquinas is right or not in refusing to admit the possibility of reasonable objections to the articles of faith will thus depend on whether it is right to think of knowledge as produced by intellectual virtues, and on whether Christian faith is an intellectual virtue. (His view of faith as a virtue in the intellect, but not an intellectual virtue, does not recommend itself very strongly.) These are the central questions of this book; the truth of Aquinas's views on them will be investigated when these questions are examined.

This account of faith as believing First Truth has considerable merits when considered on its own, as does the first account of faith that is described above. The problem for Aquinas's view of faith is reconciling the two. The incompatibility between them has already been brought out, in the discussion of the difficulties with Aquinas's view of the cause of the firmness of assent of faith. The source of the incompatibility between them lies in this: if the formal object of faith, the reason for believing, is God's speaking, why does faith involve a will to salvation, as the first account says it does? Our intellect can tell us that God cannot speak falsely, and knowledge of this fact is sufficient to bring us to believe what God says without in any way willing to reach him. Moreover, it is quite possible for us to see that there is a contradiction implied in God's speaking falsely, and hence that it is impossible that this could happen. Since this is so, why should faith differ from knowledge? And why should it necessarily be voluntary?

---

[52] This distinction of epistemic categories means that much contemporary debate about whether Aquinas's understanding of knowledge is internalist or externalist is beside the mark. Contemporary internalist and externalist accounts of justification usually agree in describing justification as something that can occur in both knowledge and false belief. Justification of this sort does not exist in Aquinas's thought.

The difficulty of resolving these two accounts is not one that could easily be resolved by abandoning one or the other. The description of faith as lying between science and opinion enables it to be called voluntary, and hence makes it capable of being meritorious. The description of faith as having First Truth as its object states the basic idea of faith as belief in divine revelation, and gives the grounds for belief that makes faith rational. If Aquinas were to have considered abandoning one or the other of these accounts, he would have been left with the choice of either having no explanation for the voluntariness of faith, or of having no explanation for the rationality of faith. This unresolved tension within his conception of faith is produced by a part of what has come to be called the problem of the act of faith: the difficulty of reconciling the contentions that faith is rational, that it is voluntary, and that it requires grace.

It is Aquinas's explication of two of these three contentions – the contention that faith is rational, and the contention that it requires grace – that determines his position on the role of the motives of credibility in faith. The question of the role of the motives of credibility in faith is not one that he addresses as a separate question. Like most of his predecessors, his main concern in discussing the relation of faith and reason is not with why we believe, but with what we believe. When he talks about 'arguments that compel us to faith', he has in mind arguments for the propositions believed in faith, not arguments for the reasonableness of believing.[53] Nonetheless he has a clear position on the role of motives of credibility.

His understanding of grace and his assertion that faith requires grace mean that he cannot accept that faith be rationally grounded on the motives of credibility. Since grace means the conferral of a property that surpasses created nature, if the act of believing requires grace, it is impossible for faith to be based on the motives of credibility. This is because the comprehension of these motives and the inference from them to Christianity's being divinely revealed is within human power. Aquinas holds (*2a2ae* 6, 1) that not only the proposal of the truths to be revealed in faith, but also the act of assenting to them, requires grace. The former requires grace because some of the things to be believed in faith surpass human reason, and thus can only be known through God's revealing them. As for the latter, he argues that there are two causes that can be suggested as causing men's assent to the articles of faith. One is external inducements, like miracles and human persuasion. But these cannot be sufficient causes, since some of those who see miracles and hear preaching believe, and others do not. There must therefore be some internal cause for belief. The Pelagians claim that this cause is the choice of our will, but this is false. Because man in assenting to the teachings of faith is elevated above his nature, it is necessary that this assent be found within him as a result of a supernatural principle affecting him interiorly, which is God. Thus the *habitus* of faith is infused by God, not by any natural cause. Significantly, unlike previous scholastic theologians, Aquinas does not postulate the existence of

---

[53] *3 Sent.* d. 24 a. 2 sol. 2 ad 4: 'argumenta quae cogunt ad fidem, sicut miracula, non probant fidem per se, sed probant veritatem annuntiantis fidem.' Aquinas, 1933, vol. 3, p. 770.

acquired faith as well as infused faith. Infused faith, for him, is the only faith there is in Christian believers.

It might be pointed out that Aquinas describes the devils, who are without faith, as believing on the basis of signs, and that this is hard to reconcile with the claim that Christian faith is not based on signs. But he thinks of the knowledge of faith possessed by Christians as entirely different from that possessed by devils; believing is said equivocally of the faithful and devils (*D. V.* 14, 9). Belief in the articles of faith can serve as a foundation for *scientia* in Christian believers, but the belief of devils in the articles of faith cannot serve as principles that give rise to new knowledge (*De malo*, 16, 6). The faith of the devils is compelled by the evidence of signs, but the faith of humans is voluntary. One might ask how the faith of the devils can be compelled by signs, while the faith of humans cannot be; Aquinas's explanation would probably be that the devils have much greater intellectual powers and access to evidence than humans do.

It might also be asked how it is that Aquinas can claim that the divine origin of the Christian revelation is shown by many evident proofs (cf. *Summa contra gentiles*, 1, 4), while at the same time denying that belief in this revelation is based on these proofs. Although Aquinas does not address this question, it is not hard to see how it could be answered on the basis of his views. These evident proofs are not strong enough to force humans to believe against their wills. Since this is so, someone who is presented with the claims of the Christian religion will choose not to believe, if he has a bad will; and if he has a good will, he will choose to have infused faith. Fr. R.-A. Gauthier's remarks on Aquinas's application of the term 'convincere' to unbelievers are worth recalling. 'It is important to remind ourselves of something that often seems to have been forgotten, which is that 'convincere' does not mean to *convince* someone of their error, that is, to *persuade* them that they are in error, but rather to *convict* them of error; to provide a (juridical) proof of their error.'[54]

This reason for thinking that faith cannot be rationally grounded on the motives of credibility does not exclude the possibility of these motives entering into the rational grounding of faith, and even being a necessary condition for it, although they are not sufficient to bring it about. However, these possibilities are not compatible with Aquinas's views. He could not hold that the motives of credibility are necessary to justify faith, because he holds that the justification can work the other way round. He says that 'faith in itself is sufficient to bring us to believe everything that accompanies or follows or precedes faith.'[55] This includes the motives of credibility. But if faith can on its own bring us to believe the motives of credibility, they cannot be needed for producing faith. Nor in his view can the motives of credibility enter in to the rational grounds of faith for some people, while not being necessary for faith in others. Faith in his view has one and only

---

[54] Gauthier, introduction to vol. 1 of St. Thomas Aquinas, *Summa contra gentiles*, 1961, p. 98 (my translation of Gauthier).
[55] '... fides, quantum in se est, ad omnia quae fidem concomitantur, vel sequuntur, vel praecedent sufficienter inclinat': *3 Sent.* d. 24 q. 1 a. 1 sol. 2; Aquinas, 1933, vol. 3, p. 769 (my translation).

one formal object. But faith can exist without the motives of credibility. In line with the Fathers, he holds that a perfect faith does not require signs, and that miracles are neither necessary nor sufficient for faith (*2a2ae* 2, 10; *In Ioan.* c. 2 l. 3 n. 5). The word of God is of such a power that as soon as it is heard it ought to be believed.[56] But if there is only one rational ground for believing, only one formal object, and this formal object can exist in the absence of the motives of credibility, then these motives cannot be part of that rational ground. Aquinas's reason for thinking that there can only be one such formal object has already been described; only belief in infallible First Truth speaking can make faith a virtue in the intellect. The implications of his view that there is only one formal object of faith are spelt out in his discussion of the status of theology in human knowledge. In *1a* q. 1 a. 8 he concludes from the fact that Sacred Scripture has no superior science that '...if an opponent holds nothing of what has been divinely revealed, then no way lies open for making the articles of faith reasonably credible; all that can be done is to solve the difficulties against faith that he may bring up. For since faith rests upon unfailing truth and the contrary of faith cannot really be demonstrated, it is clear that alleged proofs against faith are not demonstrations, but charges that can be refuted (solubilia argumenta).'[57]

The character of our assent to the articles of faith also excludes the possibility of the motives of credibility playing any part in the reason for our believing. Aquinas asserts that the *habitus* of faith makes known the articles of faith in the same way as the intellect makes known the principles of a science that are grasped through *intellectus*.[58] Faith, like assent to such principles, does not proceed from inference.[59] But if the motives of credibility were to form part of our reason for believing, it would have to be through serving as a basis for inference to the truth of the articles of faith; since there is no such inference, they cannot be part of our reason for believing.

Aquinas does not deny that such motives can play a role in bringing about faith. He only denies that they enter in to the reason for believing.

> There are three things that lead us to faith in Christ. First, natural reason; ... second, the witness of the Law and the Prophets; ... third, the preaching of the Apostles and others. But when a man has been led to believe by these, we can say that it is not on account of any of them that he believes; he believes, not because of natural reason, nor because of

---

[56] *In Heb.* c. 4 l. 1: 'Verba enim Dei sic sunt efficacia, quod statim audita debent esse credenda. Ps. XCII, 7; "Testimonia tua credibilia facta sunt nimis."' Aquinas, 1953a, p. 380.

[57] St. Thomas Aquinas, *Summa Theologiae*, vol. 1, 1963, pp. 28–31.

[58] *3 Sent.* d. 23 q. 2 a. 1 ad 4: 'lumen infusum, quod est habitus fidei, manifestat articulos, sicut lumen intellectus agentis manifestat principia naturaliter cognita.' Aquinas, 1933, vol. 3, p. 721. *D. V.* 14, 8 ad 16: 'ipsum autem testimonium veritatis primae se habet in fide ut principium in scientiis demonstrativis.' Aquinas, 1972, p. 461. See also *Super Boet. de Tr.* 2, 2 ad 4.

[59] *D. V.* 14, 1 ad 2: 'fides dicitur non inquisitus consensus, in quantum consensus fidei vel assensus non causatur ex inquisitione rationis; tamen non excluditur per hoc quin in intellectu credentis remaneat aliqua cogitatio vel collatio de his quae credit.' Aquinas, 1972, p. 438.

the witness of the law, nor because of the preachings of others, but because of first truth in itself.[60]

One role that signs can play is to strengthen and confirm the virtue of faith (*Quodl.* 2, q. 4 a. 1 ad 4). Aquinas is not very clear on the role that signs can play in bringing to faith those who do not yet possess it. He does, however, say that faith is both preceded and followed by intellectual activity, and that the reasoning that precedes faith inclines the will to choose to believe, rather than bringing the intellect to assent to a proposition.[61]

Aquinas's position on the role of the motives of credibility, and his refusal to postulate acquired as opposed to infused faith, is a return to the patristic position described in the previous chapter. Like the patristic position, his view faces the crucial question – some might say the crucial objection – for positions of this sort; what is it, if not the motives of credibility, that leads us to think that the teachings of the Christian faith are spoken by God, and hence to believe them?

Fr. John Jenkins has offered an account of Aquinas's view on this question, in his *Knowledge and faith in Thomas Aquinas.*[62] He presents Aquinas in the *Summa theologiae* as ascribing to two of the Gifts of the Holy Spirit, the Gifts of Understanding and Science, the role of enabling the believer to accept that the propositions of faith are to be believed, and of enabling the believer to actually believe them. But this interpretation cannot be maintained. Aquinas holds that the theological virtues (of which faith of course is one) are presupposed by the Gifts, as the roots from which they are derived (*1a2ae* 68, 4 ad 3). Just as the intellectual virtues are placed before the moral virtues and regulate them, so the theological virtues are placed before the Gifts and regulate them (*1a2ae* 68, 7). In particular, the Gift of Understanding is the fruit of the virtue of faith (*2a2ae* 8, 8 ad 1). If the Gifts of Understanding and Science are founded on faith and presuppose it, it does not seem possible for them to have an essential role in bringing faith into existence. That they do not have this role in Aquinas's view is clear from the fact that he

---

[60] *In Ioan.* c. 4 l. 5 n. 2: 'Inducunt nos ad fidem Christi tria. Primo quidem ratio naturalis. Ad Rom. I, 20: "Invisibilia Dei a creatura mundi per ea quae facta sunt, intellecta conspiciuntur." Secundo testimonia Legis et Prophetarum. Rom. III, 21: "Nunc autem iustitia Dei sine Lege manifestata est, testificata a Lege et Prophetis." Tertio praedicanto Apostolorum et aliorum. Rom. X, 14: "Quomodo credent sine praedicante?" Sed quando per hoc homo manuductus credit, tunc potest dicere, quod propter nullum istorum credit: nec propter rationem naturalem, nec propter testimonia legis, nec propter praedicationem aliorum, sed propter ipsam veritatem tantum; Gen. XV, 6: "Credidit Abraham Deo, et reputatam est ei ad justitiam."' Aquinas, 1952, p. 124.

[61] *3 Sent.* d. 23 q. 2 a. 2 sol. 1 ad 2: 'per hoc quod dicit Damascenus quod fides est non inquisitus consensus, excluditur inquisitio rationis intellectum terminantis, non inquisitio voluntatem inclinans. Et ex hoc ipso quod intellectus terminatus non est, remanet motus intellectus, inquantum naturaliter tendit in sui determinationem. Unde fides consistit media inter duas cogitationes, una quarum voluntatem inclinat ad credendum, et haec precedit fidem; alia vero tendit ad intellectum eorum quae jam credit, et haec est simul cum assensu fidei.' Aquinas, 1933, vol. 3, p. 728.

[62] John Jenkins, *Knowledge and faith in Thomas Aquinas*, 1997, pp. 192–4.

states that the Gifts cannot exist without charity (*la2ae* 68, 5). But faith can exist in us without charity; so the Gifts cannot be necessary for faith. This reasoning would not follow if Aquinas had held, as some theologians did, that formless faith is different from formed faith and disappears with the advent of charity, but he explicity denied that this was so (*D. V.* 14, 7).

If the Gifts do not lead us to faith in Aquinas's view, what does? He asserts that two things are needed for faith; exterior preaching, and an interior call from God.[63] Without this call, even when miracles are present to provide evidence for faith, belief is impossible and unbelief is without fault.[64] The Son and the Holy Spirit cooperate in bringing believers to faith;

> For just as the effect of the mission of the Son is to lead us to the Father, so the mission of the Holy Spirit is to lead the faithful to the Son. Since the Son is begotten wisdom itself, he is truth itself. John 14, 6; 'I am the way, the truth and the life.' And therefore the effect of a mission of this sort is that men are made to become participants in the divine wisdom, and knowers of the truth. For the Son hands over teaching to us, since he is the Word; but the Holy Spirit makes us capable to receive this teaching. For the Son says 'He [sc. the Holy Spirit] will teach you all things'; because no matter what men teach from without, unless the Holy Spirit gives understanding of what they teach, their labour in teaching is in vain; for unless the Holy Spirit is present in the hearts of the hearers, the words of teachers are useless.[65]

But the question of how the Holy Spirit acts in us so as to make us believe is not answered by Aquinas. This is probably because it would not have struck him as a question urgently in need of investigation. We do not have to understand this action of the Holy Spirit in order to cooperate with it. A defence of the rationality of the faith that results from this action would require an account of the nature of

---

[63] *In Rom.* 10, 1.2: '... ad fidem duo requiruntur: quorum unum est cordis inclinatio ad credendum et hoc non est ex auditu, sed ex dono gratiae; aliud autem est determinatio de credibili et istud est ex auditu. Et ideo Cornelius qui habebat cor inclinatum ad credendum, necesse habuit ut ad eum mitteretur Petrus, qui sibi determinaret quid esset credendum.' Aquinas, 1953a, p. 157.

[64] *In Ioan.* XV l.V n.4: 'Secunda quaestio est de veritate conditionalis utrum scilicet...si Christus non fecisset in eis opera quae nemo alius fecit, immunes essent a peccato infidelitatis. Responsio. Dicendum: si nos loquamur de quibuscumque miraculis, haberent excusationem, si in eis facta non fuissent per Christum. Nullus enim potest ad Christum venire per fidem nisi tractus; supra VI, 44: "Nemo potest venire ad me, nisi Pater, qui misit me, traxerit eum." Et ideo Cant. I, 3, dicit Sponsa: "Trahe me post te: curremus in odorem unguentorum tuorum." Unde si nullus esset qui eos traxisset ad fidem, excusabiles essent de infidelitate.

Sed est attendendum, quod Christus attraxit verbo, signis visibilis et invisibilius, scilicet movendo et instigendo interius corda. Prov. XXI, 1: "Cor regum in manu Dei." Est ergo opus Dei instinctus interior ad bene agendum, et qui ei resistunt, peccant: ... Est ergo hoc quod Dominus dicit, "Si opera non fecissem in eis quae nemo alius fecit", intelligendum non solum de visibilius, sed etiam de interiori instinctu et attractu doctrinae: quae quidem si in eis non fecisset, peccatum non haberet.' Aquinas, 1952, p. 388.

[65] *In Ioan*, XIV l. 6 n. 6, Aquinas, 1952, p. 367 (my translation).

the role of the Holy Spirit in bringing us to believe, but Aquinas did not think it necessary to offer such a defence. To find such a defence, we need to look at a later thinker who lived at a time when Christianity was more widely challenged.

John Owen   John Owen was the Puritan vice-chancellor of the University of Oxford, and Oliver Cromwell's right-hand man in ecclesiastical affairs. Owen does not have the theological breadth or philosophical ability of Aquinas, but, unlike Aquinas, he explicitly argues for his position on the role of the motives of credibility in faith. Although often prolix and sloppy in his manner of expressing himself, he was a sharp and perceptive thinker, and his position on the motives of credibility was a major advance. Regrettably it seems to have been too major an advance for his contemporaries or successors, since it was never taken up or built upon.

Owen wrote two works on the rational grounding of Christian faith, *Of the Divine Original, Authority, Self-Evidencing Light, and Power of the Scriptures* (1659), and *The Reason of Faith: or, the grounds whereon the Scripture is Believed to be the word of God with faith divine and supernatural* (1677). His view is basically the same in these books, but the later one is a deeper and more elaborate presentation. The question he poses in them is one that would have been familiar to Aquinas: what is the formal object of faith?

> ... in our believing, or our faith, two things are to be considered: 1). What it is that we do believe; and, 2). Wherefore we do so believe it. The first is the material object of our faith, – namely, those things which we do believe: the latter, the formal object of it, or the cause and reason why we do believe them...The material object of our faith is the things revealed in the Scripture, declared unto us in propositions of truth ...[66]

Faith requires us to believe the Scriptures as divinely revealed. There are motives of credibility that can serve to show that the Scriptures are the word of God:

> There are sundry cogent arguments, which are taken from external considerations of the Scripture, that evince it on rational grounds to be the word of God. All these are motives of credibility, or effectual persuasives to account and esteem it to be the word of God ... the assent unto the divine authority and original of the Scriptures, which the mind ought to give upon them, we grant to be of as high nature as it is pretended to be, – namely, a moral certainty.[67]

These may give rise to a human faith, but they cannot be the formal object of divine saving faith. The motives of credibility are fallible grounds, but divine faith is not;

> ... there is an assent of another kind unto the divine original and authority of the Scriptures required of us, – namely, that of faith divine and supernatural. Of this no one will say that it can be effected by or resolved unto the best and most cogent of rational

---

[66] John Owen, *The Reason of Faith*, 1852, p. 16.
[67] Owen, 1852, p. 21.

arguments and external testimonies which are absolutely human and fallible; for it doth imply a contradiction, to believe infallibly upon fallible evidence.[68]

Divine faith requires grace, but a belief based on the motives of credibility does not:

> The moral certainty treated of is a mere effect of reason. There is no more required unto it but that the reasons proposed for the assent required be such as the mind judgeth to be convincing and prevalent; whence an inferior kind of knowledge, or a firm opinion, or some kind of persuasion which hath not yet gotten an intelligible name, doth necessarily ensue. There is, therefore, on this supposition, no need of any work of the Holy Ghost to enable us to believe or to work faith in us; for no more is required herein but what necessarily ariseth from a naked exercise of the reason...Now this is not faith, nor can we be said in the Scripture sense to believe hereby, and so in particular, not the Scriptures to be the word of God; for faith is 'the gift of God', and is 'not of ourselves', Eph. ii. 8 ... 'No man can say that Jesus is the Lord, but by the Holy Ghost', 1 Cor. xii. 3; but he who believeth the Scripture truly, aright, and according to his duty, doth say so. No man cometh to Christ, but he that hath 'heard and learned of the Father', John vi. 45. And as this is contrary to the Scripture, so it is expressly condemned by the ancient church, particularly the second Aurausican council, can. 5, 7: 'Si quis sicut augmentum ita etiam initia fidei, ipsumque credulitatis affectum, [....] non per gratiae donum, id est, per inspirationem Spiritus Sancti, corrigentem voluntatem nostram ab infidelitate ad fidem, ab impietate ad pietatem, sed naturaliter nobis inesse dicit, apostolicis dogmatibus adversarius approbantur'. And plainly, can. 7: 'Si quis per naturae vigorem bonum aliquod quod ad salutem pertinet vitae eternae, cogitare ut expedit, aut eligere, sive salutare, id est, evangelicae praedicationi consentire posse affirmat ansque illuminatione et inspiratione Spiritus Sancti, qui dat omnibus suavitatem consentiendo et credendo veritati, haeretico fallitur spiritu'.[69]

---

[68] Owen, 1852, p. 21.

[69] Owen, 1852, pp. 49–50. The second Aurausican council is the second council of Orange, held in 529 A.D. Owen's citation of its canons is accurate save for the fact that his citation of canon 5 leaves out the passage 'quo in eum credimus, qui justificat impium, et ad (re)generationem sacri baptismatis, pervenimus' between 'affectum' and 'non per gratiae donum'; the missing words are indicated by square brackets in the text. The full conciliar text is translated as 'Can. 5. If anyone says, that just as the increase [of faith] so also the beginning of faith and the very desire of credulity, by which we believe in Him who justifies the impious, and (by which) we arrive at the regeneration of holy baptism (is) not through the gift of grace, that is, through the inspiration of the Holy Spirit reforming our will from infidelity to faith, from impiety to piety, but is naturally in us, he is proved (to be) antagonistic to the doctrine of the Apostles ... Can. 7. If anyone affirms that without the illumination and the inspiration of the Holy Spirit, – who gives to all sweetness in consenting to and believing in the truth, – through the strength of nature he can think anything good which pertains to the salvation of eternal life, as he should, or choose, or consent to salvation, that is to the evangelical proclamation, he is deceived by the heretical spirit ... ' H. Denzinger, *The Sources of Catholic Dogma*, 1957, pp. 76–7. The records of this council were lost for a thousand years and thus made no impact on medieval discussions. However, when rediscovered, they were accepted as authoritative by the Roman Catholic Church. The council's teaching on faith was quoted and reaffirmed by the First Vatican Council, *Dei Filius*, ch. 3, and the Second Vatican Council, *Dei Verbum*, para. 5.

He considers the position that it is not the motives of credibility alone, but the motives together with the majesty, holiness and excellence of the doctrines taught in Scripture that provide the reason for faith. He rejects it because believing on the grounds of the excellence of the doctrine asserted is not faith, which consists in believing on the basis of testimony,[70] and because in fact this excellence cannot be perceived without faith, and thus is not capable of grounding it.

Owen does not think that the motives of credibility are useless. He says that the motives of credibility

> ... have all of them their use, and may in their proper place be insisted on. Especially ought they to be pleaded when the Scripture is attacked by an atheism arising from the love and practice of those lusts and sins which are severely condemned therein ... with others they may be considered as previous inducements unto believing, or concomitant means of strengthening faith in them that do believe. In the first way I confess, to the best of my observation past and present, their use is not great, nor ever hath been in the church of God: for assuredly the most that do sincerely believe the divine original and authority of the Scripture do it without any great consideration of them, or being much influenced by them ...[71]

In seeing the motives of credibility as being able to strengthen the faith of believers, Owen agrees with Aquinas. But it is not clear how they can perform this function, if, as both Owen and Aquinas assert, the formal object of faith provides a reason for believing that yields certainty, while the motives of credibility can only yield probability. It is worth noting that some later theologians, who adopted a Thomist view on the motives of credibility, more consistently denied that they are of any use in strengthening faith. Reginald Garrigou-Lagrange asserts that reliance on the motives of credibility is an imperfection that is removed in the course of progress towards Christian perfection.

> This very intimate, sublime, and highly simplified manner whereby infused faith attains to its formal motive is gradually purified more and more of every imperfect element in the passive purification of the spirit, called by St. John of the Cross the dark night of the soul. In this dolorous darkness the formal motive of faith, that is, first truth revealing, is more and more detached from every other secondary and imperfect motive which is then dolorously carried away, for instance, from the harmony of the supernatural mysteries with truths about God naturally known or our own aspirations ... Then, as the best directors of souls affirm, is not the time for rereading our apologetics but for the most humble, confiding prayer ... Thus the mystical experience of the saints confirms the assertion of theologians as follows: the formal motive of any theological virtue cannot be anything created; it cannot be a miracle or any truth naturally known ...[72]

---

[70] 'It belongs unto the nature of faith, of what sort soever it be, that it be built on and resolved into testimony. This is that which distinguisheth it from any other conception, knowledge, or assent of our minds on other reasons or causes.' Owen, 1852, p. 53.

[71] Owen, 1852, p. 71.

[72] Reginald Garrigou-Lagrange, *Grace: Commentary on the Summa Theologiae of St. Thomas, 1a2ae, qq. 109–14*, 1952, pp. 496–7.

If the motives of credibility are not the formal object of faith, what is? Owen's position on the formal object of Christian faith is the same as that of Aquinas. 'The authority and veracity of God revealing the material object of our faith ... are the formal object and reason of our faith, from whence it ariseth and whereinto it is ultimately resolved.'[73] The formal object is God's testimony: '... the power of our souls whereunto it is proposed is that whereby we can give an assent unto the truth upon the testimony of the proposer, whereof we have no other evidence.'[74] It is not God's veracity in itself that is the formal object of faith, nor God's veracity in at some time or other uttering the doctrines that are asserted in the Scriptures, but God's veracity in uttering the Scriptures, the writings, themselves.

Why believe that this is the formal object of faith? One argument is that if the Scriptures are the word of God, as faith accepts that they are, they must be recognizable as such.

> ... there seems to be a moral impossibility, that the word of God, should not manifest its own original, and its authority from thence ... A curious artificer imparts that of form, shape, proportion, and comeliness, to the fruit of his invention, and work of his hands, that every one who looks upon it, must conclude, that it comes from skill and ability. A man in the delivery of his mind, in the writing of a book, will give it such an impression of reason, that though you cannot conclude that this or that man wrote it, yet you must, that it was the product of a man, or rational creature: yea some individual men of excellency in some skill, are instantly known, by them that are able to judge in that art or skill, by the effects of that skill ... Now certainly this is strange beyond all belief, that almost every agent should give an impression to its work, whereby it may be appropriated unto him, and only the word wherein it was the design of the great and holy God, to give us a portraiture as it were of his wisdom, holiness and goodness ... is not able to declare and evince its original. That God ... should write a book ... commanding us to receive it as his, under the penalty of his eternal displeasure, and yet that book not make a sufficient discovery of itself to be his, is past all belief.[75]

God's veracity being the formal object of faith explains why the simple believe as firmly, or more firmly, than the learned. If faith were based on the motives of credibility, the faith of the learned ought to be stronger than that of the simple, since 'no assent of the mind can be accompanied with any more assurance that the

---

[73] Owen, 1852, p. 18.

[74] Owen, 1852, p. 88.

[75] John Owen, *Of the Divine Original, Authority, Self-Evidencing Light and Power of the Scriptures*, 1826, p. 437. Opponents of Owen such as Edward Stillingfleet objected to this argument on the grounds that the contents of Scripture can easily be repeated by people other than God, as appears from the many books of Christian devotion there are in the world. The reply that can be made in defence of Owen's argument is that the parallel to the work of the artificer is God's action of speaking to believers, rather than the words that are spoken; it is this action that 'declares and evinces its original'. This reply will be explicated in Chapters 7 and 8 below. It allows us to see the strength of Owen's point: there *does* seem to be a moral impossibility that the word of God, if it exists, should not manifest its origin.

evidence whose effect it is, and which it is resolved unto, will afford.'[76] But this is clearly not the case, so the motives of credibility cannot be the formal object of faith. If God's veracity is the formal object, however, there is no difficulty in the simple believing as firmly as the learned.

God's veracity can be known to be the formal object of faith in the Scriptures because that is the reason for believing that the Scriptures themselves propose. It is self-refuting to say that we believe the Scriptures as divinely revealed on the grounds of the motives of credibility, if the Scriptures themselves assert that the reason why we should believe them is simply God's veracity in uttering them. Owen claims that this is the case: '... God requires us to believe the Scripture for no other reason but because it is his word ... To this purpose do testimonies abound in particular, besides that general attestation which is given unto it in that sole preface of discourse, "Thus says the Lord"...'[77] Particular instances that he cites are the reading of the Law to the people in Deut. 31:11–13, '... that which, by the appointment of God, is to be proposed unto them that know nothing, that they may believe, that is unto them the formal reason of their believing. But this is the written word: "Thou shalt read this law unto them which have not known any thing, that they may hear and learn," etc...'[78]; Isaiah 8:19–20; and Jeremiah 23:28–9.[79] 2 Tim. 3:16 gives divine inspiration as the reason for believing the Scriptures, and this divine inspiration consists in their being spoken by God.[80] 2 Peter 1:16–21 describes the prophetic word as more sure than the voice of God heard at the Transfiguration. The parable of Dives and Lazarus (Luke 16:27–31) shows that miracles will not convince those who do not believe the teachings of the prophets.

Owen rather irritably points out that this argument is not meant to establish that the Scriptures are actually spoken by God, but only that the formal object of our believing them, if we believe them, must be God's speaking alone:

> Some, it may be, will ask whether this prove the Scripture to be the word of God, because it says so of itself, when any other writing may say the same; but we are not now giving arguments to prove unto others the Scripture to be the word of God, but only proving and showing what our own faith resteth on and is resolved unto[81]... it is not unlikely but that some persons, well-conceited of their own understanding in things wherein they are most ignorant, will pride and please themselves in the ridiculousness of proving the Scripture to be the word of God by testimonies taken out of it. But, as was

---

[76] Owen, 1852, p. 100.

[77] Owen, 1852, p. 74.

[78] Owen, 1852, p. 74.

[79] Isaiah 8:19–20: 'And when they say to you, "Consult the mediums and the wizards who chirp and mutter", should not a people consult their God? Should they consult the dead on behalf of the living? To the teaching and to the testimony!' Jeremiah 23:28–9: 'Let the prophet who has a dream tell the dream, but let him who has my word speak my word faithfully. What has straw in common with wheat? says the Lord. Is not my word like fire, says the Lord, and like a hammer which breaks the rock in pieces?'

[80] Owen, 1826, p. 411.

[81] Owen, 1852, p. 73.

said, we must not forego the truth because either they will not or cannot understand what we discourse about.[82]

Divine faith in the Scriptures as the word of God must be reasonable, not based on blind credulity:

> ... if, moreover, we are asked a reason of our faith or hope, or why we do believe things we do profess ... we do not answer, 'Because so it is, for this is that which we believe', which were senseless; but we must give some other answer unto that inquiry, whether it be made by others or by ourselves[83]... there is no doubt but that men are obliged to consider all things of that nature which are proposed unto them, and not to receive it with brutish, implicit belief; for the receiving of it is to be an act of men's own minds or understandings, on the best grounds and evidences which the nature of the thing proposed is capable of ...[84]

What are the evidences in the Scriptures themselves that enable us to recognize them as coming from God? Owen describes two sorts of such evidence. One sort is that, as an artificer leaves an imprint of himself on his work, so 'God, as the immediate author of the Scripture, hath left in the very word itself evident tokens and impressions of his wisdom, prescience, omniscience, power, goodness, holiness, truth, and other divine, infinite excellencies, sufficiently evidenced unto the enlightened minds of believers.'[85]

Another sort of evidence lies in the effect of the Scriptures on those who read them. Owen says that there are two sorts of things that are self-evidencing – light and power – and that the Scriptures bear both of these within themselves.

> Without the Scripture all the world is in darkness ... superstition, idolatry, lying vanities, wherein men know not at all what they do nor whither they go, fill the whole world, even as it is this day. And the minds of men are naturally in darkness; there is a blindness upon them that they cannot see nor discern spiritual things. With respect unto both these kinds of darkness the Scripture is a light ... thereby evidencing itself to be a divine revelation; for what but divine truth could recall the minds of men from all their wandering in error, superstition, and other effects of darkness, which of themselves they love more than truth?[86]

The Scriptures show their power through their effect on the minds and consciences of men.

> The principal divine effect of the word of God is in the conversion of the souls of sinners unto God ... of this great and glorious effect the word is the only instrumental cause, whereby the divine power operates and is expressive of itself ... The work which is effected by it, in the regeneration, conversion, and sanctification of the souls of

---

[82] Owen, 1852, p. 79.
[83] Owen, 1852, p. 16.
[84] Owen, 1852, p. 81.
[85] Owen, 1852, p. 92.
[86] Owen, 1852, p. 97.

believers, doth evidence infallibly unto their consciences that it is not the word of man, but of God.[87]

The effects of the Scripture are ones that can only be achieved by God. These include the making manifest the secrets of the heart (cf. 1 Cor. xiv. 24–5), which is only possible for God, who alone knows the secrets of the heart, and 'the work of conviction of sin on those who expected it not, who desired it not, and who would avoid it if by any means possible they could.'

> Conscience is the territory or dominion of God in man, which he hath so reserved unto himself that no human power can possibly enter into it or dispose of it in any wise. But in this work of conviction of sin, the word of God, the Scripture, entereth into the conscience of the sinner, takes possession of it, disposeth it unto peace or trouble, by its laws or rules, and not otherwise ...[88]

Recognition of these traits in the Scriptures is not naturally possible for men; it requires the assistance of the Holy Spirit. The Spirit works by removing the blindness that makes it impossible to recognize these traits.

> There are two things which hinder or disenable men from believing with faith divine and supernatural, when any divine revelation is objectively proposed unto them: – First, The natural blindness and darkness of their minds, which are come upon all by the fall, and the depravation of their nature that ensued thereon. Secondly, the prejudices that, through the craft of Satan, the god of this world, their minds are possessed with, by traditions, education, and converse in this world. This last obstruction or hinderance may be so far removed by external arguments or motives of credibility, as that men may upon them attain unto a moral persuasion concerning the divine original of the Scripture; but these arguments cannot remove or take away the natural blindness of the mind, which is removed by their renovation and divine illumination alone.[89]

This conception of the work of the Holy Spirit is one of the few divergences between Owen's view and Aquinas's view. Unlike Aquinas, Owen does not see the grace of faith as conferring a gift that surpasses the powers of any possible created nature, but only as repairing the damage to human nature done by the fall.

Owen is insistent about the action of the Holy Spirit's being the efficient cause, not the formal object, of belief. If the Spirit's action were to be the reason for our belief, its action in every believer would amount to a revelation. Belief in a direct

---

[87] Owen, 1852, pp. 94–5. Note the crucial difference between this assertion and the claim made by Origen. Origen said that the redemptive effect of the gospel shows to onlookers of this effect that the gospel originates in God; Owen says that the redemptive effect shows to the *person who is redeemed by hearing* that the gospel is spoken by God.

[88] Owen, 1852, p. 96. Owen is aware of the obvious riposte to this claim, which is that people can easily affect their own consciences by e.g. corrupting them; his answer to it is not very successful. What he ought perhaps to have replied is that, as he says elsewhere, it is only God who can confer on our consciences knowledge that it is not in their natural power to obtain, and that the Scriptures do this.

[89] Owen, 1852, p. 58.

revelation by the Holy Spirit to every individual believer, that does not involve any created messenger, is enthusiasm, which Owen vehemently rejects. Indeed it is likely that part of his motive for writing *The Reason of Faith* was to attack the Quakers, who believed in just such revelations. The formal object of faith must be something publicly available.

This brings up the obvious objection that if the evidence of the Scriptures' being God's word is public and objectively available, their divine origin should be clear to everyone; but it is not. Owen's answer is that their origin would only have to be obvious to everyone if everyone had faith; but they do not. The inability of people without faith to perceive the divine origin of the Scriptures is no more an objection against their divine origin than the inability of a blind man to see the sun is a reason to doubt that the sun is shining.

Owen, as we saw above, claims that divine faith is infallible, and that it provides an absolute, not just a moral, certainty. His justification for this claim rests on an important and original claim about knowledge.

> ... there are three ways whereby we assent unto any thing that is proposed unto us as true, and receive it as such: –
>
> (1.) By inbred principles of natural light ... in general, the mind is necessarily determined to an assent unto the proper objects of these principles ... its first apprehension of the things which the light of nature embraceth ... is this assent ...
>
> (2.) By rational considerations of things externally proposed unto us. Herein the mind exerciseth its discursive faculty, gathering one thing out of another, and concluding one thing from another; and hereon is it able to assent unto what is proposed to it in various degrees of certainty, according unto the nature and degree of the evidence it proceeds upon ...
>
> (3.) By faith. This respects that power of our minds whereby we are able to assent unto any thing as true which we have no first principles concerning, no inbred notions of, nor can from more known principles make unto ourselves any certain rational grounds concerning them. This is our assent upon testimony, whereon we believe many things which no sense, inbred principles, nor reasonings of our own, could either give us an acquaintance with or assurance of. And this assent also hath not only various degrees, but is also of divers kinds, according as the testimony is which it ariseth from and resteth on; as being human if that be human, and divine if that be so also.[90]

Owen says of testimony that

> ... this is the principal and most noble faculty and power of our nature. There is an instinct in brute creatures that hath some resemblance unto our inbred natural principles ... but as unto the power or faculty of giving an assent unto things on witness or testimony, there is nothing in the nature of irrational creature, that hath the least shadow of it ... And if our souls did want but this one faculty of assenting unto truth upon testimony, all that remains would not be sufficient to conduct us through the affairs of this natural life. This, therefore, being the most noble faculty of our minds is that whereunto the highest way of divine revelation is proposed.[91]

---

[90] Owen, 1852, p. 83.
[91] Owen, 1852, p. 88.

As far as I know, Owen is the first European thinker to present testimony as a source of knowledge that is independent of and equal to any other source.[92] This is an important step not just for theology but for philosophy as well.

Owen holds that God reveals himself to us through all these three ways, but the most important revelation, the Scriptures, is 'accompanied with more assurance than any assent which is the effect of science upon the most demonstrable principles.'[93] He is aware of the distinction between kinds of assurance that is made by Aquinas, but he has doubts about it;

> ... the schoolmen do distinguish between a certainty or assurance of evidence and an assurance of adherence. In the latter, they say, the certainty of faith doth exceed that of science; but it is less in respect of the former. But it is not easily to be conceived, how the certainty of adherence should exceed the certainty of evidence, with respect unto any object whatsoever. [94]

He does not draw this distinction in claiming that the assurance of faith surpasses all others. He argues for this claim as follows;

> ... unto the firmitude and constancy which we have in the assurance of faith, three things do concur: –
>
> (1.) That this ability of assent upon testimony is the highest and most noble power or faculty of our rational souls; and, therefore, where it hath the highest evidence whereof it is capable, – which it hath in the testimony of God, – it giveth us the highest certainty and assurance whereof in this world we are capable.
>
> (2.) Unto the assent of divine faith there is required an especial internal operation of the Holy Ghost. This rendereth it of another nature than any mere natural act and operation of our minds; and, therefore, if the assurance of it may not properly be said to exceed the assurance of science in degree, it is only because it is of a more excellent kind, and so is not capable of comparison unto it as to degrees.
>
> (3.) That the revelation which God makes of himself, his mind and his will, by his word, is more excellent, and accompanied with greater evidence of his infinitely glorious properties, – wherein alone the mind can find absolute rest and satisfaction (which is its assurance), – than any other discovery of truth, of what sort soever, is capable of; neither is the assurance of the mind absolutely perfect in any thing beneath the enjoyment of God. Wherefore, the soul by faith making the nearest approaches whereof in this life it is capable unto the eternal spring of being, truth and goodness, it

---

[92] Before discovering Owen's work I would have said that Thomas Reid was the first European to propose such a view of testimony (Indian philosophers had already been maintaining it for centuries). I have not been able to find any evidence of Reid's being influenced by Owen, but since Reid was a Presbyterian divine it is quite likely that he would have read Owen's works. It is interesting to note that Owen was led by his faith to insights about the nature of testimony that were only widely accepted by European philosophers hundreds of years later.

[93] Owen, 1852, p. 100.

[94] Owen, 1852, p. 101.

hath the highest rest, satisfaction and assurance therein, that in this life it can attain unto.[95]

This description of assent upon testimony as the highest and most noble power of our rational souls might seem overly strong, but there is an important sense in which it is true. As we shall see in chapter 6, testimony is the highest power of our rational souls, if we rank these powers according to the amount of important information they are capable of providing us with.

It is interesting to speculate on the origin of Owen's ideas. His views on the epistemology of testimony seem entirely original, as is his application of them to divine faith. His understanding of the role of grace in faith was not the universal view of English Puritans; the other main seventeenth-century Puritan thinker, Richard Baxter, held that Christian faith is based on the motives of credibility, and that divine power is not strictly needed to produce faith.[96] The close resemblance between some of his arguments against faith being based on the motives of credibility and the standard Dominican arguments for this position make it seem incredible that he was not influenced by Dominican authors (he had read Melchior Cano, for example), although he was not the man to admit that this was the case. He may also have been influenced in forming his conclusions by Clement of Alexandria, to whom he refers in his discussion. However, it should also be recognized that in his insistence on the necessity of grace for faith he was being faithful to Calvinism, which in turn was defending a central tenet it had inherited from Catholicism.

Owen's account of what leads us to believe the Scriptures can be seen to provide what is lacking in Aquinas's views on the role of the motives of credibility; an explanation of how we can recognize and believe God as First Truth speaking. His explanation brings to light two crucial issues that must be addressed in order to answer the question asked by this book. These issues are the epistemic status of testimony, and the ways in which an utterance can be recognized as coming from God. Chapters 6 and 8 attempt to resolve these issues.

---

[95] Owen, 1852, p. 102.

[96] See Richard Baxter, *The Reason of the Christian Religion*, 1707, p. 120; and his *Catholick Theologie: Plain, Pure, Peaceable: for PACIFICATION of the Dogmatical WORD-WARRIORS, WHO, 1. By contending about things unrevealed or not understood, 2. And by taking VERBAL differences for REAL, and their arbitrary Notions for necessary Sacred Truths, deceived and deceiving by ambiguous unexplained WORDS, have long been the Shame of the Christian Religion, a Scandal and a hardening to unbelievers, the Incendiaries, Dividers and Distracters of the Church, the occasion of State Discords and Wars, the Corrupters of the Christian Faith, and the Subverters of their own Souls, and their followers, calling them to a blind Zeal, and Wrathful Warfare, against true Piety, Love, and Peace, and teaching them to censure, backbite, slander and prate against each other for things they never understood: written chiefly for Posterity, when sad Experience hath taught men to hate Theological Logical Wars, and to love, and seek, and call for Peace*, 1675, p. 47.

Christian faith as partially, but not entirely, based on the motives of credibility

The Franciscan school of Alexander of Hales, as we saw, postulated the existence of both infused faith and acquired faith in the believer, and held that both are required for the virtue of faith. But this position is somewhat different from the one that will be considered here. In Alexander's *Summa*, acquired faith functions rather like the rope ladder for the preacher in *Moby Dick*, who uses the ladder to climb up into his pulpit and then pulls it up after him. It does not remain as part of the cause of belief. The idea of acquired faith remaining along with infused faith as a separate and necessary basis for belief originates with Duns Scotus. After Scotus, this position became the dominant one among Roman Catholic theologians.

Duns Scotus Scotus's discussion of the role of the motives of credibility in faith took place in an intellectual environment that differed significantly in one respect from that of Aquinas. After Aquinas's death, Peter Olivi had explicitly raised for the first time the question of whether believing on account of miracles and prophecy did not constitute believing on account of human reason.[97] The answer he offered was interestingly that believing on account of Christ's miracles did not constitute an inference from those miracles. Rather, the miracles put us in immediate contact with the divine, as if we were touching it, and it is this immediate contact that leads us to believe.[98]

Scotus, however, did not see acquired faith as non-inferential. Nor did he conceive of it as something that is left behind when infused faith is acquired, as Alexander of Hales did. His arguments for the existence of acquired faith in believers do not leave open the possibility of its being in any way dispensable. He claims that it is certain that there is acquired faith in believers on the following grounds:

1. As Augustine says in his letter against the Manichaeans, we would not believe the Gospel were it not for the teaching of the Catholic Church ('non crederet Euangelio, nisi crederet Ecclesiae Catholicae'). It is apparent from this that the sacred canonical books are not to be believed, save because the Church is first to be believed approving and authorizing these books and resting content in them (contenta in eius); for let any book have as much authority as it likes from its author, we will still not firmly adhere to it, save because we believe the church approving of it and testifying to the veracity of its authors. For this reason Augustine says that the Gospel of the Nazarene is not to be accepted, because it is not accepted by the Church. Thus therefore if there was no infused faith in me, I would still firmly believe the accounts of the canonical books on account of the

---

[97] Peter Olivi, *S. Q. Sent. III* q. 8 obj. 7 ex. 2a5ie, quoted in Roger Aubert 'Le caractère raisonnable de l'acte de foi d'après les théologiens de la fin du 13e siècle', *Revue d'histoire ecclésiastique*, 1943, pp. 64–5.
[98] Aubert (1943), p. 65.

authority of the Church, just as with acquired faith I would believe the accounts written or narrated by other famous men.[99]

(This argument is crucial in the evolution of the notion of acquired faith, because it means that such faith not only introduces infused faith and exists alongside it, but serves as a necessary foundation for infused faith.)

2. If an unbaptized Jewish child were brought up among Christians, and taught as they are, he would believe with acquired faith everything that Christians do, just as we believe with acquired faith, through hearing the assertions of our parents and others, that much time has passed and that the world did not begin at the same time as we did. I believe that there is such a city as Rome, although I have not seen it, on the assertions of people who are worthy of belief. In the same way, I firmly adhere with acquired faith to the things revealed in the Scriptures, on account of the authority of the Church.[100]

3. Suppose a baptized person to believe all the articles of faith, but then to err concerning one of them. Error about one article does not entail error about all of the articles, because there is no necessary connection between heresies. He will then believe the other articles without infused faith, because infused faith is destroyed by heresy. His belief must therefore be acquired faith. But acquired faith does not come into being in the instant that infused faith is destroyed by heresy, for error does not dispose to faith; rather, it is an indisposition to it. So acquired faith must have existed before the loss of infused faith.

4. In Romans ch. 10, the Apostle says 'How can anyone believe without hearing? And how can they hear without a preacher? And how can anyone preach without being sent?' Thus according to the Apostle, no-one can believe without hearing someone preach the things that are to be believed. But this is only true of acquired faith. Such a faith can occur in someone who hears the preaching and accepts it but lacks charity, being in a state of mortal sin. A person who lacks charity cannot have infused faith; rather, he believes on account of his natural reason, hearing the preacher and seeing the miracles that he works, and knowing that it is impossible that God should testify to the truthfulness of a false preacher through working miracles. Thus, faith in a preacher arises through acquired faith.

These arguments do not adequately get to grips with the Thomist position that they oppose. The first argument assumes that believing the Church must be different from believing God and hence must constitute believing with acquired faith, something Aquinas might not have granted. He would simply have denied that the faith of an unbaptized Jewish child of the sort described is the same as the infused faith of a Christian, and that such a child would have developed faith in the same way as Christians do. He explicitly states that heresy is adopted for reasons different than the ones that lead an orthodox Christian to believe, so he would have said that a different form of belief does come into existence at the moment heresy

---

[99] *Opus Oxoniense, In III Sent.* d. 23 q. 1 schol., in Duns Scotus, *Quaestiones in lib. III sententiarum,* in *Opera,* vol. 7, 1639a, p. 460; see also *Reportata Parisiense, In III Sent.* d. 23 q. 1. schol. 1, in Duns Scotus, *Reportata parisiense,* in *Opera,* vol. 11, 1639b.
[100] Scotus, 1639a, p. 460.

begins; error is no obstacle to the will for power and self-aggrandizement, which is the motive for belief that Aquinas ascribes to heretics. As for the fourth argument, it assumes that infused faith cannot exist without charity, which Aquinas denies. However, arguments that covertly assume the most debatable points connected with them often have controversial success, so it is not surprising that Scotus's position was influential.

If acquired faith leads us to believe Christian teaching, what need is there for infused faith, and what reason do we have to suppose that it exists? Scotus opposed the view that infused faith exists in order to provide greater certainty than is possible for acquired faith, using arguments of considerable interest. He maintained that acquired faith has a certainty that is greater than that of opinion, involving no fear of the negation of the proposition believed through it being true. He reasoned as follows: I do not believe that the world began to exist when I did. I do not have *scientia* of the fact that it existed before me, but nor is this conviction *opinio*. Rather, I believe firmly and undoubtingly that this is so on the basis of acquired faith in the assertions of people whose veracity I firmly accept. Just as I do not hesitate concerning the veracity of the people who say this, which is like a principle, so I do not hesitate concerning the truth of what they assert, which is like a conclusion. There can be no doubt about the truthfulness of God, whose absolute veracity can be naturally known. Nor can there be any doubt about the approbation given to the Scriptures by the Church. Therefore, there is no doubt about the truth of the revelation given in the Scriptures, which is firmly assented to on the basis of acquired faith.[101] Those who possess this acquired faith are not able to doubt or disbelieve.[102] We can and ought to believe more greatly those witnesses who are more truthful, and to believe more in a larger number of witnesses. The Catholic Church is the most truthful community in existence, because she condemns falsehood and praises truthfulness the most; therefore we can believe her testimony with the greatest certainty. She is especially to be believed where she most strongly condemns falsehood, which is in that which concerns faith and morals. Therefore the wayfarer can most firmly believe on the basis of his natural reason the teachings of the Church concerning faith and morals.[103]

Scotus rejects Aquinas's contention that First Truth is the formal object of infused faith. If we assent to 'God is three and one' because it is divinely revealed, we must assent all the more to 'This is revealed by God', just as when we assent to a conclusion on the grounds of a principle, we must assent all the more to the principle. If it is answered that we assent in turn to 'It is revealed by God that God is three and one' because God reveals it, we are left with an infinite regress, and left without any firm reason for believing. Moreover, the formal object of a *habitus* must be a real being, not a merely intellectual being (*ens rationis*). 'It is revealed by God that God is three and one' is a proposition, an intellectual being, not a real being; so it cannot be the formal object of the *habitus* of faith. (An illustration of

---

[101] Scotus, 1639a, p. 460.

[102] Scotus, 1639a, p. 469.

[103] *Quodl.* q.14, in Duns Scotus, *Quaestiones quodlibetales*, in *Opera*, vol. 12, 1639c, p. 356.

Scotus's point about the formal object of a *habitus* is the formal object of sight; this would be light, or colour, not propositions like 'this thing is coloured' – it is not propositions that we see.) An obvious Thomist reply to this objection would be that the formal object of faith is God's action of speaking, which is a reality, not propositions of the form 'God reveals that X'. But this reply is not available if we accept Scotus's view that our belief that God reveals things is based on the Church's telling us that he reveals them.

Why then suppose that there is such a thing as infused faith? Scotus's answer to this question is that we must believe it purely as a matter of faith, because the Scriptures and the doctors of the Church tell us that it exists.[104] The reason for its existence is that since the image of God is present in both the will and the intellect, both the will and the intellect must be perfected by Christ in his healing of the soul. The will is perfected by charity, and the intellect is perfected by infused faith. These virtues are the result of grace, and have God alone as their efficient cause. There is a parallel between Scotus's view of faith and his view of charity. Unlike Aquinas, he thinks it naturally possible for men to love God in himself above all created things. The virtue of charity does not enable men to do this in itself, it only enables them to do it in a more perfect way; just as the virtue of infused faith does not enable men to believe what God reveals, it only enables them to believe in a more perfect way. Acquired faith and infused faith have the same object, divine revelation. Our belief in revelation, if we are in a state of grace, is based on both of these faiths.[105]

Presupposed to Scotus's account of faith is a conception of grace that is different from that of Aquinas's. Since he thought that the action of an infused virtue was the same as that of an acquired one, he could not hold, as Aquinas did, that grace confers properties on man that surpass created nature. In Scotus's view, the grace that operates in infused faith is grace *quoad modum*. With grace of this sort, it is the means by which something is brought about, not the end result of the action of grace, that is supernatural. An example would be the conferring of the gift of tongues on the Apostles at Pentecost. The result of this gift (speaking in Arabic, and so on) would be something that is attainable through natural human powers, but the way in which it was conferred – by a miraculous divine intervention – was not.

This bare appeal to faith as a reason for believing in infused faith might seem rather unsatisfactory. However, an examination of the long history of Roman Catholic theologians who follow Scotus on the question of the role of the motives of credibility in faith tends to bring out the merits of this bare appeal. This history is a repeated series of unsuccessful attempts to explain why (given the supposed necessity of the motives of credibility as a rational justification for belief) there must also be such a thing as infused faith.[106] It is a testimony to Scotus's insight

---

[104] *Opus Oxoniense, In III Sent.* d. 23 q. 1 schol., Scotus, 1639a, p. 468.

[105] *Opus Oxoniense, Quod.* q. 14, Scotus, 1639c, p. 353.

[106] Most Roman Catholic theologians from the time of Scotus onwards (virtually all of them outside the Dominican Order) accepted some form of this second position on the role of the motives of credibility. Different variants of it were given by Cajetan, Suarez, De Lugo,

that he saw the uselessness of attempting such explanations, and refrained from giving them.

An assessment of the strength of Scotus's position will partially depend on how far one feels bound to agree with the authorities he quotes in support of his postulation of infused faith. If one does not accept his theological reasons for believing in infused faith, however, his arguments in support of acquired faith will lead us towards believing in acquired faith as the sole foundation for Christian belief, and it may be that, historically, this was their main effect.

Later adherents of the Scotist position added some precisions to his account of the relations between acquired and infused faith that are worth noting.[107] Theologians from the fourteenth to the seventeenth century distinguished between the act of believing itself, whose content was 'Christianity is divinely revealed and hence true'; the judgement of credibility, whose content was 'It would be reasonable and morally permissible for me to choose to believe that Christianity is divinely revealed'; and the judgement of credentity, whose content was 'It is morally obligatory for me to choose to believe that Christianity is divinely revealed.' The judgement of credibility was necessary in order for an act of divine faith to be a rational and morally good act, and the judgement of credentity was necessary in order for unbelief to be morally wrong. All agreed that the role of the motives of credibility was to establish the truth of the judgement of credibility, and that this judgement could only be based on these motives. Most of them held that these motives were not sufficient to establish beyond a reasonable doubt for the average believer the fact that Christianity is divinely revealed, but that was not the role that the baroque scholastics generally assigned to them. The motives of credibility were only required to establish that it was legitimate to choose to believe; the act of belief itself was not based on them, but simply on the authority of God revealing. When it came to the judgement of credentity they were divided. Since this judgement presupposes the judgement of credibility, the motives of credibility are necessary for it, but many theologians held that they were not sufficient, because they thought this judgement required grace. All agreed that the act of believing with divine faith required grace.

From the middle of the seventeenth century until the mid-twentieth century, however, a much stronger version of the Scotist position came to predominate in

---

Billot, and Rousselot. For a history of these theories, see A. Gardeil, 'Crédibilité', *Dictionnaire de théologie catholique*, and Roger Aubert, *Le problème de l'acte de foi*, 2nd edn, 1950.

[107] This history is taken from Guy de Broglie, 'La vraie notion thomiste des "praeambula fidei"', *Gregorianum*, 1953; for more detail, see Gardeil's article 'Crédibilité', and Harent's article 'Foi', in the *Dictionnaire de théologie catholique*, as well as Aubert, 1950. The first position described is a very summary account of the highly sophisticated kind of view on faith held by the baroque scholastics, such as Bañez, John of St. Thomas, De Lugo, Suarez, Molina, and the Carmelites of Salamanca. These views, and the disputes about them, are a neglected subject of great interest. My excuse for not including them in this historical account, despite the loss that results from largely ignoring baroque scholasticism, is that they would require a volume for themselves, and that the thinkers I do discuss introduce all the really fundamental considerations that are necessary for a discussion of faith.

Catholic theology.[108] This saw the motives of credibility as establishing beyond a reasonable doubt the two premises that God had revealed the Christian religion (in its Catholic form), and that God necessarily told the truth. The judgement of credibility was then the judgement that it was morally legitimate to choose to believe on the basis of these premises the conclusion that Christian teachings were true, and the judgement of credentity was the judgement that it was morally obligatory to make this choice; the act of faith was the making of the inference itself, an act that was supposed to require divine grace for its performance. This position involved the doubtful view that the making of this straightforward deductive inference could be voluntary, and the absurd view that the making of this inference could require divine grace. It is amazing that such a defective position could have been so widely held for so long. What made possible its success, aside from the general intellectual weakness of the Catholic Church at the time, was that the main interest of Catholic theologians was defending their position against Protestants and unbelievers. Emphasizing the strength of the motives of credibility that could be alleged in favour of Catholic claims was useful for this purpose; the incoherence of their position did not bother the Catholics themselves, and was not going to be used against them by Protestants or unbelievers, who after the seventeenth century usually accepted that the motives of credibility were the only foundations for Christian belief, and were therefore not going to criticize this view for giving a derisory role to grace.

Common to all the later versions of the Scotist position is the assertion that the motives of credibility are necessary for faith because they are necessary for the judgement of credibility. This is the ground upon which the Thomist position is rejected. We can therefore ask: why are they necessary for this judgement? It is quite legitimate to claim that the judgement itself is necessary if faith is to be a virtuous act; the question is why it must be rationally based on the motives of credibility. Stanislas Harent, in the course of arguing against the Thomist position (which he wrongly terms 'fideism'[109]), gives three reasons for holding this. The first, which is an elaboration of one of Scotus's arguments, is that without the motives of credibility faith would either fall into an infinite regress, holding that we believe because God had revealed, we believe God has revealed because he has revealed it, and so on, or else into a vicious circle, where we have faith because of God's revealing, and we hold that God has revealed because faith tells us so. The second is that faith is essentially a mediate sort of knowledge, which must therefore be based on some immediate knowledge, which is constituted by the

---

[108] On this see de Broglie (1953).

[109] See Harent, article 'Foi', *Dictionnaire de théologie catholique*. 'Fideism' is a term that has been given a wide range of meanings. In applying the term to the Thomist position (which of course he did not call by that name) Harent meant to accuse it of being heretical; but those versions of fideism which the Roman Catholic Church has condemned are the position that natural reason cannot arrive at moral and religious truths (such as the existence of God), so that any knowledge of these truths must be based on faith, and the position that the motives of credibility do not give good evidence for the assertion that Christianity is divinely revealed. Neither of these positions are part of Thomist views of faith.

motives of credibility. The third is that the same rules apply to divine faith as to human faith. We trust human witnesses because we have evidence of their knowledge and veracity. And when we believe someone speaking through an intermediary, such as a written document, we not only verify the speaker's knowledge and trustworthiness, but we check to see if the intermediary is genuine; we actually owe it to the speaker to do this.

The foundation of all of these arguments is the notion that belief in testimony is a mediate form of knowledge, that must be based on evidence for the knowledge and veracity of the speaker if it is to be rational. This notion, as we have seen, was rejected by Owen in his elaboration of the Thomist position. In order to decide between the Scotist and the Thomist positions it is necessary to determine whether it is correct or not, a task that will be undertaken in Chapter 6.

The different elaborations of the Scotist view that have been offered raise the question of where to draw the line between Thomist and Scotist views. A Thomist will not require a believer to know the motives of credibility that indicate that Christianity has been divinely revealed, since these motives do not on his view enter in to the act of faith. But could he hold that the act of faith requires reasonable belief that there are no good objections to believing? The purest form of Thomism would be that the only rational consideration producing belief is the voice of God. For such a view, the only rational requirement for belief aside from hearing God's voice would be that one does not have what would strike one as good reasons for thinking that Christianity is not divinely revealed; and the role of the motives of credibility, if they have one, would be to dispel such putatively good reasons and thus make faith possible. A further question for this view would be how good these putative reasons would have to seem to prevent the assent of faith. If they seemed to show beyond a reasonable doubt that Christianity is not divinely revealed, it seems right that God would not bring about the assent of faith unless through some extraordinary grace, since that would mean overriding one's natural reason and violating the Thomist principle that grace builds upon nature. So in such a case the motives of credibility would ordinarily be necessary to serve as a preparation for faith. Whether they would also be ordinarily necessary when the reasons against Christianity being divinely revealed seemed strong but not conclusive is harder to say.

Christian faith is entirely grounded on the motives of credibility

The view that Christian belief is based entirely on an inference from the motives of credibility did not appear for almost fifteen hundred years after the time of Christ, but once upon the scene it rapidly became influential and even predominant. It is desirable to give a sketch of the historical circumstances in which this radical departure from previous Christian thought came about.

The context in which it developed was what has been called the sceptical crisis of the sixteenth and seventeenth centuries, a crisis provoked by two developments;

the recovery of ancient Greek scepticism, and the intellectual conflict between Catholics and Protestants.[110]

The thought of the sceptical schools of Hellenistic philosophy was little known in the Middle Ages. The only complete sceptical works that have survived, Sextus Empiricus's *On the Pyrrhonic Hypotyposes* and *Against the Mathematicians*, did not come to light until the sixteenth century. Once they became known, however, the battery of sceptical arguments they contained, which defended the Pyrrhonist position that we should neither believe nor disbelieve but suspend judgement, had a powerful effect. They were found appealing by Christian thinkers, who used them to argue that since reason was useless, we have to rely on revelation instead. (A similar position was advanced by Erasmus in *The Praise of Folly*, which mocked philosophy and appealed to a faith that was not based on reason, but Erasmus did not make use of philosophical tools to attack reason.) Pico della Mirandola took this line in opposing the Renaissance revival of pagan humanism, in his *Examen vanitatis doctrinae gentium* (1520). The most important figure of this Christian Pyrrhonism was Michel de Montaigne. Montaigne read Sextus Empiricus in 1575 and was convinced by him, abandoning his prevous Stoicism and striking a medal to celebrate the event. He made the case for scepticism in his *Apologie de Raimond Sebond* in 1580, where he used Sextus Empiricus's arguments to undermine the claims of reason. He advocated the acceptance of faith that is based on grace rather than reason, and the following of nature rather than rational deliberation when faith had nothing to say. His views had a surprising success in France. His disciple Fr. Pierre Charron systematized his ideas in his *De la sagesse* (1604) and *Le petit traicté de la sagesse* (1635). Saint-Cyran, one of the founders of Jansenism, enthusiastically supported Charron's ideas, and persuaded the Sorbonne to condemn the Jesuit François Garasse for criticizing Charron's positions. Cardinal Bérulle, the founder of the French school of spirituality that had a decisive effect on Counter-Reformation Catholicism, accepted Charron's views, as did the learned convert from Protestantism Cardinal du Perron. (Du Perron, when dining with Henry III, offered to give convincing proofs of the existence of God; after delighting the King by expounding them, he then offered to give equally convincing proofs that God did not exist. The enraged king threw him out.) There seem to be two main reasons for the success of this Christian Pyrrhonism in France. One was that it was thought to be useful as a tool for attacking Calvinism, and the other was the Augustinianism of French theology at the time, which led to a low opinion of the capacities of fallen human nature.

Its use as a method of attack arose in the debate between Catholics and Protestants over the rule of faith. This debate, which became the central issue in Reformation polemics, addressed the question of the nature of the rule that should determine what Christians believe to be part of the Christian revelation. The Protestants held that Scripture alone should be the rule, with no interpreter having

---

[110] This crisis, and its influence on religious thought, are discussed in the standard work of Richard Popkin, *The History of Scepticism from Erasmus to Spinoza*, 1979, in Henry van Leeuwen, *The Problem of Certainty in English Thought, 1630-1690*, 1963, and Louis Bredvold, *The Intellectual Milieu of John Dryden*, 1959.

the authority to decide what its meaning was. The Catholics held that the teachings of the Church were the rule of faith. (This did not amount to denying that the Scriptures were a rule of faith, only to denying that they were the only one. Catholic views on how this rule related to Scripture, and to divine revelation, were complicated and various. Some of the Catholic positions on these questions are described in chapter 7 below. These variations are not relevant to the controversy over the rule of faith, since the Catholic position here was simply that Christians do have to accept that the Christian faith is what the Catholic Church says it is; the different explanations of why this is the case do not affect this basic position.) Protestants attacked the Catholic position by claiming that the evidence of tradition that was supposed to prove the Catholic view was absent or unreliable, and that the Catholic Church had contradicted itself in the past. Catholics attacked the Protestant position by claiming that Scripture on its own was insufficient to determine the contents of Christian faith. This line of attack was perfected by François Veron, a priest who devoted his life with considerable success to converting Protestants. He described his approach in militant terms as a '*machine de guerre de nouvelle intention*', able to overcome any Protestant resistance. It involved, firstly, arguing that the contents of Protestant belief could not be reconciled with the view that Scripture alone is the norm of belief. He pointed out that the doctrines that Protestants profess in their confessions are not actually stated in Scripture. Even if it were the case that they were logically deducible from Scripture – which he denied – this would not mean that they were compatible with the principle of 'sola Scriptura', because the Scriptures do not contain any logical rules of deduction, or state that it is necessary or legitimate to believe their logical consequences as well as what they actually assert. Secondly, it involved arguing that the Scriptures alone cannot suffice as a rule for any faith, because of doubts that can be raised over their text, authorship, translation and meaning.[111] These doubts mean that the Scriptural message must remain uncertain unless interpreted by an authoritative Church. Veron did not extend his sceptical arguments to human reason generally, as the Christian Pyrrhonists did; he confined his sceptical attack to the Protestant position on the rule of faith.

It is worth noting that some form of the Thomist view of faith must lie behind both Christian Pyrrhonism and Veron's *machine de guerre*, since these hold that faith is independent of reason. This fact had an effect on Protestant thought,

---

[111] This line of argument, common to most Catholic polemicists at the time, had important consequences. The Oratorian Richard Simon laid the foundations of modern biblical criticism in the late seventeenth century, in the course of offering sceptical arguments about the Scriptures in order to prove the uselessness of Scripture alone as a rule of faith, and the consequent necessity for a living teaching authority. It is interesting to note the contrast between this seventeenth-century Catholic approach and the rejection of sceptical positions on the Scriptures by the Pontifical Biblical Commission in the early part of the twentieth century. This contrast probably resulted from the change in Catholic thought from a reliance on the supernatural authority of the Church to justify Catholic positions to a reliance on arguments from historical evidence. This change is discussed in Chapter 7 below. It is significant that Bossuet, who exemplified this change (as is mentioned in Appendix II), was the main critic of Simon's views on the Bible.

particularly because Protestants came to identify Christian Pyrrhonism with Catholicism.[112]

The need to respond to these Catholic lines of argument was one of the principal factors that led to the emergence of the view that the motives of credibility were the rational grounds for Christian faith. The other was a division that emerged between Protestants. Calvin held that it is through an internal inspiration of the Holy Spirit that we come to grasp both that the Scriptures are the Word of God, and what the meaning of the Scriptures is. This became an important issue when Michael Servetus denied the doctrine of the Trinity. Servetus thought that the Holy Spirit was not telling him that the doctrine of the Trinity was the truth, but Calvin was getting a different message from the Holy Spirit, so he had Servetus burned at the stake. The French Protestant theologian Sebastien Castellio was horrified by this treatment of Servetus. In order to furnish an argument for religious toleration, he offered what seems to be the first explicit presentation of Christian faith as being based on the motives of credibility. In his *De haereticis, an sint persequendi*, he protested against Servetus's execution, on the grounds that the meaning of Scripture is often genuinely obscure, and that the answers to debated questions are not so obvious that everyone should be compelled to accept them, a fact that is evident from the existence of religious differences; why should anyone be willing to die for the denial of the obvious? In consequence, no-one can be sure enough of the truth in religous matters to be justified in killing heretics. When the Calvinist theologian Theodore Beza attacked this work, Castellio wrote but did not publish *De arte dubitandi* (1563), which extended his argument for the uncertainty of religious doctrines to human knowledge generally. In it, he argued from the fallibility of human rational faculties to the desirability of caution in making judgements.

Intellectually, Castellio's objection was not a telling criticism of the Calvinist view, since it was open to the simple reply that the meaning of the Scriptures is perfectly obvious to those who have faith, and is only denied by sinners. Practically, however, the implementation of this Calvinist response posed difficulties. The shift from the idea of an inspired Church to that of an inspired individual conscience made possible an exercise of power that was much more abrupt and peremptory than was the case in Catholic countries, if, as with Calvin, the possessor of the individual conscience in question also held supreme political authority. Acceptance of the authority of an inspired Church can still leave room for argument over what that Church is saying, and although these arguments can be ended by appeal to the decisions of Popes or Councils, such decisions take time to be made if they are made at all (consider the lapse of time between Duns Scotus's arguing for the doctrine of the Immaculate Conception and Pius IX's defining it in 1854). But the authority of an inspired individual like Calvin, who is immediately

---

[112] This identification was not entirely correct. We find this view in Sir Thomas Browne, for instance, who said 'since I was of understanding to know we know nothing, my reason hath been more pliable to the will of faith; I am now content to understand a mystery without a rigid definition.' Sir Thomas Browne, *Religio Medici*, in *Sir Thomas Browne: The Major Works*, 1977, p. 70.

available to settle all questions, does not permit such leeway; and there will be individuals who disagree, while both claiming inspiration, but there is only one Church. So the Calvinist view, although logically consistent, was bound to cause practical difficulties.[113]

These difficulties contributed to a further evolution of division among Protestants, which occurred in Holland. When the Protestant theologian Jacobus Arminius rejected Calvin's views on predestination, a synod was held at Dort that reaffirmed the Calvinist doctrines and condemned Arminian views. The supporters of Arminianism were persecuted; one of them, van Oldenbarnevelt, was beheaded, and another, Hugo Grotius, was sentenced to life imprisonment (he escaped by being smuggled out of prison in a chestful of books). However, the Calvinists failed to extinguish the Arminians, whose ideas represented an important development in thought on Christian faith. They responded to the difficulties involved in individual inspiration by denying not only that the state had the right to punish heresy, but also that a church could impose any beliefs as conditions of membership. Their professions of faith were meant only as expositions of what the persons who subscribed to them believed, not as descriptions of what Christians ought to accept. Their most important thinker was Grotius. Although now remembered chiefly as an international jurist, Grotius was in fact bored by the law; his chief interest was in religious questions. He wrote in Dutch verses a treatise on the truth of the Christian religion which he intended for the use of seafarers, who in his view tended to waste their time at sea, and who would by reading it employ themselves profitably and be rendered capable of giving arguments for the conversion of the unbelievers they would meet in their travels. When translated

---

[113] The Calvinist view also made it difficult to distinguish between articles of faith and theological opinions, and to distinguish between error and heresy. Every theologian will be inclined to argue for his views by claiming that they are expressed in the Scriptures. But if, in cases where this claim is made, the inspiration of the Holy Spirit is held to invariably produce, not only the text of the Scriptures, but also a believer's understanding of the meaning of the text, it is difficult to give any rationale for distinguishing between denying an article of faith and rejecting someone's theological opinion. This is because on this view, if it is assumed that I have faith, my thinking that the Scriptures make a certain claim will entail not only that I think that this claim is divinely revealed, but that it *is* divinely revealed. And if some other Christian disagrees with me on this claim, that person cannot be understood by me as having the virtue of faith while being in error about what God has said on this particular issue, because faith, involving as it does the production by the Holy Spirit of correct belief about the meaning of the Scriptures, leaves no room for error. Such a person must necessarily be a heretic, rather than the victim of an innocent mistake. Again, this is a view that is logically defensible, but that is liable to cause difficulties in practice. It will mean that people who subscribe to a church confession will have to agree on every theological question that they think to be important. Given the diversity of human opinion, this is likely to lead to one or the other of two dangers. Either a church's confession of faith will be quite detailed, in which case people with divergent opinions will be disaffected and leave, or – in order to secure agreement – it will be rather general, which will make people who hold views that are not included in it think that it permits denial of divinely revealed truths. These practical difficulties, which have manifested themselves at various times in history, provide an incentive to suppress the role of the Holy Spirit in bringing about faith.

into Latin, this work had an enormous success throughout Europe. Based to a great extent on the work of the Protestant Philippe du Mornay, it had two crucial starting points. One of these was the character of the certainty it assigned to Christian faith. Referring to Aristotle's view that different kinds of subject matters require different kinds of proof, Grotius claimed that belief in the Christian revelation required no more than the moral certainty that is available from evidence that makes a conclusion probable beyond a reasonable doubt. The other starting point was Grotius's clear assertion that Christian faith is based on an inference from the motives of credibility. The substance of the work proceeds to set out the evidence for the existence of Christian revelation, and to argue that it makes this revelation overwhelmingly probable.

William Chillingworth The influence of Grotius and Arminianism made itself felt upon William Chillingworth, a seminal figure in the development of the view that faith is based on the motives of credibility (and indeed in philosophy generally).[114] While at Oxford, Chillingworth converted to Catholicism as a result of his contacts with the Jesuit John Fisher (whose real name was John Percy), who convinced him of the necessity of an infallible guide in matters of Christian faith. He went to France and entered the seminary at Douai, but was not happy there[115] and entertained some doubts about the reasons that had led him to Catholicism. Returning to England in a state of uncertainty about all religious belief, he went to Great Tew in Oxfordshire, where he became a member of the intellectual circle that surrounded Lord Falkland. His doubts were resolved by reading Grotius's work on the truth of the Christian religion, and he returned to the Anglican church. (Grotius seems to have been the chief influence on his religious thought, but he had also read Castellio.) He wrote his main work, *The Religion of Protestants a Safe Way to Salvation*, as a reply to the Catholic controversialist Matthias Wilson (who wrote under the alias of Edward Knott). In it he laid out the essential features of a response to both the Catholic polemic of the counter-Reformation and the pyrrhonist crisis of the sixteenth and seventeenth centuries.

The epistemological foundation of this response, which served as a defence against both Catholicism and pyrrhonism, was a defence of the possibility of moral certainty. Such certainty was said to result from the possession of overwhelming evidence in favour of a proposition, that nonetheless did not entail the impossibility of the proposition's being false. In such a case, although the bare possibility of the proposition's being false would remain, this possibility would not make it rational

---

[114] In addition to his ideas on epistemology, he put forward the claim that it is illegitimate to infer 'is' statements from 'ought' statements.

[115] John Aubrey remarks: 'About anno 1630 he was acquainted with one who drew him and some other scholars over to Doway, where he was not so well entertained as he thought he merited for his great Disputative Wit. They made him the porter (which was to trye his temper, and exercise his obedience) so he stole over and came to Trinity College again, where he was fellowe ... I have heard Mr. Thomas Hobbes, Malmsb. (who knew him) say, that he was like a lusty fighting fellow that did drive his enimies before him, but woulde often give his own party smart back-blowes.' John Aubrey, *Brief Lives*, 1958, pp. 63–4.

to have any doubt of the proposition's truth, or any fear of its falsehood. This moral certainty was held to be proof against the sceptical arguments of the pyrrhonists. It was also held to give an answer to the Catholic argument, which Chillingworth had at one time found convincing, that an infallible authority was necessary to serve as a foundation for Christian faith. It could be conceded, in Chillingworth's view, that fear of a proposition's falsehood or doubt of its truth was incompatible with faith. But if we accept that moral certainty can eliminate fear or doubt, we do not need to hold, with some Catholic controversialists, that there is need of infallible evidence for believing, or to draw, as Aquinas did, a distinction between the certainty of evidence for a proposition and the certainty of adherence to it. This conception of moral certainty was not original; as we have seen, it was proposed by Duns Scotus. But Chillingworth's presenting it as the principal foundation for our beliefs about the world, as part of a rebuttal of the Pyrrhonist position, was an important departure from the Aristotelian views hitherto prevalent (found for example in the thought of Sir Francis Bacon), which held that we could achieve knowledge rather than moral certainty about things in the world through understanding their natures. His assertion that we can have no more than moral certainty for our beliefs about the world in general serves to buttress his claim that moral certainty is sufficient for religious belief, since it makes the demand for an assurance greater than moral certainty for religious belief seem an exorbitant one.

Chillingworth holds that the motives of credibility can provide us with moral certainty about both the fact and the content of Christian revelation. This moral certainty is sufficient to enable belief about revelation to achieve its purpose, which is to motivate us to act in accordance with these beliefs; people reasonably risk their lives on the basis of less moral certainty than is available for revelation, as when they trust their doctor's advice on the treatment of a life-threatening illness. An infallible ground for belief is thus unnecessary, and unattainable, because the motives of credibility, which are what provide our reason for believing, are only able to provide moral certainty, since they involve trusting human testimony. (Even the certainty available from logical and mathematical reasoning, which the motives of credibility do not attain to, is not strictly speaking infallible in Chillingworth's view, because our reasoning capacities can err.) Chillingworth rejects the possibility of a reasonable distinction between certainty of evidence for a belief and certainty of adherence to it; he thinks that the strength of adherence to a belief should be proportioned to the evidence available for it.

The principal evidence for Christianity's being divinely revealed are the miracles that attended its promulgation, which we know about through reliable human testimony. We know that this revelation is found in the books of Scripture, because of universal human tradition to the effect that these books were written by the prophets, apostles and evangelists, who witnessed or received the promulgation of this revelation. We cannot know that any of this revelation is to be found in unwritten traditions that are not contained in Scripture, because there is no good evidence for the existence of such traditions. Chillingworth replies to Catholic criticisms of the Scriptures as a rule of faith by stating that our certainty about the fact of revelation does not extend to knowledge of the meaning of everything expressed in Scripture, only to knowledge of the fundamental teachings of Christianity, which are what we need to know in order for revelation to do its work of saving us.[116] He weakens this answer somewhat by refusing to specify what exactly these teachings are,[117] and also by holding that all that is required for salvation is to do one's best to find out what God has revealed in the Scriptures, rather than to actually accept any particular teachings contained therein. This last position comes closer to abandoning the idea of the need for a rule of faith than to defending the Scriptures as such a rule. He explicity rejects the possibility of anyone's being morally obliged to hold a particular understanding of Christian revelation. Speaking of his own changes of religious allegiance, he says '…this man thinks himself no more to blame for all these changes, than a Traveller, who using all his diligence to find the right way to some remote city, where he had never been (as the party I speak of had never been in Heaven), did yet mistake it, and after find his error, and then amend it.'[118]

Chillingworth suffered for his beliefs; after being wounded and taken prisoner by the Roundheads in the Civil War, he was mercilessly harassed on his deathbed by a Presbyterian minister named Francis Cheynell, who urged him to renounce his reliance on human reason, and threw a copy of *The Religion of Protestants* into his grave at his funeral with the wish that it would rot along with its author. However, his views achieved posthumous success in the Anglican Church. They were the basis for the thought of the Latitudinarians, a group of theologians who achieved influence in the Church of England after the Restoration in 1660 and dominated it after the fall of James II in 1688. The main Latitudinarian thinkers included John Tillotson, John Wilkins, Edward Stillingfleet, Joseph Glanvill and Edward Fowler. Their basic positions were those of Chillingworth, and it was through them that his ideas achieved their widest influence. They accepted his conceptions of the role of moral certainty in the attainment of knowledge, and applied it to science, holding the goal of science to be the attainment of probable theories that cover the evidence rather than an unattainable knowledge of the real nature of things. These conceptions became the guiding principles of the Royal Society, of which Wilkins was a founder and Glanvill was an early member. Chillingworth's views on this

---

[116] It is worth pointing out the difference between the idea of fundamentals of Christianity that was held by Chillingworth and by Protestants generally, and that held by their Catholic opponents, some of whom were willing to say that all the fundamentals of Christianity were to be found in Scripture. Chillingworth meant by the fundamentals of Christianity all the doctrines that were necessary to be believed as matters of faith. The Catholics meant by fundamentals the starting points or basic truths of the faith, which determine but do not exhaust what is necessary to be believed. This difference of understanding can still cause confusion in ecumenical discussions.

[117] This may have been partly due to his holding a minimizing view of these fundamentals; he did not for example think that Arianism could be considered as incompatible with Christian belief, and he only subscribed to the 39 Articles on the understanding that subscription meant allowing these articles to be legitimate understandings of the Christian message ('articles of peace'), rather than being an actual profession of belief in them.

[118] Chillingworth, quoted in Pierre Des Maizeaux, *An Historical and Critical Account of the Life and Writings of William Chillingworth*, 1725, p. 26.

topic were also espoused by Robert Boyle. The Latitudinarians were responsible for the introduction of the standard of proof beyond a reasonable doubt into the common law.[119] They were more theologically orthodox than Chillingworth himself was; they generally accepted the doctrine of the Trinity, the Nicene teaching on the incarnation and divinity of Christ, and the resurrection of the body. Their chief opponents in theological matters were the Catholics rather than the Nonconformists. Their theological positions were thus influenced by debates with English Catholic writers, many of whom were converts from Anglicanism.[120]

John Tillotson John Tillotson was the most important theorist of faith among the Latitudinarian theologians. Originally a Calvinist and Nonconformist, he became disgusted with Calvinism partly through his experience with the Presbyterian ministers active around the time of Cromwell's death. The crucial event in his intellectual history was his reading of Chillingworth's *The Religion of Protestants*, which set the pattern for his own thought. After the Restoration in 1660 he became one of the most popular preachers in London. As with the other Latitudinarians, he took the Roman Catholics to be his principal intellectual opponents, and devoted his polemical efforts to refuting their positions. Holding these views, he not surprisingly supported William of Orange against James II, and was made Archbishop of Canterbury after James's fall from power. His thought had a great influence on English Christianity. His sermons were presented as models to Anglican clergymen during the eighteenth century, and were often simply repeated verbatim by lazy parsons. He was the principal influence on John Locke's religious thought. After Tillotson's death, Locke lamented in a letter to the Dutch Arminian theologian Philippus van Limborch that he had lost his main adviser in religious questions.[121] The apologetic works of Bishop Butler and William Paley assume the position of Tillotson and the other Latitudinarians as a starting point; Paley's work was required reading for Cambridge undergraduates throughout the nineteenth century, and indeed into the twentieth, when Malcolm Muggeridge was made to

---

[119] See Theodore Waldman, 'Origin of the Legal Doctrine of Reasonable Doubt', *Journal of the History of Ideas*, 1959.

[120] For an account of these thinkers see George Tavard, *The Seventeenth-Century Tradition: A Study in Recusant Thought*, 1978. Among the more important were Thomas White, Richard Smith, Hugh Cressy, Christopher Davenport, William Rushworth, Henry Holden, and John Sergeant. Cressy (who took the name of Serenus in religion) was a member of the Great Tew circle and knew Chillingworth before his conversion.

[121] Locke to Philippus van Limborch, Dec. 1694: "As soon as I find leisure I shall examine your *Theologia Christiana* diligently, for I think that I ought now to give my mind for the most part to such studies, and I wish so much the more that I were with you because now that that great and candid searcher after truth [Tillotson], to say nothing of his other virtues, has been taken from us, I have scarcely anyone whom I can freely consult about theological uncertainties. Others will make known sufficiently how great a man the English public weal has lost, how great a pillar the Reformed Church. I have assuredly lost, to my very great hurt and grief, a friend of many years, steadfast, candid and sincere." Letter 1826, in John Locke, *The Correspondence of John Locke, Vol. V*, 1979, pp. 237–8 (editor's translation from the Latin original).

read it (and characteristically found it a disincentive to belief). Through Locke, Butler and Paley, Tillotson originated a series of intellectual progeny that continues to this day.

The main sources for Tillotson's position on faith are his *Rule of Faith*, which was written as a reply to the Catholic controversialist John Sergeant, and a series of sermons on the text of Hebrews 11:6, 'but without faith it is impossible to please God.' Tillotson gives a clear definition of faith as simply being belief in some proposition: 'Faith is a persuasion of the mind concerning any thing; concerning the truth of any proposition, concerning the existence, or futurition, or lawfulness, or convenience, or goodness, of any thing, or the contrary: or concerning the credit of a person, or the contrary.'[122] He claims that this is the common and usual understanding of the term 'faith', although 'from hence by a metonymy it comes to be put for the argument whereby this persuasion is wrought in us', or for 'the object of this persuasion'.[123] He is aware of the scholastic definition of faith as belief in someone's testimony, but rejects it as a definition applying to faith in general or religious faith in particular. Religious faith he conceives of as including three things: a persuasion of the principles of natural religion, which are known by the light of nature; a persuasion of truths that are revealed; and a persuasion of the existence of supernatural revelation. This is the faith he conceives to be described by the Scriptures as necessary to salvation. It cannot correspond to the scholastic definition, because it includes a persuasion of divine revelation, and 'a persuasion of divine revelation cannot be called Faith; because it is irrational to expect that a man should have another divine revelation to assure him, that this is a divine revelation: for then for the same reason, I must expect another divine revelation to assure me of that, and so on without end.'[124] Within religious faith he distinguishes divine faith, which is 'an assent to a thing upon the testimony and authority of God',[125] and Christian faith, which is the doctrine of the gospel revealed to the world by Jesus Christ. The peculiar content of Christian faith, which is not found in natural religion or other divine revelation, is the message that Christ is the Messiah and the divine Son of God.

This conception of religious faith explains why without faith it is impossible to please God. Tillotson expounds this text as meaning that 'unless we believe that he is, and that he will reward those that seek to please him, it is impossible, that is, it is unreasonable, to think men should attempt to please him.'[126] This account of the necessity of faith is what leads Tillotson to include the principles of natural religion in religious faith, on the assumption that a knowledge of God's existence and his readiness to reward those who seek him must be based on natural religion.

---

[122] John Tillotson, *Works*, 3rd edn, 1722, vol. 2, p. 428. I have modernized Tillotson's spelling.
[123] Tillotson, 1722, vol. 2, p. 428.
[124] Tillotson, 1722, vol. 2, p. 441.
[125] John Tillotson, *The Works of the Most Reverend Doctor John Tillotson ... being all that were published by his Grace himself*, 5th edn, 1707, p. 654.
[126] Tillotson, 1722, vol. 2, p. 426.

Assent to divine revelation may properly be called divine faith upon three grounds; 'not only in respect of the matter and object of it, which are divine things, such as concern God and revelation: and in respect of the divine effects it hath upon those who believe these things: (for in these two respects a persuasion of the principles of natural religion may be said to be a divine faith) but likewise in respect of the argument whereby it is wrought, which is a divine testimony.'[127] He vacillates about whether it should called divine because of the work of the Holy Spirit, its efficient cause; in some places he admits this, but in others he denies it, because 'the Spirit of God doth not, speaking properly, persuade us immediately of the truth of the things supernaturally revealed; but mediately, by persuading us of the truth of revelation: for to believe a thing to be true, which we are persuaded is revealed by God, is so natural and consequent upon such a persuasion, that it doth not seem to require any new work of the Spirit.'

The purpose of divine faith is to provide the basis for action. The proper and genuine effect of divine faith is the conformity of our hearts and our lives to what we believe. Tillotson goes so far as to say that if we truly believe, this conformity will inevitably follow.

... A true divine faith supposeth a man satisfied and persuaded of the reasonableness and necessity of being religious: that it is reasonable for every man to be so, and that it is necessary to his interest. Now there needs no more to be done to put a man upon anything, but to satisfy him of these two things ... This shews why there is so little true religion in the world: t'is for want of faith, without which it is impossible for men to be religious ... For did men believe these things, they would be religious: they would not dare to live in any known sin or impiety of life: unless we can presume that a man can be seriously unwilling to be happy, and to have a longing desire to be miserable and undone forever. For whoever believes the principles of religion, and the precepts, and promises, and threatenings, that are contained in this holy Book, and yet after all can continue in sin, he must not only put off the principles of a reasonable creature, but must quit the very inclinations of his nature: that is, he must knowingly resist that which he naturally desires, which is happiness: and must embrace that, which of all things that can be imagined he must abhor, and that is misery.[128]

It should be recognized that although Tillotson's view that sincere believers cannot sin is outlandish, his reasoning is quite cogent, so cogent that it might be conclusive were it not for the personal experience that shows it to be false.

When it comes to the reasons for which we assent to a proposition as coming from God, Tillotson distinguishes between two groups. The first are the people who receive a revelation directly from God without any intermediary, and the second are the people who receive revelation through the report of the first group. Tillotson offers some not very convincing speculations about the grounds the first group had for believing. However, these speculations are not relevant to the grounds that he assigns for the belief of the second group, so all that is really necessary for his account of the faith of the second group is that we admit the

---

[127] Tillotson, 1722, vol. 2, p. 439.
[128] Tillotson, 1722, vol. 2, p. 462.

possibility of God's enabling people to know (somehow or other) that he is directly revealing things to him; and, as Tillotson remarks, admitting this possibility does not raise any problems.

The grounds of belief for the second group are the miracles that accompanied the proclamation of the Christian message by the initial group. These miracles amounted to God's endorsement of the initial group's assertion that they brought a divine revelation. Tillotson clarifies the nature of the miracles that can reasonably be alleged to support a claim to be the bearer of divine revelation.

> ... But here you must distinguish between doubtful and unquestionable miracles. I call those doubtful miracles, which, though a man cannot tell how they can be done by any natural power, yet do not carry that full conviction with them as to be universally owned and acknowledged for arguments of a divine power. Such were those which the Magicians did by their enchantments. I call those unquestionable, which considering their quality and number, and the public manner of doing them, are out of all question. Such were the miracles of Moses, and of our Saviour. Now a doubtful, and a single, and a private wonder, or miracle, as I may call it, can give no confirmation to a thing in opposition to a revelation, or a doctrine confirmed by many, and public, and unquestionable miracles...that the greatest and most unquestionable miracles are to carry it, is evident; because this is all the reason why Moses was to be credited above the Magicians, because he wrought more and greater wonders than they did[129]...In particular the great weight of the Gospel is laid upon the miracle of Christ's resurrection from the dead, which our Saviour mentioned as the only sign that should be given to that generation, that is, the clearest[130]...

It is because Christianity has the greatest and most unquestionable miracles that it ought to be believed rather than, say, Islam. Tillotson claims that the Scriptures support his view that miracles are the grounds for belief, citing texts in which Christ gives his miracles as grounds for believing him, such as Matt. 11:2 and John 5:36 ('the works which the Father has granted me to accomplish, those very works which I am doing, bear me witness that the Father has sent me.') The Thomist reply to this argument was, as we have seen, that the works Christ is referring to include the inward work of grace in the believer, without which faith could not be produced. (It could also be pointed out that some of these works, like those in Matt. 11:2, are presented by Christ as proving his mission because they fulfil the prophecies, and thus presuppose faith.) Tillotson does not consider this Thomist reply.

These miracles can produce three degrees of assent in the second group, all of which oblige them to believe divine revelation.

> 1). If we have the evidence of our senses for it, that is, if we see them wrought. This evidence the disciples of our Lord had, and the Jews, and therefore their unbelief was inexcusable ...

---

[129] Tillotson, 1722, vol. 2, pp. 444–5.
[130] Tillotson, 1722, vol. 2, p. 448.

2). If we have the credible report of eye-witnesses of those miracles, who are credible persons, and we have no reason to doubt of their testimony; that is, if we have the reports immediately from the mouth of those who were eyewitnesses of them ...
3). If the credible report of eye-witnesses concerning such miracles be conveyed to us in such a manner, and with so much evidence, that we have no reason to doubt it. For why should we not believe a credible report conveyed to us in such a manner, as we have no reason to question, but that it hath been faithfully conveyed and transmitted to us? ... And this is that assurance which we who live at this distance from the age of Christ and his Apostles, have of the miracles wrought in confirmation of the Scripture.[131]

This last assurance amounts to as good historical evidence as one could ask for: '... that such miracles were wrought, is evident from as credible histories, as we have for any of those things which we do most firmly believe ... Even the rudest of the vulgar, and those who cannot read, do believe upon very good grounds that there was such a king as William the Conqueror; and the miracles of Christ and his Apostles are capable of as good evidence as we have of theirs.'[132] This historical evidence results from the universal human tradition that the books of the Scripture were written by the Prophets, Apostles and Evangelists, who recorded these miracles and were credible witnesses. It is because there is no such human tradition for the Catholic claim that unwritten apostolic traditions have been preserved by the Catholic Church that the Scriptures alone should be the Christian rule of faith; it is only in the Scriptures that a reliable historical record of the original divine revelation to the initial group has been preserved.

At this point Tillotson's views begin to look oddly familiar. They are like the ghostly opponent that liberal and modernist theologians attack when they want to discredit orthodox Christian belief. It is not that these theologians have necessarily read Tillotson, or anyone like him; it is that this is the kind of view they assume would have to be advanced in order to substantiate orthodox claims to knowledge of divine revelation. The existence of this assumption is a revealing indicator of the influence that Tillotson's sort of understanding of faith has achieved. It also provides an explanation, from a Thomist standpoint, of how modernist theologians have continued these attacks for centuries without either destroying orthodox Christianity or having doubts about the effectiveness of their arguments. These arguments raise difficulties for the sort of belief that they are aimed at, but from a Thomist point of view such belief is not Christian faith at all.

Tillotson holds that the evidence of miracles provided by the Scriptures gives moral certainty that Christianity is divinely revealed.

Aristotle hath long since observed, how unreasonable it is to expect the same kind of proof for every thing, which we have for some things ... conclusions in natural philosophy are to be proved by a sufficient induction of experiments; things of a moral nature by moral arguments, and matters of fact by credible testimony ... None can demonstrate to me, that there is such an island as Jamaica; yet upon the testimony of credible persons, and authors who have written of it, I am as free from all doubt

---

[131] Tillotson, 1722, vol. 2, p. 448.
[132] Tillotson, 1707, p. 625.

concerning it, as from doubting of the clearest mathematical demonstration[133]... Is Mr. S[ergeant] sufficiently assured that there is such a place as America? and can he demonstrate this to any man, without carrying him thither? Can he show by any necessary argument, that it is not impossible that all the relations concerning that place should be false? ... and yet I suppose notwithstanding the possibility of this, no man in his wits is now possessed with so incredible a folly as to doubt whether there should be such a place. The case is the very same as to the certainty of an ancient book, and of the sense of plain expressions[134]...

The Scriptures provide the testimony of credible persons about the miracles they relate, and thus put them and the revelation they establish beyond a reasonable doubt. Tillotson's remark about Aristotle follows the beginning of Grotius's *On the Truth of the Christian Religion*, and his position on moral certainty follows Chillingworth in alleging that such certainty can remove any fear or doubt.

Tillotson's views here should be seen in their context, which was his debate with the Catholic apologist John Sergeant. Sergeant had idiosyncratically maintained, not only that faith was incompatible with doubt and required infallible grounds in order to exclude doubt, but also that the human tradition that could be alleged in support of the teachings of the Catholic Church and of her claim to authority provided such an infallible ground. (This view later got him in trouble with the Inquisition, and had to be modified.) Tillotson objected that no human faculty, let alone belief in testimony, could provide infallible grounds, and that if such grounds were available they would take away the merit of faith, because they would render it involuntary. Moreover, such grounds would not be necessary, because moral certainty suffices to attain the purpose of faith.

> ... For what degree of assent, and what security of the means, which convey to us the knowledge of Christianity, are necessary to the true nature of faith, is to be estimated from the end of faith, which is the salvation of men's souls. And whoever is so assured of the authority and sense of the Scripture, as to believe the doctrine of it, and to live accordingly, shall be saved. And surely such a belief as will save a man hath the true nature of faith, though it be not infallible.[135] ... We have abundantly more assurance of the recompense of another world, than we have of many things in this world, which yet have a greater influence upon our actions, and govern the lives of the most prudent and considerate of men ... Men venture to take physic upon probable grounds of the integrity and skill of their physician; and yet the want of either of these must hazard their lives ... Men venture their whole estates to places which they never saw; and that there are such places, they have only the concurrent testimony and agreement of men; nay perhaps, have only spoken with them that have spoken with those that have been there. No merchant ever insisted upon the evidence of a miracle to be wrought, to satisfy him that there were such places as the East and West Indies, before he would venture to trade thither. And yet this assurance God hath been pleased to give the world of a state beyond the grave, and of blessed immortality in another life[136]...

---

[133] Tillotson, 1707, preface.
[134] Tillotson, 1707, pp. 688–9.
[135] Tillotson, 1707, preface.
[136] Tillotson, 1722, vol. 1, p. 79.

Tillotson followed Chillingworth in maintaining that the Scriptures expressed themselves clearly on every doctrine that is necessary for salvation. He denied that the existence of disputes among Protestants was a good reason for calling the sufficiency of Scripture into question, saying that '... if nothing were to be accounted sufficiently plain, but what is impossible a great wit should be able to wrest to any other sense, not only the Scriptures, but all other books ... and all truths would fall into uncertainty'[137]; he insisted that Catholics would have to actually produce an important doctrine upon which Scripture was unclear to prove their claims. (He was willing to back up this assertion about the Scriptures by giving arguments to show that the doctrines held by Protestants were clearly expressed in them, but this brave attempt does not succeed. Instead of manifest obviousness he can only give a scholar's confidence in his own case, a notoriously frail reed.)

Although Tillotson followed tradition in saying that faith is produced by the action of the Holy Spirit, he changed the sense of this assertion. He allows for two ways in which faith is produced by the Holy Spirit. 'First, in respect of the outward evidence which the Spirit of God gives us to persuade us to believe. Secondly, in respect of the inward efficacy and operation of the Spirit of God upon the minds of men in believing.'[138] But he states that it is the first way that makes faith most properly to be called the gift of the Holy Spirit, and he is careful to explain that the inward operation of the Spirit is in no way absolutely necessary for faith. The evidence of miracles is sufficient on its own to produce divine faith, because 'our understandings are naturally endowed with a sufficient power to assent to any truth that is sufficiently propounded to them.'[139] The inward operation of the Spirit in producing belief may occur through his strengthening our understandings, or suggesting the evidence for revelation to our minds, or bringing us to remember it, or holding our minds intent upon this evidence until it has its effect on us, or removing impediments to belief (such as prejudices imbibed from our education, or desires that disincline us to believe).[140] These are all things that God may and probably often does do, but that do not have to happen in order to produce faith. They are simply help that he may provide for its attainment.

Tillotson was aware of theologians who denied that faith is based on the motives of credibility, and he attacked their position.

> ... I know there hath been a very rude clamour been raised by some persons, (but of more zeal I think than judgement) against the use of reason in matters of faith; but
> 1. Divine revelation doth not endow men with new faculties, but propoundeth new objects to the faculties, which they had before. Reason is the faculty whereby revelation is to be discerned ...

---

[137] Tillotson, 1707, p. 659.
[138] Tillotson, 1722, vol. 2, p. 455.
[139] Tillotson, 1722, vol. 2, p. 456.
[140] Tillotson, 1722, vol. 2, pp. 456–7.

2. Faith (as we are now speaking of it) is an assent of the mind to something as revealed by God: Now all assent must be grounded upon evidence; that is, no man can believe any thing, unless he have, or thinks he have some reason to do so. For to be confident of a thing without reason, is not faith; but a presumptuous persuasion, or obstinacy of mind.

3. This will yet be more evident, if we consider the method that must of necessity be used to convince any man of the truth of religion ... The most natural method surely, were this, to acquaint him with the holy Scriptures ... He would ask us, 'why we believe that book?' The proper answer would be, 'Because it is the word of God' ... But then he would ask, 'Why we believe it to be the word of God, rather than Mahomet's Alchoran, which pretends no less to be of divine inspiration?'

If any man now should answer, that 'he could give no reason why he believed it to be the word of God, only he believed it to be so, and so every man else ought to do without enquiring after any farther reason, because reason is to be laid aside in matters of faith'; would not the man presently reply, 'that he had just as much reason as this comes to, to believe the Alchoran, or anything else'; that is, none at all?

But certainly the better way would be to satisfy this man's reason by proper arguments that the Scriptures are a divine revelation, and that no other book in the world can with equal reason pretend to be so ...

Before I pass from this argument, I cannot but observe, that both the extremes of those who differ from us in matters of religion are generally great declaimers against the use of reason in matters of faith ...

I have often wondered that people can with patience endure to hear their teachers and guides talk against reason ... One would think this but an odd way to gain authority over the minds of men; But some skilful and designing men have found by experience, that it is a good way to recommend themselves to the ignorant, as nurses use to endear themselves to children, by perpetual noise and nonsense.[141]

The Thomist reply to Tillotson's argument from the necessity of the motives of credibility for converting unbelievers will be that these motives suffice for the sole purpose to which we can put them, which is showing that the objections of unbelievers are worthless, but that they are not necessary for our persuading unbelievers to believe, because this is not a task that falls to us. On the Thomist view it is God who produces belief, rather than us, so Tillotson's objection that we cannot produce belief without an appeal to the motives of credibility begs the question. His appeal to reason also begs the question, by assuming that belief in divine revelation has to be based on evidence for that revelation if it is to be reasonable. But that does not mean it is wrong. As with the Scotist position, Tillotson's objection to Thomist views on faith turns on the question of whether belief in testimony must be justified by evidence.

In the light of the history we have examined, it is clear that Tillotson had an important role in a revolution in the understanding of Christian faith. Despite the abundance of documentation for this revolution, it is difficult to give a satisfactory explanation for it. This is because no good answer is apparent for this question: how did the notion of the necessity of grace for the act of faith disappear in

---

[141] Tillotson, 1722, vol. 1, pp. 18–19.

Tillotson and the Latitudinarians? This disappearance did not lie simply in their rejecting any such necessity, but also in it not occurring to them that they needed to defend this rejection.

This rejection was a complete break not only with patristic and medieval thought, but also with the English Reformers. Tyndale spoke contemptuously of acquired faith. 'So now with an historical faith I may believe that the Scripture is God's by the teaching of them; and so I should have done, though they had told me that Robin Hood hath been the scripture of God: which faith is but an opinion, and therefore abideth ever fruitless; and falleth away, if a more glorious reason be made unto me, or if the preacher live contrary.'[142] The Puritan divine William Whitaker attacked the Catholics for basing belief on acquired rather than infused faith:

> ... The papists say that we believe the Scripture upon the word and authority of the church. I ask, therefore, what sort of faith is this, – whether acquired or infused? They call that acquired which is gained by our own exertions and human topics of persuasion; that infused, which the Holy Spirit hath disseminated and inspired into our hearts. If they say it is acquired, (as they must needs say, because the authority of the church is in the place of an external means of persuasion), I say, that it is not sufficient of itself to produce in us a certain conviction; but in order that we should believe any thing firmly, there is need of the internal infusion of the Spirit ...[143]

Richard Hooker distinguished between certainty of evidence and certainty of adherence along the lines of Aquinas, assigning the highest certainty of adherence to faith, and holding that 'the simplicitie of faithe which is in Christe taketh the naked promise of God his bare word and there it resteth.'[144] The English reformers agreed with the Catholic opponents of the Latitudinarians that Christian faith required an infallible basis in order to exclude all doubt.

Some causes can be suggested for this disappearance. One is the influence of Chillingworth, who could not easily have countenanced a necessity of grace for faith without admitting, as he was unwilling to do, that he had sinned against grace at some point or other in his religious peregrinations. A second is the fact that the Catholic opponents of the Latitudinarians did not press the point of the necessity of grace for faith, partly because they chose for practical reasons to fight on the grounds of the motives of credibility for faith, and partly because some of them (like Sergeant) did not have much room for grace in their own accounts. A third is the hatred and contempt of the Latitudinarians for the Calvinists, who were the chief Protestant proponents of the necessity of grace for faith. (Tillotson's preferred approach to Nonconformist objectors to Anglicanism was locking the objectors in jail.) But when these causes are taken into account there remains a

---

[142] William Tyndale, *An Answer to Sir Thomas More's Dialogue, The Supper of the Lord*, CUP, Cambridge (orig. pub. 1531), 1850, p. 51.

[143] William Whitaker, *A Disputation on Holy Scripture against the Papists, especially Bellarmine and Stapleton* (Latin original 1588), 1849, p. 355.

[144] Richard Hooker, *Laws of Ecclesiastical Polity*, in *Folger Library Edition of the Works of Richard Hooker*, vol. 1, 1990, p. 77.

mystery that is difficult to resolve. We can, however, say that this revolution could not have occurred without the birth in the early Middle Ages of the idea of acquired, as opposed to infused, faith, and the subsequent incorporation by Scotus of acquired faith into Christian faith. It is a natural evolution from the Scotist conception. As we saw in looking at the Scotist view, if we accept the existence of acquired faith it is difficult to give a satisfactory explanation for the necessity of infused faith, so the further step of suppressing infused faith entirely is a natural one to take. The mystery lies in why the theologians who took this step faced so few challenges, and had so much success.[145] This success makes the birth of the idea of acquired faith, and its subsequent usurpation of the title of Christian faith from infused faith, the most important turning points in the history of the Christian understanding of faith.[146] Whether they were also turning points in the history of the abandonment of Christianity by European civilization is an interesting question that lies beyond the scope of this book.

(Although I disclaim the ambition to investigate the hypothesis that the triumph of acquired faith was a central factor in the European abandonment of Christianity, I will try to clarify the hypothesis that is being suggested, in order to distinguish it from related hypotheses that have been proposed in the past. Leslie Stephen also saw Latitudinarian thought as a crucial step towards unbelief. He remarked of the Latitudinarians that '... in many of their arguments it is sufficient to substitute Revelation for Rome to make the attack on Catholicism available for an attack upon all supernatural authority.'[147] The Latitudinarians did indeed provide individual arguments that were useful to unbelievers; Hume's taking his argument against miracles from Tillotson's argument against transubstantiation is a famous example. But Stephen's view on the effect of basing faith on natural reason is not one I would accept. Stephen makes an unbeliever's assumption that there really are good rational objections to faith, which an acceptance of supernatural authority is necessary to face down. If we accept his conclusion about the tendency of Latitudinarian thought to produce unbelief, it will be for a different reason. It will not be because the Latitudinarians unwittingly provided good arguments against faith, but because the sort of belief they tried to produce was not Christian faith at all.)

---

[145] These theologians were often criticized on the grounds of Socinianism. But this criticism cannot be equated with a criticism of their dispensing with the necessity of grace for faith, because Socinus, while denying that faith rested on anything except unaided human reason, also rejected the doctrines of the Trinity, original sin, the divinity of Christ, and divine foreknowledge. It is thus often unclear whether attacks on Socinianism were aimed at Socinus's view of faith, or at his views on other Christian doctrines. When it is clear, it is generally because these attacks agree with Socinus about faith.

[146] The fact that neither of these changes corresponds to disagreements between Catholics and Protestants illustrates how the Reformation divides obscure important theological differences as often as they reveal them.

[147] Leslie Stephen, *History of English Thought in the Eighteenth Century*, vol. 1, 1876, p. 78.

John Locke   Locke's views on the rational grounding of Christian faith are substantially those of Chillingworth and Tillotson, two of his favourite authors; neither his religious nor his epistemological views are very original – he is more the culmination of a school of thought than the beginning of a new school – and his account of faith is less developed and sophisticated than Tillotson's. Where he represents an advance on Tillotson is in the account of knowledge that he uses to underpin his views on faith.[148] His epistemology is the most philosophically complete and satisfactory version of the general Latitudinarian conception of knowledge. It is this epistemology, together with the great influence he has retained long after Tillotson has been largely forgotten, that make it desirable to examine his views. A Latitudinarian conception of faith will stand or fall with this kind of epistemology; that is why it will be set forth at some length.

Locke resembles Aquinas to some extent in distinguishing between knowledge and assent that is not knowledge. Knowledge is infallibly certain, and assent to what is known is not voluntary.[149] Where he differs from Aquinas and Aristotle is in holding that knowledge is not limited to propositions whose truth is known through grasping the meaning of their terms. He admits knowledge of self-evident propositions and knowledge arising through demonstration from known propositions,[150] but he departs from the Aristotelian view in claiming that we can obtain knowledge of singular contingent facts through sense experience. Thus he asserts:

> KNOWLEDGE, as has been said, lying in the Perception of the Agreement, or Disagreement, of any of our *Ideas*, it follows from hence...That we can have no Knowledge farther, than we can have Perception of that Agreement, or Disagreement: Which Perception being, 1. Either by *Intuition*, or the immediate comparing any two *Ideas*: or, 2. By Reason, examining the Agreement, or Disagreement of two *Ideas*, by the Intervention of some others: Or, 3. By *Sensation*, perceiving the Existence of particular Things.[151]

Besides knowledge, the mind is capable of judgement:

> Thus the Mind has two Faculties, conversant about Truth and Falshood.

---

[148] On the crucial role played by religious considerations in Locke's epistemology see Richard Ashcraft, 'Faith and Knowledge in Locke's Philosophy', in *John Locke: Problems and Perspectives*, 1969. The importance that Locke attached to religious questions, reflected in his letter to van Limborch quoted above, is also indicated by the fact that after 1683 most of his note-taking is devoted to theological issues; on this see John Marshall, 'John Locke and Latitudinarianism', in *Philosophy, science and religion in England 1640–1700*, 1992.

[149] Locke is not however entirely consistent on the question of whether knowledge is not voluntary.

[150] Locke's understanding of self-evidence and of demonstration is not the same as that of Aristotle or Aquinas, but this difference is not pertinent to our investigation.

[151] John Locke, *An Essay concerning Human Understanding*, 4th edn, 1975, pp. 538–9.

First, Knowledge, whereby it certainly perceives, and is undoubtedly satisfied of the Agreement or Disagreement of any *Ideas*.

Secondly, Judgement, which is the putting *Ideas* together, or separating them from one another in the Mind, when their certain Agreement or Disagreement is not perceived, but *presumed* to be so; which is, as the Word imports, taken to be so before it certainly appears. And if it so unites, or separates them, as in Reality things are, it is *right Judgement*.[152]

Judgement deals with the sphere of probability:

§2. Our Knowledge, as has been shewn, being very narrow, and we not happy enough to find certain Truth in every thing which we have occasion to consider: most of the Propositions we think, reason, discourse, nay act upon, are such, as we cannot have undoubted Knowedge of their Truth: yet some of them border so near upon Certainty, that we make no doubt at all about them; but *assent* to them as firmly, and act, according to that Assent, as resolutely, as if they were infallibly demonstrated, and that our Knowledge of them was perfect and certain. But there being degrees herein, from the very neighbourhood of Certainty and Demonstration, quite down to Improbability and Unlikeness, even to the Confines of Impossibility; and also degrees of *Assent* from full *Assurance* and Confidence, quite down to *Conjecture, Doubt* and *Distrust* ...

§3. *Probability* is likeness to be true, the very notation of the Word signifying such a Proposition, for which there be Arguments or Proofs, to make it pass or received for true. The entertainment the Mind gives this sort of Propositions, is called *Belief, Assent*, or *Opinion*, which is the admitting or receiving any Proposition for true, upon Arguments or proofs that are found to perswade us to receive it as true, without certain Knowledge that it is so. And herein lies the difference between Probability and Certainty, Faith and Knowledge, that in all the parts of Knowledge, there is intuition; each immediate Idea, each step has its visible and certain connexion; in belief not so ...

§4. *Probability* then, being to supply the defect of our Knowledge, and to guide us where that fails, is always conversant about Propositions, whereof we have no certainty ... The *grounds of it* are, in short, these two following:

First, The conformity of any thing with our own Knowledge, Observation, and Experience.

Secondly, The Testimony of others, vouching their Observation and Experience. In the Testimony of others, is to be considered, 1. The Number. 2. The Integrity. 3. The Skill of the Witnesses. 4. The Design of the Author, where it is a Testimony out of a Book cited. 5. The Consistency of the Parts, and Circumstances of the Relation. 6. Contrary Testimonies.

§5. Probability wanting that intuitive Evidence, which infallibly determines the Understanding, and produces certain Knowledge, *the Mind if it will proceed rationally, ought to examine all the grounds of Probability*, and see how they make more or less, for or against any probable Proposition, before it assents to or dissents from it, and upon a due ballancing the whole, reject, or receive it, with a more or less firm assent, proportionably to the preponderancy of the greater grounds of Probability on one side or the other ...[153]

---

[152] Locke, 1975, p. 653.
[153] Locke, 1975, pp. 655–6.

If testimony clashes with experience, there are no exact rules about which to prefer:

> The difficulty is, when Testimonies contradict common Experience, and the reports of History and witnesses clash with the ordinary course of Nature, or with one another; there it is, where Diligence, Attention, and Exactness is required, to form a right Judgement, and to proportion the *Assent* to the different Evidence and Probability of the thing; which rises and falls, according as those two foundations of Credibility, viz. Common observation in like cases, and particular Testimonies in that particular instance, favour or contradict it. These are liable to so great a variety of contrary Observations, Circumstances, Reports, different Qualifications, Tempers, Designs, Over-sights *etc.* of the Reporters, that 'tis impossible to reduce to precise Rules, the various degrees wherein Men give their Assent.[154]

Locke contrasts belief in testimony with simply accepting the opinion of others:

> There is another, I confess, which though by it self it be no true ground of *Probability*, yet is often made use of for one, by which Men most commonly regulate their Assent, and upon which they pin their Faith more than any thing else, and, that is, *the Opinion of others*; though there cannot be a more dangerous thing to rely on, nor more likely to mislead one; since there is much more Falshood and Errour amongst Men, than Truth and Knowledge.[155]

Opinion cannot give rise to knowledge:

> Not that I want a due respect to other mens Opinions; but after all, the *greatest reverence is due to Truth*; and, I hope, it will not be thought arrogance, to say, That, perhaps, we should make greater progress in the discovery of rational and contemplative *Knowledge*, if we *sought* it in the Fountain, *in the consideration of things themselves*; and made use rather of our own thoughts, than other mens to find it. For, I think, we may as rationally hope to see with other Mens Eyes, as to know by other mens Understandings. So much as we our selves consider and comprehend of Truth and Reason, so much we possess of real and true Knowledge. The floating of other Mens Opinions in our brains makes us not one jot the more knowing, though they happen to be true. What in them was Science, is in us but Opiniatrety ...[156]

In this discussion of opinion, Locke (as he does so often) fails to make his views clear. C. A. J. Coady describes this passage as 'individualist rhetoric',[157] but it is not clear that he is right in implying that Locke means to disparage testimony as a way of forming beliefs. The context of the above passage is an attack on people who accept the philosophical doctrine of innate ideas on the authority of others. Testimony is being rejected here as a basis for 'rational and contemplative knowledge', not as a basis for judgements of probability. It is only in the sphere of

---

[154] Locke, 1975, p. 663.
[155] Locke, 1975, p. 657.
[156] Locke, 1975, p. 101.
[157] C. A. J. Coady, *Testimony*, 1992, p. 13.

knowledge, not in the sphere of probable judgement, that Locke rejects testimony as a ground for belief. (It may be however that Locke also means to attack those who simply accept the testimony of others without weighing this testimony in the manner he recommends above.)

Faith is a form of belief in testimony:

> *Reason* therefore here, as contradistinguished to Faith, I take to be the discovery of the Certainty or Probability of such propositions or Truths, which the Mind arrives at by Deductions made from such *Ideas*, which it has got by the use of its natural Faculties, *viz*, by Sensation or Reflection.
>
> *Faith*, on the other side, is the Assent to any Proposition, not thus made out by the Deductions of Reason; but upon the Credit of the Proposer, as coming from GOD, in some extraordinary way of communication. This way of discovering Truths to Men we call *Revelation*.[158]

It is not knowledge:

> To you and me the christian revelation is the true ... Now do you or I know this, (I do not ask, with what assurance we believe it; for that, in the highest degree, not being knowledge, is not what we now enquire after.) Can any magistrate demonstrate to himself ... not only all the articles of his church, but the fundamental ones of the christian religion? For, whatever is not capable of demonstration (as such remote matters of fact are not) is not, unless it be self-evident, capable to produce knowledge, how well grounded and great soever the assurance of faith may be wherewith it is received; but faith it is still, and not knowledge; persuasion, and not certainty. This is the highest the nature of the thing will permit us to go, in matters of revealed religion, which are, therefore, called matters of faith: a persuasion of our own minds, short of knowledge, is the last result, that determines us in such truths. 'Tis all God requires, in the Gospel, for men to be saved ...[159]

In consequence, no allegedly revealed statement can be accepted if it contradicts what we know:

> For since no evidence of our Faculties, by which we receive such *Revelations*, can exceed, if equal, the certainty of our intuitive Knowledge, we can never receive for a Truth any thing, that is directly contrary to our clear and distinct Knowledge, *v.g.* The *Ideas* of one Body, and one Place, do so clearly agree: and the Mind has so evident a Perception of their Agreement, that we can never assent to a Proposition, that affirms the same Body to be in two distant Places at once, however it should pretend to the Authority of a divine *Revelation*: Since the Evidence, *First*, That we deceive not our selves in ascribing it to GOD; *Secondly*, That we understand it right, can never be so great, as the Evidence of our own intuitive Knowledge, whereby we discern it impossible, for the same Body to be in two Places at once. And therefore, *no Proposition can be received for Divine Revelation*, or obtain the Assent due to all such, *if it be contrary to our clear intuitive Knowledge*.[160]

---

[158] Locke, 1975, p. 689.

[159] John Locke, *A third letter concerning Toleration*, in *Works*, 5th edn, 1751a, p. 312.

[160] Locke, 1975, pp. 691–2.

This is of course a stock argument aimed at the doctrine of transubstantiation, taken from the Latitudinarians; it is found in Chillingworth and Tillotson. Owen also argues against this doctrine on the grounds that for reasons somewhat like those offered by Locke we can know it to be false. But there is a significant difference between Locke's argument and Owen's argument. Locke, unlike Owen, argues from the superiority of natural knowledge over any claim to revelation. Owen does not believe that natural knowledge is superior to that provided by revelation, or deny the status of knowledge to faith; he only argues that since it is impossible for the two sources of knowledge to disagree, and since we know that transubstantiation must be false, the doctrine of transubstantiation cannot be revealed. (This of course is a weaker argument from a polemical point of view than Locke's argument, since Catholics could just turn it around and say that since we know transubstantiation to be true the objections against it must be false. The polemical value of Locke's position probably contributed to its success.)

This superiority of reason over faith is said by Locke to exist even in cases of immediate revelation. (Locke does not explicitly describe how such immediate revelation is to be recognized, although he says that Moses and others who took themselves to be receiving it did not simply accept what some disembodied voice told them, but had evidence in the form of miraculous signs to accredit the revelation they received.[161]) When revelation is not immediate, acceptance of it is not only subject to the test of reason, but rests upon reason:

> ... but to all those who pretend not to immediate *Revelation*, but are required to pay Obedience, and to receive the Truths revealed to others, which, by the Tradition of Writings, or word of Mouth, are conveyed down to them, Reason has a great deal more to do, and is that only which can induce us to receive them.[162]

Locke does not directly set out to show how reason is supposed to establish the claims of Christian revelation. He may simply have thought that this task had been sufficiently addressed by the apologists of his day, and not thought it necessary to take on the task himself. His views can however be gleaned from his remarks on the subject, even though he does not attempt an apologetic proof. The Christian religion in his view prevailed in the first ages of the church 'by its own beauty, force and reasonableness',[163] without the aid of force or actual miracles:

> you will not say ... that all, or the greatest part of those, that embraced the Christian religion, before it was supported by the laws of the empire...had actually miracles done before them, to work on them ... The greater part then, of those who were converted ...

---

[161] '... the holy Men of old, who had *Revelations* from GOD, had something else besides that internal Light of assurance in their own Minds, to testify to them, that it was from GOD. They were not left to their own Perswasions alone, that those Perswasions were from GOD; But had outward signs to convince them of the Author of those Revelations.' Locke, 1975, p. 705.

[162] Locke, 1975, p. 693.

[163] Locke, 1751a, p. 457.

were wrought upon, by bare preaching, and such miracles as we still have, miracles at a distance, reported miracles.[164]

The means that God has appointed to make men hear and consider are "'exhortation in season and out of season", &c. together with prayer for them and the example of meekness and a good life.'[165] The evidence of the reports of Christ's miracles is enough to require us to believe his message:

> The evidence of our Saviour's mission from heaven is so great, in the multitude of miracles he did, before all sorts of people, that what he delivered cannot but be received as the oracles of God, and unquestionable verity. For the miracles he did were so ordered by the divine providence and wisdom, that they never were, nor could be denied by any of the enemies, or opposers of Christianity.[166]

Locke affirms the necessity of grace for belief. But he is agnostic on what the action of grace consists in: "Twill be idle for us, who know not how our own spirits move and act, to ask in what manner the Spirit of God shall work upon us.'[167] He forestalls a possible objection to his view by arguing thus:

> Perhaps it will farther be urged, that this is not a 'saving faith': because such a faith as this the devils may have, and 'twas plain they had ... To which I answer, 1. That they could not be saved by any faith, to whom it was not proposed as a means of salvation, nor ever promised to count for righteousness. This was an act of grace shown only to mankind ... 2. I answer; that though the devils believed, yet they could not be saved by the covenant of grace; because they performed not the other condition required in it, altogether as necessary to be performed as this of believing; and that is repentance.[168]

This answer is significant as indicating that he did not think of the faith of the devils as differing in its rational grounds from the faith of Christian believers.

Part of Locke's case for his understanding of faith consists in his attack on enthusiasm, which he presents as being the alternative to his view:

> §4. *Reason* is natural *Revelation*, whereby the eternal Father of Light, and Fountain of all Knowledge communicates to mankind that portion of Truth, which he has laid within the reach of their natural Faculties: *Revelation* is natural *Reason* enlarged by a new set of discoveries communicated by GOD immediately, which *Reason* vouches the

---

[164] Locke, 1751a, p. 458.

[165] John Locke, *A second letter concerning Toleration*, in *Works*, 5th edn, 1751b, p. 283.

[166] John Locke, *The Reasonableness of Christianity as delivered in the Scriptures*, in *Works*, 5th edn, 1751c, pp. 574–5. Locke espoused Unitarian and Socinian views in this work, and pared down the revelation that Christ made in addition to the truths of natural religion to the simple assertion that he was the Messiah, a position that made it easier for him to defend the compatibility of the revealed message with reason. This conception of Christ's message is a development of Tillotson's views, since Tillotson thought that Christ's revelation was that he was the Messiah and the Son of God.

[167] Locke, 1751c, p. 582.

[168] Locke, 1751c, p. 559.

Truth of, by the Testimony and Proofs it gives, that they come from God. So that he that takes away *Reason*, to make way for *Revelation*, puts out the Light of both, and does much what the same, as if he would perswade a Man to put out his Eyes the better to receive the remote Light of an invisible Star by a Telescope.

§5. Immediate Revelation being a much easier way for Men to establish their Opinions, and regulate their Conduct, than the tedious and not always successful Labour of strict Reasoning, it is no wonder, that some have been very apt to pretend to Revelation, and to perswade themselves, that they are under the peculiar guidance of Heaven in their Actions and Opinions ...[169]

§8. Though the odd Opinions and extravagant Actions, Enthusiasm has run Men into, were enough to warn them against this wrong Principle so apt to misguide them both in their Belief and conduct: yet the Love of something extraordinary ... so flatters many Men's Laziness, Ignorance, and Vanity, that when they are once got into this way of Immediate Revelation ... 'tis a hard matter to get them out of it. Reason is lost on them, they are above it: they see the Light infused into their Understandings, and cannot be mistaken; 'tis clear and visible there; like the Light of bright Sunshine, shews it self, and needs no other Proof, but its own Evidence ...

§9. This is the way of talking of these Men: they are sure, because they are sure: and their Perswasions are right, only because they are strong in them. For, when what they say is strip'd of the Metaphor of seeing and feeling, that is all it amounts to ...[170]

§13. Light, true Light in the Mind is, or can be nothing else but the Evidence of the Truth of any Proposition; and if be not a self-evident Proposition, all the Light it has, or can have, is from the clearness and validity of those Proofs, upon which it is received.[171]

This is simply a repetition of the usual Latitudinarian polemic. As an argument for his view it is not of any value. Enthusiasm is not the only alternative to his position on belief in revelation as resting on the motives of credibility, so the discrediting of it does not prove his position. Nor does he here furnish any independent reasons for this position; he simply assumes it as true. When one compares his thought on this subject with that of John Owen, one would have thought them reversed in time. Owen, arguing against the Latitudinarians, anticipates Locke's points and provides replies to them, but Locke does not engage at all with Owen's arguments. In this he was simply following his Latitudinarian predecessors. His failure in this respect is less blameable than theirs, since he was not a trained theologian. He would not have felt called upon to engage with the thought of Owen, for reasons intellectual, sociological, political and religious. Owen's close association with Cromwell would not have been seen as an indication of Christian wisdom, and the political defeat and widespread detestation of Puritanism had removed Puritan thought from the mainstream of theological discussion. More generally, the experience of interminable religious conflict made reason seem attractive as a basis for religious belief to people who had not yet had the opportunity to lose their illusions about its power to settle religious questions.

This failure to engage with alternatives to his view does not mean that Locke's position is implausible. The two essentials of his view, 1) that testimony does not

---

[169] Locke, 1975, pp. 698–9.
[170] Locke, 1975, pp. 699–700.
[171] Locke, 1975, p. 703.

give knowledge, and 2) that our belief in the existence of revelation is based on human testimony, are both quite defensible; and if they are true, his position on the roles of the motives of credibility is the correct one. Whether they are true or not is a question that must be addressed in the discussion of knowledge, testimony and revelation to which we shall now turn.

Chapter 5

Knowledge as the Product of Intellectual Virtue

Having reached the end of an incomplete and selective historical survey of thought on the question of the rational grounds for faith, the next step is to address the philosophical issues that this survey has revealed as being crucial for a resolution of the question. The first issue that needs to be addressed is one that surfaced in the discussion of Aquinas; it is the question of whether knowledge is the result of the exercise of intellectual virtues. I will maintain that it is.

An intellectual virtue will be understood to be a capacity whose function is to arrive at true beliefs, and whose operation consists in the production of true beliefs. (It is worth recalling that 'believing' in this context is simply meant to be thinking a proposition to be true, so that having a belief in a proposition p is simply thinking that p is true.) In order to clarify what such an intellectual virtue is, it is helpful to stress the 'consists in'; an intellectual virtue's operation *consists in* producing true beliefs. 'Consists in' here is to be understood in the sense of identity, not in the sense of constitution. That means, as we saw in Chapter 4 in our discussion of Aquinas, that if a belief is not true, it cannot have been produced by the operation of an intellectual virtue. This sort of intellectual virtue is different from many of those currently discussed by epistemologists. It is not an ability that has a good success ratio in attaining the truth, but that need not be and cannot be infallible.[1] Such an ability would not be an intellectual virtue in the broadly Thomist sense given here (which will be the sense used from now on), because its exercise can result in false belief. Nor is it the sort of intellectual virtue discussed by Linda Zagzebski. Zagzebski defines virtue in general as 'a deep and enduring acquired excellence of a person, involving a characteristic motivation to produce a desired end and reliable success in bringing about that end';[2] she defines motivation in turn as 'a disposition to have a certain motive, and a motive is an emotion that initiates and directs action to produce an end with certain desired features'.[3] She considers that intellectual virtues belong to this broad category of virtue. The basic intellectual virtues, understood in a Thomist sense, are not acquired excellences. Their exercise does not in itself involve emotion, motivation, deliberation or choice; it is not an activity of the will, and it delivers knowledge independently of any activity of the will.

---

[1] See for example Ernest Sosa, *Knowledge in Perspective*, 1991, p. 275.
[2] Linda Zagzebski, *Virtues of the Mind*, 1996, p. 137.
[3] Zagzebski, 1996, p. 136.

Having contrasted the broadly Thomist view that is proposed with those described above, it should be noted in what sense it is 'broadly Thomist'. It is Thomist in that it agrees with Aquinas that knowledge is the result of the operation of intellectual virtues, which are capacities to attain the truth; but it does not endorse the specific list of intellectual virtues that Aquinas thinks humans to possess (sc. *intellectus* and *scientia*). Nor does it give exactly the same characterization of intellectual virtue as Aquinas does. The differences between this characterization and that of Aquinas will emerge by the end of the discussion.

Why believe that knowledge is the result of the operation of intellectual virtues?

Three lines of argument will be offered for thinking that knowledge is the result of the operation of intellectual virtues.

The first is that the basic ways in which we acquire knowledge are intellectual virtues, because the statements that describe their activity are factive. It is often remarked that knowledge itself is factive. By calling knowledge factive, we assert that from 'I know that p', where p is some proposition, it follows that p is true. But it is also the case that the basic ways in which we get knowledge are factive. From 'I see that p' it follows that p. The same is true of other ways of getting knowledge through the senses, like 'I hear that p'. 'I remember that p' is also factive.

The argument that arises from the factiveness of statements about the exercise of our basic knowledge-providing capacities is a straightforward one. Statements about the exercise of these capacities, like 'I see that p', 'I remember that p', and so on, can only be factive if the intellectual powers whose activity they describe infallibly produce true beliefs. If it were possible for their exercise to give rise to false beliefs, the expressions that describe them could not be factive. Since they infallibly produce true beliefs, they are all capacities whose operation consists in arriving at the truth in some particular way, and they are intellectual virtues.

The second line of argument is that if our beliefs are not produced by intellectual virtues, then it is not in our power to bring it about that our beliefs are true, and the propositions that are the objects of our beliefs cannot be known. (We should distinguish between it being in our power to bring it about that our beliefs are true, and it being in our power to prove or provide evidence that our beliefs are true; these are not the same.) This is so because a belief-forming mechanism that is not an intellectual virtue will by definition not provide truth all the time, and can at best provide it most of the time. But if the mechanism that leads to our formation of a belief can only deliver truth most of the time, the fact that on a given occasion it actually does deliver truth cannot be entirely due to us and to the operation of our intellectual capacities. There will always be an element of accident and luck, from our point of view, in such a mechanism's actually doing what it does most of the time. And if there is an element of accident or luck in a belief-producing mechanism's giving rise to true beliefs, the beliefs that it gives rise to cannot constitute knowledge.

Part of the assumption about knowledge that underlies this line of argument is put forward by John McDowell in a discussion of the acquisition of knowledge from testimony.[4] He considers whether the knowledge that we acquire from believing a person's assertion can result from an argument that concludes that the person in question is telling the truth, on the basis of evidence that we possess about the person's trustworthiness. He argues that this cannot be the case, because such evidence leaves open the possibility that the person is not telling the truth. What concerns us here is not his conclusion about testimony (although this conclusion will be discussed further on), but the premise from which he argues to it. He describes this premise as follows:

> I have been exploiting a principle to this effect; if we want to be able to suppose that the title of a belief to count as knowledge is constituted by the believer's possession of an argument to its truth, then it had better not be the case that the best argument he has at his disposal leaves it open that things are not as he believes them to be. If it does, what we are picturing is an epistemic position in which, for all the subject knows, things are not as he takes them to be; and this is not a picture of something that might intelligibly amount to knowing that they are that way. The argument would need to be conclusive; if you know something, you cannot be wrong about it.
>
> ... Think of a roulette wheel with ninety-nine red slots and one white one. Given the task of predicting the outcome of a given spin, one will of course predict red... Suppose one makes one's prediction, the wheel is spun, and the result is red. Did one's prediction then amount to knowledge? Surely not: for all one knew, the result was going to be white. The fact that one had a result that established a high probability for the outcome that one predicted – so that one had excellent reasons for one's prediction – makes no difference at all to that. We can alter the example to make the probability higher, but I cannot see how changing the figures can make any difference of principle: if there is one white slot out of thousands or millions, one does not know that the result will not be white. I think the moral is that being known (a property of propositions) cannot be intelligibly seen as some region at the high end of a scale of probabilification by considerations at the knower's disposal, perhaps with room for argument about how high the standards need to be set.[5]

McDowell makes this point about arguments that leave some possibility of their conclusion's being false, but he seems to extend the point to a more general characterization, that of 'considerations at the knower's disposal.' And the logic of his point means that it applies to all our belief-forming cognitive capacities, not just to the making of inferences that only yield probable results. If there is a possibility of the operation of any of these capacities producing beliefs that are false, such operations cannot give us knowledge, because they will give rise to 'an epistemic position where, for all the subject knows, things are not as he takes them to be.'

Because McDowell's position on knowledge excluding the possibility of error is now widely rejected, it is worth pointing out that it is not just his idiosyncrasy; it is the rule rather than the objection in the history of philosophy. The reasons for its

---

[4] John McDowell, 'Knowledge by Hearsay', in *Knowing from Words*, 1994.
[5] McDowell, 1994, pp. 200-1.

current unpopularity can in part be traced to historical developments that have been mentioned above. As we have seen, one reaction to the sceptical crisis of the sixteenth and seventeenth centuries was to scale back the proposed areas of operation of knowledge so that they were not thought of as including the findings of science, and to limit the claims of science to the attainment of high probability amounting to moral certainty, rather than to knowledge. When in the twentieth century science came to be thought of by many philosophers as the paradigm for human knowledge, this view of science as resting on moral certainty rather than knowledge (in itself quite plausible) was replaced by an identification of high probability with knowledge. However, another reaction to the sceptical crisis was Descartes' epistemology. This required knowledge to possess certainty in a very strong internalist sense, so strong that most of the beliefs we think of as knowledge end up being disqualified for that status. As a result, the idea that knowledge involves certainty was discredited. We will give reasons below for thinking that both these developments of thought should be repudiated.

McDowell's claim that if you know something you cannot be wrong about it does not on its own get us to the conclusion that knowledge must be the result of the exercise of a capacity to attain the truth. In order to arrive at this conclusion, it is helpful to consider the account of knowledge that has been given by Alvin Plantinga. Plantinga describes warrant as 'that property – or better, quantity – enough of which is what makes the difference between knowledge and mere true belief.'[6] (This description is contentious and open to question, since it assumes that the property that confers the status of knowledge on a true belief can be shared to some degree by beliefs that are not knowledge.) According to Plantinga, a belief is warranted if it is produced by a belief-producing mechanism that has the purpose of producing true beliefs, and this mechanism is functioning properly according to a good design plan in the environment in which it was designed to operate. A design plan specifies a way of working whose operation is intended to realize the purpose of the thing designed. A good design plan is a plan that does realize this purpose, most or all of the time, in the environment for which it was designed.

However, satisfaction of these conditions does not suffice to produce knowledge. This can be seen from the following example. Suppose God creates a person *S* with a mental constitution that causes *S* to non-inferentially come to believe, whenever he meets a man with blue eyes, that that man is a used-car salesman. God arranges that all the blue-eyed men in *S*'s vicinity are used-car salesmen, and whenever *S* meets a blue-eyed man, he forms his belief accordingly. (To avoid confusing the issue, suppose that he never gets independent evidence of these men being used-car salesmen.) God forms *S*'s mental constitution and arranges *S*'s environment in this way in order to bring it about that *S* forms a true belief about the used-car salesman status of the particular blue-eyed men that he meets. *S*'s belief would be warranted in Plantinga's view, and would actually constitute knowledge, because it is true, results from the operation of a design plan aimed at true belief that is operating in the environment for which it is designed,

---

[6] Alvin Plantinga, *Warranted Christian Belief*, 2000, p. xi.

and its design plan is a good design plan for the environment in which it is designed, indeed a perfect one since it can never produce false belief. But obviously *S*'s belief would not in fact be knowledge, and would not even be reasonable.

The failure of Plantinga's account shows that McDowell's contention that if you know something you cannot be wrong about it does not suffice as a description of knowledge, although it is quite true. In the above example *S* cannot be wrong about his belief, because God has arranged things so that he cannot be wrong. But *S* does not possess knowledge. The reason for this is that his inability to be wrong in his belief does not result from his own powers. Although *S* cannot go wrong, his disposition to form the belief that someone is a used-car salesman is not a power to form true beliefs. The disposition to believe that blue-eyed men are used-car salesmen would be the same disposition, even if the beliefs that resulted from it were not true. *S*'s success in arriving at true beliefs would have had to have resulted from the exercise of his own cognitive powers in order for it to be knowledge; and since the powers in question would have to be ones that could not go wrong, they would, if they provided knowledge, be intellectual virtues.

The third line of argument is that the alternative to the intellectual virtue position does not work. If the beliefs that are presented as candidates for knowledge are not produced by intellectual virtues, their status as knowledge must rest upon capacities that give truth at best most of the time (capacities that give truth none or almost none of the time are obviously not in the running as knowledge-producers). Call a conception of knowledge of this sort a probabilistic view of knowledge (the term is meant only as a handy tag, not as an accurate summary of what the view states). If this is how our knowledge arises, we must assign some weighting to the beliefs we accept as known if we are to be rational. As Locke says, we must proportion our belief to the evidence. The nature of the proportioning that is necessary is controversial. Some philosophers will speak of the degree of assent we give to beliefs, while others will refuse to accept that assent is a matter of degree and talk instead about assigning a probability to a proposition; for convenience's sake I will speak of the degree of assent that is given to a proposition, without meaning to thereby embrace a position on the nature of the weighting that propositions must have on the probabilistic view. The probabilistic view of knowledge demands that beliefs have such a weighting, because from the point of view of theoretical rationality the degree of assent afforded to a belief ought not to be stronger (or weaker) than the grounds that provide the rational motivation for the belief, and the probabilistic view implies that such grounds will come in varying degrees.

The problem for the probabilistic view of knowledge is that it is impossible to determine the right degree of assent. In arguing for this impossibility, I will assume the soundness of the arguments made by William Alston,[7] which establish that we have no way of knowing that our senses are reliable at all. I will not reproduce the details of his arguments, but their broad outline is that there are no *a priori* grounds

---

[7] In William Alston, *The Reliability of Sense Perception*, 1993.

for supposing that our senses are reliable, and that arguments for their reliability that are based on *a posteriori* evidence would be vitiated by epistemic circularity – they would, in attempting to establish the trustworthiness of a certain sort of reason for believing, necessarily assume its trustworthiness. I will take it that the case Alston makes is a successful one; his argument seems conclusive, and I have found no good rebuttals of it. The construction of a parallel argument for memory is straightforward. There are no *a priori* reasons for thinking that our memory is reliable, and any *a posteriori* evidence for its reliability is going to have to make use of beliefs that rest at least partially on what we remember. When it comes to our faculties of logical inference or intuition, a somewhat different approach is needed. It might be said that the concepts of logical inference and intuition imply that they infallibly produce or preserve truth. The question at issue would be whether our actual reasoning processes are instances of logical inference or intuition, or not. Since we would rely on these processes in any investigation of this question, such an investigation cannot avoid epistemic circularity.

The implication of these arguments for the degrees of assent due to our basic belief-forming processes is clear; if we cannot know that they are reliable at all, we cannot know the degree of reliability that any of them possess, and we cannot know the degree of assent that ought to be given to them. Since the probabilistic view of knowledge requires that we know the degree of assent that is due to the propositions we know, it cannot work.

It should be pointed out that the options that have been proposed as attempts to provide a positive answer to the simple question of whether our basic cognitive faculties are reliable or not, do not work when it comes to the more complex question of the degree of reliability that should be attributed to these faculties, and hence the degree of assent that should be awarded to the beliefs produced by them. One such option is Alston's defence of the rationality of taking these faculties to be reliable, that bases itself on the practical rationality of using these faculties;[8] another is George Santayana's defence of a simple 'animal faith' in their deliverances.[9] These options are not available, because when it comes to degrees of assent there is not a single stance that can be presented as justified by practical rationality or acceptable through animal faith. These two defences only conclude that our basic cognitive capacities are reliable; they do not tell us *how* reliable they are. If it is granted that our basic cognitive capacities are reliable, it will still be the case that there are a myriad different ways in which we can assign degrees of reliability to their operations, and hence degrees of assent to the beliefs produced by them; and practical reason or animal faith do not provide criteria for choosing between them.

In fact neither Alston's nor Santayana's defences succeed even as responses to the simple question of reliability. Both of them apply equally to a situation where we do in fact possess reliable belief-forming processes, or intellectual virtues, and to a situation where we do not (e.g. where we are very stupid, or deceived by an evil demon). As defences of the rationality or propriety of our beliefs, they work

[8] See Alston, 1993, ch. 5.
[9] See George Santayana, *Skepticism and Animal Faith*, 1923.

just as well in the latter type of case as the former. But this cannot be right. Although our beliefs are (arguably) rational in the former situation, they certainly are not in the latter; they are mistakes or delusions. Since these defences do not distinguish between the two situations, they cannot be true.

The intellectual virtue account does not demand that we assign degrees of assent to beliefs that are produced by intellectual virtues, and it does not require us to know that beliefs which are known are produced by intellectual virtues, in order for these beliefs to count as knowledge. It is thus not open to the objection raised against probabilistic views of knowledge in the third line of argument given above. But it does offer the possibility of knowing that we know, at least some of the time, through checking the output of one belief-forming process with another. This process must of course ultimately rest upon the output of a process or processes that are not checked, but if it is the case that we have some intellectual virtues to start with, it enables us to sometimes distinguish between real and apparent knowledge.

The intellectual virtue account also suggests the possibility of a reply to sceptical challenges about sense experience, memory and other basic sources of belief, because it enables us to reasonably believe that we have knowledge from these sources. Whether or not our beliefs actually are produced by intellectual virtues, it is undoubtedly true that it *seems* that the beliefs we count as knowledge are produced by seeing, remembering, etc.; that is, by processes that are intellectual virtues. If we accept that these processes are intellectual virtues, and that beliefs constitute knowledge when they are produced by the operation of intellectual virtues, it will then be true that it seems that we have knowledge in many cases. It is a principle of reasonable belief (although not of knowledge) that if something seems to be so, in the absence of evidence to the contrary it is reasonable to take it to be so. (The distinction between knowledge and reasonable belief will be explicated below.) 'It seems to me that p' here is not to be understood as meaning 'I am inclined to believe that p', but rather as 'it experientially appears to me that p'. We can thus have a reasonable belief that we have knowledge. Of course this reasonable belief can be mistaken – that is the difference between reasonable belief and knowledge; but it is none the less reasonable. This kind of appeal to reasonable belief cannot be used to salvage the evidential conception of knowledge. Although it can seem to me that I see something, it cannot seem to me that the process that produced a belief of mine has a certain degree of reliability, or deserves a certain degree of assent.[10]

---

[10] Would this mean that it would be reasonable to believe that e.g. we were perfectly deceived in our sense experiences, since a perfect deception would seem exactly the same to us as would actual possession of knowledge from the senses? We must distinguish between seeming like, and seeming exactly the same as. A perfect deception would seem exactly the same as the real experience it deceptively simulates, but it would not seem like a deception; it would seem like the real experience. Two things can seem exactly the same, without both of them seeming like what they actually are. That is the point of describing a deception as deceptive; it does not seem like what it actually is.

An advantage of the intellectual virtue account of knowledge is that it does not fall victim to Gettier cases, which all describe situations that it would not classify as instances of knowledge. An example would be the Mr. Nogot case; Mr. Nogot, who works in my office, tells me that he owns a Ford, and shows me legal documents to prove his ownership. He has always been trustworthy in the past, and on the basis of his assertion I come to believe that someone in the office owns a Ford. This belief is true, because unbeknownst to myself someone else in the office besides Nogot owns a Ford. But Nogot, in fact, is lying and has forged the documents. Such a case is meant to furnish a counterexample to analyses of knowledge as justified true belief, because the belief in question is justified and is true, but is not knowledge. It does not, however, furnish a counterexample to the intellectual virtue account of knowledge. This account would not classify this case as an instance of knowledge; my believing Mr. Nogot is not believing someone who is truthfully speaking from knowledge (something that is more fully discussed in the next chapter), and hence is not the result of the exercise of an intellectual virtue. (The same point can be made about the alternative case where Mr. Nogot thinks he is telling the truth, but his Ford was destroyed by a meteorite five minutes before he makes the claim.) It is not possible to go through all the many kinds of Gettier cases that have been proposed, and I will simply maintain that in all of the cases the belief that is being discussed is not an instance of knowledge, because it is not produced by an intellectual virtue; the reasoning needed to establish this is straightforward in every such case. The immunity of the intellectual virtue account to Gettier counterexamples is linked to a feature that was pointed out in our discussion of Aquinas, which is that such a conception of knowledge does not admit the possibility of a justification that can exist in both knowledge and false belief.

Objections to the intellectual virtue conception

This rejection of an almost universally accepted view of knowledge will give rise to objections, which must be dealt with.

One objection is that the intellectual virtue conception is based upon an excessively plain diet of examples. The forms of knowledge acquisition discussed above have been simple acts of observation, memory or inference. But much of our knowledge is not produced by simple acts of these sorts. Instead, it is inferred from masses of different pieces of evidence. This is especially true of the sciences, where this kind of inference is the norm. But such inference is not always or even usually deductive. It frequently yields no more than (often very high) probability. The knowledge it gives rise to is therefore not produced by the exercise of intellectual virtues.

The answer to this objection will accept that knowledge can result from a mass of different observations. The intellectual virtue view does not deny this; it only rejects the possibility of such knowledge arising from inductive inference from evidence. It holds that if conclusions that are based on reasoning from a mass of evidence constitute knowledge, they are not arrived at through inductive inference; and if they are arrived at through inductive inference, they are not knowledge.

Some knowledge that arises from a mass of different observations is not the result of inference at all. Consider coming to know the shape of a bit of landscape that cannot be observed from any one place, but that can be observed by walking around it all day. This process need not involve any inference. And the inference that does occur when knowledge is obtained from a mass of observations need not consist in concluding that the proposition known is made probable by the evidence for it. Take the case of coming to know a person's character traits. A complicated and not immediately apparent character trait, like being neurotic or duplicitous or trustworthy, can only be known through a good deal of observation of the person in question under a variety of circumstances. Such observation can be supplemented by inference, but the inference need not be probabilistic (it might e.g. consist in drawing a conclusion from one's observations that eliminates a possible explanation for someone's behaviour).

One might object that a very large proportion of scientific conclusions really are the result of probabilistic reasoning, which is often explicitly formalized to some extent through statistics. But a large proportion of scientific conclusions do not constitute knowledge, something most scientists will readily admit. The prestige and useful results of science give scientific methods and conclusions a high profile in the study of reasoning and rational belief, which can lead us to forget that its procedures and findings are not typical of human knowledge acquisition. The work of scientists is to investigate what is unknown and difficult to discover. It lies by its very nature at the farthest limits of human capacities to know about the physical world. As such, it will have to proceed most of the time by making complicated inferences from a mass of diverse evidence; and a large part of the hypotheses that scientists consider and investigate will in the nature of the case be things that are not known, because scientists are interested in what they are unsure of, not what they are sure of. That is why a large proportion of scientific conclusions do not constitute knowledge. In fact, once something becomes known through scientific investigation, scientists often lose interest in it. An example would be the question of whether the earth is at the centre of a number of rotating spheres, or is moving around the sun through empty space. This was a subject of debate between astronomers when they did not know which of the answers was right, but only had probable reasons in favour of one theory or another. Now that they can be said to know that the earth is moving through empty space, they do not concern themselves with the truth of the statement that the earth is moving around the sun through empty space. It will still be used in their theories, but it will not be something that they investigate or test against the data.[11] Another example would

---

[11] This will likely provoke the objection that physicists thought they knew Newtonian physics to be true, and did not make its basic assertions a subject for investigation for a long time, but turned out to be wrong. I would simply reply that science deals with things difficult to know because remote from the senses, and this means that scientists will often think that they know things when they do not, and that that is what happened in the case of

be the existence of atoms. At one time, one could speak literally of the 'atomic theory'; the existence of atoms was treated as a hypothesis that was judged by how well it explained the data. Now, however, this is no longer the case. Scientists investigate the properties of atoms, but they do not investigate whether or not they exist.

Two points need to be added to this defence of the contention that inductive reasoning does not give us knowledge of its conclusions. The first is that the fact that conclusions reached through inductive reasoning are not known does not mean that inductive reasoning does not give us knowledge. It does; it gives us knowledge of probabilities. Although Prob(p) cannot give us knowledge that p, we can know that Prob(p). Much of the knowledge that science gives us is of this sort. Probability is thus not excluded from the sphere of knowledge.[12]

The second point to be added is that as well as knowledge of probabilities, there is something like the *opinio* (and *suspicio*) that Aquinas talks about. There is such a thing as reasonable belief in a proposition, that is not knowledge. Such belief in a proposition can arise from the balance of probability being in its favour, or it can arise from more fundamental principles of inductive inference that are prior to any assessments of probability. Examples of such principles are the principle that everything else being equal a simpler explanation is more likely to be true than a complex one, and the principle, mentioned above, that if something appears to us to be the case then in the absence of contrary evidence it probably is the case. (Acceptance of this principle should not be understood as acceptance of the view that our judgements about what is the case are normally based on judgements about what seems to us to be the case. I do not think that this is true. But there are non-typical occasions upon which we do base our judgements about what is the case upon what seems to us to be the case, and in these situations we make use of this

---

Newtonian physics. The ease of their being mistaken in thinking that they possess knowledge does not mean that they cannot possess it.

[12] As we have seen, this is not how Aquinas would have described the relation between probability and knowledge. For him, the probable belonged to one sphere, the sphere of opinion, and knowledge belonged to another sphere, and the two did not overlap; hence he could not admit such a thing as knowledge of probabilities. Ian Hacking, in *The emergence of probability*, 1975, has advanced the claim that the concept of inductive evidence as we now know it emerged in the seventeenth century. 'Concepts of testimony and authority were not lacking: they were all too omnipresent as the basis for the old medieval kind of probability that was an attribute of opinion. Testimony is support by witnesses, and authority is conferred by ancient learning. *People* provide the evidence of testimony and authority. What was lacking was the evidence provided by *things*' (Hacking, 1975, p. 32). Hacking's contention that the notion of evidence provided by things did not exist prior to the seventeenth century has been questioned. I will venture, as a totally unsupported conjecture, the suggestion that what was lacking in the middle ages and before was the idea of a knowledge of probabilities. This absence would explain the lack pointed out by Hacking of any mathematics of randomness or probability prior to the seventeenth century. Mathematics was universally held to belong to the sphere of knowledge both before and after the seventeenth century. If probability and knowledge are mutually exclusive, the idea of a mathematics of probability is a contradiction.

principle.) Reasonable belief is important and indeed necessary in life, but it is not knowledge. (Knowledge of probabilities can serve as a foundation for reasonable belief, but even when this happens they are not the same; it is not only that the former is knowledge and the latter is not, but also that the proposition assented to is different – for the former it is Prob(p), for the latter it is p.) We can agree with the Latitudinarians against Aquinas that such reasonable belief is capable of producing moral certainty, and of excluding doubt or fear of being mistaken. We can note however that reasonable belief that is strong enough for moral certainty is still not the same as knowledge. For if we find out that some proposition that we believed ourselves to know is in fact false, we will say that we did not know it after all. However, if we find out that some proposition turns out to be false that we took ourselves to have a reasonable belief in, a reasonable belief that was strong enough for moral certainty, we need not conclude that our belief in it was not reasonable, or that the degree of our reasonable belief was too strong.

Having said these things, the complete answer to the objection that there is such a thing as probable knowledge will be that the webs of rational motivations for our beliefs will belong to one of the three kinds that are described above – those that give knowledge and do not rest on inductive inference, those that give knowledge of probabilities, and those that give reasonable belief – and that none of these kinds give knowledge of some proposition p that is based on inductive evidence that makes p probable.

This classification enables us to respond to a doubt that might arise in relation to the argument about degrees of assent to beliefs that is used above, which is that we *do* as a matter of fact rank our beliefs differently, with a higher rank being given to some than to others, and that the absence of such a ranking would make us irrational. The response is that rationality does require us to rank our beliefs according to different orderings, but that none of these rankings distinguish between degrees of assent that ought to be given to beliefs that lie in the sphere of knowledge. With knowledge of probabilities, the propositions whose probabilities are known are (or should be) ranked according to their probability, and our reasonable assenting to propositions whose exact probability is not known will also be ordered according to some (perhaps very rough) ranking of probability. Within the sphere of knowledge, there will be a principle of evaluation of beliefs that will not rank beliefs according to probability or degree of assent. If two beliefs contradict one another, it will follow that they cannot both be true, and thus cannot both be known. If it seems to us that we have come to know something that contradicts a belief that we previously took to be knowledge, we will therefore be required to choose between them, and this choice will be guided by principles that tell us which ought to be taken to be real rather than apparent knowledge. Such principles will not rank beliefs according to probability or degrees of assent, because they will be about when beliefs should be taken to be false, and thus about when beliefs should be rejected rather than given a particular degree of assent.

One could object that the different parts of our knowledge are not really on the same footing. Some beliefs that we know, like 2+2=4, are known more securely than others, like the existence of Australia (for people who have never been there).

But the difference in security, in these cases, does not consist in one of these beliefs being more likely to be mistaken than the other. Rather, it lies in our possession of other beliefs, beliefs about the possibility or conceivability of grounds that could convince us that something we take to be knowledge really is not. We cannot conceive of there being evidence that would convince us that we do not know that 2+2=4, but we can conceive of this in the case of a belief that there is such a place as Australia.

There is a further objection to the intellectual virtue account of knowledge that is related to the probable knowledge objection, or is perhaps a version of it. It is that it is unreasonable to say that knowledge must be the result of the operation of intellectual virtues, because our knowledge-gathering capacities are obviously not infallible. The factiveness of expressions that describe acts of seeing, remembering, etc., do not provide a reason for thinking that these acts are the activities of infallible capacities, because such factive statements are not statements about the exercise of particular kinds of capacities. Rather, they are success-statements, statements about the successful exercise of capacities. 'Seeing' is like 'winning'. It means that a cognitive activity has been exercised successfully, just as 'winning' means that a competitive activity has been exercised successfully. Compare the expressions 'winning' and 'competing'. If you say 'I won', that means you competed successfully. But the fact that 'I won' means that you competed successfully does not imply that if you did not win you were not competing, but rather engaging in some different sort of activity. In both winning and losing you are engaged in the same activity, that of competing. The difference between the two is that in one case, circumstances enable your activity to reach its goal, and in the other case they do not. It need not lie in anything that *you* do. The same is true of the exercise of our cognitive capacities. When they succeed, and yield us knowledge, they are not necessarily doing anything different from when they do not yield us knowledge.

Why might we suppose that this account of our cognitive capacities, rather than the intellectual virtue account, is the right one? One reason that I think underlies the view that our knowledge-gathering capacities are not infallible is the belief that exactly the same capacities can be seen to be operating in the cases of knowledge and of false belief. An example would be seeing a real barn, and seeing a clever papier-mache copy of a barn that is visually indistinguishable from the real barn to the observer. The same capacity, seeing, here gives rise to both true and false belief; in the first case it gives knowledge of what is seen, but in the second case it clearly does not.

What is to be made of this contention? We must ask what is meant by saying that the same capacities can be seen to operate in the production of both knowledge and false belief. They are not literally seen to operate with the eyes, and if 'seen to operate' is understood to mean 'known to operate', the assertion simply begs the question. What can be admitted to be true is that we sometimes cannot observe any difference between the exercise of capacities that operate in the production of knowledge, and the exercise of capacities that operate in the production of false belief. But from the fact that in a given case we cannot observe any such difference, we cannot conclude that the same capacities actually are operating. This conclusion would only follow if we were to hold that every aspect of the exercise of our conceptual capacities must be open to introspection. But we know that this is not true. Leaving aside the many physiological features of sense perception about which we know nothing, there are aspects of our purely mental activity about which we need not be aware. We can first infer a conclusion from some premises, and only after making the inference consciously reconstruct the steps by which we derived the conclusion; and even this may not always be possible. We therefore cannot conclude that because we sometimes do not observe any difference in the exercise of capacities that produce knowledge and those that produce false belief, it is really true that the same capacities are operating. This appearance may explain why people think that knowledge-producing capacities are fallible, but it does not support their belief.

This disagreement over whether the same capacities operate in the production of knowledge and in the production of false belief is closely linked to debates in the philosophy of perception. Philosophers have raised the question of whether we are doing the same thing in both veridical and illusory sense perception. Examples like that of the real and fake barns given above have been used to argue that we are. The conclusion that we are doing the same thing in both veridical and illusory sense perception has in turn led to the conclusion that both veridical and illusory experiences must have the same kind of object. Since the object of an illusory experience cannot be an object in the world, mental entities – sense-data – have been postulated as the objects of both veridical and illusory perception.

This view has in turn led to rebellion on the part of philosophers who did not think that perception involved sense data, and did not think that sense data were legitimate entities. The point of telling this familiar story is that philosophers have been led by their rebellion against sense-data to deny the starting point from which sense-data theorists began, and reject the contention that we are doing the same thing in both veridical and illusory sense perception. McDowell follows this path:

> … On any question about the world independent of oneself to which one can ascertain the answer by, say, looking, the way things look can be deceptive; it can look to one exactly as if things were a certain way when they are not…It follows that any capacity to tell by looking how things are in the world independent of oneself can at best be fallible. According to the tempting argument, something else follows as well: the argument is that since there can be deceptive cases experientially indistinguishable from non-deceptive cases, one's experiential intake – what one embraces within the scope of one's consciousness – must be the same in both kinds of case. In a deceptive case, one's experiential intake must *ex hypothesi* fall short of the fact itself, in the sense of being consistent with there being no such fact. So that must be true, according to the argument, in a non-deceptive case too …
>
> This line of thought is an application of the Argument from Illusion. I want now to describe and comment on a way of resisting it.
>
> We might formulate the temptation that is to be resisted as follows. Let the fallible capacity in question be a capacity to tell by experience whether such-and-such is the case. In a deceptive case, what is embraced within the scope of experience is an appearance that such-and-such is the case, falling short of the fact: a *mere* appearance. So what is experienced in a non-deceptive case is a mere appearance too …

But suppose we say – not at all unnaturally – that an appearance that such-and-such is the case can be *either* a mere appearance *or* the fact that such-and-such is the case making itself manifest to someone. As before, the object of experience in the deceptive cases is a mere appearance. But we are not to accept that in the non-deceptive cases too the object of experience is a mere appearance ... On the contrary, we are to insist that the appearance that is presented to one in these cases is a matter of the fact itself being disclosed to the experiencer.[13]

McDowell's disjunctive account of experience is important for the question of the nature of the capacities that give us knowledge. It means that the capacities exercised in veridical and illusory perception need not be said to be the same. If it was maintained that the same capacity was exercised in both cases, the capacity would then be a disjunctive one – the capacity to *either* experience a mere appearance *or* to experience an actual state of affairs – and it is absurd to say that such a capacity is a single real capacity, instead of a logical construct from two different capacities. But if we then conclude that different capacities are being exercised in veridical perception and in illusion, we end up postulating a capacity for veridical perception; and such a capacity would be an intellectual virtue.

This link between the intellectual virtue conception and the philosophy of perception results from a more fundamental connection between intellectual virtue and the nature of our cognitive capacities. As we have seen, if the intellectual virtue conception is rejected, the operations of our cognitive capacities must be thought of as analogous to competing, with operations of a given capacity that produce knowledge being compared to winning, and operations of the same capacity that produce false belief being compared to losing. What enables us to see both winning and losing as forms of the same activity is that we do not take the differences in external reality that distinguish winning from losing, such as crossing a line ahead of rather than behind someone else, to make a difference to the activity that the competitor is engaged in. If we are to reject the intellectual virtue conception of knowledge, we need to postulate a similar kind of independence of reality for our cognitive capacities. The difference between a belief's being false and its being known depends on (although it does not consist in) whether or not reality is as the belief portrays it, so if the same cognitive capacity can give rise to both knowledge and false belief, the differences in reality that distinguish those two states of affairs cannot affect the nature of the capacity that is being exercised in them. Philosophers who hold that the same cognitive capacities give rise to both knowledge and false belief have thus been led to separate these capacities from the realities that the capacities are designed to inform us about, and the way in which they have done this arises from the fact that our senses, and our other cognitive capacities, take objects. If the same cognitive capacities can produce both knowledge and false belief, then either the same cognitive capacities can take essentially different kinds of objects, one kind in the

---

[13] John McDowell 'Criteria, Defeasibility and Knowledge', in *Perceptual Knowledge*, 1988, pp. 210–11. For another disjunctive account of perception, see Paul Snowdon, 'Perception, Vision and Causation', in *Perceptual Knowledge*, 1988.

case of knowledge and another in the case of false belief, or the objects for the exercise of our cognitive capacities must be the same in both knowledge and false belief. The first of these alternatives is a non-starter, and accordingly has not been much espoused by philosophers. The nature of a cognitive capacity may not be exhausted by the kind of objects it takes, but it cannot be independent of the kind of object it takes either; there is for example no sense in talking about seeing a sound. Instead, philosophers have tended to opt for the second option, asserting that our cognitive capacities have the same kinds of objects in both knowledge and false belief, and they have secured the required independence from external reality by moving these objects inside the mind, and describing them as mental realities that are distinct from what the knowledge or the false belief in question is actually about. When applied to sense perception, this move has involved the postulation of sense-data. With regard to memory, a form of this approach is taken by David Hume, who describes memory as being an idea in the same sense that a mental image is an idea, and distinguishes memory from imagination by the allegedly superior force and vivacity of the ideas of memory when compared to the ideas of imagination. This permits Hume to assert that false memories can have the same sort of object as true ones; 'an idea of the imagination may acquire such a force and vivacity, as to pass for an idea of the memory, and counterfeit its effects on the belief and judgment.'[14]

The difficulties with this kind of approach are familiar ones. A first objection is that our cognitive capacities, when delivering knowledge, take realities as their objects, rather than the sort of objects that it postulates. A second objection is that these postulated objects, such as sense-data, do not in fact exist (even in the cases where our cognitive capacities do not deliver knowledge). A third objection is that the postulation of such objects cuts off our cognitive capacities from reality in a way that makes it impossible to suppose that they achieve their goal of providing knowledge. This third objection can take various forms. One form is the old objection that there does not seem to be any reason for us to think that the world should be as our sense-data are supposed to represent it, since according to the sense-data account of perception we can never experience the world independently of these sense-data. Another, more fundamental form is that our knowledge cannot actually be *about* external realities if it does not take these realities themselves as its object. This I take to be part of what McDowell has in mind when he talks about there being no gap between thought and the world, and about the external world itself as entering into the space of reasons. Space does not permit a discussion of the strength of these objections. I will simply assert that a large number of philosophers have found them convincing, that I agree with these philosophers, and that I will assume that the objections are decisive ones. If this assumption is granted, it furnishes support for the intellectual virtue conception, for it means that there is no workable way of maintaining that the same capacities are exercised in the production of both knowledge and false belief.

---

[14] David Hume, *A Treatise of Human Nature*, 1911, vol. 1, pp. 88–9.

One might raise the following objection to this conclusion. It is that this line of argument concentrates on sense experience, where the difficulties with the idea of sense data make it plausible. Our cognitive capacities are however not simply equivalent to our perceptual capacities. We say that knowledge generally, as well as sense experience, is produced by our cognitive capacities. However, knowledge, or at least one kind of knowledge, takes propositions as its object. The reasoning applied above to sense experience works awkwardly when applied to knowledge of this sort. When knowledge of some reality is propositional knowledge, then the reality known and the proposition known ought not to be described as identical. After all we describe propositions as being *about* reality; and this description supposes that propositions and the realities they are about are not the same things. But this means that we have an object of knowledge, a proposition, that is not the reality that is known.

It is impossible to do more than sketch a reply to this objection. What is clear is that such a reply must deny that propositions should be considered as entities that occupy an intermediary place between our minds and reality. This denial will have to appeal to some form of content externalism, that sees the content of propositions as being determined by the realities they are about. Since propositions just are their content, this kind of externalism means that there is some sense in which propositions are identical with the realities they are about, and thus that there is no difficulty in taking both propositions and realities to be the immediate objects of knowledge. I offer arguments for content externalism in Appendix I. However, these arguments cannot do full justice to this substantial topic, and, as with the arguments against sense data and in favour of direct realism in perception, I must point the reader towards the case that other philosophers have made for content externalism, and express my confidence in its soundness.

This discussion suggests avenues for further philosophical exploration. One avenue would be to investigate the mutual interdependence of the intellectual virtue conception of knowledge, direct realism in perception, and content externalism. The discussion above would seem to indicate that the intellectual virtue conception of knowledge and direct realism mutually imply one another, and that these in turn imply content externalism. Another avenue would be to argue that if content is determined by reality, then it is reality that must furnish content, and that since we get to reality through the exercise of intellectual virtues, all our grasp of content must therefore originate in knowledge. However, we cannot go down these avenues here, as they are not part of our topic.

I owe a lot to McDowell in the account of intellectual virtue that has been developed here. It might however be said that I am departing radically from his views, because he explicitly states that our capacities to tell by experience how the world is are fallible. But it is not actually clear whether or not this is so, because he does not spell out the way in which these capacities are supposed to be fallible. The intellectual virtue account will admit that our intellectual virtues can be fallible, in the sense that they can fail to operate. Take the power to recognize a statement as tautologous. (The recognition in question will be a recognition that operates simply by grasping the statement, rather than by working out a proof of its tautologousness.) This power can obviously operate when the statements in question are fairly simple, but fail to operate when they become more complex. It is no less of an intellectual virtue for such failure, because whenever it does operate it produces a true belief. The same is true of perception. We might be able to see things when they are close to us, but be unable because of shortsightedness to see them when they are far away. The failures of these capacities do not remove their status as intellectual virtues, because they do not consist in these capacities providing us with mistaken beliefs.

A last objection that might be made against the intellectual virtue account is that it falls victim to the difficulties of reliabilism. It could be considered a form of reliabilism, broadly construed, since intellectual virtues are perfectly reliable. Alvin Plantinga gives a version of a standard objection, aimed at a reliabilist account of Alvin Goldman's:

> ... There is a rare but specific sort of brain lesion (we may suppose) that is always associated with a number of cognitive processes of the relevant degree of specificity, most of which cause its victim to hold absurdly false beliefs. One of the associated processes, however, causes the victim to believe that he has a brain lesion. Suppose, then, that S suffers from this disorder and accordingly believes that he suffers from a brain lesion. Add that he has no evidence at all for this belief: no symptoms of which he is aware, no testimony of which he is aware, no testimony on the part of physicians or other expert witnesses, nothing. (Add, if you like, that he has much evidence against it; but then add also that the malfunction induced by the lesion makes it impossible for him to take appropriate account of this evidence.) Then the relevant type [of cognitive process] (while it may be hard to specify in detail) will certainly be highly reliable; but the resulting belief – that he has a brain lesion – will have little by way of warrant for S.[15]

Examples of this sort do not pose a problem for the intellectual virtue account, because possession of such a brain lesion (and of any belief-forming process that results from it) is not possession of a capacity to arrive at the truth.

This response may however meet what can be called the strange source objection. Suppose the brain lesion in Plantinga's example always gave rise to true beliefs, instead of mainly false ones? Or suppose, to avoid the objection that it is not possible for a brain lesion to be a source of true beliefs, that someone found that whenever they made a guess about what the weather would be like the next day, their guesses turned out to be true? Would not these cases be intellectual virtues, according to the definition given here? And yet one is reluctant to say that they provide knowledge.

I think that this objection is met by a standard reliabilist reply, which is that since we do not as a matter of fact have brain lesions or guessing capacities that reliably provide us with true beliefs, our intuitions about whether or not they would give us knowledge cannot be trusted. Cases like this kind of brain lesion go too far beyond the range in which we normally apply the concept of knowledge, and thus our application of this concept to them is necessarily uncertain. But this reply might be modified by some observations about how we actually treat purported

---

[15] Alvin Plantinga, *Warrant: The Current Debate*, 1993, p. 199.

instances of strange sources of knowledge. When people claim to have obtained knowledge through the exercise of psychic powers of some kind, we do not usually react by attempting a conceptual analysis of whether such powers could confer knowledge, but by investigating whether the beliefs that are supposedly produced by them are true or not (and are not known by other means). The assumption behind such investigation seems to be that if these supposed powers really did produce true beliefs, we would accept them as sources of knowledge.

The case that can be made for an intellectual virtue account of knowledge is a strong one, and I shall take it to be conclusive. One might ask whether this account is a form of the horror of 'classical foundationalism'. This view is defined by Plantinga as follows:

> (CF) A belief is acceptable for a person if (and only if) it is either properly basic (i.e., self-evident, incorrigible, or evident to the senses for that person), or believed on the evidential basis of propositions that are acceptable and that support it deductively, inductively, or abductively.[16]

Such foundationalism has been much blown upon by philosophers of religion who see it as the culprit in philosophical justifications of unbelief, their criticism being that it first sets up an excessively high standard for reasonable belief and then wrongly condemns religious faith for not satisfying this standard. It will be argued that Christian faith has a degree of certainty that would in fact satisfy the demands of classical foundationalism, if the certainty requested by such foundationalism is understood as being the result of production by an intellectual virtue, so this criticism will not be found acceptable. But in any case the intellectual virtue account of knowledge need not conform to classical foundationalism. A classical foundationalist version of the intellectual virtue view would hold that all reasonable beliefs about what is probable would have to ultimately be based on beliefs that are known through the exercise of intellectual virtue. This position could certainly be argued for, but it is not part of the intellectual virtue account itself; this account could allow for there being basic beliefs that are simply probable. Whether or not there are such beliefs is not relevant to the questions being investigated here.

The intellectual virtues that have been postulated so far are memory, sense experience, belief in conceptual truths on the grounds of their being self-evident, and deductive inference. It should be pointed out that some of these intellectual virtues would not have been accepted as such by Aquinas. For him, empirical knowledge was a contradiction in terms[17], and he could not have admitted that

---

[16] Plantinga, 2000, p. 84.

[17] The idea of empirical knowledge was a contradiction in terms for Aquinas, in the sense that he did not believe that the deliverances of the senses could constitute knowledge. He did think that the senses could contribute to knowledge through enabling us to know the natures of physical things, and that we could have knowledge about things that can be seen, heard, and so on, in the sense of having *scientia* of universal statements about such things through grasping their natures; but he did not think that sense experience could in itself provide knowledge.

memory and sense experience were virtues that could give rise to knowledge. He also required that knowledge be of what is seen, i.e. that some fact about a belief that entails the belief's being true be itself open to intellectual introspection. It is because the things that are believed through faith are not seen by the intellect to be true that faith is not in his opinion an intellectual virtue. This requirement needs to be precisely stated: 'open to intellectual introspection' should not be understood as meaning 'immediately and unfailingly evident to intellectual introspection'. As Alasdair Macintyre points out,[18] Aquinas, following Aristotle, asserts that it is difficult to know that we know. He does not, like Descartes, understand the content of knowledge to be clear and distinct ideas, whose truth is supposed to be immediately and unfailingly evident to intellectual introspection. The intellectual introspection that he has in mind is something that itself requires the exercise of intellectual virtues that we do not automatically possess. It is nonetheless possible, on his view, to know that we have *intellectus* or *scientia* of some proposition. Both self-evidence and logical deduction are processes that are open to intellectual introspection.

The intellectual virtue account given here does not follow Aquinas on this issue; it accepts that the deliverances of the senses can be knowledge, and does not require that knowledge be of what is seen. Aquinas, if presented with this account, might ask why the operation of such a virtue should be considered sufficient, rather than merely necessary, for the production of knowledge. Why is it wrong to insist that the truth of propositions must be seen by the intellect, if these propositions are to be known? The answer I would give is that the empiricist philosophers who came after Aquinas (and the Hellenistic philosophers who came before him) were right in claiming that the deliverances of the senses can constitute knowledge. To be precise, I agree with those empiricist philosophers who claim that the deliverances of the senses can give us knowledge about the world, not just about how things seem to us to be. Aquinas denied that sense experience gives us knowledge of its objects.[19] But I hold that he is wrong about this. Of course we can think that we know things through sense experience, when we do not; just as we can think we understand a proposition to be self-evidently true when it is not. In neither case does the possibility of deception rule out knowledge where no deception exists. We all in fact accept that this is the case, and that what we see or hear can be as trustworthy and certain as our grasp of self-evident principles. Our acceptance that this is so is in possession, so to speak; the burden of proof is on someone who would deny that it is the case, and this burden has not been and cannot be satisfied. But the truth of the propositions we come to know through

---

[18] In Alasdair Macintyre, *First principles, final ends, and contemporary philosophical issues*, 1990.

[19] He would not necessarily deny that sense experience can give us practical certainty of what it is that we experience. But if we understand by knowledge the grasp of truth that the intellect seeks to obtain in its activity, and possession of which constitutes realization of the goal of the intellect, he would not consider sense perception to provide knowledge of what is experienced; knowledge would in his view only be attainable through *intellectus* and *scientia*.

sense experience cannot be discerned by intellectual introspection. Nor is there some introspectible feature that enables us to distinguish veridical from illusory perceptions. We cannot therefore demand that the possession of an intellectual awareness of such a dissimilarity be a condition for the possession of knowledge.

This is not to deny that Aquinas's requirement that knowledge be of what is seen applies to knowledge of logical or conceptual truths. It may be right to hold that this is true of knowledge in these particular spheres. It may be that the root of his mistake about knowledge does not lie in his imposing this requirement, but in restricting the sphere of knowledge to truths of this sort, for which this requirement is arguably a reasonable one. The basic difference between his account of knowledge and the one presented here could be seen as consisting not in the acceptance or rejection of his requirement, but in a difference over what lies within the sphere of the intellect. If sense experience gives us knowledge, the operations of the senses must be seen as being operations of the intellect as well, something that Aquinas would never accept. The intellect will thus be something much more embodied and connected with the physical world than Aquinas would have it to be.

In rejecting Aquinas's view that knowledge is of what is seen, and in offering the existence of knowledge acquired through the senses as a justification for this rejection, I am departing from Locke as well as from Aquinas. Locke was reluctant to grant that our senses could give us knowledge of the world in a strict sense:

> There is, indeed, another *Perception* of the Mind, employ'd about *the particular existence of finite Beings without us*; which going beyond bare probability, and yet not reaching perfectly to either of the foregoing degrees of certainty [sc. those of intuition and demonstration], passes under the name of Knowledge. There can be nothing more certain, than that the *Idea* we receive from an external Object is in our Minds; that is intuitive Knowledge. But whether there be any thing more than barely that Idea in our Minds, whether we can thence certainly infer the existence of any thing without us, which corresponds to that idea, is that, whereof some Men think there may be a question made, because Men may have such Ideas in their Minds, when no such thing exists ... I answer, that we certainly finding, that Pleasure or Pain follows upon the application of certain Objects to us, whose Existence we perceive, or dream that we perceive, by our Senses, this certainty is as great as our Happiness, or Misery, beyond which, we have no concernment to know, or to be. So that, I think, we may add to the two former sorts of Knowledge, this also, of the existence of particular external Objects, by that perception and consciousness we have of the actual entrance of *Ideas* from them ...[20]

Locke is irritatingly inconsistent here in trying to both deny and affirm that our senses give us knowledge of external objects. However, it is his denial that is consistent with his description of knowledge as arising from the mind's perceiving with certainty the agreement or disagreement of ideas. This description involves a stronger constraint that Aquinas's contention that knowledge is of what is seen, because it requires an immediate and completely obvious perception that the conditions of knowledge are fulfilled. This constraint cannot be satisfied by beliefs about external objects that are founded on sense experience, a fact that led later

---

[20] Locke, 1975, pp. 537–8.

empiricist philosophers to try and base our empirical knowledge upon what it seems to us that we are experiencing; something that they followed Locke in claiming to be immediately and unquestionably evident. Both Locke's constraint and Aquinas's constraint are what would now be called internalist requirements for the possession of knowledge. The intellectual virtue account given here, in rejecting them, is to that extent proposing an externalist conception of knowledge.

This externalism contradicts the Stoic view, cited by St. Augustine and mentioned in Chapter 2, that associated knowledge with perception of truth, and claimed that 'nothing could be perceived unless it was so manifestly true that it could be distinguished from what was not true through a dissimilarity in indications'.[21] This view has a deep appeal, an appeal that may have served to motivate conceptions of knowledge like those of Aquinas, Descartes and Locke. Given its strength and the support it has received, it is not satisfactory to simply dismiss this appeal as unreasonable. Rather, we should see it as resulting from a legitimate demand that has been extended beyond its proper sphere. This is the demand that insists that knowledge must not depend on chance to any degree at all. When this demand is legitimate, it is met by intellectual virtues, which, when they operate, necessarily do discriminate between truth and falsehood. It becomes excessive, however, when it is interpreted as requiring not only that knowledge in fact result from a discrimination between truth and falsehood, but that we be aware, whenever we have knowledge, that such discrimination has taken place. The desire is to rule out not just any actual possibility, but any epistemic possibility, of our being mistaken in cases where we have knowledge; it may arise, in some cases, from conflating these two sorts of possibility. This desire springs from legitimate aspirations – the fear of error, and the desire for truth. It would indeed be good if we could in fact always tell whether or not a belief was produced by the exercise of an intellectual virtue. If this were the case, we would be far better situated with respect to the truth, and far less endangered by error. But this desirable state is not in fact within the compass of human capacities, and to insist on its attainment as a condition for knowledge is unreasonable.

Since the intellectual virtue account that is proposed here has an externalist character, the description of it as 'Thomist' is a loose one. The next thesis that I will propose will make this Thomist label looser still. If one is inclined to accept the idea of intellectual virtues, then memory, sense experience and deductive inference would be fairly uncontroversial candidates for this status. Belief in testimony, however, would not be accepted as an intellectual virtue so easily. St. Thomas and Locke rejected the idea that it could provide knowledge. The rejection of Aquinas's and Locke's constraints on knowledge makes it possible to claim that testimony can provide knowledge. In the next chapter I will argue that such a claim is true, and consider the nature of knowledge acquired through testimony.

---

[21] St. Augustine, *Contra Academicos*, 1951, pp. 79–80. Cf. Cicero, *Acad.* 2. 59.

Chapter 6
Knowledge from Testimony

Having given an account of knowledge as the product of the exercise of intellectual virtue, we turn next to the question of the epistemic status of belief in testimony, which is the sort of belief that is involved in faith in a purported divine revelation. We believe on the basis of testimony when we believe a proposition p on the basis of someone's asserting that p. Attributions of belief that take a person as their object, as e.g. 'I believed Albert', refer to beliefs formed in this way; they mean 'I believed Albert when he said that p'. Although we have an intuitive notion of what it is to offer testimony and what it is to believe someone's assertion, these notions ought to be explicated and clarified for the purposes of our discussion. Testifying certainly involves making assertions about how things are, but it cannot simply be equated with the making of such assertions. A guess is an assertion, and so is an abusive remark like 'You are a lying bastard'. A piece of testimony is an assertion that:

a) presents itself as intended to communicate information, and
b) is vouched for by its speaker; that is, the speaker presents himself as knowing what he asserts.

The everyday notion of testimony may not be as sharply defined as this, but the conception described in this definition is central to this everyday notion, and is adequate for the purposes of our discussion.

Believing someone's testimony is not the same as believing that some proposition p is true because X asserts it, as Elizabeth Anscombe has pointed out: '… suppose I were convinced that B wished to deceive me, and would tell the opposite of what he believed, but that on the matter in hand B would be believing the opposite of the truth. By calculation on this, then, I believe what B says, on the strength of his saying it – but only in a comical sense can I be said to believe *him*.'[1] We believe a person when we think that they are saying what they believe to be true, and that they are speaking from knowledge. Believing X that p need not, it seems, involve coming to know p through believing X. We can say to someone 'I believe you', even when we already know that what they are asserting is true.

The principal question that needs to be settled in connection with the epistemic status of belief in testimony is whether such belief can be the result of the exercise

---

[1] G. E. M. Anscombe, 'What Is It to Believe Someone?', in *Rationality and Religious Belief*, 1979, p. 145.

of an intellectual virtue. There are two facts that together lead to an affirmative answer to this question. These are:

1. Beliefs that result from accepting someone's testimony can have the status of knowledge, not merely probable opinion.
2. Their status as knowledge is not usually derived from some source of knowledge other than testimony.

The truth of this first assertion can be seen through considering the extent and the certainty of our beliefs that rest upon testimony. As J. L. Mackie has remarked, 'the greater part of what each one of us knows comes to him by testimony'.[2] Few of our beliefs about the world have or could have had their origin in our own observation; all our knowledge of history, our knowledge of parts of the world that we have not seen, our knowledge of facts about ourselves that we are not in a position to verify (such as our date of birth or the identity of our parents), our knowledge of science, all originate in the assertions of others. Cooperative intellectual enterprises, like the sciences, rely on the practice of accepting others' assertions. Scientists are not in a position to verify by their own observation the evidence that they need to formulate and test their theories, and even their own collection of evidence requires them to rely on the assertions of others (e.g. in their use of weights and measures). John Hardwig[3] gives an illuminating example of the importance of testimony in scientific practice. He cites a physics experiment, too complex to be completed in the lifetime of one man, that incorporated the work of 99 different researchers. All of these researchers were experimentalists, who would not have been concerned with actually constructing theories that would have made use of their data; the theoreticians who made use of it were entirely dependent on these experimentalists, who did work that the theoreticians themselves would not have been capable of. A striking example of the importance of testimony is archaeology, where the evidence that is investigated is destroyed in the process of being collected, leaving behind only a record of its nature.

The members of the massive group of beliefs that are produced by testimony are not in any way epistemically inferior to other beliefs because of their source. As Scotus pointed out, a belief that arises from testimony can be as certain as any other belief. We therefore ought not to deny the status of knowledge to beliefs that arise from testimony.

It remains to be determined how beliefs produced by testimony attain the status of knowledge. The question of whether testimony is an autonomous source of knowledge was posed rather late in the history of Western philosophy. As we have seen in the discussion of Origen given above, it was a philosophical commonplace in the ancient world that we are dependent on testimony for many of our beliefs and actions, but the philosophers who held this view did not think of testimony as providing knowledge. David Hume seems to have been the first European

---

[2] J. L. Mackie, 'The Possibility of Innate Knowledge', *Proceedings of the Aristotelian Society*, 1970, p. 254.
[3] John Hardwig, 'Epistemic Dependence', *Journal of Philosophy*, 1985.

philosopher to both admit testimony as a source of knowledge and argue for its dependence on other sources. In his *Enquiry concerning Human Understanding*, he asserts:

> ... we may observe, that there is no species of reasoning more common, more useful, and even necessary to human life, than that which is derived from the testimony of men, and the reports of eye-witnesses and spectators. This species of reasoning, perhaps, one may deny to be founded on the relation of cause and effect. I shall not dispute about a word. It will be sufficient to observe that our assurance in any argument of this kind is derived from no other principle than our observation of the veracity of human testimony, and of the usual conformity of facts to the reports of witnesses.[4]

This is a reductionist view of testimony, that seeks to derive the warrant provided by testimony from another, more basic source of knowledge. It rejects the second assertion about testimony made above, which claims that testimony is an autonomous source of knowledge. Reductionist views of testimony were prevalent for a long time after Hume, but have recently been challenged by several philosophers.[5] If we accept such a view, it is not possible to think of belief in testimony as an intellectual virtue in the full sense. On a reductionist view a complete list of the intellectual virtues that provide humans with knowledge would not have to include belief in testimony. The autonomy of testimony must be defended if it is to be described as an intellectual virtue.

Hume does not specify how testimony is based on observation of the conformity of facts to the reports of witnesses, and there are various ways in which this supposed inference could be understood. One way would be:

1. For every person whose testimony I believe, I observe a conformity between the facts and the reports they make.

It should be noted that we cannot rely on the testimony of others as to such conformity in arguing for (1), since this would involve us in epistemic circularity; we would be trying to establish an epistemic principle through reasoning that made use of that very principle. This being said, it is clear that (1) is false. With most of the people we believe, we never have the chance to observe any conformity between the facts and the reports they make. A better attempt would be:

2. For most occasions when I check by observation an assertion that I have heard someone make, I find that the assertion turns out to be true.

From this, we could conclude inductively that most of the assertions that people make are true.

---

[4] David Hume, *An Enquiry concerning Human Understanding*, 3rd edn, 1975, p. 111.
[5] For examples of such challenges, see Peter Geach, 'Faith', in *The Virtues,* 1977; the papers in B. K. Matilal and A. Chakrabarti *Knowing from Words,* 1994; and the excellent work by Coady, 1992.

There are several objections that could be raised to this line of reasoning, but we need only consider one decisive objection, which is that it too is vitiated by epistemic circularity. In order to judge that what people say is true, you must attribute a meaning to their utterances. You can only understand utterances as having a particular meaning if you understand the language in which they are made, and you can only come to learn a language through trusting that most of the assertions made to you by the people who teach you the language are true. In learning a language, we can only figure out what states of affairs are claimed by statements to obtain by observing a correlation between statements and the states of affairs that they describe; by observing that e.g. whenever someone says 'this is a fork', a fork is present. But this correlation will only exist if most of these statements are true. We obviously cannot know that such a correlation exists, because we could only know that if we already understood the language, so in learning we just assume that this is the case. Assuming that the correlation exists means assuming that people tell the truth most of the time, which is what (2) is supposed to establish.

Our trust in testimony thus cannot be rationally founded on observation of conformity between facts and the reports of witnesses, and it does not seem that such observation is what actually motivates us to believe in people's testimony; we do not base our trust in people on reasoning of the kinds described above. We should ask if there are other forms of inference upon which our reliance on testimony could be based.

A possible argument for the reliability of testimony would be an argument from analogy. I know that when I make assertions, I am knowledgeable and sincere most of the time. By analogy from my own case, I reason that other people are too.

This argument does not suffer from epistemic circularity. However, the analogy it makes use of is weak. There is only one of me, and I differ in character and intellect from other people. Aside from the counterintuitive implication that habitual liars would be much less justified in believing others' assertions than honest people would be, such an argument would not make it more probable than not that most of the assertions other people make are true. If we admit that probable evidence can give knowledge, something that has been argued against in the previous chapter, it will still be the case that a very high level of probability will be needed to confer the status of knowledge on a belief. This analogical argument cannot confer such a high level of probability, and hence cannot make testimony a source of knowledge. But testimony can give us knowledge; so its justification cannot rest on this argument.

It is worth mentioning that this argument is a philosopher's argument. It is not reasoning that most people make in thinking about whether to believe testimony, so it cannot be the ground of the actual testimony-based knowledge that people have.

Elizabeth Fricker has offered a characterization of the way in which we derive knowledge from testimony, that presents it as involving inference from information that is at least partially independent of anyone's testimony. She sees trust in a person's testimony as resulting from an assessment of their psychological makeup:

A speaker's sincerity and competence, or lack of them, are aspects of her psychology – in the case of competence, in a suitably 'broad' sense, which takes in relevant parts of her environment. Assessment of them is part of, or a prediction from, a more extended psychological theory of her. So, in order to assess a speaker's trustworthiness, a hearer needs to piece together at least a fragment of such a theory of the speaker – an ascription of beliefs, desires, and other mental states and character traits to her. Thus it is commonsense psychology or person-theory, and the related epistemic norms for attribution of these states, that we must look to, to see how trustworthiness can be evaluated [6] ...

Indeed the primary task for the hearer is to construct enough of a theory of the speaker, and relevant portions of her past and present environment, to explain her utterance: to render it comprehensible why she made that assertion, on that occasion. Whether the speaker's assertion is to be trusted will, generally speaking, be fall-out from this theory which explains why she made it; and it is difficult to see how sincerity and competence could be evaluated other than through the construction of such an explanation. [7]

Fricker's account cannot be said to describe the vast majority of cases where we acquire knowledge from testimony. In most cases we do not have the evidence necessary to construct an explanation of the sort she requires, and we often do not have any evidence at all. Suppose I turn to the book *Teach Yourself Ancient Greek*, by Gavin Betts and Alan Henry, and read in it that the aorist first person singular of the verb λέγω is εἶπον. I know nothing at all about Gavin Betts or Alan Henry, and cannot even make a start on constructing the sort of theory of their behaviour that Fricker asks for. But that does not mean that I am not warranted in believing them, or that I do not get knowledge from their assertion. I do come to know the form of this irregular verb from their testimony. Fricker might claim that commonplace person theory tells us the authors of grammar books are unlikely to lie or be mistaken. But a theory that would give us this result would be very different from the kind of theory that Fricker envisages, since she requires us to construct a psychological picture, not just of kinds of witness, but of every individual who we choose to believe, and of their motivation on every individual occasion where they make an assertion that we believe. In fact we believe that certain kinds of witness are reliable simply because we are told that they are. Most of us know very few people well enough to be able to construct the kind of account of them that Fricker asks for. What is more, Fricker's view would rule out the possibility of acquiring knowledge through a chain of testimony, where the person we believe is himself telling us something that he learned from the testimony of another. In such a case, we will not be in contact with the person or persons whose original testimony gave rise to the testimony that we are hearing. We could try to determine whether the immediate speaker we hear is the kind of person who is good at determining whether people are telling the truth or not, but the cumulative uncertainty involved in these evaluations will drag the level of probability of the result of our theorizing

---

[6] Elizabeth Fricker, 'Against Gullibility', in *Knowing from Words*, 1994, p. 148.
[7] Fricker, 1994, p. 149.

very low; and such investigations will be impossible for chains of testimony that involve more than two links.

Attempts to base knowledge from testimony upon other sources of knowledge thus do not succeed. We might however consider a more modest goal, that of trying to show that belief in testimony makes use of other sources of knowledge even if it is not entirely derived from them, and hence that testimony is neither autonomous nor wholly derivative. This goal could be approached by pointing out that in believing people, we do not simply assume that whatever anyone says is true if there is not evidence to the contrary. We only believe people if they appear competent in the subject-matter with which their assertion is concerned. This is less evident when we consider subject matters where any normal person is competent, such as their name, their psychological states when these are of a kind readily available to introspection, the weather when they left the house in the morning, and so on. But it becomes apparent when we think of subject-matters where special knowledge is required. For these subject-matters, we demand signs of competence if we are to be prepared to believe people. We will believe a doctor's advice on health and medical treatment, but not that of a person who lacks medical training (unless we have other evidence that can substantiate an untrained person's claim to be telling the truth). We require evidence for competence; if you go into a doctor's office you will find his medical certificate on the wall. Thus, believing people involves inference from evidence.

In reply to this argument, it can be said that although we only believe people who appear to be competent, our believing people who show signs of competence does not amount to our inferring from evidence that people are competent, in the way that we might infer from someone's suffering from fever, enlargement of the lymph nodes, anaemia, and pains in the limbs and joints, that they are suffering from trypanosomiasis. If knowledge from testimony is to rest at least partially on inferring from evidence that people are competent, such inference would have to provide knowledge. Do we in fact know independently of trust in testimony that e.g. people wearing white coats and having a certain kind of certificate on their walls are competent in medical matters, or that topographical details on a map marked 'Ordnance Survey' are reliable? We do not have evidence for these signs being marks of competence in the way that a researcher can have evidence for the above-mentioned symptoms being signs of trypanosomiasis, and the signs are not signs of competence in the way that the symptoms are signs of trypanosomiasis. They are socially established conventions for identifying competence, not natural signs of it, and we accept them, not because we have evidence independent of testimony that they indicate competence, but simply because we have been told that they do.

If we do not typically infer from evidence that people are competent, what is it that we do? It would seem that when they are competent, and appear to be competent, we just observe that they are competent. Although it is true that their possession of signs of competence makes them appear to be competent, we do not want to say that we infer their being competent from their appearing to be competent, any more than we want to say that we infer that a particular person is old from their appearing to be old. Rather, we observe that people are old, and observe that they are e.g. doctors. It is true that if challenged as to our claim about someone's age we might defend it by saying that they appear to be old. But our offering the fact that someone appears to us to be old as a justification or defence for our claim that he is old, does not mean that our belief or our knowledge that he is old is based on his appearing to be old, or that it is his appearing to be old rather than his actually being old that is the immediate object of our observation. Of course people can appear to be competent when they are not, just as they can appear to be old when they are not. But this does not mean that when they actually are old or competent, we cannot directly observe that they are.

In the case of competence, there is also the possibility of the socially established conventions for establishing competence not being successful. Imagine a society where it is thought that shamans have the power to discern the cause of someone's death, and where the sign of being a shaman is having a few shrunken heads hanging at one's belt. If these shamans do not have the power to discern the causes of people's death, then their appearance of competence – if it is such – is illusory. Social conventions have to succeed in their goal of identifying competence, if they are to enable us to observe competence. We do not however have to know that they succeed in particular cases in order for them to enable us to observe competence, and as a rule we are not in fact able to know that they succeed in particular cases; it just has to be the case that they succeed, and that we understand them. If this were not so, we could not be said to know that people are competent, and we would not get knowledge from testimony.

Since belief in testimony is not in normal cases even partially dependent on other sources of knowledge, we can conclude that testimony is a full-fledged intellectual virtue. Michael Dummett has pointed out how belief in testimony resembles another basic intellectual virtue:

> The analogy between memory and testimony is very strong. In forming a belief, or adding an item to one's stock of knowledge, on the strength of a memory, one does not, in the normal case, arrive at it by any process of inference ... Exactly the same holds good for coming to believe or to know something by being told it. In the normal case, this is not effected by any process of inference. There are, again, special cases. I may know, from experience, that a particular informant is generally unreliable, through dishonesty or proneness to error, or that he is especially unreliable about a certain subject-matter. I may therefore consider, concerning something he has told me, the probabilities that he is mistaken or deceiving me, and decide that, in that specific case, the probability of either supposition is low, and so conclude to the probable truth of what he said. But such reflections are exceptional. If someone tells me the way to the railway station, or asks me whether I had heard that the Foreign Secretary has just resigned, or informs me that the Museum is closed today, I go through no process of reasoning, however swift, to arrive at the conclusion that he has spoken aright: my understanding of his utterance and my acceptance of his assertion are one: I simply add what he has told me to my stock of information.[8]

---

[8] Michael Dummett, 'Testimony and Memory', in *Knowing from Words* , 1994, pp. 260–61.

We can agree with Dummett that it is possible to conclude to the probable truth of what someone says on the basis of evidence as to his trustworthiness on a particular occasion. Because this will only give us a probable conclusion, however, it will not count as coming to know the truth of what he says. It will only be the normal form of accepting testimony – simply believing someone we take to be trustworthy – that can give us knowledge.

Dummett's account of believing and knowing from testimony presents such knowledge as not only autonomous, but non-inferential. One could give an account of knowledge from testimony that presented it as both autonomous and inferential. On this view, we would observe that S says that p, and from 'S says that p' infer that p. Our acceptance of testimony as an autonomous source of knowledge would consist in our accepting the form of this reasoning as valid. However, Dummett's account of knowing from testimony as non-inferential seems better than this view. It corresponds to the actual psychological reality of our acquiring knowledge from testimony, a process that, as Dummett says, does not involve the making of any inference. An inferential view makes it difficult to see how testimony could provide us with knowledge, since the inferential patterns involved ('S says that p, therefore p', or perhaps 'S says that p and appears to be truthful and knowledgeable, therefore p') would not be invariably truth-preserving, and thus would only give probable belief rather than knowledge; and, as the previous chapter argued, probable belief is not knowledge. On the non-inferential view, acquisition of knowledge from testimony would closely resemble the acquisition of knowledge from other basic intellectual virtues. Compare seeing; when I see that the window is broken, my perception can give rise to two different beliefs, the belief that the window is broken and the belief that I see that it is broken. If I was challenged as to how I know that it is broken, I would give the grounds for my claim to knowledge by saying 'I saw that it is broken'. But this does not mean that my belief that the window is broken is inferred from my belief that I saw that it was broken. Rather, my perceiving that it is broken gives rise to both my belief that it is broken and my belief that I saw that it is broken; and my perceiving that it is broken is not something that is independent of its actually *being* broken, so that its actually being broken is included in my reason for believing that it is. Testimony works in the same kind of way. I perceive that S honestly and knowledgeably says that p, and this perception gives rise both to the belief that S does this and to the belief that p, but the latter belief is not based on the former.

The view that our hearing and understanding the testimony of a knowledgeable, truthful person is our coming to know has been put forward by Dummett, John McDowell and the Nyāya school of philosophers in India.[9] Following C.A.J. Coady,[10] we could use *learn* (written in italics) to describe coming to know through testimony. *Learning* that p will be believing a person who truthfully

---

[9] I depend for this characterisation of the Nyāya philosophers on Arindam Chakrabarti, 'Telling and Letting Know', in *Knowing from Words*, 1994, and B. K. Matilal, 'Understanding, Knowing, and Justification' in *Knowing from Words*, 1994. For McDowell, see his 1994.

[10] See Coady, 1992, pp. 135–6.

asserts that *p* and knows that *p*. Like seeing and remembering, *learning* will be factive.

There is a difference between the view presented here and the positions of other philosophers who see testimony as an autonomous source of knowledge. Some philosophers justify the autonomy of testimony by appealing to 'a kind of *presumptive right* to take every understood utterance as knowledge-generating and hence knowledge-imparting'.[11] This is not compatible with the intellectual virtue account of testimony presented here, which holds that we can observe people to be knowledgeable and trustworthy. Depending on such a presumptive right in forming beliefs based on testimony need not be a matter of making inferences, but it will amount to following a rule, a rule that could roughly be described as 'accept that testimony is true in the absence of evidence of ignorance or deceit on the part of the speaker'. Following a rule is not observing. One can raise questions about the epistemic justification of following such a rule, but not about the epistemic justification of observing things; one can only ask whether one *has* observed something or not. A 'presumptive right' of this kind needs to be postulated in order to justify acceptance of testimony as an autonomous source of knowledge, if we think that our intellectual capacities stop short of the world. But on the intellectual virtue view, knowledge from testimony does not stop short of the world: what makes belief in someone's testimony reasonable, is the *actual* honesty and knowledge of the person being believed; there is no need or room for a presumptive right to be inserted between believer and person believed in order to warrant trust on such occasions. This explains how Aquinas can hold that someone who believes God when God is really speaking, believes for a different reason than someone who thinks himself to be believing God speaking but is mistaken.

The frequent occurrence of deceit and misinformation is likely to furnish objections to this description of the acquisition of knowledge from testimony. We often believe deceitful or misinformed people, sometimes without ever suspecting that they are untrustworthy, and even, in some cases, without having any evidence or means for determining that they are untrustworthy. These are not cases of *learning*, in the sense given above, but we are not able to determine that they are not.

This objection amounts to the demand referred to in the previous chapter, that knowledge be of what is seen. But this demand is unreasonable, as the discussion in that chapter brought out. Similar objections could be raised to seeing and remembering. We can experience hallucinations or misidentify things we see, and we can have false memories; and in some circumstances there may be no means available to us to rectify our mistakes, so that we will be stuck with the condition of thinking that we have knowledge when we do not. Since these possibilities do not prevent seeing and remembering from being intellectual virtues, the possibility of unidentifiable deceit need not prevent *learning* from being an intellectual virtue. It is fair to require, as McDowell does, that we be doxastically responsible if we are to gain knowledge from seeing, testimony or some other avenue of knowledge:

---

[11] Chakrabarti, in Matilal and Chakrabarti, 1994, p. 8.

We can protect the idea that acquiring knowledge by testimony is not a mindless reception of something which has nothing to do with rationality, but yields a standing in the space of reasons, by insisting that the knowledge is available to be picked up only by someone whose taking the speaker's word for it is not doxastically irresponsible ... A person sufficiently responsible to count as having achieved epistemic standing from someone else's words needs to be aware of how knowledge can be had from others, and rationally responsive to considerations whose relevance that awareness embodies. That requires him to form beliefs on the say-so of others in a way that is rationally shaped by an understanding of, among other things, the risks to which one subjects oneself in accepting what people say.[12]

If we are doxastically responsible we will be aware of the ways in which hearing, seeing, believing others, etc., can go wrong, and responsive to signs of their going wrong. But this responsiveness does not have to include the power to always identify cases where they do go wrong. To demand this power is to ask for something more than human, and to misconceive the nature of knowledge.

Accepting *learning* as an intellectual virtue is not compatible with a conception of knowledge as being an autonomous possession of the individual. If learning is an intellectual virtue, some of our knowledge is dependent on what other people do. Human knowledge is to some extent a collective enterprise. The remarks made above about observing signs of competence show that this dependence is not limited to the necessity for the people we believe to be knowledgeable and trustworthy if we are to be able to *learn* from them. These signs are usually determined by socially established conventions. The creation of such signs is the work of a society, not of an individual. This means that much of our *learning* depends on the actions of a society as a whole, not just on the trustworthiness of the individuals whom we believe. Such dependence lessens our autonomy even more radically than our dependence on the word of individuals, whom we can to some extent evaluate.

Ought we to regret this lack of autonomy, or restrict the sphere of our knowledge to the tiny area in which such autonomy can be claimed to exist? The ideal of autonomy does not make it worthwhile to submit ourselves to this restriction. Even our intellectual virtues that do not involve trusting other people depend on the universe's cooperating by providing suitable conditions for their exercise. The sense of sight would be no good to us in a place that had an atmosphere opaque to visible light. Real autonomy in our acquisition of knowledge is thus a chimera. Moreover, we can console ourselves for the sacrifice of autonomy involved in acquiring knowledge through testimony by reflecting that this sacrifice makes possible the vast extension in our capacity to know that results from the ability to acquire the knowledge of others, an ability that makes human culture and civilization possible.

It might be objected that accepting this sacrifice of autonomy runs counter to the argument given in the previous chapter, to the effect that knowledge must result

---

[12] McDowell, 1994, pp. 210–11.

from the exercise of our own powers. It certainly requires a modification or at least a clarification of this argument, which specifies that 'our own powers' refers to the powers in humanity as a whole, not just to the powers found in a particular individual. This in turn leads to an understanding of knowledge as communal that is a radical departure from most philosophical tradition. It means that a particular bit of my knowledge may necessarily be the product of the exercise of other people's epistemic powers as well as of my own. But this departure is justified by the fact that testimony does in fact provide us with knowledge.

We have introduced Coady's term *learning*, to describe coming to know through testimony. A further term is needed to describe the act of conveying knowledge to someone through providing him with one's testimony. There is no ordinary English word that has this meaning, so I will follow Coady's example and coin a new term, *telling*, written in italics, to express it. '*Telling*' does not have the same meaning as the ordinary English word 'telling', since the latter word does not imply comprehension, belief and knowledge of what is told in the person being told, whereas '*telling*' implies the existence of all these things in the person who is *told*. We *learn* through someone else's *telling* us something. Christian faith involves God's *telling* things to the faithful. The notion of being *told* something by God is not as straightforward as the notion of being *told* something by a mere human. In order to understand what is involved in being *told* something by God, we need to have an analysis of the nature of *telling*. Our discussion of the acquisition of knowledge from testimony enables us to work out such an analysis.

Telling is a way of imparting knowledge; when I *tell* A something, I impart knowledge to him in a particular way. The question is, in what way? Just causing A to know that *p* is not *telling* him that *p*. I can do this without making use of my knowledge that *p*, and even without myself knowing that *p*. With *telling* this is not so. I have to know that *p* in order to enable A to know that *p* through my *telling* him. As well as my knowing that *p*, A has to take me to know that *p*, and has to take my knowing that *p* as being included in the grounds for his knowing that *p*.

It may of course be the case that A already knows that *p*. We can take this possibility into account by describing *telling* not in terms of a speaker S's bringing A to know that *p*, but in terms of S's making his knowledge that *p* available to A. We define this as follows: S makes his knowledge that *p* available to A just in case S would bring A to know that *p* if A did not already know that *p*. We explain how S would bring A to know that *p* in terms of the case where S actually does bring A to know that *p*, so the description of making knowledge available can simply be read off from the description of the actual transfer of knowledge through testimony; it is this description that lets us know how *telling* works.

Since A has to take S to know that *p* in order to come to know *p* through S's *telling* him, a condition for S's *telling* A that *p* is the following:

S *tells* A that *p* only if:

1.   S intentionally brings A to recognize that S knows that *p*.

In order for S to *tell* A that p, A has to know that he is being *told*, since his reason for believing p is precisely that S *tells* him it. Since (1) is part of *telling*, then, S has to bring A to know that (1) is occurring; and a further requirement for S's *telling* A that p is:

2. S intentionally brings A to recognize that S intends to do (1).

'S knows that p' entails p, so A's realizing that S knows that p lets A know that p, and it makes A's knowing that p derive from S's knowing that p. *Telling* requires honesty in the teller; and S can intend to bring A to realize that S knows that p only if S thinks that he *does* know that p, which excludes S's thinking that p is false. The occurrence of conditions (1) and (2) would thus seem to be sufficient for *telling* to occur.

This account of *telling* appears to resemble the account of meaning that has been given by Paul Grice. One might therefore suppose that it falls victim to the objections that have been raised against Gricean accounts. But this is not the case. One sort of objection to Gricean accounts is that their account of linguistic meaning takes for granted the concepts of thought and content. This is held to be illegitimate, because these concepts are thought of as things that cannot themselves be explained independently of possession of a capacity to use language. Another objection is that Gricean accounts fail in the end to account for the concept of language meaning, because they explain the meaning of language in terms of thoughts that have content, without explaining what it is for thoughts to have content. Whether or not these objections to Grice's views are well founded, they do not apply to the account of *telling* that has been given here, because, unlike Gricean accounts, this account of *telling* does not present itself as giving an analysis of linguistic meaning. It is simply an account of a particular way of conveying and acquiring knowledge. Whether this account can be used to explain linguistic meaning, or whether *telling* must be held to presuppose the existence of language, is not something that is determined by the account itself, and is not a question with which we need to concern ourselves.

Another sort of objection to Gricean accounts consists in the suggestion of counterexamples. Consider this example of a Gricean account:

'U meant something by uttering x' is true iff;
1. U intended, by uttering x, to induce a certain response in A
2. U intended A to recognize, *at least in part from the utterance of x*, that U intended to produce that response
3. U intended the fulfilment of the intention mentioned in (2) to be at least in part A's reason for fulfilling the intention mentioned in (1).[13]

This account falls victim to a counterexample that Grice himself mentions:

---

[13] Paul Grice, *Studies in the Way of Words*, 1989, p. 94.

A man is playing bridge against his boss. He wants to earn the boss's favor, and for this reason he wants his boss to win, and furthermore he wants his boss to *know* that he wants him to win (his boss likes that kind of self-effacement). He does not want to do anything too blatant, however, like telling his boss by word of mouth, or in effect telling him by some action amounting to a signal, for fear that the boss may be offended by his crudity. So he puts into operation the following plan: when he gets a good hand, he smiles in a certain way; the smile is *very* like, but not *quite* like, a spontaneous smile of pleasure. He intends his boss to detect the difference and to argue as follows: 'That was not a genuine giveaway smile, but the simulation of such a smile. That sort of simulation might be a bluff (on a weak hand), but this is bridge, not poker, and he would not want to get the better of me, his boss, by such an impropriety. So probably he has got a good hand, and, wanting me to win, he hoped I would learn that he has a good hand by taking his smile as a spontaneous giveaway. That being so, I shall not raise my partner's bid.'

In such a case, I do not think one would want to say that the employee had meant, by his smile (or by smiling), that he had a good hand, nor indeed that he had meant anything at all.[14]

Although the employee's smile does not mean anything, it satisfies the account of meaning given above. But the counterexample is not a difficulty for the account of *telling* that has been proposed, because the second condition in this account is not fulfilled; the boss does not think that the smile is intended to bring him to know that the employee has a good hand. The immunity of the account of *telling* to this counterexample is a result of a crucial difference between it and Gricean accounts. All Gricean accounts of meaning define meaning entirely in terms of a speaker U's acting with a certain intention. The account of *telling*, however, defines *telling* in terms of both the speaker's acting with a certain intention and the hearer's belief about this intention. We can see how including the hearer's belief about the speaker's intention in the definition of telling means that the definition is not open to the counterexample given above. Consider a different counterexample proposed by Stephen Schiffer, that is aimed at a reformulation of Grice's analysis that was designed to get around the counterexample quoted above:

A, thinking she is unobserved by S, sees S applying lipstick to her husband Harold's shirt, and reasons thus: 'S is manufacturing evidence that Harold has been unfaithful. S intends me to see the lipstick stains and to infer that they got there as a result of Harold's close encounter with a lipstick-wearing female. But dear old S wouldn't try to deceive me in this way if he didn't know that Harold had been unfaithful. So Harold must have been unfaithful.' Since that is exactly how S intends A to reason, he satisfies the conditions of [S] for meaning that Harold has been unfaithful. Yet S, in manufacturing the evidence, does not *mean* that Harold has been unfaithful.[15]

The same observation can be made about this counterexample as about the last one; the second condition for *telling* (assume for simplicity's sake that S knows that Harold is unfaithful) is not realized, because S does not bring A to recognize that S intends to bring A to realize that S knows that Harold is unfaithful. In this

---

[14] Grice, 1989, pp. 94–5.
[15] Stephen Schiffer, *Remnants of Meaning*, 1989, p. 245.

case, too, it is the fact that the definition of *telling* includes the hearer's recognition of the speaker's intentions that means that the counterexample does not apply to it. I will not go further into the exuberantly complicated series of analyses and counterexamples that have been given by Grice, his followers and their opponents. I will only remark that, as Anita Avramides points out, the common thread in all the counterexamples that have been given to the Gricean account above and to its successors is the possibility of deceit.[16] The speaker's act in the counterexamples fails to conform to our notion of communication, because the hearer is deceived about the intention of the speaker's act. Such deception is excluded by the second condition for *telling*, so none of these counterexamples work against it.

This discussion brings out the fact that the similarity between the account of *telling* and Gricean analyses of meaning is not as great as one might at first sight take it to be. The fact that objections to Gricean accounts do not apply to the account of *telling* does not mean that it raises no important philosophical questions. How we manage to *tell* people things, and how we manage to do it through the use of language, are important issues that require philosophical investigation. But such investigation is not required for our inquiry. All we need to know is that we do *tell* people things, and that the two conditions given above are sufficient for our doing so. Our investigation has shown that this is the case; and that permits us to go on to consider the question of God's *telling* us things.

---

[16] Anita Avramides, *Meaning and mind*, 1989, p. 51.

Chapter 7

The Nature of Divine Speaking

In Chapter 1 it was argued that there is such a thing as divine speaking. The subject that will now be addressed is the nature of this divine speaking. There are three questions that are crucial to an analysis of divine speech:

1. Is divine speaking direct, or deistic?
2. Is divine speaking God's speaking and not any non-divine human's speaking, or is the speaking of some humans who are not divine also God's speaking?
3. If God speaks in the speaking of humans who are not divine, where and how does this speech happen?

Direct vs. deistic divine speaking

The term 'deistic' was introduced by Eleonore Stump to characterize Richard Swinburne's conception of divine revelation.[1] I shall understand a deistic conception of divine speaking to be the following: according to such a conception, God conveys the Christian message by speaking to an initial group, which is (roughly) made up of the prophets and the apostles. Those who do not belong to this initial group (the vast majority of believers, whom we can call the typical Christian believers) learn about the Christian message by hearing the reports of members of this initial group (or reports of these reports, etc.; for simplicity's sake I will take coming to know the reports of this initial group through a chain of testimony to be included under the description of believing the reports of the initial group). They do not hear it through hearing God himself when he speaks, but only through hearing the reports of the initial group; and these reports are not God's speaking. (There are various ways in which God's speaking to the initial group could have happened. He could have done so through sending visions, for example, or in the teachings of Christ, whose utterances were God's utterances. We need not consider how a deistic view should explicate God's speaking, since the features of the deistic view that we will consider will not be affected by how this is understood.) The typical believer, unlike the members of the initial group, will not actually encounter any divine utterances; he will only have access to human reports

---

[1] In Eleonore Stump, review of Richard Swinburne's *Revelation*, in *The Philosophical Review*, 1994. I do not claim that Stump was right in describing Swinburne's views in this way.

of divine utterances. He will thus come to accept the message that God conveys to humanity by reasoning like this:

God said that *p* to *X*; therefore, *p*.

The direct view of divine speaking, on the other hand, asserts that God himself speaks to everyone who has Christian faith, not just to an initial group, and that Christian faith involves believing God himself when he speaks.

Although the deistic view has been espoused by many Christian thinkers, it faces insuperable objections.

1.
On the deistic view, the typical believer is not believing God, but is rather believing other people when they make claims about what God said to them. This leads to a number of difficulties.

i) It means that belief in what God says does not as such involve the personal relationship with God that would exist if the believer actually believed God himself. The accusation falsely made against propositional views of revelation in general really does apply to the deistic view; it takes the belief involved in faith to have propositions *rather than* the person of God as its object. (The prevalence of deistic views of divine speaking may go some way towards explaining why many theologians have found this argument against propositional views of revelation convincing.) In contrast, the direct view of divine speaking holds that belief does take the person of God as its object, since belief in testimony, as Anscombe points out, takes the person who is believed as its object. Such belief also of course involves believing the propositions asserted by the speaker who is believed; it does not permit the separation between belief in propositions and personal encounter that is involved in the deistic view.

ii) It does not allow for the moral relation with God that believing God sets up. There are debates over whether or when belief in propositions is voluntary, and over whether or how belief in propositions is subject to moral obligation or evaluation. But believing persons is clearly subject to moral evaluation, and hence voluntary. Consider Othello. We can say that he ought to have believed Desdemona's protestations of innocence, because a man has an obligation to believe his wife when she denies having committed adultery and there is no good evidence that she is not telling the truth. Othello's failure here is not, or not only, in his failing to make adequate investigation into whether or not Desdemona had committed adultery, or in his failing to trust her in the sense of failing to act on the assumption that she is telling the truth about her innocence. In addition to his other moral failures, he fails specifically in his refusing to believe Desdemona when she asserts her innocence. Generalizing, we can say it is a morally good thing to believe those who deserve our trust, and a a bad thing to disbelieve them. We feel this to be true when we encounter someone who refuses to believe our assertions without good reason. We not only take such a person to be acting unreasonably, we resent him as doing us an injustice. Of course it is possible to be innocent in disbelieving a trustworthy person. But if we have every reason to take someone to be trustworthy, but do not believe him, our disbelief is morally blameworthy. That is why being suspicious and untrusting is generally taken to be a category of moral failure, not just of epistemic failure. If we believe God himself when he speaks, the moral relation that exists when we trust someone who deserves our trust is set up between us and God, and we have the merit of believing God as we should. But on the deistic view, this is not so. (I do not here use 'merit' in any technical theological sense, but only in the ordinary sense of the goodness involved in doing a morally good action.) This moral aspect of belief in testimony helps to clarify the nature of the personal encounter involved in believing a person that is mentioned above. Such belief involves having a certain attitude towards the person believed, that of taking him to be knowledgeable and trustworthy; expressing this attitude, in trusting him; and rendering him what is due in justice to his knowledge and truthfulness.

iii)   It means that our belief in what God has said rests ultimately on human faith, that is, on believing humans rather than believing God. There does not seem to be any necessity or role for grace in arriving at such human faith. As Locke remarks, 'to all those who pretend not to immediate *Revelation*, but are required to pay Obedience, and to receive the Truths revealed to others, which, by the Tradition of Writings, or word of Mouth, are conveyed down to them, Reason has a great deal more to do, and is that only which can induce us to receive them.'[2] How could grace be necessary for us to determine whether or not someone is telling the truth when they claim that God spoke to them?

2.

If the Scriptures have God as their author, then the typical believer, in believing the Scriptures, is believing what God himself says. But this cannot be reconciled with the deistic view. The Scriptures cannot on this view plausibly be seen as addressed solely by God to the initial group, and not also being human utterances. They were not written by Christ himself, or dictated by a voice from heaven; rather, they are clearly the product of the minds and efforts of their human authors.[3] We can see in the different canonical books the signs of the characteristic purposes and mentalities of their human authors. But if these books were not human utterances, but simply written at God's dictation, these purposes and mentalities would have no place, because the books would not be compositions of their human authors',

---

[2] Locke, 1975, p. 693.
[3] Thus for example Luke describes himself as writing an orderly account for Theophilus (Luke 1:3). Cf. the discussion of views of inspiration in Chapter 2.

but solely of God's. Who would be willing to say that St. Paul did not himself choose what to write in his canonical letters, but simply wrote down what the Holy Spirit dictated to him? The Scriptures, on the deistic view, should thus be considered as the utterances (or reports of the teachings or utterances) of the initial group. On the deistic view, this rules out the contention that the Scriptures are uttered by God. The Scriptures can only be a record of what God said, not themselves said by God. But the contention that the Scriptures are said by God is firmly established by Scripture and tradition.

Scriptural evidence for this contention is to be found in the New Testament. In Matt. 19:4–5, Christ attributes the words of the book of Genesis to God, saying 'Have you not read that he who made them from the beginning made them male and female, and said "For this reason a man shall leave his father and mother and be joined to his wife, and the two shall become one flesh"?'. The words that are cited (Gen. 2:24) are not put into God's mouth in the book of Genesis, but are simply stated in the text itself. In Acts 1:16, the Holy Spirit is described as speaking through men. In Heb. 3:7 (citing Ps. 95:7), Acts 4:25–6 (citing Ps. 2:1), Acts 13:34–5 (citing Is. 55:3 and Ps. 16:10), the Scriptures are cited as the words of God. In Rom. 3:2, Heb. 5:12 and 1 Pet. 4:11, passages from the Old Testament are described as the oracles of God. In Heb. 1:5–14, 'God said' is asserted of a number of scriptural citations. Rom. 1:2 speaks of what the Word of God uttered through his prophets in the holy writings. 2 Tim. 3:16 describes the Scriptures as God-breathed (qeo,pheustoj). 2 Pet. 1:20–21 asserts that 'no prophecy of scripture is a matter of one's own interpretation, because no prophecy ever came by the impulse of man, but men moved by the Holy Spirit spoke from God'. This understanding of the Scriptures as being spoken by God reflects and endorses the universal view of Jews in New Testament times.[4]

The idea that the Scriptures have God as their author is also universally accepted by the Fathers (see e.g. Tertullian, *Apol.* 31, Gregory of Nyssa, *Contra Eunom.* 7, Irenaeus, *Adv. Haer.* 2.28.2–3, Eusebius, *H.E.* 5.28, Origen, *De prin.* 1.48, Basil, *In Ps.* 1.1, Jerome, *In Mich. Proph.* 2.7, *In Is.* 29.9, Chrysostom, *In Gen. hom.* 21.1, and the passage from Augustine's *The Harmony of the Gospels* quoted in Chapter 2 above). It is a natural interpretation of the line in the Creed that describes the Holy Spirit as having spoken through the prophets, a line that on any interpretation is hard to reconcile with a deistic conception. It was accepted by the Reformers as well as by Catholics,[5] and was in fact universally accepted by

---

[4] On this see A. T. Hanson, *The Living Utterances of God*, 1983.

[5] The Second Helvetic Confession, for example, states that 'we believe and confess the Canonical Scriptures of the holy prophets and apostles of both Testaments to be the true word of God, and to have sufficient authority of themselves, not of men. For God himself spake to the fathers, prophets, apostles, and still speaks to us through the Holy Scriptures.' (John H. Leith, *Creeds of the Churches*, 1973, p. 132.) The First Vatican Council in its constitution *Dei Filius* describes God as the author of the Scriptures, saying of them that 'Spiritu sancto inspirante conscripti Deum habent auctorem' (Tanner and Alberigo, *Decrees of the Ecumenical Councils*, 1990, vol. 2, p. 806), and the Second Vatican Council in *Dei Verbum* para. 12 describes God as having spoken through the Scriptures, 'Deus in sacra

Christians until the seventeenth century. It tended to be presupposed rather than explicitly discussed in much theological consideration of revelation, which from the Middle Ages onwards concentrated on the question of inspiration, first of prophecy and then of the Scriptures, rather than on the status of the Scriptures as spoken by God; inspiration was generally conceived of primarily as a property of those who prophesized or who wrote the Scriptures, rather than a property of the utterances they produced. (This conception, it should be pointed out, is significantly different from the meaning of θεόπνευστος in 2 Tim. 3:16, which is a property of the Scriptures rather than of their authors.)[6] But this very status as an unquestioned presupposition testifies to its acceptance as a fundamental doctrine.

It thus conforms to the Vincentian canon of a doctrine that was accepted always, everywhere and by everyone, 'quod ubique, quod semper, quod ab omnibus creditum est'. This canon ought not to be understood as referring to doctrines that are accepted by literally everyone at every time, because if it were, it would not be a means for settling differences of opinion about what to believe (since the mere fact of disagreement about a doctrine would mean that it did not satisfy the canon). Rather, it should be understood as referring to doctrines that were accepted always and everywhere by everyone prior to being questioned. Any doctrine that was explicitly accepted by all Christians for a long time from apostolic times onwards would satisfy this canon.[7] On the broadly Catholic view that this book takes as a starting point, the fact that the claim that the Scriptures are uttered by God is explicitly asserted by the Scriptures themselves and by subsequent tradition means that it must be accepted as true. But the degree of agreement among Christians in the past about this claim is so great that such a broad Catholic view is not needed to justify its acceptance from the point of view of Christian belief. It is implausible to accept Christianity as a religion of divine origin, if it could err so fundamentally about such an important principle for so long.

3.

If the Scriptures are spoken by God, they give knowledge to those who believe them, since God is completely truthful and knowledgeable. The deistic view does not in principle rule out the possibility of the typical believer's acquiring knowledge from God's speaking. If the typical believer accepts the trustworthy testimony of a member of the original group who claims 'God said p to me', he can thereby come to know that God said p to that person, and hence that p. But testimony of this sort is as a matter of fact almost never available. This means that

---

scriptura per homines more hominum locutus sit' (Tanner and Alberigo, 1990, vol. 2, p. 976).

[6] Mangenot remarks that the Fathers generally described the human authors of the Scriptures as θεοφερόμενοι or πνευματοφόροι rather than θεόπνευστοι. E. Mangenot, 'Inspiration de l'Écriture', *Dictionnaire de théologie catholique* vol. 7(2), col. 2069.

[7] It is significant that the doctrine that God is the author of the Scriptures satisfies the Vincentian canon, because this fact shows that the level of agreement demanded by the canon is not so high as to prevent any substantive theological claim's satisfying it.

on the deistic view there is no way of reliably determining what God actually said in communicating the Christian message, and there is thus no way of knowing what this message actually is; which makes Christianity pointless as a religion.[8] This is because the Scriptures, if they are considered to be simply a human record of what God said in the past, cannot be called a reliable record. Many of the utterances attributed to God in the Bible were not actually said by him in the way that the Bible presents them as having been said. God obviously did not communicate the book of Deuteronomy to Moses on Mount Sinai. Of the reported divine utterances in the Bible that could possibly have happened as the Bible described, many cannot be supported by good historical evidence, if the Bible is considered simply as a human record. This is true of God's speaking to the patriarchs, to Moses, to the prophets.

One might say that the Scriptures are not purely human records, because they are divinely inspired. But until the Middle Ages, divine inspiration was traditionally taken to be that which (however conceived of) brought it about that the Scriptures were spoken by God; or else to be simply the fact of their being spoken by God. This conception of divine inspiration does not enable one to say that the Scriptures are of more than human value as evidence for what God said, but are not themselves spoken by God.

It is true that from the Middle Ages onwards, a rather different conception of divine inspiration came to be generally accepted. This conceived of divine inspiration as being a property of the individual human writers of the Scriptures, rather than simply as a property of the Scriptures themselves. This resulted from seeing the inspiration of Scripture as resembling prophetic inspiration, which is a charism of a particular individual. It had the consequence of identifying the inspired meaning of the text, which Christians were required to accept as a matter of faith, with the meaning of the utterances of its individual human authors. But this later view of inspiration led to serious misunderstandings of the text, which posed unnecessary difficulties for Christian believers. This is because the meaning that we will ascribe to a text if we take it simply as written by an individual human author will be different from the meaning that we will ascribe to it if we take it as having God for its author.[9] An obvious form of misunderstanding is reading meanings into the text that are not there, and that are false or objectionable. Thus it is quite likely that the individual who wrote the creation account that is found in the first chapter of the book of Genesis really thought that the universe was brought into being in six days, and that the author of Psalm 137 really meant to bless those who bashed out the brains of Babylonian children. The later view of inspiration commits us to accepting these beliefs and sentiments as true and estimable, when they obviously are not. (Something like the later view of inspiration probably lies

---

[8] The defence that some Christians have made, in the teeth of the evidence, of the ideas that the Scriptures are the product of divine dictation, or at least that they are straightforward historical records, probably results from their assuming the deistic view. Divine dictation views of inspiration certainly emerged after deistic views of divine speaking became dominant.

[9] This important point is well brought out by Swinburne, 1992.

behind C. H. Dodd's assertion, quoted in Chapter 2, that the Bible contains much
that is untrue or immoral.) The older view does not require us to accept these
things, because it does not imply that the beliefs and sentiments of these
individuals are the meaning that God expresses in the text. A less obvious but
perhaps more damaging result of this view of inspiration lies in denying the
existence of meanings of the Scriptural text that are actually there. Thus the
Christological content of the Old Testament is denied because individual authors of
the Old Testament did not have Christ in mind when they wrote.[10] This is an area
where the differences between the older and the newer views of inspiration have
some of their most striking results. An example is mentioned by Yves Congar, who
notes with some disquiet how the Fathers freely appealed to passages in the Old
Testament to argue for their views about how the Christian Church is structured.[11]
They could do this because they were not bothered about what the original human
authors of the text had in mind. Many of them might indeed have said if asked that
the nature of the Church was a mystery of the New Law that no-one could have
known about before the coming of Christ. They could have said this without
inconsistency because the meaning they sought in reading the Scriptural text was
the meaning that it has when understood as divine speech, rather than what the
individual human authors had in mind when they wrote the bits that make it up.

Attempts to get around the problems posed by the later view of inspiration have
just made things worse. An example is the makeshift theory of the *sensus plenior*
of Biblical texts, which postulated that the individual authors of the Scriptures
managed in some way to express in their writings a meaning that surpassed what
they understood or had in mind; where the expression of this meaning is thought of
as an act of the human authors themselves. This theory was once much appealed to
by Roman Catholic theologians to defend the existence of Christological references
in the Old Testament. It is true that, as the theory supposes, the writings and
utterances of a speaker can mean something different from what the speaker takes
them to mean. This is because the rules of meaning for a language are determined
by the linguistic community, not by the individual. (It would not be true if words
simply meant what the speaker intended them to say, as Humpty Dumpty claims in
Alice in Wonderland; but he was wrong, as the episode in the book demonstrates.)
But when this happens, it is because of the ignorance or error of the speaker about
the rules for the meaning of the language he is using, and it is not satisfactory to
see part of the Scriptural message which Christians are supposed to believe as
springing from ignorance or error. It might be said that the view that the Bible has
God as its author requires the *sensus plenior* theory, because it requires us to say
that the meaning of the Scriptural text is not equivalent to the meaning that the
individual authors of the text had in mind. But the *sensus plenior* theory is not
limited to this true assertion. It also says that what we believe when we believe the

---

[10] I take the New Testament as my authority for asserting that many texts of the Old
Testament are about Christ. There are innumerable New Testament passages that could be
cited to this effect; for a fascinating discussion of the New Testament use of Old Testament
texts as referring to Christ, see C. H. Dodd, *According to the Scriptures*, 1952.

[11] Yves Congar, *Tradition and traditions*, 1966, pp. 80–81.

Scriptural text is the utterances of these individual authors. It does not explain the difference between what these individual authors meant to say and the meaning that we believe when believing the Scriptures as being due to our believing someone other than these individuals, viz., God,[12] when we accept what the Scriptures say; it explains the difference by saying that the individual authors somehow did not fully understand what they meant when they composed the texts that have been put together to form the Bible. This explanation is not credible.

The later view of inspiration should thus be rejected, and it cannot be used to defend the accuracy of the descriptions of divine speaking in the Scriptures. If the position that the Scriptures are spoken by God is rejected, therefore, we are left with the conclusion that the Scriptural descriptions of divine speaking cannot be relied upon. And even if it could, the converse of the point made by James Barr in chapter 2 would apply. Barr pointed out that the Scriptures were not simply a record of non-communicative divine actions; divine speaking is essential to the account of God's actions that they give. But it is also true that the descriptions of divine speaking in the Scriptures are not self-sufficient, and do not provide the whole Christian message on their own independently of the context in which they are set. This does not pose a problem if the context itself, the Scriptural text, is held to be spoken by God. But if it is only the reports of divine speaking in the Scriptures that tell us what God said, the divine message will be torn from the context that is obviously intended to provide much of its meaning, and will be truncated, incomplete and uncertain. If this is the case, it will follow that God intended to speak to mankind in order to communicate a message of the highest importance, but that he did not bother to do so in a way that would make it possible to determine what that message actually was, and this is implausible.

Public vs. private revelation

The arguments in the preceding section establish that divine speaking is direct rather than deistic. The mere statement that divine speaking is direct does not on its own settle the question of whether such speaking occurs in the speaking of humans who are not divine, or whether it does not. The qualification 'who are not divine' is meant to exclude the teaching of Christ from the question. His teaching was undoubtedly divine speech by a human, since he was both God and man; what is meant to be considered is the question of whether the speech of men other than Christ was also divine, and whether such speech is the means by which God speaks to the typical Christian believer. It should be made clear that the divine speaking in question is speaking that conveys the Christian message, speaking belief in which is an act of Christian faith, and disbelief in which is contrary to faith. (Belief in such speaking is referred to as an act of Christian faith rather than as required by Christian faith, because all acts of divine speaking that communicate the Christian faith are being discussed here, and it does not seem reasonable to assert that

---

[12] This does not mean that we are never believing the individual human authors of the texts of the Scriptures when we believe the Scriptures, only that we need not be doing so.

Christian faith requires one to believe every act of divine speaking that communicates that faith; one can be a believing Christian without having read the whole Bible.) Christian mystics have often recorded experiences of divine speaking that did not occur in the speaking of humans who were not divine, through visions, for example. Such experiences seem perfectly possible, but they are not the kind of divine speaking that is being investigated here. They are not addressed to all humanity, but only to particular individuals, and hence believing them cannot be an act of faith on the part of the typical believer. (The typical believer can believe that they occurred, but this can only happen through trusting the report of the person to whom they were actually addressed, which would be an act of human faith. Whether believing them would be an act of divine faith on the part of the person to whom they are actually addressed is a question that will not be investigated here.)

Some of the early Quakers seem to have held the view that God speaks directly to every believer through an inner inspiration of the Holy Spirit, and not through the speech of humans who are not divine. This view was what John Owen and others described and opposed as enthusiasm. I do not have anything to add to the standard polemic against enthusiasm, which I believe makes its case adequately, and I will only mention briefly the main points that have been made against it. Enthusiasm does not seem compatible with the biblical assertions that faith comes by hearing and that no-one can believe without being taught by a preacher (Romans 10:14, 10:17). It cannot explain why the only people that believe or know about the Christian message are in fact those who have heard about it from other humans. It is an individualistic view of faith, that does not see it as necessarily involving communion with others, and deprives Christ of a role in our believing God; it does not have God speak to us through his incarnate Son. Many Christians (including myself) do not notice any such inner speaking; if it is there, why aren't we aware of it? Are the vast majority of professed Christians who do not notice any such speaking, deceiving themselves when they believe that they have Christian faith? It cannot explain why God has produced in so many Christians a view of Christian faith that says that enthusiasm is false. Were Owen and a vast number of other Christians (a majority of those who have thought about the question) misunderstanding what God said to them when they held as a matter of faith that enthusiasm is false? Finally, an enthusiast position that says that God speaks *only* in the inner inspiration of the Holy Spirit, and not in any other way, is incompatible with the view that the Scriptures are spoken by God. The Scriptures were written by men, so if they are spoken by God it follows that God's speaking is also the speaking of men who are not divine.

This is an appropriate place to discuss the views of Alvin Plantinga on the rational grounds for Christian belief, as set forth in his book *Warranted Christian Belief*, views which have some resemblance to enthusiasm. One cannot however speak as if Plantinga had only one position on this subject. Rather, his book contains two different positions that are of different merit.

Plantinga describes the acquisition of Christian faith as resulting from a three-tiered process. The first part of the process is God's producing the Scriptures as their principal author. The second part is the presence and activity of the Holy

Spirit in the soul, by which the ravages of sin, including the noetic damages that it causes, are repaired to a greater or lesser extent. This presence and activity is a supernatural gift, not a faculty that belongs to human nature. The third part of this process is that by virtue of this action, Christians come to believe, accept, endorse and rejoice in the great things of the Gospel. This is faith, which involves both knowledge and will. The part of the will in faith is both affective (loving and being grateful to God) and executive (accepting the offered gift of salvation and committing one's self to the Lord). This description of the role of the will in faith resembles that of Aquinas in the affections and intentions that it postulates in the believer, but it does not seem to agree on the action that these affections and intentions give rise to. For Aquinas, as we have seen, it is the act of believing itself that results from the desire for God and the intention to pursue him above all other things; but for Plantinga the affections and intentions that form part of faith follow from or accompany believing God, rather than giving rise to this belief.

The different positions that are to be found in Plantinga's discussion have to do with whether or not Christian faith is belief on God's testimony. On the one hand, he frequently asserts that it is. He states:

> On the model, there is both scripture and the divine activity leading to human belief. God himself (on the model) is the principal author of Scripture. Scripture is most importantly a message, a communication from God to mankind: scripture is a word from the Lord. But then this just is a special case of the pervasive process of testimony, by which, as a matter of fact, we learn most of what we know. From this point of view, Scripture is a much a matter of testimony as is a letter you receive from a friend. What is proposed for our belief in Scripture, therefore, just *is* testimony – divine testimony. So the term 'testimony' is appropriate here. However, there is also the special work of the Holy Spirit in getting us to believe, in enabling us to see the truth of what is proposed. Here Thomas Aquinas's terms 'invitation' and 'instigation' are more appropriate ... it is the instigation of the Holy Spirit, on this model, that gets us to see and believe that the propositions proposed for our belief really *are* a word from the Lord.[13]

But Plantinga also says something different about the way in which we come to believe. He describes an encounter with the Scriptures, or with a report of what is said by the Scriptures, as an *occasion* for belief, rather than as giving rise to belief through our accepting the Scriptures as divine utterances. He asserts that when we read Scripture or are told of it, or in some other way encounter a Scriptural teaching:

> What is said simply seems right; it seems compelling; one finds oneself saying 'Yes, that's right, that's the truth of the matter; this is indeed the word of the Lord.' I read 'God was in Christ, reconciling the world to himself'; I come to think: 'Right; that's true; God really was in Christ, reconciling the world to himself!' And I may also think something a bit different, something *about* that proposition: that it is a divine teaching or revelation, that in Calvin's words it is 'from God'. What one hears or reads seems

---

[13] Plantinga, 2000, pp. 251–2.

clearly and obviously true and (at any rate in paradigm cases) seems also to be something the Lord is intending to teach.[14]

Here, faith is described as being produced by something other than belief in God's testimony. It is simply an immediate conviction of the truth of the Christian message. Plantinga does not clearly say whether or not this immediate conviction and the recognition that the message is from God can both be said to give rise to belief in the Christian message, but he implies in some passages that it is the immediate conviction that produces belief, not the recognition of its divine origin, and that this recognition is a concomitant of belief in the message rather than a ground for it. He says:

> [Calvin] does not mean to say, I think (at any rate this is not how the model goes), that the Holy Spirit induces belief in the proposition *the Bible* (or the book of Job, or Paul's epistles, or the thirteenth chapter of First Corinthians) *comes to us from the very mouth of God*. Rather, upon reading or hearing a given teaching – a given item from the great things of the gospel – the Holy Spirit teaches us, causes us to believe that *that* teaching is both true and comes from God. So the structure here is not: what is taught in Scripture is true; *this* (e.g. that in Christ, God was reconciling the world to himself) is taught in Scripture; therefore, this is true. It is rather that, on reading or hearing a certain teaching *t*, one forms the belief that *t*, that very teaching, is true and from God.[15]

As the discussion of testimony above has shown, it is quite right to deny that belief arising from testimony is inferential, and thus it is true that belief in God's testimony will be a basic belief (and a properly basic belief, since it will be believing someone who is knowledgeable and truthful). But Plantinga, who asserts that the belief involved in faith is properly basic, does not seem to have in mind the proper basicality that belongs to belief in truthful knowledgeable testimony. Rather, this proper basicality attaches to the immediate conviction that believers possess of the truth of the great things of the gospel. And since in this immediate conviction the Holy Spirit causes us to believe that the teachings of the gospel are true, the conviction that God teaches these things cannot form part of our grounds for believing in their truth, because this belief has already been produced by the immediate conviction.

Call these two different accounts of how Christian faith is produced the testimony account and the immediate conviction account. The immediate conviction account is not a tenable one; it is open to a number of insuperable objections:

1.

It does not explain why faith should constitute knowledge or reasonable belief. Why should the fact that believers have immediate conviction of the truth of their beliefs make this conviction reasonable? Lots of people have firm unshakable convictions that are totally unjustified. Plantinga would presumably reply that this

---

[14] Plantinga, 2000, p. 250.
[15] Plantinga, 2000, p. 260.

immediate conviction is rational and provides knowledge because it is produced by the inner inspiration of the Holy Spirit, and a conviction so produced satisfies the conditions he has laid down for a belief to be warranted. It is brought about by God, our designer, with the purpose of getting us to believe truths, and operates in the environment – hearing the truths of the gospel announced to us – in which it is designed to operate; and since it is brought about by God it cannot fail in achieving its purpose.

If the conditions that Plantinga lays down for beliefs to be warranted were correct ones, it would be true that if this immediate conviction was actually produced by the Holy Spirit, it would provide knowledge. But, as we have seen in chapter 5 above, these conditions are not sufficient for warrant. The counter-example to Plantinga's analysis of warrant given in Chapter 5 also shows that the immediate conviction that he describes as giving rise to faith would produce irrational belief. The production of S's belief about the blue-eyed man being a used-car salesman happens in the same way as the production of belief in Christian teaching does on the immediate conviction account. Since S's belief is irrational, Christian belief would be irrational as well if it was formed in the way the immediate conviction account describes.

2.

It does not describe this immediate conviction as belief in divine speaking. Thus, on the immediate conviction view, belief does not involve the personal and moral relationship with God that belief in divine speaking does. It is open to the reproach of taking belief in propositions rather than belief in God as its object.

3.

As with enthusiasm, it faces the question of why, if it is true, it is not held by Christian believers generally. In the historical survey of the reasons for Christian belief given above, all the thinkers examined have given God's testimony as the reason for belief, and none of them have mentioned anything like Plantinga's immediate conviction, which, as has been pointed out, excludes God's testimony as the reason for belief. Why should they and everyone else who agreed with them have failed to notice that faith actually works in the way that Plantinga says it does, and instead thought that it involves belief in God's testimony? What is more, this conviction that faith is based on God's testimony has been held as a doctrine of faith. If God produces immediate belief in the truths of the Christian faith in the way Plantinga describes, how is it that the conception of these truths that has actually been held by most theologians throughout history implies that Plantinga's account is wrong?

4.

Christians disagree over important matters of faith. How, on the immediate conviction view, can these disagreements be explained and resolved?

One reply to this objection might be that most Christians do not disagree over important matters of faith; they agree on the essentials of faith, and only disagree over nonessentials. But this is not so. One example among many would be over the permissibility of divorce for Christians. Roman Catholics, and some others, hold that Christ's teaching absolutely forbids divorce between baptized Christians, and that a Christian who divorces his or her Christian spouse and marries someone else commits adultery. Other Christians hold that it is indeed permissible for Christians to divorce and remarry. Another example is the doctrine of the Real Presence of Christ in the Eucharist. If Christ is really physically present in the Eucharist, it is obligatory to worship the Eucharistic elements as divine; but if he is not, such worship will be idolatry.

Another reply would be that disagreement is due to sin on the part of people who hold wrong beliefs about the faith, and that the way to make sure that your convictions about faith are the right ones is to refrain from sinning. I do not want to deny that mistaken beliefs about faith can be due to the sin of the believer, and that disagreements over the content of the faith are sometimes, even often, the result of such mistaken beliefs. But it is unreasonable to say that this is always the case. It is dangerous as well as unreasonable, because it tends to give rise to the following line of thought: if sin is the only explanation for mistaken belief, it must be that everyone who holds a mistaken belief does so out of sin. Since sin deserves punishment, it follows that those who hold mistaken beliefs deserve to be punished. That is the way most Christians thought until the eighteenth or nineteenth centuries, with horrible results that are too well known. These results eventually helped them to see that the assumption that mistaken belief can only be due to sin is wrong. Christians can hold mistaken views about the teachings of the Christian faith in entire innocence.

Plantinga could (and I suspect would) hold that the way to settle doubts or disputes about the faith is by appealing to the Scriptures, whose content believers accept as being spoken by God. But any answer that will emerge from such an appeal will be accepted because it is spoken by God, and therefore not because of immediate conviction. This is incompatible with his immediate conviction understanding of faith.

For these reasons the immediate conviction account should be rejected. Such a rejection would improve Plantinga's view of faith, because he would then be left with only his testimony account, according to which God speaks in the Scriptures and the inner action of the Holy Spirit leads us to recognize and believe this speech. This account is simply the position of Christian tradition on this subject, as we have seen. It is not affected by the problems with his theory of warrant and knowledge, because he does not need this theory in order to say that testimony provides us with knowledge; we know that testimony can be a source of knowledge, independently of any philosophical theorizing about what knowledge is. What he does need though, and does not provide, is some explanation of how the Holy Spirit enables us to recognize and believe God's speech in the Scriptures. Arriving at such an explanation will be the goal of the next chapter.

Views of how God utters the Christian message

In the two preceding sections it has been shown that divine speaking is direct rather than deistic, and that the Scriptures are uttered by God. These results are important, but they do not give a complete account of where the divine speech that communicates the Christian faith is to be found. The task of giving such an account is a most difficult one, and I will not attempt a complete and definitive fulfilment of it. Instead I will set out the main possibilities for an answer to the question of where this divine speech is to be found, indicate their advantages and disadvantages, and try to explore the nature and merits of a particular answer that has not been much considered by theologians in modern times.

Three different answers to this question will be considered. In order to provide a nomenclature of a neutral sort, they can be christened the scriptural view, the magisterial view and the ecclesial view. On the scriptural view, which is that of traditional Protestantism, God speaks in the Scriptures, and Christians (at least after apostolic times) believe his speech only in believing the text of the Scriptures. On the magisterial view, which is that generally held by Roman Catholics, God speaks in the Scriptures, but believing God's speech requires more than believing the text of the Scriptures. It also requires believing those teachings of the Church which are authoritatively promulgated as being divinely revealed, although the Church's act of promulgating these teachings is not divine speaking. On the ecclesial view, God speaks in the Church's teaching, and believing God consists in believing the Church when she teaches. This will include believing the Scriptures, because the Scriptures are a part, indeed the principal part, of the Church's teaching; but it will not consist only in believing the Scriptures, because God speaks in parts of the Church's teaching that are not the Scriptures.

The scriptural view has the advantage of harmonizing with the traditional views that the Scriptures are spoken by God, and contain everything necessary for salvation. However, it faces several objections. One is the fact that it does not provide a way of determining what the text of the Scriptures is. This objection is not made decisive by the fact that nowhere in the Scriptures is there a description of what the text of the Scriptures is supposed to be, because an adherent of the scriptural view could claim that the content of the text of the Scriptures is shown rather than said. The fact that a text was part of the Scriptures would be shown by some feature that it possesses, like its eminent truth or goodness, or its effect on its readers. But the trouble with this answer is that there are significant differences between Christians over the text of the Scriptures. Roman Catholics and Protestants notoriously disagree over which books should be included in the canon of the Scriptures. What is more, it is an open question within Catholic theology whether or not the Septuagint should be taken to be inspired.[16] This dispute is not over whether the Septuagint is an inspired translation of the Hebrew text (which it obviously is not, since there are substantial differences between the two). Rather, it

---

[16] Thus Richard F. Smith S.J. remarks that 'the inspiration of the LXX, though supported by weighty arguments, may not be said to be fully established.' Richard F. Smith, 'Inspiration and Inerrancy', *Jerome Biblical Commentary*, 1968, p. 512.

is over whether the Septuagint *itself* is an inspired text. And the Septuagint is quite a big book. How can texts be shown in the ways described to be part of the Scripture, if there is so much disagreement over them? It is not credible that God has shown to some people (on any account a minority of Christian believers), but not to others, that certain texts are what compose the Scriptures.

A further objection to the scriptural view is that the text of the Scriptures taken on its own is silent and/or unclear on important questions of faith. A good example is the Scriptural teaching on divorce. The Scriptural text on its own is not clear on whether divorce can ever actually be permitted. Three texts (Luke 16:18, Mark 10:10–12 and 1 Cor. 7:10–11) give complete prohibitions of divorce. Two texts, Matthew 5:32 and 19:9, say that divorce is forbidden except in the case of πορνεία. One cannot, by looking at the Scriptural text alone, determine what πορνεία is supposed to mean in that particular context, and whether the Matthean texts are really offering an exception to the blanket prohibitions of the other texts or not.[17] Another example would be the nature of the Holy Spirit. Is the Holy Spirit a divine being distinct from Christ and the Father? The text of the Bible hardly gives a decisive answer to this question when taken on its own. A further example is the question of what if any is the structure that the Christian Church should take. Is it right, or not, to claim that an ordained priesthood and episcopate is a divinely established feature of the Church? A list of such questions could go on for a long time. It is notorious that over centuries of dispute appeals to the text of the Scriptures have not succeeded in resolving these issues. This is not because the partisans of one side or another were not in good faith in seeking the truth about them in the Bible, or not clever or knowledgeable enough to determine what the text said; the Biblical text taken on its own is genuinely insufficient for their resolution. And it is not reasonable to suppose that God should choose to speak to mankind in order to convey a message of the first importance, but that he should not bother to make this speech clear on crucial points of this message.

One might ask: is not this line of argument simply Veron's '*machine de guerre*'? It is. Veron's weapon is an effective one against the target of the scriptural view. Its effectiveness can be seen in the positions of Protestant thinkers like Temple and Dodd, whose rejection of the traditional Protestant espousal of the scriptural view is probably partly motivated by the realization that it involves insuperable difficulties. But an endorsement of Veron's strategy raises the question

---

[17] See the interesting discussion by Raymond F. Collins, *Divorce in the New Testament*, 1992. Some theologians have interpreted πορνεία as meaning adultery, and have conceived of the Matthean text as providing a real exception to the prohibition of divorce. Others, following Joseph Bonsirven, *Le divorce dans le Nouveau Testament*, 1948, have interpreted it as meaning marriage within the prohibited degrees of affinity (following St. Paul in 1 Cor. 5:1), and thus as not providing a real exception. The average believer could hardly be expected to master these scholarly debates, which in any case do not decisively settle the question of the meaning of the Scriptural text. But the content of Christ's teaching on divorce is essential information for many average believers, who face the question of whether or not they can morally get divorced and remarry; they cannot settle for ignorance on this question.

of why the scriptural view has survived it for four hundred years. This cannot be explained as simply being due to the stupidity of its adherents; there has to be some shortcoming in the strategy itself. And this is indeed the case. If the scriptural view is rejected some alternative must be proposed in its stead. The alternative that has been proposed by Catholics since the Reformation has been the magisterial view. As I shall argue, this view has its own insuperable problems. These problems are what have prevented the scriptural view's difficulties from leading to its demise.

It is worth pointing out the difference between this objection to the scriptural view, and the objection that was raised to the deistic view. Neither of these are the objection that the position being criticised simply makes it very difficult to find out the contents of the divine message. It would be possible to reply to this objection by saying that this difficulty is part of God's probation for believers, intended to ensure that only those people who are sincerely determined to find out the truth will arrive at it. (Someone who took an Augustinian view of faith and grace would not find this reply satisfactory, because on such a view all good action must begin with faith and cannot precede it, and hence such probation can serve no useful purpose, but that is by the way.) But this reply is not available to the objection to the deistic view, which is that on the deistic view it is not merely difficult, but in principle impossible given the available evidence, to get an accurate idea of what God has said in speaking to humanity. Nor is it available to the objection to the scriptural view, which is not that it is in principle impossible to know what God has said, but rather that on the scriptural view what God has actually said does not possess a clear and determinate meaning, so that there is no coherent divine message to discover.[18]

The possibility of resolving such questions is an advantage of the magisterial view, which says that as well as believing the Scriptures we must believe with the assent of faith those propositions which the Church teaches as dogmas of faith, although the Church's teaching is not itself divine speaking. This is the view generally held by Roman Catholics. A standard version of it is the following, which is taken from a Roman Catholic theology manual of a traditional sort:

> Theology like faith accepts, as the sources of its knowledge, Holy Writ and Tradition (remote rule of faith) and also the doctrinal assertions of the Church (proximate rule of faith) ...[19] By dogma in the strict sense is understood a truth immediately (formally)

---

[18] This objection was raised a long time ago by John Henry Newman: '... we are brought to this strange conclusion, that God has given us a revelation, yet revealed nothing, – that at great cost, and with much preparation He has miraculously declared His will; that multitudes have accordingly considered they possessed it, yet that, after all, He has said nothing so clearly as to recommend itself as His to a cautious mind; that nothing is so revealed as to be part of the revelation, nothing plain enough to act upon, nothing so certain that we dare assert that the contrary is less certain.

Such a conclusion is a practical refutation of the objection which leads to it. It surely cannot be meant that we should be undecided all our days. We were made for action, and for right action, – for thought, and for true thought.' John Henry Newman, *Tract 85*, 1969, p. 84.

[19] Ludwig Ott, *Fundamentals of Catholic Theology*, 4th edn, 1960, pp. 2–3.

revealed by God which has been proposed by the Teaching Authority of the Church to be believed as such ...

Two factors or elements may be distinguished in the concept of dogma;

a) An immediate Divine Revelation of the particular Dogma (revelatio immediate divina or revelatio formalis), i.e. the Dogma must be immediately revealed by God either explicitly (explicite) or implicitly (implicite), and therefore be contained in the sources of Revelation (Holy Writ or Tradition).

b) The Promulgation of the Dogma by the Teaching Authority of the Church (propositio Ecclesiae). This implies, not merely the promulgation of the Truth, but also the obligation on the part of the Faithful of believing the Truth...

Dogma in its strict sense is the object of both Divine Faith ... and Catholic Faith (fides catholica); it is the object of Divine Faith ... by reason of its Divine Revelation; it is the object of Catholic Faith ... on account of its infallible doctrinal definition by the Church. If a baptised person deliberately denies or doubts a dogma properly so-called, he is guilty of the sin of heresy[20]...

Dogmas are classified ... c) According to the mode by which the Church proposes them, as: formal Dogmas (dogmata formalia) and Material Dogmas (dogmata materialia). The former are proposed for belief by the Teaching Authority of the Church as truths of Revelation; the latter are not so proposed, for which reason they are not Dogmas in the strict sense[21]...

Corresponding to the purpose of the Teaching Authority of the Church of preserving unfalsified and of infallibly interpreting the Truths of Revelation   (D 1800) the primary object (obiectum primarium) of the Teaching office of the Church is the body of immediately revealed truths and facts. The infallible doctrinal power of the Church extends, however, secondarily to all those truths or facts which are a consequence of the teaching of Revelation or a presupposition of it (obiectum secondarium). Those doctrines and truths defined by the Church not as immediately revealed but as intrinsically connected with the truths of Revelation so that their denial would undermine the revealed truths are called *Catholic Truths* (veritates catholicae) or Ecclesiastical Teachings (doctrinae ecclesiasticae) to distinguish them from the Divine Truths or Divine Doctrines of Revelation (veritates vel doctrinae divinae). These are proposed for belief in virtue of the infallibility of the Church in teaching doctrines of faith or morals (fides ecclesiastica).

To these Catholic truths belong:

Theological Conclusions (conclusiones theologicae) properly so-called. By these are understood religious truths, which are derived from two premises, of which one is an immediately revealed truth, and the other a truth of natural reason. Since one premise is a truth of Revelation, theological conclusions are spoken of as being mediately or virtually (virtualiter) revealed. If however both premises are immediately revealed truths, then the conclusion also must be regarded as immediately revealed and as the object of Immediate Divine Faith (fides immediate divina).

Dogmatic Facts (facta dogmatica). By these are understood historical facts, which are not revealed, but which are intrinsically connected with revealed truth, for example, the legality of a Pope or a General Council ... The fact that a defined text does or does not agree with the doctrine of the Catholic Faith is also, in a narrower sense, a 'dogmatic fact' ...

---

[20] Ott, 1960, pp. 4–5.
[21] Ott, 1960, pp. 5–6.

> *Truths of Reason*, which have not been revealed, but which are intrinsically associated with a revealed truth, e.g. those philosophic truths which are presuppositions of the act of Faith (knowledge of the supersensual, possibility of proofs of God, the spirituality of the soul, freedom of the will), or philosophic concepts, in terms of which dogma is promulgated (person, substance, transubstantiation, etc.)[22]

The advantage of the magisterial view over the scriptural view is clear; the teachings of the Church settle those essential questions of faith that the text of the Scriptures alone do not enable us to decide, and give a means of interpreting the Scriptures when their meaning is unclear. But it also faces grave difficulties, which explain why this advantage has not proved decisive in the centuries since Veron's time.

Some of these difficulties pertain to particular formulations of the magisterial view, and can be addressed by adjusting it. The idea of divine revelation being the remote rule of faith and the doctrinal assertions of the Church being the proximate rule of faith has already been found unsatisfactory by Catholic theologians. This distinction between remote and proximate rule means that we cannot believe the Scriptures simply on account of their being spoken by God, but must believe them on account of the Church's having proposed them for belief as having been spoken by God. This position is now generally rejected by Catholic theologians, because it cannot be reconciled with the view that divine revelation, in the sense of divine communication, is the formal object of divine faith.[23] The division of dogmas into material and formal, and the claim that divine utterances only become dogmas in the strict sense when they are proposed for belief by the Church as such, is even more unsatisfactory. It attributes to teachings of the Church that are not utterances of God an authority and a power to compel belief that is not possessed by the spoken word of God himself. This is intolerable.

All these objections can, however, be accommodated by adopting a more reasonable form of the magisterial view, to the effect that believers must have divine faith not just in the doctrinal assertions of the Church, but in both these assertions and the utterances of God in the Scriptures. But this accommodation will not serve to defuse the more fundamental difficulties that the magisterial view faces. A first difficulty is the fact that (as Tillotson among others pointed out) there

---

[22] Ott, 1960, pp. 8–9. 'D 1800' refers to Denzinger's *Enchiridion*.

[23] Catholic theologians thus felt the force of criticisms like Whitaker's, mentioned in Chapter 4. This rejection is documented, as mentioned above, in Gardeil's *Dictionnaire de théologie catholique* article 'Crédibilité'. A standard Catholic theological manual, that of van Noort, Castelot and Murphy, states: 'The proposal of a truth by the Church is nothing more than the normal means by which the truths contained in the treasury of Scripture and Tradition are made known to us in secure fashion so that we may cling to these truths exclusively because of the authority of God revealing. Consequently when Augustine says: "I would not believe the gospel unless moved to do so by the authority of the Catholic Church", he does not mean that the Church's authority is the motive or formal reason why we believe the gospel. He simply means that the Church's authority is the normal means for knowing what should or should not be accepted as belonging to the gospel.' G. van Noort, *Dogmatic Theology, vol. III: The Sources of Revelation*, 1961, pp. 200–201.

is an extensive tradition to the effect that the whole of Christian revelation is to be found in the Scriptures. Since the magisterial view demands that ecclesial tradition be followed, it seems therefore to refute itself.

A second difficulty is offering an explanation of how the Church comes to know those extra teachings she pronounces which are not to be found in the Scriptures. Appealing to the inspiration of the Holy Spirit is not helpful; for how is this inspiration supposed to operate? The idea that the Holy Spirit directly informs the Church of these teachings is repugnant. It does not seem to be reconcilable with the traditional view (discussed below) that revelation was completed with the Apostles, or with the traditional view that the Apostles had the charism of inspiration in a way that the Church does not. And no-one can give an explanation of how this direct informing of the Church is supposed to happen.

Adherents of the magisterial view have attempted to answer these difficulties by appealing to unwritten tradition. The idea is that those teachings of the Church that cannot be found in the Scriptures originate in divine revelation that was not written down in the Scriptures, but was passed down from the apostles through word of mouth in an unwritten tradition. This view was thought to be the teaching of the Council of Trent. However, it has now been largely abandoned. There is no historical evidence for such unwritten traditions,[24] and the idea of their existence was not thought of until the Middle Ages.[25] Historical investigation has shown that this view was not actually taught by the Council of Trent, and the Second Vatican Council deliberately refused to affirm the existence of such traditions.[26] In line with Yves Congar and others, I see no objection to postulating that there are some traditional practices that originated with the Apostles (possible examples would be infant baptism and the practice of keeping Sunday rather than Saturday as a holy day), but the idea of there being doctrines to which the assent of faith must be given that were handed down solely through unwritten tradition seems implausible for the reasons given in the literature on the subject, and I will take it that it is false. So this solution to these difficulties can no longer be proposed.

The non-existence of such unwritten traditions renders insoluble another difficulty with the magisterial view. How can we have divine faith in the pronouncements of the Church, if these pronouncements do not utter teachings that were said by God? Traditionally the magisterial view answered this question by

----

[24] See R. P. C. Hanson *Tradition in the Early Church*, 1962.

[25] See Congar, 1966, and George Tavard, *Holy Writ or Holy Church*, 1959. This theory is reflected in the passages quoted from Ott above that talk about Scripture and Tradition being the sources of revelation. However, in the nineteenth century Catholic theologians, sensitive to the lack of historical evidence for such unwritten traditions, began to define tradition as being the teaching of the magisterium of the Church. This obviously makes it impossible to talk of tradition as a source of revelation upon which Church teaching is based, or as something that should be believed in addition to the Church's doctrinal assertions. On this subject see Congar, 1966, and J. P. Mackey, *The modern theology of tradition*, 1962.

[26] On this question see Congar and Dupuy, *Vatican II: La Révélation divine*, 2 vols., 1968 (especially B.-P. Dupuy, 'Historique de la constitution', in vol. 1), J. R. Geiselmann, *Die Heiliger Schrift und die Tradition*, 1962, and J. R. Geiselmann 'Un malentendu éclairci. La relation Écriture–Tradition dans la théologie catholique', *Istina*, 1958.

saying that the teachings of the Church were simply indicating what God had already said in Scripture or unwritten tradition, and that believers then assented to these utterances because God said them rather than because the Church taught them. But we now know that those teachings of the Church that are not stated in Scripture do not usually originate in apostolic traditions either, so no justification could be made for the magisterial view's demand that they be believed with divine faith, even if we accepted a deistic rather than a direct understanding of revelation.[27] This problem is especially acute if we hold with Ott that believers must have divine faith not just in propositions that have been uttered by God, but also in propositions taught by the Church that are logically deducible from propositions uttered by God. It is arguable that divine faith *requires* belief in the latter sort of propositions, but such belief cannot be an *exercise* of divine faith, because it is *ex hypothesi* belief in propositions that God never uttered.

A final difficulty with the magisterial view arises from the fact that, for the reasons given above, the deistic view is wrong. Divine faith should be conceived of not as just believing that God said something, but as believing God speaking. But the whole idea of the magisterial view is that we should believe with divine faith teachings of the Church that are not divine utterances. This is incompatible with the direct view of divine speaking.

The magisterial view thus does not stand up to examination. Its shortcomings, and those of the scriptural view, provide reasons for accepting the ecclesial view: a negative reason, which is that the possible alternatives to the ecclesial view do not work, and a positive reason, which is that the ecclesial view gives answers to the objections that are fatal to the scriptural and magisterial views. The ecclesial view, as described above, states that the doctrinal teachings of the Church are God's speaking. On this view the Scriptures are God's speaking because they are a part of the teaching of the Church, indeed the principal part of it, the part for which all the other teaching is commentary and exposition. The meaning of the Scriptures will not be incomplete or unclear, because this meaning will not arise from the Scriptural text taken in isolation from its context in the teaching activity of the Church. Nor will it be impossible to explain how divine faith can be given to the doctrinal assertions of the Church, because these assertions will be God speaking.

There are also reasons for adopting the ecclesial view that are independent of the inadequacy of the alternatives to it.

---

[27] As we have seen, a somewhat similar argument was made by Veron, but with an important difference from the one offered here. When he claimed that it was illegitimate for the Protestants to hold beliefs logically deduced from the Scripture because the Scripture did not license such deductions, he was attacking the Protestants for violating their own rule of faith, rather than for presenting statements that were not actually uttered by God as suitable objects for divine faith. His line of argument does not rule out the possibility of a rule of faith that asserts that logical deductions from the Scripture must be believed as a matter of faith; it only points out that the Protestant rule of faith does not permit this assertion.

1.

There is a substantial body of tradition that supports it. Before and even during the Middle Ages it was common to include the writings of the Fathers, conciliar canons and sometimes even theological works in the category of *Scriptura sacra*.[28] Patristic writings were sometimes described as θεόπνευστος, inspired. St. Gregory of Nyssa describes St. Basil's *Hexameron* as θεόπνευστον, and says that it has been justly described as equal to the words of Moses himself.[29] St. Augustine describes the work of St. Jerome as truly written to the dictation of the Holy Spirit.[30] Leontius of Byzantium states that the Fathers could not have contradicted one another, because they did not speak of themselves, but rather the Holy Spirit spoke through them.[31] St. John Damascene describes the Fathers as θεόπνευστοι.[32] The works of St. Gregory the Great were often described as inspired. Anselm of Laon writes of Gregory's *Moralia*, 'Videamus quod dicat Sanctus Spiritus in Moralibus', 'Let us see what the Holy Spirit says in the *Moralia*'.[33] The Second Council of Nicaea speaks of the 'God-spoken teaching of our holy fathers'.[34] There are numberless texts that describe the councils of the Church as inspired; they are sometimes put on a level with the Gospels. This is especially true of the council of Nicaea, whose creed is described by St. Athanasius as ῥῆμα τοῦ Κυρίου (*Ad Afros*, 2). St. Cyril of Alexandria asserted that the Holy Spirit spoke in the Fathers of that Council:

> ... let us show as far as possible in what way the mystery of the economy of salvation devised by Christ has been announced to us by Holy Scripture. Then, also, what the Fathers themselves have spoken who set forth the standard of blameless faith, since the Holy Spirit taught them the truth; for, according to our Saviour's words, it was not they themselves who spoke but 'the Spirit of God and Father who speaks through them'.[35]

St. Gregory the Great stated that he accepted and believed the four councils of Nicaea, Constantinople, Ephesus and Chalcedon just as he accepted and believed

---

[28] Congar (1966), pp. 92–3.

[29] St. Gregory of Nyssa, *In Hexameron*, P.G. 44, 61–64. He promises to give an exposition that follows the divinely inspired commentary of St. Basil, 'μετὰ τὴν θεόπνευστον ἐκείνην τοῦ πατρὸς ἡμῶν εἰς τὸ προκείμενον θεωρίαν' (p. 61).

[30] St. Augustine, *Ep.* 82, 2. This passage is admittedly from a letter to Jerome himself, and could plausibly be construed as flattery that Augustine did not really believe. But it is still significant that Augustine could have felt it possible to say such a thing even as flattery.

[31] Leontius of Byzantium, *Adver. Nestor.*; P.G. 86, 1356 A.

[32] St. John Damascene, *De fid. orth*, IV, 17; P.G. 86, 1176 B.

[33] Anselm of Laon, *Sententiae*, 1895, p. 29.

[34] 'τῇ θεηγόρῳ διδασκαλίᾳ τῶν ἁγίων πατέρων ἡμῶν'; Tanner and Alberigo, 1990, vol. 1, pp. 135–6. On this tradition see Congar, 1966, especially his Chap. 3, Excursus B; Gustave Bardy, 'L'Inspiration des Pères de l'Église', in *Recherches de Science Religieuse*, 1952; D. van der Eynde, *Les normes de l'enseignement chrétien dans la littérature patristique des trois premières siècles*, 1933.

[35] Letter 1, in St. Cyril of Alexandria (1987), p. 17.

the four gospels.[36] The Third Council of Constantinople describes itself as divinely inspired.[37]

Yves Congar describes this tradition as having been prevalent until the twelfth century:

> God acts in the Church, and thus what is there legitimately done is done from him. This is the conviction of the whole Catholic tradition. It has nevertheless been conceived of in two ways, roughly spread over two periods which, in the West, hinge at the twelfth century. I say 'roughly' because one can find, in the first period, various indications of the spirit underlying the second, particularly in Rome; just as, in the second period, one finds considerable survivals from the spirit of the first. However, ten years' close study of the texts has convinced me that the following facts are true: the Gregorian Reform and its influence, decisive for an epoch as full of life as the twelfth century in the West, marked a definitive turning-point: the transition from an appreciation of the ever active *presence of God* to that of *juridical powers* put at the disposal of, and perhaps even handed over as its property to, 'the Church', i.e. the hierarchy. For the Fathers and the early Middle Ages, the sacred actions are performed *in* the Church, according to the forms of the Church, and are rigorously sacred as such. But their *subject* is *God*, in an actual and direct way. Ecclesiastical structures are much more the manifestation and form of *God*'s action than a subject whose internal quality or power could constitute an adequate basis for the certain production of the expected effect. The categories of thought are less those of (efficient) causality than those of the manifestation of the invisible via the visible, and a symphony of the two – the invisible retaining a primacy of presence and operation.[38]

Congar relates this change to a change in the political and legal conceptions of the Latin West:

> Even outside the immediate ecclesiastical context the actual world of ideas concerning authority changed. The Middle Ages had built their politico-juridical ideas on Holy Scripture, the Fathers and Germanic law. On one side, they tempered the rights of the sovereign by community rights, and on the other, they saw the powers exercised by members of the hierarchy, civil or ecclesiastical, as subject to laws, to the common good, to justice, to right order, which excluded in principle the discretionary use of their power. All this underwent a far-reaching change, beginning in the fifteenth century – the renaissance of Roman law, dating from the twelfth century, bore its fruit slowly. In Roman law the subject of law is always an individual will, in the public law it is the State, conceived of as a person, not the people themselves. As a result there is a

---

[36] 'Praeterea, quia corde creditur ad justitiam, ore autem confessio fit ad salutem, sicut sancti Evangelii quatuor libros, sic quatuor concilia suscipere et venerari me fateor.' St.Gregory the Great, *Ep*. XXV; P.L. 78, 478.

[37] 'ἡ καθ' ἡμᾶς ἁγία καὶ οἰκουμενικὴ θεοπνεύστως ἐπεσφράγισε σύνοδος'; Tanner and Alberigo, 1990, vol. 1, p. 125.

[38] Congar, 1966, pp. 134–5. His remarks on the categories of thought in the earlier tradition being those of a manifestation of the invisible via the visible, *rather* than those of efficient causality (as if these two are incompatible), seem prompted more by his discomfort with the view of the earlier tradition than by a real difference in this respect between the earlier and the later view.

tendency to make the State absolute, and with it the princely power that embodies it. The modern theory of sovereignty had its roots much earlier than the sixteenth century, but at that time it took on a new absolutist form (J. Bodin, Machiavelli), rigorously submitting the community to its head. These ideas were to show their full force in the political theories of the civil order, often hardly Christian, but echoes of them are found in the public law of the Church and the theology which translated this into ecclesiological doctrine.[39]

Congar's extensive documentation of this earlier tradition, and his description of the reasons for its being supplanted, are the more notable because he himself rejects it.

Congar's assertion that the earlier view lost its predominance in the twelfth century, with nothing more than 'considerable survivals' after that time, has been shown to be mistaken by the important work of J. Ermel on the Council of Trent.[40] This work was based on the rather tardy publication of the acts and preparatory documents of that Council at the end of the nineteenth century, made possible by the opening of the Vatican archives. Ermel has shown that the earlier view was explicitly held and argued for by important figures at the fourth session of that Council in 1546, and that it represented the general view held by the fathers of the Council at that session. This was the session that discussed the sources of Christian faith, and that produced a document listing the books of the Scriptures and stating that divine revelation was to be found in both Scriptures and apostolic traditions. Alphonsus de Castro OFM, a theologian who played an important role in this session, explicitly presented the earlier view in his *Adversus omnes haereses*. There, he stated that we believe the Scriptures not because of the men who wrote them, but because of God who inspired them, and asked what would prevent the Holy Spirit from inspiring the church who speaks, just as much as the evangelist who writes?[41] He took this line in the debates at the Council. Jerome Seripando, the general of the Augustinians at the time, also explicitly stated the ecclesial view in his *De Traditionibus*, where he said that the Holy Spirit had revealed through the general councils, according to the necessities of the times, many truths that are not openly stated in the Scriptures.[42] During the conciliar discussions, Bonuccio, the general of the Servites, objected to the claim that divine revelation was to be found partly in Scripture and partly in tradition, on the grounds that all of revelation was in Scripture; but he explicated this by saying that Scripture includes not only the books listed as composing it, but also many other texts, such as the canons of the apostles, general councils, and the decretals of the popes.[43] The general view at this session of the council was that the truths of faith were to be found in three places; the text of Scripture, unwritten apostolic traditions, and the teachings of the Church. An interesting modification of this view added a fourth to this list, that of

---

[39] Congar, 1966, pp. 179–80.

[40] J. Ermel, *Les sources de la foi*, 1963.

[41] '... Quid ergo prohibet divinum spiritum astare ecclesiae loquenti, perinde ac Evangelistae scibendi?' Lib. XIV, fol. VIII, quoted in Ermel, 1963, p. 38.

[42] Ermel, 1963, p. 55; see Seripando, *De Traditionibus*, tract. XII.

[43] Ermel, 1963, p. 136.

logical deductions from the text of Scripture and the traditions of the apostles. This addition shows that the teachings of the church were explicitly considered to be something different from logical deductions from Scripture and apostolic tradition.

Ermel offers an explanation of how it is that the teachings of the church failed to be mentioned in the council documents along with Scripture and apostolic traditions, despite the demands of the council fathers that it be included as a source of divine revelation. He asserts that the fourth session of the council was ended before the text on the sources of revelation was completed, and the complaints of the fathers about the incompleteness of the resulting document were placated by the promise that the question of the teaching of the Church as a source of divine revelation would be taken up in the next session; however, at the beginning of that session the organizers proceeded straight to the issue of original sin in order to save time, and the document on the sources of revelation was left incomplete. This historical account, although plausible, is speculative. What is not speculative, given the evidence Ermel provides, is the general acceptance of some form of the ecclesial view at the fourth session of the council. Ermel explains the replacement of the ecclesial by the magisterial view (something already visible in the writings of Melchior Cano not many years after the fourth session of the council) as being due to a misinterpretation of the document produced by the fourth session as restricting the sources of revelation to Scripture and apostolic tradition, a misinterpretation no-one was in a position to correct until the acts of the council were published more than three and a half centuries later, and to the pressure of controversy with Protestants. On the one hand the notion of continual inspiration of the Church was disliked as something the Protestants could apply to themselves, and on the other hand an appeal to the inspiration of the teachings of the Catholic Church was not useful in arguing against Protestants, who would deny that it existed. A purely historical appeal to the facts of church tradition was the only thing that could be of use in attacking them. The relative weight to be given to Ermel's explanations of this change on the one hand, and Congar's on the other, is not easy to determine; no doubt all of these factors played a role.

In the transition from the ecclesial to the magisterial view we can see part of the motivation of the Protestant Reformation, whose rejection of the attribution to human authority of powers that belong only to God was entirely just, as the criticism of the magisterial view has brought out. As applied to the views of the fathers of the fourth session this rejection was somewhat question-begging, since these views held that the exercise of the powers of the Church was an exercise of divine power; but the Protestants were not in a position to know what these fathers had thought, since they had no access to the acts of the council.

This favourable remark about the motivation of the Reformers may be found excessively paradoxical, on the grounds that it criticizes the magisterial view for making overweening claims about the Church's teaching authority in the course of putting forward an even stronger claim about the nature of that authority. A quick reply would be that it is not the magisterial view's claims about the Church's teaching authority as such that are being criticized, since both the magisterial view and the ecclesial view hold that these teachings demand the assent of faith. Rather, it is the rationale proffered for this authority by the magisterial view that is found insufficient. But it should also be said that the differences between the magisterial view and the ecclesial view over the rationale of the teaching authority of the Church have implications for the way in which this authority is exercised. If the teaching of the Church is an activity of Christ speaking in his Body, the Church, then this teaching must be done in such a way that it truly can be said to be the activity of that Body, and all the members of the Body can play a part in it. These implications can be seen to operate in the differences between the way in which Church teaching was determined and promulgated in Congar's first period, especially in the patristic era, and the way in which it was determined and promulgated in post-Tridentine Roman Catholicism. The intensive conciliar activity of the patristic era, not only in the great ecumenical councils but in a multitude of smaller assemblies and synods, the active involvement of the laity in the Arian crisis, the central role played by monks in the Iconoclast controversy – all reflect an understanding of how the teaching of the Church is an activity of the Body of Christ, in which the whole of that body can be involved. In contrast, the teaching of the Church came increasingly to be seen in the Roman Catholic Church after the Council of Trent as analogous to an administrative decision by a highly placed official. This was a logical working-out of the magisterial view, that produced damaging effects of many kinds.[44]

2.

The ecclesial view has a theological foundation in the doctrine of the Mystical Body of Christ.

The idea that the Church is the body of Christ is amply testified to in the Scriptures. The Fathers, in the course of the Arian controversy, insisted that the union of Christians with Christ was not merely a union of mind and will, but a real union of being; the union of charity between Christians, and between Christians and Christ, does not constitute this union of being, but is a consequence of it.[45] But the voluntary actions of a person's body are the voluntary actions of the person himself. If the Church is in a real sense Christ's body, it follows that the Church's actions are Christ's actions. (Of course not every action of a member of the Church will be an action of the Church. The actions of a member of the Church will be actions of the Church when they are done by someone who is furthering the mission of the Church, which is the sanctification of humanity, and who is sent by Christ to further this mission through these actions.) Since a principal activity

---

[44] Another problem with the magisterial view was the damage it did to Catholic understandings of Church tradition. Roman Catholics, accepting the expedient of postulating unwritten traditions as a way of defending the magisterial view, came more and more to think of tradition as having the function of supporting dogmas that lacked any explicit scriptural foundation. The *ressourcement* movement in theology attempted to correct this understanding, but without much success. This defective view meant that when belief in unwritten traditions was abandoned, Catholics tended to not see tradition as having any point or authority at all.

[45] On this see the classic work by Émile Mersch, *The Whole Christ*, 1938, and E. L. Mascall, *Christ, the Christian and the Church*, 1946.

of the Church is preaching the Gospel, it is Christ who preaches in the Church's preaching. Most discussion of the Church as the body of Christ has focused on the nature of the link between Christians and Christ that makes Christians members of Christ. There has also been a good deal of discussion of how the link between Christ and his members means that Christ himself suffers in his members, and that we love Christ in loving those who are members of him (cf. Matt. 25:40, Acts 9:4). There has been less consideration of how Christ acts in his members. But this topic has not gone entirely without notice. Augustine speaks of how Christ prays in the prayer of Christians:

> When each of you sings a verse, it is still this one man that sings, since you are all one in Christ. We do not say, 'To Thee, O Lord, have we lifted up our eyes', but 'To Thee, O Lord, have I lifted up my eyes' [Ps. 122:1]. You should of course consider that each one of you is speaking, but that primarily this one man is speaking who reaches to the ends of the earth.[46]

The English Cistercian Isaac of Stella offers these reflections on the Church's forgiveness of sins:

> The Bridegroom, who is one nature (*unum*) with the Father, is one person (*unus*) with the Bride ... What was natural and proper to her He took unto Himself, and what was proper to Himself and divine He has given to her ... This interchange accounts for the dignity of confession and for the power to remit sins. Christ has said; 'Get thee hence and show thyself to the priest' (Luke 5:14). This power becomes no less truly and solely Christ's by belonging to the Church; nay, it would not belong to the whole Christ unless it did belong to the Church. In like manner this power is no less truly and solely God's power by being Christ's, and would not belong to the whole God, so to speak, if it were not Christ's.[47]

We can make a similar statement about divine speaking, and say that this activity becomes no less truly and solely Christ's by belonging to the Church, and that it would not belong to the whole Christ unless it belonged to the Church. A Scriptural warrant for this assertion can be found in Luke 10:16: 'He who hears you hears me, and he who rejects you rejects me, and he who rejects me rejects him who sent me.'[48] The ecclesial view together with the doctrine of the Church as the Body of Christ offers an explanation of Christ's words in the Gospel of Luke: 'I came to cast fire on the earth; and would that it were already kindled! I have a baptism to be baptized with; and how I am constrained until that is accomplished!' (Luke 12:49). The baptism that he refers to is the baptism of his death. The question that this passage poses is why Christ should be constrained until he has

---

[46] St. Augustine, *In Ps.* 142 (quoted in Mersch, 1938, p. 424). See this work and also *In Ps.* 54, *In Ps.* 85, *In Ps.* 122, in St. Augustine, *Enarrationes in Psalmos LI–C*, 1956b, *Enarrationes in Psalmos CI–CL*, 1956c.

[47] Isaac of Stella, *Sermo* II, P.L. 194, 1731 (quoted in Mersch, 1938, p. 448).

[48] Cf. also John 13:20: 'He who receives any one whom I send receives me; and he who receives me receives him who sent me.'

experienced the baptism of his death. We can understand why others might be constrained until then, because they will be enslaved by the yoke of sin that Christ's redemptive death removes, but why should *Christ* be constrained? This can be understood if we hold that only after his death will Christ act in his Body, which is redeemed through that death. Since his Body extends throughout the world, he can act in it much more extensively than he could as one man in Palestine. The ecclesial view also lets us see how the Church can be described as the pillar and foundation of the truth (1 Tim. 3:15). It is because Christ is the pillar and foundation of the truth, and he speaks in the Church's speaking.

3.

The idea that Christ speaks in the teachings of the Church, and that the Scriptures are the principal part of this teaching, coheres with what has been learnt about the nature of the Scriptures and about the way in which they have been traditionally understood. An important finding of modern scriptural scholarship has been the extent to which the books of the Bible were written in order to express the faith of the community that produced them. This is exactly how the ecclesial view expects them to be. On the ecclesial view, the human author of the Scriptures is the Church.[49] This harmonizes with the fact that until the late Middle Ages, the meaning of the Scriptures was taken to be the meaning of the Scriptures as expounded by the Church. The ecclesial view also casts light on the methods of Scriptural interpretation found in the Scriptures themselves. For instance, many of

---

[49] Similar views have been argued for by Karl Rahner, *Inspiration in the Bible*, 1961, R. A. F. Mackenzie 'Some Problems in the Field of Inspiration', *Catholic Biblical Quarterly*, 1958, J. F. Mackenzie, 'The Social Character of Inspiration', *Catholic Biblical Quarterly*, 1962. The ecclesial view accepts the traditional position that the meaning that God intends to communicate in the Scriptures is the meaning intended by their human authors, if it is understood that the human author of the Scriptures is the Church. Of course in some cases the meaning of the individuals who wrote the parts of the Scriptures will also be the meaning of the Church. And in these cases it may also be true that God was speaking in the individual's actual writing of the text in question, which is not the same thing. For example, the individual Paul's writing his canonical letters would be the Church's writing these letters, and hence God's writing them, since Paul was writing ex cathedra, in his capacity as apostle. The ecclesial view can also accept the traditional scholastic understanding of Biblical inspiration, according to which God, as the author of the Scriptures, is the principal efficient cause of them, with the human authors being the instrumental cause, just as a man writing with a piece of chalk is the efficient cause of the writing, with the chalk being the instrumental cause. However, the action of the human instrumental cause in producing the Scriptures should not be understood as the action of writing the words of the Scriptures down on papyri, but rather as the collective activity of human minds and wills that was involved in the Church's composition of the Scriptures. The former 'divine dictation' kind of understanding of the action of the instrumental cause of the Scriptures was not the patristic one, as the discussion of patristic views of inspiration in chapter 2 brings out. Its emergence among both Catholics and Protestants is likely the result of the assumption, discussed in Louis Bouyer, *Du Protestantisme à l'Église*, 1954, that divine and human action are mutually exclusive, so that the Scriptures' being produced by conscious human effort would imply that they are not also produced by God.

the New Testament authors attribute messianic significance to texts that did not have such significance when they were originally written. The ecclesial view can explain these attributions without finding the authors guilty of inventing meanings, by pointing out that this messianic significance was generally accepted by Jews at the time of the writing of the New Testament. The very fact of this general acceptance meant that the texts in question had a new meaning conferred on them that they did not possess when first written. This meaning was conferred on them by their being used to convey this meaning as part of the faith of Israel. (A presupposition of this last explanation is that God speaks not just in the teaching of the Christian Church, but in the teaching of the People of God generally; which would include Israel as well as the Church – cf. Matt. 23:1: 'The scribes and the Pharisees sit in Moses's seat.')

The ecclesial view, while being supported by the findings of Scriptural scholarship, has an implication for the goals of this scholarship that ought to be pointed out. Much study of the New Testament has focused on the question of which parts of its teaching originate in the early church, and which parts originate in Christ himself. The ecclesial view means that this is a question to which there can be no answer. (There is no doubt an answer to the question of which statements were physically uttered by Christ in person and which were not (although there does not seem to be enough historical evidence to find out this answer), but even if the answer to this question were known, it would not give us an answer to the question of what teachings originated in Christ himself as opposed to in the Church.) Since many years of scholarly investigation of this question have proved barren of solid results, this implication of the ecclesial view is not one that should disturb Scripture scholars.

The ecclesial view must face the difficulties of reconciling its assertions with the tradition that revelation ceased with the death of the last Apostle, and of accounting for the primacy of the Scriptures. Resolving the former difficulty gives the key to a resolution of the latter.

The doctrine that public divine revelation was completed with the Apostles is a central part of the common Christian tradition, held by Catholics, Orthodox and Protestants alike, and originating in the earliest Fathers of the Church, who were all anxious to maintain that they 'hold and declare the faith given from the beginning by the great God and our Saviour Jesus Christ to the Holy Apostles.'[50] This tradition is supported by the theological rationale that the purpose of revelation is to bring the message of salvation. But salvation comes in Christ, who is the Way, the Truth and the Life. With Christ's incarnation, passion and resurrection, and the sending of the Holy Spirit, the way to salvation has been fully established, and thus the message of salvation is complete. There is no more to be said about the way to salvation, and thus nothing that can be added to revelation.[51] This is obviously

---

[50] Council of Constantinople II, in Denzinger, 1957, no. 212, p. 85.

[51] This point is made by the *Catechism of the Catholic Church*:
'65 ... Christ, the Son of God made man, is the Father's perfect and unsurpassable Word. In him he has said everything; there will be no other word than this one. St. John of the Cross, among others, commented strikingly on Hebrews 1:1–2:

difficult to reconcile with the view that God speaks to us in the teachings of the Church up to the present. There are in fact two difficulties posed for the ecclesial view by the doctrine that revelation was completed by the Apostles. The first is that the ecclesial view states that God continues up to the present to speak in a manner that commands the assent of faith. Since such speech is divine revelation, this implies that revelation continues up to the present. The second is that the ecclesial view, as described above, holds not only that God continues to speak after the death of the last Apostle, but that he says new things. According to the ecclesial view the teachings of the ecumenical councils are spoken by God. However, many of these teachings were not uttered in the Scriptures, and cannot plausibly be said to have descended from the Apostles via an unwritten tradition. They were thus never said before the death of the last Apostle, and it is hard to see how they could fail to be considered as new revelations.

This is obviously true for most of the doctrinal assertions taught by the Roman Catholic Church as matters of faith. But it is also true for the teachings of the councils that are recognized by both Catholics and Orthodox as ecumenical and binding, and for the Nicene Creed, which is adopted as a profession of faith by churches that are not Catholic or Orthodox. Nowhere in the Scriptures is it stated that e.g. Christ is consubstantial with the Father, or that Christ does not have a single will that is both divine and human. These statements may be logically deducible from the Scriptures, but they certainly are not said in them. One might reply that these teachings are Catholic truths in Ott's sense. It is possible to make a case for the Church's having the authority to teach propositions that are not divinely revealed, and hence for their being such a thing as Catholic truths and ecclesiastical faith, in Ott's sense of these terms. The question of whether or not the Church possesses such a power falls outside the scope of this book. But the teachings of the councils recognized by Catholics and Orthodox are not proposed for belief as Catholic truths. Rather, they claim to be passing on the teachings of the apostles, and claim the assent of divine, rather than simply of Catholic, faith.

The first difficulty is not as severe as the second one; it could be claimed that God's repeating things that he had already said does not constitute a true addition to revelation. However, it is harder to explain why his saying new things should not be such an addition. (The difficulty of providing such an explanation may be a motivation for the magisterial view.) But an explanation needs to be attempted. The teachings of the Church that were not pronounced in or before apostolic times are not dispensable parts of Christian belief, because, as we have seen, the

---

In giving us his Son, his only word (for he possesses no other), he spoke everything to us at once in this sole Word – and he has no more to say ... because what he spoke before to the prophets in parts, he has now spoken all at once by giving us the All which is His Son. Any person questioning God or desiring some vision or revelation will be guilty not only of foolish behaviour but also of offending him, by not fixing his eyes entirely on Christ and by living with the desire for some other novelty.'

Catechism of the Catholic Church, 1994, p. 22; quoting *The Ascent of Mount Carmel* 2, 22, 3–5, in St. John of the Cross, *The Ascent of Mount Carmel*, in *The Collected Works of St. John of the Cross*, 1979).

Scriptural text on its own does not settle important questions of faith, and there are no unwritten traditions available to settle these questions. But, as we have also seen, these teachings can only claim the assent of faith if they are God's speaking.

The ecclesial view and the doctrine of the completion of revelation can be reconciled in the following way. The purpose of God's act of revelation is to bring us into contact with salvific realities. The fundamental salvific realities, to which all the rest of revelation is ordered, are the divine persons of the Trinity. Created persons who play an essential role in the economy of salvation are also part of revelation. Persons are not the only salvific realities that are revealed. The people of Israel and the Church are also revealed. Things, like the sacraments, and events, like the Resurrection, are revealed. The moral teachings in Scripture are fundamentally revelations about certain features of human nature, those features which determine the good for man and the way to reach it. The teaching that no new revelation has been given since the time of the Apostles should be understood as asserting that since the Apostles, no new salvific realities have been revealed by God to mankind. An addition to revelation would thus consist not in God's repeating an utterance that he had already made, or in his saying something that he had not said previously, but rather in his asserting the existence of a new salvific reality, whose existence had not been revealed before the death of the last Apostle. This account of the completion of revelation harmonizes with the theological rationale for believing that revelation was completed by the time of the Apostles, since it allows us to explain how God had said everything he had to say by this time; God's utterance was complete because he had told us about all the things he intended us to know.

This resolution of the difficulty posed for the ecclesial view by the doctrine of the completion of revelation is in fact a resolution of the problem of the development of doctrine. The development of Church doctrine has posed a theological problem for the reasons given above; many parts of the teaching of the Church are not actually asserted in Scripture, and were not taught by God before the death of the last Apostle. They must be understood as developments of what God taught before the death of the last Apostle. But this raises problems; why should these developments not be considered as new revelation, and hence illegitimate? And how can these developments claim the assent of faith? If we understand the completion of revelation in the way suggested, these developments do not have to be described as new revelation, because they do not proclaim the existence of new salvific realities. They would arise from the deepening of the Church's understanding of the salvific realities that already exist, and from the Church's mission from God to proclaim the truth about these realities.[52] They

---

[52] This account of doctrinal development is taken from Newman; for more on Newman's view see Appendix II. It should be pointed out that this account of development and of the completion of revelation is not intended to explain why doctrine in fact developed the way it did, or to provide a theory to account for the directions that doctrinal development takes. It is only intended to explain how doctrinal development of the sort that has taken place in the Church can occur without violating the Christian teaching that revelation was brought to completion by Christ and the Apostles. In fact I doubt if it is possible to discover a theory

claim the assent of faith because the Church's teaching of them is God's speaking. The problem raised above, of how the Holy Spirit is supposed to inspire the Church in making pronouncements that claim the assent of divine faith and that were not expressed until after apostolic times, is thus solved. This inspiration operates through the Church's encounter with salvific realities, the understanding of these realities that she is given by the Holy Spirit, and the mission she has received from God to proclaim the truth about these realities.

The only strong objection that can be made to this conception of the development of doctrine would come from those who question whether it is right to interpret the tradition of the Church on the completion of revelation as referring to the realities that are revealed. Since this tradition does not explicitly consider the distinction between the propositions that are revealed and the realities that these propositions are about, it is difficult to judge this objection; it is difficult to determine on what side of a distinction people's ideas fall, when they themselves did not draw that distinction. It may be that the tradition on the completion of revelation does not at all distinguish between propositions taught by the Church and the realities these propositions are about. In that case it would be ambiguous. It would not rule out the conception of the completion of revelation that has been offered, and could not justify objections to it.

However, I think it would be wrong to understand it as entirely ambiguous, given what has been said about the development of doctrine in Church tradition before the sixteenth century. Aquinas, for example, referring to Heb. 11:6, says that all the articles of Christian faith are implicit in the belief that God exists and has a providential care for man's salvation (*2a2ae*, 1, 7). It is difficult to understand this as meaning that all the propositions that make up the Christian revelation are logically implied by the proposition that God exists and has a providential care for our salvation. It makes more sense to interpret it as referring to the realities that the Christian revelation is about, and as asserting that all those realities that God has revealed to us are described, in a general way, by the statement that God exists and has a care for our salvation.[53]

If we accept the view of the completion of revelation that has been proposed, it becomes possible to account for the Christian tradition about the primacy and sufficiency of the Scriptures. This primacy and sufficiency arise from the fact that it is in the Scriptures that the existence of all revealed salvific realities is made known. Not everything that the Church teaches about these salvific realities is actually asserted in the Scriptures. But every teaching about these realities is dependent on the Scriptures, and starts with the Scriptures, because every such teaching requires that these realities be known to exist, and it is the Scriptures that tell us that they exist. It is because the Scriptures tell us about all the realities

---

that will predict future developments of doctrine, or fully explain those that have already taken place. The Church's growth in understanding of salvific realities is something that is directed by God's providential plan for humanity, whose details we are not in a position to know about.

[53] For a different explanation of what Aquinas may have meant, however, see Appendix I.

connected with our salvation that they can be said to contain everything needed for our salvation.[54]

One might find this conception of the development of doctrine unsatisfactory, on the grounds that it will often be unclear exactly which salvific realities were revealed before the death of the last apostle, or which realities are described in the Scriptures. For example, it is clear that the existence of the Church is revealed in the Scriptures. But what about a sacramental priesthood? Is it revealed to exist by the Scriptures? If the Scriptures do not distinctly hold that it exists, can its existence be said to be revealed when the existence of the Church is revealed, since it is a part of the Church? Many problems like this are bound to arise in connection with controversies about the content of revelation.

The answer to this is that the account of the primacy of the Scriptures that has been proposed is not meant to permit the text of the Scriptures to answer all such questions, or to serve as an all-sufficient guide for distinguishing between legitimate developments and corruptions (although it does not mean that it can never serve this purpose). But on the ecclesial view there is no need for the Scriptures to do this. The Church settles questions about what sacred realities are revealed in the Scriptures; that is what she is there for.

This conception of the development of doctrine makes it possible for the ecclesial view to answer a significant objection that arises to the magisterial and ecclesial views; how can it be that there is a need of further teaching after the time of Christ and the apostles, as these views claim in objection to the scriptural view? If there really is such a need, were not those Christians who lived before this further teaching lacking in something necessary? That would mean that the teaching given by Christ and the apostles was lacking in some important respect, which is absurd.

If the completion of revelation is seen as the completion of the propositions made known through divine speaking, this objection is unanswerable. It could be answered if the further teachings were identified with unwritten apostolic traditions; this was the move made by Catholic theologians in the past. But, as we have seen, advances in historical knowledge mean that this move is no longer a tenable one. (The collapse of belief in unwritten oral traditions during the twentieth century probably explains the incoherence[55] (or even silence) into which current Roman Catholic thought on faith has lapsed.)

---

[54] Accepting that God speaks and imparts new information after the death of the last apostle, as the ecclesial view permits us to do, would seem to enable us to dispense with the notion of Catholic truths and Catholic faith as defined by Ott above. The Church teachings that have been seen as belonging to the category of Catholic truths in this sense (as e.g. that the Council of Nicaea was an ecumenical council whose teachings are binding on Christians) could be seen as directly uttered by God, and faith in them could thus be seen as divine faith. This would have the advantage of avoiding the sort of problems with the idea of Catholic faith and Catholic truths that have been described by F. Marín-Sola, *L'evolution homogène du dogme catholique*, 2nd edn, 1924.

[55] Examples of this incoherence are Fr. George Tavard's talking about 'the vision of a trans-logical development within the analogy of faith' (Tavard, 1978, p. 196), and Fr. Jan Walgrave's section on 'The Dangers of Conceptual Thought', in Jan Walgrave, *Unfolding*

On the view of the completion of revelation that has been suggested, however, the need for further teachings can be explained as arising from the appearance of questions about salvific realities that had not previously occurred to anyone, where a wrong answer to such a question would lead to a rejection or a serious misapprehension of these realities. Thus, for example, the question of whether one should rebaptize baptized Christians who had apostasized, but then repented and asked for readmission to the Church, might not have arisen during the lifetimes of the apostles, and thus their silence on it (supposing they were silent) would not have meant that there was anything lacking in the message they communicated to their hearers. In the absence of the question actually having to be posed, this message would have lacked nothing that was required for its salvific effect; but when it was posed, it is clear that the answer would have a profound effect on the understanding of the sacrament of baptism, and hence that a correct answer would be essential for a proper grasp of this salvific reality.

The ecclesial view of divine speaking is given support by the Thomist understanding of sacramental causality. I will not undertake to argue for this understanding of sacramental causality, since space does not permit such argument and since I do not have anything to add to the standard reasons given by the Thomist school in its favour. I will only point out how this understanding, if it is found to be correct, can be used to support the ecclesial view.

Aquinas holds the following positions on grace and the sacraments;

- Only God can cause grace.
- The sacraments truly cause grace, and are not merely signs or occasions of grace.
- The form of the sacraments are the words uttered by the minister.
- It is the form of the sacraments that causes grace.

There are complications that can arise from these positions, due to the diversity of the sacraments. It is not necessary for our purposes to go in to these complications,

---

Revelation (1972). Walgrave gives a good summary in this book of the incoherent positions that have come to dominate Catholic thought. Thus he mentions L. Charlier's view that 'faith is not in the first place an acceptance of positions in human language, but a supernatural communion with the self-revealing God Himself, pointed to by means of the revealing word' (Walgrave, 1972, p. 338), and H. de Lubac and M. Köster's view that 'even in human knowledge there is a pre-propositional, global apprehension of its object that gradually becomes explicit and articulate in an analytic rather than strictly inferential way ... Similarly, under the impact of God's reality upon the mind through the illuminating grace of faith, man apprehends this revelation as a whole, and development of doctrine is a gradual translation of that global apprehension into forms of human language' (Walgrave, 1972, p. 341). The incoherence of views such as these was discussed in Chapter 2. Of course, their emergence in the Roman Catholic Church was facilitated by the prevalence of incoherent philosophical trends that could be used to buttress them, but it was not necessitated by these trends; coherent philosophical alternatives were available to Catholics. I am inclined to think that the problem of the development of doctrine was the nerve point, pressure upon which caused Roman Catholic theology of faith to collapse into nonsense.

and we can avoid them by considering only the sacrament of baptism. Aquinas explains the contention that the sacraments are causes and not just signs or occasions of grace as follows:

> Some, however, assert that the sacraments are not the cause of grace in the sense of actually producing any effect, but rather that when the sacraments are applied God produces grace in the soul. And they put forward the example of one who on offering a leaden denarius receives a hundred pounds by order of the king. This is done not because the denarius he offers is in any way the cause of him receiving so great a sum of money. Rather this effect is produced solely by the king's will ... But on any right understanding of the matter this way of interpreting the sacraments does not attribute any further force to them beyond that of a sign. For a leaden denarius is no more than a certain kind of sign of the royal prescription directing that the man presenting it is to receive a certain sum of money ... On this interpretation, then, the sacraments of the New Law would be nothing more than signs of grace. Yet we have it on the authority of many of the saints that the sacraments of the New Law not merely signify but actually cause grace.[56]

From the positions that the sacraments truly cause grace, that it is the utterance of words by the minister that causes grace, and that only God can cause grace, it follows that it is God who utters the words of the sacrament. This does not make it any less true that the minister utters the words; indeed these positions require that the minister utter the words if God is to utter them. But if it is God who utters the words, it follows that God speaks now in the celebration of the sacraments, and that God's speaking has not ceased with the death of the apostles, but continues to happen in the present, as the ecclesial view maintains.[57] This conclusion is supported by the traditional view (cf. St. Augustine, *In Ioan.* 1, 33, hom. 5, n. 18; Eph. 5:25–6) that it is Christ who primarily baptises in the sacrament of baptism. If it is Christ who primarily baptises, as well as the human minister who performs the baptism, then the action of the human minister is Christ's action. Since an essential part of the minister's action is saying 'I baptise you in the name of the Father, Son and Holy Spirit', this speech act must also be Christ's speech act. A similar point is made by St. Ambrose, who, in his *On the Mysteries*, attributes the power of the sacrament of the Eucharist to Christ's word:

> In the time of Eliseus the Prophet, one of the sons of the prophets lost the head of his axe, and it sank immediately. He who had lost his axe sought the help of Eliseus: Eliseus also threw a piece of wood into the water, and the axe floated. Surely we realize that this also happened contrary to nature, for the substance of iron is heavier than the liquid of waters.

---

[56] *3a*, 62, 1, in Aquinas, 1974, p. 53.

[57] Aquinas speaks of the words that are the form of a sacrament as being God's instruments in bringing about grace, which might be thought to be difficult to harmonize with God himself being the speaker of these words. However, he also says that all Christ's actions and sufferings are instrumental causes of our salvation (*3a* 48, 6), and that these actions can be predicated of the Son of God (*3a* 16, 4), so the fact that the words uttered in a sacrament are instrumental causes of grace need not on his view prevent them from being uttered by God.

52. So we notice that grace is capable of accomplishing more than nature, and yet thus far we have only mentioned the benediction of a prophet. But if the benediction of man had such power as to change nature, what do we say of divine consecration itself, in which the very words of the Lord and Saviour function? For that sacrament, which you receive, is effected by the words of Christ. But if the word of Elias had such power as to call down fire from heaven, will not the words of Christ have power enough to change the nature of the elements? You have read about the works of the world: that 'He spoke and they were done, He commanded and they were created.' So, cannot the words of Christ, which were able to make what was not out of nothing, change those things which are into the things that were not? For it is not of less importance to give things new natures than to change natures.[58]

As well as demonstrating the existence of parallel cases of divine speaking, this argument about the sacraments can be generalized. One can reason that all the sanctifying acts of the Church must be divine acts, because such acts confer grace, and only God can confer grace. But the preaching of the Word is a sanctifying act, because it brings about saving faith. Therefore, it must be a divine act.

The kinds of speech acts involved in the utterances that effect the sacraments are more complicated than simple assertion, and I will not attempt to analyse them or explain how they can be both human and divine utterances. However, if it is accepted that the sacraments involve divine utterances, we must accept that human speaking can also be divine speaking. And in the case of the Church's preaching of the Christian message, we can, using the analysis of belief in testimony that has been provided, attempt an explanation of how human speaking can be divine speaking.

When God speaks to us and we believe him, we acquire knowledge of what he tells us. God's speaking to a believer is thus an instance of *telling*. *Telling*, as we have seen, can be analysed thus:

S tells A that *p* when:

- *S* knows that *p*
- *S* intentionally brings *A* to recognize that *S* knows that *p*
- *S* intentionally brings *A* to recognize that *S* intends *A* to recognize that *S* knows that *p*.

The first condition of the analysis of *telling* is automatically fulfilled in God's case for any true proposition, because God knows everything. This implies that God will *tell* a hearer *A* that *p* through the utterance of a messenger *B*, when God, by causing *B* to make some statement, intentionally brings *A* to recognize that God knows that *p*, and intentionally brings *A* to recognize that God intends that *A* recognize that God intends to bring *A* to recognize that God knows that *p*. These

---

[58] *The Mysteries*, in St. Ambrose, *Theological and dogmatic works*, 1963, p. 25. It is admittedly unclear whether Ambrose meant by 'the word of Christ' only the words that Christ uttered, or an actual utterance of Christ's. However, the comparison between the word of Elias and the creative word of God suggests the latter interpretation.

conditions are fulfilled when God sends someone to proclaim a message that the messenger announces as originating with God, and the hearer of this message recognizes that God has sent this messenger to announce the message. The hearer's recognition that God has done this is something that will be discussed in the next chapter. But the question of God's sending a messenger to announce a message is something that can be explained by the understanding of the sacraments that is argued for above. The nature of this sending is puzzling; how can anyone say today that God has actually, literally sent them to announce a message? The account of the sacraments that has been given, and its implications, let us see how this can happen. The sacrament of baptism is on this understanding an action of God himself, that involves a sending of the recipient by God. Baptism incorporates the recipient into Christ, which gives him a share in Christ's mission, and a share in Christ's priesthood. It would seem plausible therefore to say that this sacrament enables the speaking of its recipient to be God's speaking, when the recipient announces part of the gospel message.[59] The sacrament of baptism, on this view, would bring about the fulfilment of Moses' wish in Numbers 11:29, where he says 'Would that all the Lord's people were prophets, that the Lord would put his spirit upon them!'[60] It will also bring about the fulfilment of the prophecy of Joel, referred to by Peter in Acts 2:16: 'this is what was spoken by the prophet Joel: "And in the last days it shall be, God declares, that I shall pour out my Spirit upon all flesh, and your sons and daughters shall prophesy ..." '. (Peter is referring here to the descent of the Holy Spirit at Pentecost; but compare Acts 19, where Paul baptizes some disciples in the name of Jesus, and they receive the Holy Spirit.)

This position casts light on the importance attached to confession of the faith by Christians. There is of course an ordinary human duty to stand up for and honestly announce the convictions by which you live. But confessing the faith on this view will amount to more than that. Because your confession is also Christ's speaking, it is a participation in his mission, and a form of incorporating yourself into him. That is the chief reason why it is necessary for Christians. This incorporation accounts for the glory of martyrdom. Martyrdom is not simply glorious because it involves self-sacrifice in the cause of duty. It is above all glorious because it is the highest supernatural gift, since it is the closest possible form of incorporation into Christ's mission, and hence into Christ himself.[61]

Such a position seems in fact to be required by the direct view of divine speaking that has been put forward here. Consider an African, into whose language

---

[59] On some views, it might be confirmation, rather than baptism, that performs this function.

[60] John J. Schmitt remarks that the general idea of a prophet in the Old Testament is 'one who can speak in the name of God.' John J. Schmitt, 'Pre-Exilic Hebrew Prophecy', *Anchor Bible Dictionary*, vol. 5, 1992, p. 482.

[61] One could speculate that as Christ's mission is an expression of his generation, so an incorporation into his mission is an incorporation of a kind into his generation, a generation which gives rise to him as a divine person, and not only into his human nature; and hence that incorporation into his mission is a form of the divinization referred to in Church tradition – perhaps the grounds for this divinization. But these matters are too deep for me, and I would not try to judge this speculation.

none of the Scriptures or official statements of the Church have been translated, who is taught the faith by a lay catechist. One would not want to deny that such a person can have Christian faith. But if faith involves believing God himself speaking, the speaking in question would have to be that of the lay catechist.

It is of course true that baptized persons often contradict one another about the content of Christian faith. But it has not been claimed that their speaking *must* be divine speaking, only that it *can* be. If we were to recognize a teaching authority in the Church whose assertions demanded the assent of divine faith, that authority would require some divine sending additional to baptism that would imply that (at least under certain conditions) its assertions would *have* to be divine assertions. If we were to look in Christian tradition for an account of such an extra sending, the candidate would be the sending of the apostles, which would be continued in the sending of the bishops. But the question of such a sending is not one that will be discussed here.

Chapter 8

The Nature of Divine Faith

We are now at the point of addressing the question this book seeks to answer: how is it that the Christian faithful believe God when he speaks? It is best to begin consideration of this most difficult question by asking whether Christian faith is rationally grounded on the motives of credibility.

It might be asserted that the question of whether or not faith is based on the motives of credibility has already been settled by what has been said about belief in testimony. Such belief is not the result of inference, and when it is belief in the assertions of a knowledgeable honest person it gives knowledge rather than probable belief. But belief that is based on the motives of credibility is the result of inference, and it gives at best probable belief rather than knowledge. Therefore, belief in God's testimony cannot be based on the motives of credibility.

However, it could be pointed out (as it is in the quotation from Dummett in Chapter 6, p. 141) that non-inferential belief in testimony is not the only kind of belief in testimony. There are in fact cases where we conclude to the truth of what someone is saying on the basis of evidence for his truthfulness. This happens, for example, in courts of law, where a rather untrustworthy criminal may be believed on the grounds of its being in his interest to tell the truth. Believing someone because we have evidence that indicates he is telling the truth can be called *forensic* believing, to distinguish it from the more usual sort of belief in testimony. The conclusion that evidence for Christian faith seeks to establish is somewhat different from that usually sought in a court of law, since it has to do with the identity of the speaker rather than his knowledge and honesty (God's knowledge and honesty not being something that could be in doubt). But this does not provide any obstacle to Christians coming to believe that an utterance is made by God, and therefore true, on the basis of evidence for God's having made it.

Faith and the motives of credibility

There are, however, three reasons why Christian faith could not be a forensic belief based on the motives of credibility.

1.
The average Christian believer is not knowledgeable enough to be able to reasonably conclude from the motives of credibility that God has spoken. But the faith of the average Christian believer is theoretically reasonable. Therefore, it cannot be based on inference from the motives of credibility.

Alvin Plantinga has argued that in fact there are not any motives of credibility that would make it probable that Christian teachings have been communicated by God.[1] I will not try to determine whether or not he is right about this, confining myself to the observations that since as a matter of fact it is true (as Plantinga himself believes) that God has communicated the Christian faith, it would not be surprising to find out that the historical evidence on the whole supports the claim that he has; and that if the historical evidence is good evidence – i.e. evidence that gives us a fair idea of what actually happened – it *will* tell us that God communicated the Christian faith, because that is what actually happened. I will simply argue for a conditional; even if we take the most positive view of the strength of the evidence provided by the motives of credibility that could reasonably be supposed, these motives will still not suffice to make the faith of the average believer reasonable. Essential to the motives of credibility is a large and complicated mass of historical evidence. The average believer lacks the competence to assess this evidence, and unless he is exceptionally ignorant or stupid he knows that he lacks the competence to assess this evidence. He cannot appeal to a consensus of experts to justify a belief that the motives of credibility make it probable that God communicated the Christian faith, because there is no such consensus. It is even doubtful whether a majority of people with expert knowledge of the relevant historical evidence would agree that this evidence supports the claim of Christianity to be divinely revealed. The average believer has no way of knowing which experts are right on this question. Take, for example, the argument from the growth of the Church under the Roman Empire, which the Fathers saw as miraculous proof of its divine origin. Gibbon in his *Decline and Fall* famously offered alternative explanations for the growth of the Church that made no mention of divine assistance. Gibbon was an enormously learned man, whose knowledge commands respect even today. How is the average believer to determine whether or not he was right about the reasons for the growth of the Church? The task is obviously impossible for the average person; and it is only one of many tasks of comparable difficulty, historical and philosophical, that confront someone who would try to determine the worth of the motives of credibility alleged for the Christian faith.

Some theologians have attempted to get around this argument by claiming that possession of objectively good evidence for Christianity's being divinely revealed is not necessary for a judgement based on the motives of credibility. A typical position of this sort can be found in van Noort (as revised by Castelot and Murphy):

First of all it must be held that certitude about the fact of revelation ... is required before one can make an act of divine-catholic faith. Certitude means the firm adherence of the intellect to one side of a contradiction without fear of the opposite side. Consequently certitude is a state or mental attitude of the knowing subject: it is a relationship of a man's intellect to some proposition ... The same point can be proven by theological reasoning. The assent of faith must be firm, in fact of the firmest kind. But the will

---

[1] Plantinga, 2000, pp. 271–80.

cannot command an assent of this sort unless the fact of divine utterance is established with certitude ... On the other hand it must be noted that any species of certitude about the fact of revelation, i.e. every determination of the intellect to one side, so long as it actually excludes fear of the opposite side, suffices. The reason is this: as often as you have present a conviction of this sort, the act of the will commanding faith to be given is always prudent and reasonable. Consequently:

1. It is not necessary to have a metaphysical or physical certitude, but a moral certitude suffices. For moral certitude, i.e. that certitude that rests upon arguments that presuppose the stability of the moral order, is a genuine certitude. Even if the arguments which beget it are not most of the time so compelling as to exclude any possibility of doubt, they do at least exclude the possibility of reasonable doubt; so they suffice to beget in any sincere mind an adhesion of the mind whose firmness is not weakened by fear of the opposite ...

2. One does not need to have 'scientific' moral certitude, but these suffice: both an absolute popular certitude and also that certitude which is called respective or relative certitude.

Absolute certitude means that which rests upon arguments which necessarily demonstrate the objective truth of the matter and which consequently suffice to convince any man, even a very learned man provided he be sincere and of good will. Now if arguments of this sort are perceived less distinctly, less perfectly, and above all less reflexively, you have what is described as a popular certitude. If the arguments are known both more distinctively and more reflexively so that they can be clearly marshalled and defended you have what is known as a scientific, or philosophical certitude, which itself admits of greater or lesser degrees of perfection.

Respective (or relative) certitude prescinds from the objective value of the arguments upon which it rests. It rests upon arguments or reasons which are not connected with the truth necessarily, or are known in such a defective fashion that their necessary connection with the truth would be doubtful to sharper minds. Still, they factually suffice to convince minds that are either uncritical, or imbued with certain prejudices ...

The real reason we say 'respective' certitude suffices to prepare for faith has been pointed out above: just as often as you have factually present a firm adherence of the mind which actually excludes fear of the opposite side, the will to believe is a reasonable will. This point receives indirect confirmation from the fact that otherwise faith would be rendered impossible for many men and particularly for those of weak intelligence and children.[2]

... As regards some of the faithful, especially children and extremely dull adults, even though they may be lacking in arguments that are strictly sufficient, they are not lacking in arguments that are sufficient for themselves. Such arguments (only accidentally but nonetheless truly) suffice to exclude all prudent doubt for men of this sort and to produce in them a firm assent. Such arguments are mainly the authority of parents and of a parish priest. 'Since,' says Cardinal De Lugo, 'there do not occur to him [i.e. a child] reasons which might make a learned man hesitate with prudent fear, he cannot prudently fear, and, for his capacity, those motives are extremely strong which for other people would be weak.' [De Lugo, *De Fide*, disputation 5, no. 36.] ... Before despising this way of 'human authority' by which children and uneducated people come to the faith, one should stop to consider how correct and prudent they are in judging that

---

[2] van Noort, 1961, pp. 313–15.

even in religious matters they should follow the lead of those who are wiser than themselves and whom God has provided for them as instructors.[3]

Van Noort adds that the average believer can and ordinarily does move from relative certitude to absolute popular certitude. This absolute popular certitude seems to be the kind of certitude that the average educated person could acquire about Julius Caesar's having conquered Gaul. Such a person might not have an expert knowledge of Roman history, or be able to properly assess or even read the documentary evidence relating to this question. But he could still come to know with moral certainty on the basis of objectively good evidence that Julius Caesar conquered Gaul.

Van Noort is, however, wrong in saying that the average believer can acquire an absolute popular certitude about the fact of revelation on the basis of the motives of credibility. Such popular certitude is not available when there exists wide and deep disagreements among qualified experts about a question. This disagreement exists today over the probative value of the evidence for Christianity's being divinely revealed, so no average believer can possess absolute popular certitude about the value of this evidence. One suspects that van Noort's assurance about the possibility of absolute popular certitude for the typical believer arises from his feeling that the existence of such a possibility is required by his theory of faith.

The most that is available to the average believer when it comes to the motives of credibility is therefore relative certitude, where the believer mistakenly thinks that he has objectively good evidence for believing. But this certitude is easily defeasible, and it rests on ignorance, which is not a satisfactory basis for faith. It is true that such certitude can remove any fear of being mistaken. But van Noort is wrong in saying that the absence of any fear of being in error about a proposition can suffice to make a decision taken on the basis of that proposition practically reasonable. Take someone who feels absolutely confident that pine-needle tea is a sure-fire cure for his leukemia, and that nothing else will be any good. (Suppose pine-needle tea is known to be useless for this purpose, as it probably is.) It is easy for him to find out that his views on the curative powers of pine-needle tea are not of any value, and that there are experts on the subject of treating leukemia who reject these views to whose judgement he should defer, but his confidence is such that he has not bothered to do so, believing that any investigation of the subject would be a waste of time. This confidence will not make that person practically reasonable in treating his leukemia solely by drinking pine-needle tea. If this person is really too stupid or prejudiced for it to be possible for him to learn that his views on how to treat leukemia are not of any value, it might be argued that his action in treating himself would be practically reasonable, because he would be doing the best that it lies in his power to do. I would not agree with this contention; but even if it is true, the fact remains that mere possession of complete confidence in one's beliefs does not suffice to make an action based on those beliefs practically reasonable, because one can have such confidence without being in a

---

[3] van Noort, 1961, pp. 317–18.

state of invincible ignorance. Van Noort's argument for the practical reasonableness of the choice to believe on the part of someone who possesses merely relative certainty thus does not stand up. And it should be noted that today a believer who possesses merely relative certitude about the motives of credibility is not typically in a state of invincible ignorance about his understanding of the motives of credibility. Virtually every believer in contemporary Western society will encounter objections to the evidence that can be given for the divine origin of Christian faith, and unless he is stupid or prejudiced he will understand that he is not personally qualified to evaluate many of these objections, and that there is no consensus of experts to which he can appeal in rejecting them. In the absence of such stupidity or prejudice, therefore, his relative certainty will be at an end.

This argument shows that the Christian faith of the average believer cannot be based on the motives of credibility. It does not however exclude the possibility of epistemically favoured persons, who know enough to have good evidence for believing that the Christian message is communicated to them by God, having a faith that is based on this evidence. It thus does not give reason for thinking that a faith of this sort cannot be Christian faith; it only shows that most Christian faith is not based on the motives of credibility. However, it is rather unsatisfactory to hold that some Christian faith is based on the motives of credibility but that most of it is not. This position can in fact be excluded by further arguments that show that no Christian faith can be based on the motives of credibility.

2.

Gathering the evidence that makes up the motives of credibility might involve choice. But concluding from this evidence to the truth of Christian claims to a divine revelation will not normally (if ever) be a matter of choice and be voluntary, because inferring a particular conclusion from evidence in its favour is not normally a voluntary act. It cannot therefore be commanded, praised or rewarded. But the act of believing itself, as distinct from acts like investigating evidence that can prepare for belief, is commanded by God, and is praised and rewarded; conversely, disbelief is blamed and punished.

The noun 'faith' (πίστις) and the verb 'to believe' (πιστεύω) have more than one sense in the New Testament. In some cases, 'faith' refers to something other than the act of believing someone's testimony (as for example Romans 3:3, where 'πίστις' describes God's trustworthiness rather than the act of believing); and there are many cases where it could be disputed whether 'πίστις' should be understood as the act of believing testimony. There are however many passages where it clearly means trusting someone's testimony. Examples are Matthew 9:28–29; Mark 13:21, 16:11–13; Luke 22:67; John 2:22, 3:12, 4:21, 4:50, 5:24, 5:46, 8:46–47, 10:24–25; Acts 8:12, 27:25; Romans 10:16–17; 2 Thessalonians 1:10; 2 Timothy 1:12; 1 John 5:10. And the absence of belief of this kind is blamed, while its presence is praised. Clear instances of blame are found in Mark and 1 John. Mark 16:9–14 runs:

Now when he rose early on the first day of the week, he appeared first to Mary Magdalene, from whom he had cast out seven demons. She went out and told those who had been with him, as they mourned and wept. But when they heard that he was alive and had been seen by her, they would not believe it. After this he appeared in another form to two of them, as they were walking into the country. And they went back and told the rest, but they did not believe them. Afterwards he appeared to the eleven themselves as they sat at table; and he upbraided them for their unbelief and hardness of heart, because they had not believed those who saw him after he had risen.

1 John 5:10 simply states 'He who does not believe in God has made him a liar, because he has not believed in the testimony that God has borne to his Son.'

Belief in God's testimony, on the other hand, is described by St. Paul in his letter to the Romans as a worthy act that brings God's favour. Paul says that Abraham was justified on account of his believing God when God promised that Sarah would bear a child in her old age: 'In hope he believed against hope, that he should become the father of many nations; as he had been told, "So shall your descendants be" ... No distrust made him waver concerning the promise of God, but he grew strong in his faith as he gave glory to God, fully convinced that God was able to do as he had promised. That was why his faith was "reckoned to him as righteousness".' (Romans 4:18, 20–22.) Paul makes the same point in Galatians. 'Let me ask you only this: Did you receive the Spirit by works of the law, or by hearing with faith? ... Does he who supplies the Spirit to you and works miracles among you do so by works of law, or by hearing with faith? Thus Abraham "believed God, and it was reckoned to him as righteousness" '. (Galatians 3:2, 5–6.)

Even the choice that is involved in gathering the evidence that makes up the motives of credibility need not be suitable to be commanded, praised or rewarded. Suppose that faith can be based on the motives of credibility. Suppose further that someone who hates Christianity, because he violates the moral code that it asserts, investigates the evidence for it in order to be able to refute it, and finds to his chagrin that this evidence conclusively supports its claims; and then believes against his will, rather like the devils.[4] Suppose again, still assuming that faith is based on the motives of credibility, that another person investigates the evidence for Christianity in order to serve God as an apologist; but, due to some error in his reasoning or the evidence he finds, mistakenly comes to the conclusion that Christianity must be false. Here we have belief resulting from actions that have bad motives, and disbelief resulting from actions that have good ones. This cannot be reconciled with the Scriptural portrayal of belief as such being praiseworthy and commanded. This implies that the assumption upon which these hypothetical cases are based, that of belief being based on the motives of credibility, must be false.

In fact, the only moral imperative that can properly be uttered with respect to

---

[4] Chateaubriand claims that something like this happened to him: 'Je connaissais les ouvrages des Pères mieux qu'on ne les connaît de nos jours; je les avais étudiés, même pour les combattre, et entré dans cette route à mauvaise intention, au lieu d'en sortir vainqueur, j'en étais sorti vaincu.' François de Chateaubriand, *Mémoires d'Outre-Tombe*, vol. 1, 1951, p. 451.

investigating the evidence for the truth of some assertion is to do your best to find out the truth. There cannot be a moral requirement to believe a certain conclusion on the basis of investigation, unless such investigation is bound to turn up evidence that will convince any reasonable person. But, as we have seen, investigation of the motives of credibility is not bound to turn up evidence that will convince any reasonable person. It cannot therefore be justifiable to command someone to believe on the basis of the motives of credibility. Such a command would give warrant to the accusation sometimes made by unbelievers, to the effect that Christian faith demands a slavery of the intellect. (The impression that Christian faith demands such a slavery may well be due to some extent to the idea current among Christians themselves that faith is based on the motives of credibility.)

Even if we (unjustifiably) abandon the commands to believe that are found in Scripture and tradition, we are left with the praise and reward that is promised to belief, and this praise and reward is just as impossible to reconcile with a belief based on the motives of credibility as is the command to believe. That is because if we grant that belief in divine speaking can be based on the motives of credibility, it is perfectly possible, as described above, to arrive at a belief that is based on the motives of credibility by acting on bad motives; and such a belief cannot be a suitable object for praise and reward. It could be said that not all belief, but only belief that arises from an investigation of the motives of credibility that is based on the right motives, is praised and rewarded. But in such a case it will not be the belief, but only the acting upon right motives, that will be worthy of praise and reward. Seeking the truth upon right motives, if this search is understood as an investigation of the motives of credibility, is something that is possible for both those who become believers as a result of their search and for those who do not, so there will in this case be nothing about belief itself that is worthy of praise and reward. In this case the person who as a result of seeking the truth upon right motives manages to arrive at belief, will be luckier or cleverer than the person who seeks the truth upon right motives but does not manage to arrive at belief; but that will not make him *better*, or more worthy of reward.

Behind the incompatibility of a belief based on the motives of credibility with a belief that can be commanded, praised or rewarded, there is a deeper issue. At least part of the reason why belief is commanded, praised and rewarded lies in the moral relation that is set up by belief between the believer and God. But this moral relation depends on belief's being voluntary. Since the act of believing, when we believe a person's testimony on the basis of evidence for his telling the truth, is not typically voluntary, we do not, when believing in this way, set up the moral relation that exists when we accept someone's testimony simply because we trust them, the moral relation whose violation is referred to in 1 John 5:10 ('he who does not believe God has made him a liar'). But this moral relation exists in Christian faith.

3.
Divine grace is necessary for Christian faith, but it is not necessary for arriving at the conclusion that God has spoken on the basis of the motives of credibility. The evidence that is offered as the basis for the motives of credibility (as for example

miracles, transformation of people's lives, the growth of the Church) is something that can be known by unaided human powers, and the inference from this evidence to the conclusion of the truth of Christian claims is an inference that can be grasped by unaided human powers. Therefore, a faith that is based on the motives of credibility cannot be the same as Christian faith.

The nature of the divine grace that is in question here needs to be clarified. God's action in speaking is undoubtedly a form of divine grace. But Christian tradition has held that not only God's act of speaking, but also the Christian believer's act of believing God when he speaks, involves the action of divine grace, and is not possible without it. This grace has been conceived of as God's action, and as a free gift that cannot be earned or claimed as a debt of justice. Anything that requires the action of divine grace cannot therefore be brought about by unaided human powers. But since arriving at the judgement that God has spoken on the basis of the motives of credibility is at least in principle possible for unaided human powers, such a judgement cannot be said to require divine grace, and thus cannot be an exercise of Christian faith.

We need to be clear on what this line of reasoning does not require us to suppose. It does not require that the grace necessary for faith be sanctifying grace. It does not require that this grace be supernatural in Aquinas's sense, that is, that it gives a gift that is beyond the power of any possible created being. It does not involve an account of the way in which divine grace and the human action of believing are related. Nor does it claim that everyone, simply through the exercise of human powers, can come to know the evidence upon which the motives of credibility are based, and grasp the inferences that follow from this evidence, or that anyone has ever actually done this. It only claims that these things can in principle be done through the exercise of unaided human powers, and that faith cannot be arrived at in this way, because it cannot be achieved without grace. The modal claim, the 'cannot', is the key element here. One can conceive of God's direct action bringing it about, or making it possible, for someone to believe on the basis of the motives of credibility that God has spoken, rather as Tillotson supposes may happen. In this case the action of grace (perhaps in conjunction with some actions or properties of the believer) would be a sufficient condition for a belief that is based on the motives of credibility. But it cannot be a necessary condition for belief based on the motives of credibility, because such belief is in principle accessible to unaided human powers. One might say that there are some people who as a matter of fact are not able to acquire, through natural means, knowledge of the evidence that makes up the motives of credibility, or possession of the mental training and powers that are needed to arrive at the conclusion that God has spoken on the basis of this evidence. In the absence of such natural means, it would be true that there are people for whom grace would be necessary if they were to be able to believe on the basis of the motives of credibility. But grace is not necessary for Christian faith only when natural means for arriving at faith are absent, but absolutely: and it is necessary not just for some people who lack the natural means to arrive at it, but for everyone; and not just for all actual believers, but for all possible believers. That is because the help of grace is essential for Christian faith. But it cannot be essential for faith that is based on the motives of credibility, because it is at least possible for some humans to arrive at such a faith using only their own powers, even if this possibility is realized seldom or not at all. Since grace is essential for Christian faith, but is not essential for a belief based on the motives of credibility, these two things cannot be the same.

It might be claimed that grace is necessary to influence the will in order to bring about a belief that is based on the motives of credibility. It is often the case that people refuse to believe something they do not want to believe, even in the face of overwhelming evidence. It could be argued that the attachment to sin that results from our fallen state will inevitably produce an unconquerable aversion to belief, and hence that people will inevitably refuse to believe what the motives of credibility tell them, unless their wills are reformed by grace. This position would enable one to hold that grace is necessary for faith without ruling out the possibility of belief's being based on the motives of credibility. However, this claim cannot be reconciled with the fact that believing God's speaking can coexist with serious deliberate sin. Since this is the case, a good will cannot be necessary for faith, and the grace that brings about such a good will cannot be necessary for faith either.

There is a further argument that could be used against the possibility of grace being based on the motives of credibility, if we accept Aquinas's conception of grace as involving a supernatural gift. A grace that brought about a faith that was based on the motives of credibility would not involve such a supernatural gift, because it would not involve bringing about a result that surpassed the powers of created being. It would only be supernatural *quoad modum*; it would be the means of bringing about the result (sc. a divine action that is not also the action of any secondary cause) that would be supernatural, not the end result itself, which would be something that could be brought about by created being. (In Aquinas's view, as we have seen, a faith based on the motives of credibility in fact is brought about by the powers of created being in the case of the devils, who believe because of the evidence of the signs of revelation.) Aquinas does not deny that there is such a thing as grace *quoad modum*. An obvious example would be miracles of healing that produce a result that might have been brought about by medical treatment or the powers of nature. (If someone loses a limb and God causes a new one to grow back, the result – possession of the limb – is one that is brought about by nature in the course of normal human development. It is the manner of arriving at the result, not the result itself, that is miraculous.) But he does not consider that the grace required for faith can be of this kind, because faith is a theological virtue, and in his view theological virtues must involve a gift of grace that is essentially supernatural.

It is worth pointing out that the argument from the supernatural character of grace is different from the argument from the necessity of grace. Aquinas's view of grace is a theological opinion rather than a part of Christian faith. I cannot go into the question here of whether his opinion is the right one, and so will only remark that if the case for his view of grace is a good one, that will imply that the motives of credibility cannot be the rational grounds for Christian faith.

The motivation for requiring the motives of credibility

A belief that is based on the motives of credibility is thus not Christian faith. Arguments that prove this conclusion have in fact been around for hundreds of years; we have seen them in the account of Owen's views given above, and the same arguments have been offered by Dominican theologians since the Middle Ages. The question this raises is why the position they oppose has persisted despite the existence of decisive objections to it. The answer that has emerged from our historical survey is that everyone assumed that a reasonable belief in someone's testimony must necessarily be based on evidence of the honesty and knowledgeableness of the person believed. This assumption can be seen even in the semi-Scotist position of Cardinal Billot, who was one of the very few thinkers prior to the twentieth century to draw a distinction between forensic belief and the usual sort of belief in testimony. Billot's originality in this respect, and the neglect into which his ideas have currently fallen, make it worthwhile to set out his views. In his *De virtutibus infusis*, he writes:

> Belief (credere) is therefore said in its proper sense when the intellect firmly adheres to something testified to, not on account of intrinsic reasons for its truth, but solely because of the testimony of another. But on the other hand this is said in two ways ...
>
> In the first way, assent is on account of evidence for the veracity of the witness (propter evidentiam in attestante), if given purely and simply because it is evident to the intellect that the witness cannot deceive or be deceived in testifying; for instance, because it is evident to me that something is witnessed to by him who is First Truth, or because it is evident to me, after consideration of all the circumstances of someone's human testimony, that no error or deception has stolen in to it. Then, the evidence is not merely a prerequisite to assent, but is the very motive upon which assent is founded, and the proper measure for its firmness and certitude. In this case the believer does not put his faith in the witness, but only in the evidence which he has of the veracity of the testimony. Believing in this way is not honouring the witness by as it were signifying in act that he is veracious. For in this case a person will believe without distinction and for the same reason the testimony of anyone, even of someone who is reckoned the vilest and most mendacious of men; as appears by the example of a judge who firmly believes that which a party to an action in court acknowledges against himself, on account of the fact that it is clear that the witness cannot on that occasion be deceived or lying. The faith of the judge is founded on that evidence, and in no way on the dignity or authority of the witness, which in the judge's estimation is entirely absent ...
>
> In the second way, however, it comes to pass in an entirely different way that assent is given to the testimony of a witness; not on account of evidence for the veracity of the testimony, but on account of the dignity possessed by the witness. This differs from the first sort of belief in many ways. Firstly, because even if perfect evidence for the veracity of the witness is to be had, this evidence is not the formal object of assent ... Secondly, because ... it suffices for the first sort that the witness is known not to be *de facto* in error or lying; which can happen *per accidens*, irrespective of the morals and characteristics of the witness. But in the second, the motive for assent is the dignity of the speaker, and his right to a docile assent and submission of the mind. But this dignity does not exist in one who *per accidens* does not err and tells the truth, but only in him who at least in a certain order is instructed by knowledge [*scientia*], and especially who possesses veracity. Thirdly, because faith whose motive is evidence for the veracity of

the witness requires a determination of the will; but when this evidence is perfect, this determination follows necessarily and without possibility of impediment. But in faith whose motive is the utterance of an authority whom one ought to believe, the will is always free to cause the intellect to obey or not to obey this duty ... Fourthly, in that the degree of firmness of this faith is always according to the measure of the authority that is known to exist in the speaker, whatever be the perfection of the evidence through which this authority becomes known to me. And so, even if the evidence which I have of the divine infallibility and veracity is not unsurpassable, nevertheless, because I always know the authority of God (if he exists) to prevail over anything else, if I believe on account of the authority of God, I always believe with an assent that is firmer than any other assent. Fifthly and lastly, because he who believes on account of evidence for the veracity of the witness, even if that witness is God, does not believe on account of an uncreated motive; for the evidence that can be proposed for anyone's utterance is always something created. But he who believes on account of the authority of God insofar as it is understood precisely as such, truly makes an act of a theological virtue, because in his account he rests upon something that is not distinct from God.[5]

Billot's view is that the motives of credibility give us evidence that justifies belief of the first sort, belief founded on evidence of the veracity of the witness. However, this evidence is not our reason for having faith. Faith is a belief of the second sort, and its formal object is not the motives of credibility, but simply the authority of God who reveals. The motives of credibility are not the reason for faith, they are merely a necessary prerequisite for it. Thus, his theory is proposed as solving the problem of the act of faith. Faith is rational because believers have the motives of credibility; it is voluntary because its formal object is the authority of the speaker, which always gives rise to voluntary belief; it is produced by grace because faith on the grounds of God's authority, unlike a belief based on the motives of credibility, requires grace. His theory is of interest because it grasps and describes the difference between forensic belief in testimony and the usual sort. However, Billot fails to see that belief on the bare credit of the proposer *is* the usual sort of belief in testimony, and that this belief possesses epistemic authority on its own, with no need of being supplemented by evidence for the truthfulness of the person believed. The authority he attributes to belief on the bare credit of the proposer is a purely moral authority, not an epistemic one. He assumes that we must have good evidence for someone's veracity if we are to be reasonable in believing them. That is why he thinks that the motives of credibility are necessary for belief, even though they are not its formal object.

But, as we have seen, he is mistaken in thinking this; and an understanding of the fact that he is mistaken is the key to solving the problem of the rational motivation for faith. The fact that the usual sort of belief in testimony is not the same as forensic belief, and is capable of constituting knowledge, removes both the supposed necessity postulated by Tillotson and his followers for belief in God's testimony being founded on inference from evidence of his speaking, and the supposed necessity for the motives of credibility to serve as a basis for the

---

[5] L. Billot, *De virtutibus infusis: commentarium in secundam partem S. Thomae*, 1921), vol. 1, pp. 209–13, my translation.

judgement of credibility that is maintained by the Scotists. It provides the answer to the question of how belief in God's speaking comes about if it is not based on the motives of credibility. Such belief occurs in the way belief in testimony usually occurs, through simply trusting the person believed; God speaks to us, and we believe him. (In order for this to occur, the direct account of revelation must be true, because if it were not, God would not actually speak to every Christian believer. But we have seen that it is true.) A forensic belief in God's speaking cannot be the basis of Christian faith, for the reasons we have seen. Therefore, such belief must rest on the usual form of belief in testimony. The Thomist view of the formal object of faith is thus the correct one.

The basis of Christian faith

This position on how we come to believe God's speaking requires further elaboration. Although the acquisition of knowledge from testimony does not rest on inference from evidence about a speaker's knowledgeableness and honesty, we have seen that it requires recognition of the speaker's competence in the subject matter he is talking about. In the case of God's speaking, what needs to be recognized is the identity of the speaker, since once we realize that it is God who is speaking to us the speaker's knowledge and honesty is guaranteed. This recognition is necessary if we are to able to believe God when he speaks, so an account of how Christians believe needs to explain how this recognition happens. Before attempting such an explanation, however, it will be useful to recall how the recognition of a speaker's competence works. Our recognition of a speaker's competence does not mean that we infer a speaker to be competent from evidence that we observe. Nor does it mean that, having recognized such competence without inference, we then go on to infer from this recognition that the speaker is telling the truth. The factors that enable someone to recognize a speaker's competence do not form part of the *reason* for believing that speaker. The reason why we believe someone is simply that we take them to be knowledgeable and honest in what they are saying.[6] The factors that enable us to recognize their competence do not enter in to this reason. Neither, therefore, will the factors that enable us to recognize that God is speaking enter in to our reason for believing; they will not, as Aquinas and Owen put it, be part of the formal object of our belief.

The answer to the question of the nature of how Christians recognize that God is speaking to them is given by Owen. It is the effect of an utterance upon a hearer that enables the hearer to recognize it as being spoken by God. It does this because the effect is something that only a divine utterance could produce, and the hearer recognizes it as being so.

There does not seem to be any reason why there should be a limit to the kinds of effects on a hearer that can only be produced by God, so I will not try to give an

---

[6] Because God's knowledge and truthfulness are uncreated, it thus follows, as many theologians have wished to maintain, that the formal object of faith is uncreated.

exhaustive list of them. Although such a list may not be possible, Owen seems to give a helpful general characterization of the kinds of effect in question when he remarks that there are two things that are self-evidencing; light and power. A divine utterance can be recognized as divine when it enlightens us in a way that only God can, or when it changes us in a way that only God can.

Owen gives an important example of enlightenment when he speaks of the enlightenment of the conscience by the Scriptures as showing the hearer that the Scriptures are spoken by God. He asserts (as quoted above) that 'Conscience is the territory or dominion of God in man, which he hath so reserved unto himself that no human power can possibly enter into it or dispose of it in any wise. But in this work of conviction of sin, the word of God, the Scripture, entereth into the conscience of the sinner, takes possession of it, disposeth it unto peace or trouble, by its laws or rules, and not otherwise ...'[7] This assertion is open to the objection that our consciences can be changed by human power, both our own and other people's, and that both for good and for ill. We can act so as to reform or corrupt our consciences, and other people can influence our consciences in the directions of reformation or corruption. The reply to this objection is that such actions and influences can only work to actualize potentialities that our consciences already possess. But these potentialities are not unlimited. It is common for people to undoubtingly believe that evil actions they do are good, and to not be able to grasp, or be able to be brought by others to grasp, that these actions are not good. A conscience that is seared in this way does not have the power to realize that the evil actions in question are not good, or to be brought to realize this by other people. If such a conscience is brought to realize, through hearing the gospel preached, that the actions it thought good were in fact evil, this cannot happen through the action of any natural power. It can only happen through an exercise of divine power. If it is a particular speech act that brings about such an enlightenment, and only a divine act can bring this enlightenment about, it follows that this speech act must be a divine act. One might agree with this reasoning, but ask why the fact that the speech act in question is divine should entail that we recognize it as divine. The answer is that part of what is involved in the enlightenment of conscience is a realization of the past blindness of one's conscience. One can realize, as a result of being enlightened, not only that one's conscience was wrong in the past, but also that it was seared; that it was not capable of being right. If one realizes this, and realizes that it was a particular utterance that brought about the enlightenment of one's conscience, one can realize that this utterance possessed a power that belongs only to God.

A seared conscience can be enlightened not just with respect to one's own conduct, but with respect to general moral principles. Someone may be genuinely unable to understand that we ought to love our enemies (even though they themselves do not have any enemies and thus never violate this precept). In being brought to understand by the proclamation of the gospel that we should love our enemies, their consciences are enlightened by divine power.

---

[7] Owen, 1852, p. 96.

Some people can thus recognize utterances as divine through the enlightenment of their seared consciences. I expect however that Owen would go farther than this, and say that everyone's conscience is seared to some extent as a result of original sin, so much so that it is only the exercise of divine power that can give us some idea of the real nature of our condition as sinners. That is why unbelievers are so often scandalized by the Christian view of the sinfulness of fallen man; it is impossible for someone who remains in the state of fallen humanity to see that this view is correct. Everyone who, through believing the gospel, comes to an understanding of our real condition as sinners will thus be enlightened in a way that will enable them to realize that the gospel is spoken by God.

An understanding of the truth of moral judgements and principles is not the only sort of enlightenment that can be conferred by the divine word. We can also be enlightened about the goodness and desirability of the Christian life, and of the gifts and rewards promised us by Christ. For example, one can understand that it is right to forgive one's enemies without at all being able to see it as good and desirable, or as anything other than a hateful necessity laid on us by Christ's command. The same can be said of suffering for Christ's sake. Enlightenment of those people who are born unable to understand these things (probably the whole human race) is a sign of divine power.

It has not been argued that any one of these forms of blindness must afflict everyone. However, it seems plausible to say that as a result of original sin everyone will suffer from some one of these forms of blindness (or others that have not been mentioned), and thus that everyone can realize that the gospel is being spoken to them by God through being enlightened in some way.

The former kind of enlightenment mentioned in the paragraph above, that removes the blindness that results from original sin, is described by Owen, who asserts, as we have seen, that:

> Without the Scripture all the world is in darkness ... superstition, idolatry, lying vanities, wherein men know not at all what they do nor whither they go, fill the whole world, even as it is this day. And the minds of men are naturally in darkness; there is a blindness upon them that they cannot see nor discern spiritual things. With respect unto both these kinds of darkness the Scripture is a light ... thereby evidencing itself to be a divine revelation; for what but divine truth could recall the minds of men from all their wandering in error, superstition, and other effects of darkness, which of themselves they love more than truth?[8]

In seeing our fallen state as producing the blindness and sin that is dispelled by the Scriptures, Owen does not allow for the sort of effect of the divine utterance that would be required on the Thomist view of grace in an unfallen state. Since the Thomist view understands the grace required for faith as being strictly supernatural, that is, unattainable by created being as such, it holds that grace would have been needed for faith even if humanity had never fallen. We can conceive of forms of enlightenment and conversion that would have required

---

[8] Owen, 1852, p. 97.

grace, and been recognizable as effects of divine action, even in an unfallen state. Charity, since it also requires grace that is strictly supernatural, would have been unattainable even by unfallen humans, and its achievement could thus have been an effect of divine speech that was recognizably divine. Similarly, there are degrees of understanding of divine mysteries, such as the Holy Trinity and the divine indwelling through grace, that are impossible without a gift of grace that is strictly supernatural. The production of such understanding could be a recognizably divine action. It might be objected that these things are mysteries that cannot be understood. But the nature of divine mysteries is not such as to exclude any understanding at all. Rather, their nature excludes full, complete or adequate understanding. But it allows partial understanding, and such understanding is an essential element of the Christian life. (These sorts of effects of divine speaking are of course possible, and realized, in fallen humans.)

The second kind of divine action that enables the believer to recognize the gospel as spoken by God is its power to change us. Origen acknowledged this power, when he said that the transformation of evil men into good ones that is wrought by the gospel could not happen without divine power, and is proof of the divine origin of the Christian faith.[9] But he cited this power as a proof for those who behold such transformations, not as a reason why the people who are transformed believe. It is Owen who identifies this power as a means whereby God's speech can be recognized. 'The principal divine effect of the word of God is in the conversion of the souls of sinners unto God ... of this great and glorious effect the word is the only instrumental cause, whereby the divine power operates and is expressive of itself ... The work which is effected by it, in the regeneration, conversion, and sanctification of the souls of believers, doth evidence infallibly unto their consciences that it is not the word of man, but of God.'[10] This transformation is manifold. Part of it consists in producing an aversion to sin in the hearer. It is one thing to understand that our actions are bad and evil, and another thing to be averse to these actions, and to reject the sins that they exemplify. This kind of aversion can be produced by people other than God, and indeed often is produced in the course of moral education. Parents, teachers or friends can produce an aversion to bullying or dishonesty in children in part simply by telling them that these things are wrong. This aversion produced by these statements can extend past a mere repugnance for such conduct to an actual rejection of it, and to a consequent change of behaviour. But although rejection of particular sins can be produced by moral education given by mere humans, rejection of sin as a whole cannot. This is because rejection of sin as a whole cannot be produced by any natural means, since such a rejection is beyond the power of fallen human nature. The impossibility of rejecting sin as a whole is something that we find out from experience. We can recognize that, for example, temperance, chastity, or the forgiveness of someone who has gravely injured us, is something that would simply have been psychologically impossible for us in the past. It is recognized by St. Paul. Speaking

---

[9] Origen, 1965, pp. 26–7.
[10] Owen, 1852, pp. 94–5.

of the time when he was under the law of Moses, before he was set free by the law of the Spirit of Life in Jesus Christ, he says: 'I can will what is right, but I cannot do it. For I do not do the good I want, but the evil I do not want is what I do ... for I delight in the law of God, in my inmost self, but I see in my members another law at war with the law of my mind and making me captive to the law of sin which dwells in my members. Wretched man that I am! Who will deliver me from this body of death?' (Romans 7:18–19, 22–24.) When an utterance brings us to reject sin, therefore, we can thereby recognize it to be divine.

Regeneration and conversion do not simply consist of rejection of sin on its own. They consist in rejection of sin on account of conversion to God, and this conversion, the cause of rejection of sin, is the fundamental feature of regeneration. Conversion to God means loving and seeking him above all else. This love is not possible to fallen human nature (or, on Aquinas's view, to unfallen human nature). We can recognize it, once we acquire it, as something we not only did not have in the past, but could not have had. This is true not only of the basic act of loving God above everything else, but of the exercise of the virtues that flow from this love. If the preaching of the gospel brings about this basic love and the exercise of these virtues, that enables us to recognize it as a divine act. The courage of martyrs who died under torture rather than renounce their faith is sometimes cited as proof of the divine origin of that faith. The life of every Christian who is converted and regenerated involves a transformation that may be less exalted and remarkable than that of the martyrs, but is no less miraculous.[11]

The miraculous can exist in the moral order as well as in the physical. The powers and liabilities of our minds and wills are just as real and determinate as the powers and liabilities of physical things. There can thus be mental or spiritual happenings that cannot be produced by any created thing, and must therefore be due solely to the action of God, just as there can be physical happenings that cannot be produced by any created thing and must therefore be due solely to the action of God. The difference between the two is that our moral powers and liabilities can sometimes be completely understood through direct experience or introspection, whereas physical powers and liabilities cannot. We are of course largely mysterious to ourselves. But it is nevertheless possible for us to come to know some of the limitations of our minds and wills through directly experiencing these limitations. The fundamental powers and liabilities of purely physical things are not thus open to direct experience. In fact the determination of whether or not a physical event resulted from the action of a natural cause can never be simple, because of the difficulty of knowing which natural agents could have been

---

[11] In support of Owen's position, I will make the claim – which I am totally unable to substantiate – that the essentials of his view on how we recognize divine speaking occurred to me before I came across his work. I reasoned that since the motives of credibility could not be the rational motivation for belief, the only thing that could provide such a motivation was the effect of the word upon the hearer, and that that effect would have to consist in changes to the hearer's mind and will. Although my discovery of Owen's work made impossible any claim of originality on my part, the fact that I came to the same conclusion as Owen without knowledge of his writings provides some support for this conclusion.

involved in the production of an event, and what exactly the powers of these agents were. It is easy to conceive how people who were unaware of the existence of magnetism or radiation could think that the exercise of these properties surpassed the capacities of nature, and could only be due to divine action. Virtually always, the best evidence we can arrive at for a physical miracle's having happened can only be probable evidence that excludes a reasonable doubt. It will not enable us to *know* that a miracle has happened. But in the case of divine action upon our minds and wills, it will be possible for to know that a miracle has happened, because it is possible for us to know the limitations of our minds and wills. (Of course in some instances we can think we know these limitations but be mistaken, just as we can be with other kinds of knowledge, but this does not mean that in other instances we cannot truly know them.) This suggests one reason that God could have had for not arranging that Christian faith be rationally grounded on the motives of credibility. Even if a visible miracle had accompanied every occasion upon which the gospel was preached, this would not provide as strong a ground for belief as the effects that the preaching of the gospel has on the minds and wills of believers. It would only provide overwhelming probability, not knowledge, because we can only have overwhelmingly probable grounds for a physical miracle's having happened. It also lets us see how visible miracles can be a concession to weakness, as Chrysostom says. The effects of the word give us knowledge, and visible miracles do not. But the fact that we know something does not always give us the psychological capacity to feel and act in a way appropriate to that knowledge. Someone can know that a snake is harmless, and still be terrified of it and unable to stay in the same room with it. Similarly, one can know that God is speaking, and still find it difficult to feel and act as if that is the case. Visible miracles that confirm the preaching of the gospel, and other elements of the motives of credibility, will tend to make it easier to feel and act in accordance with one's knowledge that this preaching is true, even though this effect is not a rational one.

We might ask here whether the motives of credibility can serve as a help or reinforcement to faith, even though they are not the basis for it. It might be pointed out that faith can encounter a sort of resistance from seemingly plausible objections. If the motives of credibility can show that such objections are in fact baseless, they can remove a force that makes faith more difficult, although they do not thereby actually strengthen faith itself. The possibility of the motives of credibility being of use to faith in this way can be admitted, but it should be emphasized that this use is unsatisfactory in some respects. Because faith excludes the possibility of there being objections to it that have a real rational basis, the resistance that it encounters from objections cannot be a rationally based one, but must rather be the effect of irrational psychological forces, like the fear of a snake that is known to be harmless. Using the motives of credibility to deal with objections to faith leaves these irrational forces intact and untreated. Rejecting objections simply on the grounds of their incompatibility with faith, on the other hand, both acts against these forces and, unlike an appeal to the motives of credibility, is a full exercise of rationality. (An appeal to the motives of credibility is less than a full exercise of rationality because it involves treating irrational objections as if they were rational, rather than rejecting them straight out because they are known to be baseless.) Moreover, since faith is the work of grace, resorting to faith in such circumstances rather than to the motives of credibility will mean a growth in grace. It would seem then that both intellectual and spiritual maturity require abandonment of this use of the motives of credibility, and reliance upon faith alone.

Christian faith can bring about belief in God's existence as well as in his teaching. In recognizing that God is speaking to us, we recognize that there is a God. This is not the same as believing that God exists on the grounds of God's having said that he exists. Elizabeth Anscombe has pointed out the difficulty with postulating the latter form of belief, which is that a belief in God's existence is presupposed by believing anything on the grounds of God's having said it, and thus cannot be brought about by believing God.[12] But if it is the effect of God's utterances, rather than a belief in the content of these utterances, that leads one to believe that God exists, this problem does not arise. De Lugo allows for this possibility. He compares learning of God's existence through faith to hearing a shout in the middle of the night from someone that one did not previously know existed. In this case, by hearing the shout we can come to know both what the person is shouting (as e.g. that there is a fire when he shouts 'Fire!') and that the person exists.[13] This possibility gives one way of answering the difficulty noted in the discussion of Aquinas above, of how belief in God's existence can be one of the articles of faith when God's existence is presumed by faith itself.

This account of the rational grounding for Christian faith makes possible a clarification of the methods needed for theoretical and practical approaches to faith. It shows that the supposed discipline of 'fundamental theology', which largely replaced apologetics in the Roman Catholic Church after the Second Vatican Council – one specialist in the field remarks that 'the old "apologetics" has been discreetly rebaptised and is to be known henceforth as "fundamental theology"'[14] – is a nonsense. A typical definition of this subject is the following, which states that fundamental theology 'has its own proper material and formal object, namely, the self-manifestation and self-giving of God in Jesus Christ, and the intrinsic credibility of this manifestation[15]... Since revelation is the primordial mystery that conveys all the others, fundamental theology must take a dogmatic approach to this mystery ... It proceeds, therefore, from faith to understanding of faith ... On the other hand ... fundamental theology subjects this revelation event to the questions and methods of the historical sciences ...'[16] Another description states that 'First, fundamental theology (hereafter FT) is that discipline which, in the light

---

[12] G. E. M. Anscombe, 'Faith', in *The collected philosophical papers of G.E.M. Anscombe*, vol. 3, 1981. I have argued for the possibility of believing that God exists on the grounds of God's having said that he exists, in John Lamont, 'Believing that God exists because the Bible says so', *Faith and Philosophy*, 1996b.

[13] *Tractatus de virtute fidei divina*, d. 1 s. 7 n. 127, in de Lugo, *Disputationes scholasticae et morales*, vol. 1, 1891.

[14] René Latourelle and Rino Fisichella, *Dictionary of Fundamental Theology*, 2000, p. 321.

[15] Latourelle and Fisichella, 2000, p. 328.

[16] Latourelle and Fisichella, 2000, p. 329.

of faith, reflects critically on the foundations of theology and basic theological issues. Second, FT is to be distinguished from the philosophy of religion. The philosophy of religion, when it investigates religious belief ... does so by the light of reason alone ... FT, however, does it work "from the inside", as an exercise of faith ...[17] The "object" which gives FT its own identity can be stated as follows: 1) the self-revelation of the tripersonal God in Jesus Christ, 2) the credibility of the revelation, and 3) its transmission and interpretation.'[18]

In the light of our discussion of faith, it can be seen that these descriptions conflate a number of different activities that require different methods. We can distinguish four such activities:

1. Apologetics; the activity of showing that the objections raised by unbelievers to the rationality of Christian faith are unreasonable, and removing intellectual difficulties with Christian faith. This cannot base itself upon faith.
2. Evangelism; the activity of getting people, in so far as in us lies, to become Christian believers. This cannot presume faith in the people to whom it is addressed, but it must take the teachings of faith as a guide to the activity of the evangelist.
3. Understanding the nature of Christian faith (the project of this book). This assumes the fundamental teachings of the faith, which it takes as a foundation and rule (as for example in the conclusions about faith that have been drawn from the necessity of grace for faith). It belongs to the branch of theology that studies the Christian virtues.
4. Understanding the fundamental principles of the Christian faith itself. These principles are summarized in the creeds, and have to do with the Persons of the Trinity and their activity. This understanding is presupposed by (3), and belongs to systematic or dogmatic theology.

The first of these activites is separate from the others. Since it cannot base itself upon divine revelation, it is not a part of Christian theology at all, although it takes its subject matter from Christian theology. It is thus nonsensical to include it in a supposed discipline of Christian theology. The second and third depend on the fourth, but in different ways; it is the fourth which alone deserves the name of 'fundamental theology'. The assumption behind the above definitions of fundamental theology seems to be that because faith in the Christian message arises from believing God's revelation, a study of this belief is somehow more fundamental than a study of the message that God gives us when he speaks. But this is a crass mistake. It is not more fundamental in the order of knowing; rather, the message that God gives us is fundamental. (Consider a parallel: scientists have come to understand optics and human sight through evidence that they see.) Nor is it more fundamental in the order of existence, since God's redeeming us through faith rests on divine actions and intentions that are more basic (as e.g. his will to save fallen humanity, and the incarnation of Christ.) Fundamental theology, as

---

[17] Gerald O'Collins, *Retrieving Fundamental Theology*, 1993, p. 40.
[18] O'Collins, 1993, p. 41.

understood by Roman Catholic theologians, is thus not a legitimate discipline. It is instead an obstacle to the four legitimate and important activities mentioned above.

This book has concerned itself with the third activity, the study of faith. It will not embark upon a study of apologetics or evangelism, but it is easy to see that its conclusions will be of great importance for the latter activities. For example, understanding that the goal of apologetics is not conversion, and that evangelism cannot bring people to believe through apologetics (although it may use apologetics as an aid), will make a basic difference to the way that both these activities are undertaken. Understanding that evangelism must work through a transformation of the minds and hearts of its hearers will provide the fundamental principles which must govern that activity. As for apologetics, if the object of apologetics were to prove the truth of Christian claims, then the standards by which apologetics would be judged would simply be the canons of historical and philosophical investigation. But since the object of apologetics is instead to remove obstacles to belief, it should be judged by its success in addressing the difficulties actually felt by the persons to whom it is addressed. This does not mean that it can violate the canons of historical and philosophical investigation; but it does mean that it is not satisfaction of these canons per se, but rather a resolution of the problems in the mind of its audience, that should be its goal.

Previous accounts of faith have failed to resolve the problem of the act of faith. The view of faith that has been proposed gives a solution to this problem, by enabling us to see how faith can be rational, free, and the product of grace. Each of these features of faith requires consideration.

Grace

On this account, the necessity of grace for faith is easily explained. Grace is needed in order to produce the transformation in us that is necessary for us to be able to recognize divine speaking when we encounter it. The enlightenment and conversion that brings about this recognition requires that we have the capacity for these effects to be produced in us by divine speaking. We do not in our present fallen state possess this capacity. If Aquinas is right, it is impossible for us to possess this capacity on our own, simply because we are creatures. It must be conferred upon us by divine action if divine speaking is to be recognizable by us and is to have its redeeming effect. In the two things necessary for faith, divine speaking and the gift of the capacity to recognize it, we can see the missions of the Son and the Holy Spirit respectively. (One may speculate that the prevalence after Scotus of the view that the motives of credibility are required for faith is connected to the neglect by Latin Christianity of the role and importance of the Holy Spirit that began in the Middle Ages.[19])

Although grace is necessary for belief, we cannot hold unbelief to be always due to the absence or rejection of grace. It seems reasonable to say that sin can in

---

[19] For this neglect see Yves Congar, *I Believe in the Holy Spirit*, 1983. Leo XIII, in his encyclical *Divinum Illud Munus*, complained that some Catholics might say they have never heard of the Holy Spirit (para. 10).

some cases be the explanation for unbelief. Sin will explain unbelief if a person is offered the grace to believe, but deliberately chooses not to believe. This choice will both be sinful and, obviously, explain why that person does not believe. Such a choice may also be motivated by further sins that the sinner does not want to abandon or acknowledge, as he would have to do if he had faith. But simply being a sinner, and committing serious sins – as opposed to committing the specific sin of choosing not to believe – cannot explain unbelief. The mere fact of being in a state of sin (whether this is understood as suffering from original sin, or as having commited a seriously sinful act and not repented of it) cannot properly be an obstacle to grace, let alone an insuperable obstacle, because sin is the normal state of those who do not believe, a state that they cannot get out of without grace, and faith is given precisely to eliminate sin. To describe sin as an obstacle to faith is like describing disease as an obstacle to being healed; it misses the point of what is going on.

One might say that unbelief is always due to sinfully choosing not to believe. But this would be too strong. It seems right to say that natural circumstances, rather than sinful choice, can prevent one from having faith. An indisputable example of such circumstances would be living in a time and place where the gospel was never heard of. A less obvious example would be the possession of convictions that are incompatible with belief, such as a firm persuasion that it is impossible for God to exist. Consider the occasion upon which Dr. Johnson was told by an eyewitness of the siege of Gibraltar that the attackers fired red-hot cannonballs at the fortress. Because he thought this to be an impossibility, he could not believe this (perfectly true) report, and abused the person who made it for telling improbable lies. Many people, particularly in a secular society, will be in a position like this; unable to believe because they cannot escape from an erroneous conviction that they know some of the teachings, implications or presuppositions of the faith to be false. Such inability to believe need not be the result of lack of intelligence. It seems possible that, for example, John Stuart Mill's childhood indoctrination in unbelief by his father was so thoroughgoing that his great natural intelligence would never have been able to surmount it. It is of course in God's power to remove these natural circumstances through miraculous action, but clearly he does not always do so. This gives an important role to the motives of credibility and apologetics generally, particularly in a society like our own where unbelieving assumptions are widely propagated and held. They can serve to clear away natural impediments to belief.

Admitting the existence of natural circumstances that sometimes make belief impossible might be thought difficult to reconcile with the claim that faith is the remedy for sin. For if faith is the sole remedy for sin, God's allowing such circumstances to exist would seem to mean that he allows some people to inevitably be damned. I do not think that the possibility of God's allowing people to inevitably be damned can be ruled out *a priori*, because salvation is a gift of grace, and grace by definition is something that cannot be demanded or deserved, and that God can freely and rightly withhold if he wants to. Thus, God could justly deny grace to the entire fallen human race and consequently ensure their damnation. But I do think that this possibility is ruled out by God's revealed desire to bring about the salvation of the whole human race. I have assumed that God makes grace available to all humanity without exception. I cannot specify what it means for God to make grace available to all humanity without going further than my broadly Catholic starting point permits, because the existence and nature of God's desire to bring about the salvation of the whole human race has been a subject of controversy between Catholics and Protestants, between different groups of Protestants (e.g. Calvinists and Arminians), and between Catholic theological schools (most notably Thomists and Molinists). However, an account of Christian faith would be incomplete without some mention of what happens to people who do not have it. I will therefore simply assert without arguing that God's desire to bring about the salvation of humanity means that he offers to everyone without exception a real possibility of being saved. The impossibility for some people of acquiring faith therefore cannot mean that they cannot be saved, and we can infer that God offers them the grace necessary for salvation in some other way than through giving them the chance to have Christian faith. (The nature of the realness of the real possibility of salvation that God offers to everyone is itself something that theologians have argued about. Thomist theologians like Reginald Garrigou-Lagrange have claimed that those who are not predestined by God to salvation are given 'sufficient grace', which they *say* provides a real possibility for salvation; but they also hold that everyone who receives 'sufficient grace' and no other sort of grace will infallibly be damned. I will try to clarify the sort of real possibility I have in mind by stating that in my opinion some people who do not have Christian faith actually *are* saved.) The question of how God offers grace to those who are not able to believe is not one that we have the resources to answer.[20] The situations of those who cannot believe will vary, and for every such person there may be various ways in which God can offer him grace; we do not know which way God will choose, or even what these ways are. This has implications for evangelization. It means that choosing to have Christian faith is the only concrete course of action that we can know will lead to salvation. If, like Paul and Silas, we are asked 'what can I do to be saved?', the only answer we can offer is 'Believe in the Lord Jesus and you will be saved' (Acts 16:31).

What if someone is not in circumstances that make it naturally impossible for him to be able to believe? May we conclude that God will offer him the grace to believe? And, further, that this offer of the grace to believe will be the way in which God offers him the chance of salvation? And hence that if he refuses to believe he will not be saved? I will not attempt to answer these questions, and will only note that this conclusion is a natural way of accounting for those Scriptural passages which speak of the necessity of faith for salvation (e.g. Mark 16:16).

It is not simply the necessity of grace for faith that is explained by this account. It is, more broadly, the role of grace in faith. This account explains how faith can in itself redeem us, because it describes faith as involving both enlightenment and

---

[20] For this reason, I suspect that Christian attempts to construct a 'theology of non-Christian religions' are a waste of time. We cannot know enough to evaluate the purposes of these religions in God's providential plan, and it is not our business to know anyway. God's comment on such theologies would likely be 'What is that to thee? Follow thou me.'

conversion. As we have seen, this is difficult if not impossible if we take faith to be based on the motives of credibility; why should believing on the basis of these motives bring us salvation?

This description of how faith in itself redeems us avoids the problems that arise for conceptions of faith like that of Plantinga's, described above. For these conceptions, belief in God's speaking is a component of the virtue of Christian faith. The full virtue, the virtue possession of which means that the person who possesses it is justified (in the religious rather than the epistemic sense), consists in belief plus something else; where the something else is a feature of the will, of behaviour, or of the emotions (as e.g. love of God, a feeling of trusting confidence in Christ's redemptory work, living a good life, or a combination of all of these), that is separate from the act of believing God speaking. By extension, dead or formless faith is thought of as consisting in mere belief, belief minus the extra component or components needed for Christian faith. The trouble with such conceptions is that the aspects of faith that redeem us and make us acceptable to God turn out to all be concentrated in the something else. Someone who loves God and lives a good life is by that very fact saved and acceptable to God. Since the redeeming aspects of faith are separate from belief, whence the use or necessity of belief for our redemption? [21] The only function that belief can have in our salvation, on this view, is an instrumental one, that of being helpful or necessary for the achievement of the plus-component; as, for example, by providing us with information that we require in order to do the actions that will bring about our salvation. But this view of the function of belief is not consonant with Scripture and tradition. As we saw above, Scripture praises belief *itself*, not just actions that we do as a result of believing God or concomitantly with believing God. Not only is belief itself praised, it is described as bringing about our salvation, as we saw in the description of Paul's views in Romans and Galatians given above.

Advocates of a 'belief-plus' conception of the Christian virtue of faith have sometimes tried to square their views with the Scriptural texts cited above by interpreting the faith referred to in them as being something more than simply believing God when he speaks. But this interpretation does unacceptable violence to these texts. It is clear in the passage from Romans cited above, for example, that Paul is saying that Abraham was justified by the simple act of believing God when God promised that he would have a son by Sarah. Texts like those in the Epistle of James, which state that 'faith apart from works is barren' (James 2:20), do not provide support for a 'belief-plus' conception. The fact that committing sin

---

[21] Luther made this criticism in rejecting the possibility of a formless infused faith. Commenting on Galatians 5:6, he said that 'the sophists [sc. the scholastic theologians] ... say that even when faith has been divinely infused – and I am not even speaking of faith that is merely acquired – it does not justify unless it has been formed by love ... they even declare that an infused faith can coexist with mortal sin. In this manner they completely transfer justification from faith and attribute it solely to love as thus defined ...' Martin Luther, *Lectures on Galatians, 1535*, in *Luther's Works*, vol. 27, 1964, p. 28. This criticism of Luther's should not be confused with his rejection of formless faith on the grounds that all infused faith must justify; the two criticisms of formless faith are distinct.

deprives faith of its salvific value does not mean that faith is not the sole cause of salvation when sin is absent. (The fact that poison does not kill us when taken together with an antidote, does not mean that if we were to take the poison without an antidote it would not be the sole cause of our death.)

The claim that faith on its own justifies us might be met with the objection that charity on its own justifies us, and that charity is distinct from faith. The answer to this objection is that charity is a love, and love is exercised in acts. Formed faith, the faith that justifies, does not consist in choosing to believe God when he speaks and also in a separate act of choosing to love God in himself above all created things. Rather, in formed faith there is only one act, the act of choosing to believe God; and the love of God is what motivates this act. Faith is an act of charity, as Aquinas says; and it is a privileged act of charity, because it is the act that opens the door to all other acts of charity. For Christians, faith is the first act of charity, upon which all other acts of charity are built, and without which no charity is possible. It is thus misleading to describe formed or justifying faith as faith that is 'active in good works'.[22] Formed faith is *itself* the good work that justifies.[23] The orientation of the will that is required for such faith will necessarily produce other good works (at least in normal circumstances), and thus the failure to do such works will mean that the orientation of the will that is required for justifying faith cannot be present, but such works do not contribute to the justification of a

---

[22] John Webster, 'Faith', in *The Blackwell Encyclopedia of Modern Christian Thought*, 2000, p. 208. Webster has some excuse for describing formed faith in this way, because Catholics engaging in controversy with Protestants have often talked as if good works other than faith play a role in giving rise to justification, rather than simply being a necessary concomitant and result of it – have in fact espoused a 'belief-plus' theory.

[23] When speaking of justification, it is necessary to distinguish between being good and being justified. Having charity must necessarily make one good rather than evil. However, the concept of justification implies more than that one is good; it implies that one is saved, i.e. will go to Heaven, enjoy the beatific vision forever, and be gloriously resurrected. I follow the Roman Catholic view that being good is not in itself sufficient to make one deserve or attain salvation. What is needed in addition is God's decision to reward the goodness involved in charity with salvation. This is a free decision that he has in fact made and announced in his revelation (as e.g. in Matt. 25:31–46), but that he could with perfect justice have not made. We would not earn or deserve salvation even through being perfectly good. We can deserve it only in the limited sense that God is obliged to honour his promise of rewarding goodness with salvation, after he has freely chosen to make this promise of an undeserved reward. It should be noted that on this view, good works of the sort that God takes as meritorious are not possible to unaided human efforts; they can only be done through grace. Protestants often object to the Roman Catholic position on salvation, on the grounds that it describes Christians as earning their salvation through their own unaided efforts. This objection is not a very plausible one; the real difficulty in the Roman Catholic position is rather the opposite one, that of explaining how it is that human actions can be rewarded by salvation, when it looks as if it is salvation that produces the actions that are rewarded. This difficulty is apparent from the Roman Catholic teachings that (a) only acts done by those in a state of sanctifying grace are meritorious, and (b) anyone in a state of grace is already saved.

Christian. Rather, they result from a justification that has already been produced by faith.

We can elucidate this position by an improbable thought experiment. Suppose an unbeliever suffers a strange brain injury, that leaves him capable of only two coherent mental activities; the activity of believing the Christian gospel when it is announced to him, and the activity of disbelieving the gospel. If, after sustaining this injury, the unbeliever chooses to believe the gospel, and does not subsequently retract this choice, he will, in virtue of this choice, be justified. He will be in a state of sanctifying grace, he will love God above all created things, he will merit salvation, and his salvation will be guaranteed, without there being any need for further works on his part.

The claim that faith must be motivated by charity is more specific than the claim that it must be motivated by love, because charity is a particular form of love; it is love of God as he is in himself above all created things. Aquinas seems to be right in requiring this particular form of love from justifying faith. Only such a love is sufficient to exclude sin – if there is anything we love more than God, we can be motivated by this love to sin – and exclusion of sin is required in a redemptive virtue.[24]

This account of faith as bringing about our justification enables us to locate it in a more general account of the economy of salvation. Faith is produced by God's speaking to us, just as the sacraments are implied by the Thomist view to be effected by God's speaking. Both faith and the sacraments, on the views presented here, will thus be effected by God's creative Word; and people will receive the sanctifying effect of this word when they have been made ready for it by the action of the Holy Spirit. This action of the Word will be the mission of the Son, which in turn is rooted in the procession of the Son, and the preparation for faith will be part of the mission of the Holy Spirit, which is rooted in the procession of the Spirit.

One might raise an objection from the Roman Catholic point of view to this characterization of the virtue of divine faith as believing God speaking. It is that the Second Vatican Council, in its constitution *Dei Verbum*, para. 2 ff., characterized revelation as consisting in both words and deeds (i.e. deeds that are not the utterance of words); and that both these forms of revelation are described as the object of divine faith (para. 5). But if faith is believing God speaking, then the

---

[24] There is a clarification about the nature of charity that can be made. Aquinas concedes the possibility of a natural love of God above all created things, when he is loved in his capacity as creator of the world; such a love is theoretically possible to unaided human nature. The love of God involved in charity he holds to be a different love, a love of God, not as creator, but as he is in himself. This is not possible for created nature, and must be a gift of grace. Scotists have accepted that God has as a matter of fact required this latter sort of love for salvation, but claim that he could have chosen to reward the former, natural sort of love with salvation, if he had wanted to. Thomists deny that God could have chosen to reward any love aside from the love of charity with salvation. The Thomist view seems the preferable one, on the grounds that it is only the love of God as he is in himself that is actually aiming at the reward that is given in salvation. To reward any other sort of love with salvation would be giving people a reward that they are not actually seeking, which does not seem reasonable.

deeds that are not words do not seem to be a possible object of faith. So, faith cannot simply be believing God speaking. Since this characterization of revelation is accepted by many people outside the Roman Catholic Church, this objection would be felt by many non-Catholics as well.

A preliminary reply would be that we only have the required knowledge of these deeds through believing God speaking, but this does not remove the problem of how we are to give the assent of faith to deeds and not words. The first step in addressing this problem is to point to the huge weight of evidence in Scripture and tradition that describes faith as believing God speaking. The next is to explain how this evidence can be reconciled with the teaching of *Dei Verbum* by the position of Aquinas, which is that these deeds are in fact communicative acts, but they are communicative acts that are not spoken in any language, and hence not described as words. This is the position he takes when discussing the spiritual sense of Scripture:

> ... That God is the author of holy Scripture should be acknowledged, and he has the power, not only of adapting words to convey meanings (which men can also do), but also of adapting things themselves. In every branch of knowledge words have meaning, but what is special here is that the things meant by the words also mean something. That first meaning [of Scripture] whereby the words signify things belongs to the sense first mentioned, namely the historical or literal. That meaning, however, whereby the things signified by the words in their turn also signify other things is called the spiritual sense; it is based on and presupposes the literal sense.[25]

Thus God would, for example, be saying something by drowning the Egyptians in the Red Sea, not just killing them without doing anything communicative. The account of *telling* developed here could be used to explicate how this happens. We would have faith in these non-linguistic deeds when we believe God speaking in these deeds. On this interpretation, *Dei Verbum* would in a sense be rehabilitating the spiritual sense of Scripture, which has been downgraded as a source for theology, by saying that it demands the assent of faith. It would also be assigning a scope to divine speaking that is much wider than would be the case if this speaking were confined to utterances made in a human language.[26]

As well as excluding a 'belief-minus' account of formless faith, this account of the role of grace in faith gives a positive account of how faith can coexist with mortal sin, and how such formless faith can still require grace. Virtually everyone sins to some extent, so faith always coexists with some sin; by 'formless faith' I mean, as Aquinas does, the faith of sinners who are in a state of sin that will bring about their damnation if they do not repent and change their ways. Since recognition of divine speaking can be produced by enlightenment of the mind as well as by conversion, it is possible to believe God as a result of enlightenment alone, without being converted. This will be the state of those who have formless

---

[25] *1a* 10, 1, Aquinas, 1963, pp. 37–9.
[26] St. Paul clearly appeals to the spiritual sense of Scripture, as here defined, in Galatians 4:21–25.

faith. Since grace is required for this enlightenment, formless faith will require grace. One might ask why sinners might not simply remember having recognized divine speaking in the past, and believe on the basis of this memory, without any further divine action being needed to produce their belief. But even this sort of faith would require the sinner to have been given grace in the past, when he recognized divine speaking; and such past grace would not be sufficient to preserve his belief. For in order to remember something, we have to be able to grasp what it is that we remember. Without the action of grace, we would no longer be able to grasp our past enlightenment and conversion, and thus no longer be able to remember them as they were. We would be in the situation of a mathematician who had lost the parts of his brain necessary for mathematical understanding. He would no longer be able to grasp what it was that he had learnt about mathematics in the past, or what theorems he had proved, and in consequence he would not be able to remember these things. Unable to remember our past enlightenment and conversion, we would be unable to remember having heard God speaking.

Freedom

The voluntary nature of faith is easily understood from what has been said above. As remarked above, it can be seen to be voluntary because it is believing a person in the usual sense, believing upon the bare credit of the proposer; and such belief, unlike forensic belief, is voluntary.

The fact that belief is voluntary does not mean that it need be the result of deliberation and choice, and, in fact, believing any person, including God, is not typically the result of deliberation and choice. In this, faith is like the exercise of some other virtues. We can tell the truth, or act bravely, in a sense automatically; that is, without reflecting on whether or not to do so, or choosing to do so rather than do something else. But such acts are no less voluntary for their not involving deliberation or choice between alternatives. Similarly, we can believe without reflecting about it; the voluntary character of such belief appears from the fact that we could have chosen not to believe. This means that there is no need to actually make the judgements of credibility or credentity as a necessary prerequisite to faith (the judgement of credibility being the judgement to the effect that it would be legitimate to choose to believe, and the judgement of credentity being the judgement that I ought to choose to believe). Since faith need not be the result of an actual deliberation and choice in order to be voluntary, all that is needed for faith is that we not make the opposite judgements. This lets us see that the role of charity in faith need not be the one that Aquinas assigns to it. He thinks of it as the motivation for a conscious choice between alternatives. This is not ruled out by this account, but it will not be the typical way in which charity enters in to faith. Rather, we will say that in justifying faith the conversion that accompanies hearing God speaking will go deep enough to be a love of charity, whether or not this conversion involves deliberation and choice. This conversion will be tied to voluntary belief, because accepting such a conversion upon the occasion of being spoken to by God will entail recognizing this speech as divine, in the way that has been described. Recognition of this speech as divine will not on the other hand entail such a conversion, because there are other ways in which this can be recognized.

This account of the voluntary nature of faith is superior to that given by Catholic theologians like Cajetan, who have explained the voluntary nature of faith as being due to the fact that the propositions believed in faith cannot be seen to be true by the intellect, because they cannot be understood to be self-evidently true or logically deducible from self-evident truths. Cajetan claimed that it is only when a proposition is seen by the intellect to be true in virtue of its meaning, or deductively inferred from a self-evident proposition, that it compels belief. When this is not the case, he maintains that it is always possible to choose to believe or not to believe, and hence it is always possible to choose not to believe the propositions of the Christian faith that are revealed by God. But this view seems to exaggerate the extent of our power to choose our beliefs, for reasons that have been set forth in philosophical discussions of this topic.[27] Could it be right to say that I could choose whether or not to believe that I am on Earth rather than on the planet Neptune, or that I am not an amoeba, or that my head is not made of glass? But none of these propositions can be seen by the intellect to be true in virtue of their meanings.

Our examination of faith can give us some insights into the exercise of faith. Roman Catholic theologians have described faith as a virtue, that is, as a dispositional power and propensity to act well. The more recent Roman Catholic theologians have taken those acts that are exercises of the virtue of faith to be acts that have a proposition as their object. On this view we make an act of faith when we consciously think 'p is true because God says that it is'. The virtue of faith on this view is the disposition to have occurrent true thoughts of this sort. We may conjecture that this account of the virtue of faith is influenced by deistic conceptions of revelation. If we never actually encounter God speaking, the act of thinking 'p is true because God says so' will be the only way in which we can exercise our Christian faith. But since we do encounter God's speaking, and faith consists in believing him when he speaks, an act of faith will consist in the act of believing him when he speaks (as e.g when reading the Scriptures or listening to the liturgy), rather than in believing a proposition of the form 'p is true because God says that it is'. The virtue of faith will consist in the disposition to believe him when he speaks.

Rationality

The rationality of faith is also easily accounted for, given our previous discussion of belief in testimony. Faith is rational because it is belief in the word of a knowledgeable trustworthy person. Not only is it rational, it provides knowledge of what is believed. This means that Aquinas is wrong in denying the status of knowledge to faith, along with everyone else who sees faith as lying midway

---

[27] On the question of whether or not belief can be voluntary, see Bernard Williams, 'Deciding to Believe', in *Problems of the Self*, 1973.

between knowledge and opinion (and with Locke, who sees it as mere opinion, in the sense of probable belief). The correct view is that of Clement of Alexandria, Chrysostom, and John Owen, who see faith as providing us with knowledge. Its status as knowledge means that there cannot be any good reasons for disbelief, and that it is irrational (as well as sinful) for a believer to cease believing or even to take objections to faith seriously. (One may rationally take such objections seriously, in the sense of considering carefully for apologetic purposes how one can give answers to them that will be credible to unbelievers. What is not rational is for a believer to admit a real possibility of such objections ever giving good reason to disbelieve.) This follows from the account of knowledge given above. It is impossible to both know that p and know that not-p; and knowledge is superior to probable belief, so no amount of evidence that makes a proposition p merely probable can justify us in believing that p, if we know that p is false. Since faith gives us knowledge, we cannot know that a proposition that we have come to know through faith is false, and we cannot rationally accept that probable evidence against such a proposition could ever justify us in disbelieving it.

Although doubting God's word is irrational, that does not mean that it is impossible. The relations between faith and doubt are complex. Not all forms of doubt exclude faith, since we can feel doubts about things that we know perfectly well. However, there are some kinds of doubt that are not compatible with belief in a proposition, and are thus incompatible with knowing it (and hence with having faith in it). I will not address here the questions of what kinds of doubt, or what degree of doubt, may entail disbelief in a particular divine utterance, or disbelief in the Christian message as a whole, as these are difficult questions that do not fall under my topic. Nor will I try to answer the question of when doubt is a sin. As remarked above, there is a moral as well as an epistemic obligation to believe God. If the sort of doubt that is distinct from disbelief is in any way voluntary, it would seem reasonable to claim that it is a sin; but the question of whether or when doubt is voluntary is not trivial, and I will not attempt to answer it.

Some reflections about the relation of faith to other sources of knowledge, and particularly to scientific investigation, suggest themselves. We can see that it is incorrect, or at least misleading, to describe faith and science as two different methods of arriving at truth. Rather, faith is an exercise of a method of arriving at truth, belief in testimony, that is more basic than scientific investigation. It is more basic because, unlike scientific investigation, belief in testimony is a single fundamental intellectual virtue, that is required and used by science, and combined by scientists with the exercise of other intellectual virtues to arrive at results or to devise more specific means of reaching scientific conclusions. Its basic nature means that, unlike science, there is not a whole lot to say about faith as a means of arriving at knowledge. The crucial questions with respect to faith are how God speaks to us, and how we come to recognize that God is speaking to us. It is not the question of how God's speaking can give us knowledge; provided that we understand that testimony is a source of knowledge, it is obvious that believing God when he speaks must give us knowledge.

Conclusion

At the beginning of Chapter 2, we distinguished between the question of what provides the rational grounding for Christian faith and the question of what leads us to have this faith. In the course of answering the former question, we have arrived at an answer for the latter. The rational grounding for Christian faith is God's speaking to us. What brings about Christian faith is God's speaking to us, the work of the Holy Spirit in our souls enabling us to recognize this speaking, and our not refusing to believe God. Julian the Apostate was thus unwittingly correct when he said that all the wisdom of Christians could be summed up in the imperative 'Believe'. These answers in turn have enabled us to give a description of the virtue of Christian faith as such. This description turns out to be substantially that of Aquinas; the virtue of Christian faith consists in believing God when he speaks to announce the Christian message, when this belief is motivated by the love of God above all created things.

This investigation of Christian faith has been carried out from a theological perspective, the perspective of a believer. One of the things it has brought to light is that this perspective cannot be the same as that of an unbeliever. The enlightenment and conversion that bring about faith cannot be observed from the outside. They may sometimes show themselves in their effects on the believer, but such effects will not enable an unbeliever to recognize their presence. The sins of many believers mean that these effects will often be difficult or impossible to observe. Even when they are present, the unbeliever is not equipped to grasp what they are a sign of. He will in fact often be baffled and repelled by them (think of David Hume's contempt for humility and the other monkish virtues), and when he does find them attractive, he will not be able to distinguish them from the effects of natural virtue. An unbeliever cannot properly evaluate the reasonableness of Christian faith, because the evidence necessary for such an evaluation is unavailable to him. The only way for him to find out whether faith is reasonable is to, as far as lies in him, take the venture of believing; to be open to the possibility of the Christian message being spoken by God, to pray for God's assistance in arriving at the truth of this question (even if he is not sure that there is such a being as God), to refuse to be influenced against the gospel by any unwelcome implications it might have about his character and behaviour. For all those who take this venture, which itself is not possible without God's assistance, there is good hope that divine grace will show them the light that Christ came into the world to bring.

Appendix I

Content Externalism and the Development of Doctrine

In Chapter 7, an attempt was made to reconcile the ecclesial view of divine speaking, that states that the Church's teaching of the Christian message is literally God's speaking, with the traditional doctrine that revelation was completed with the apostles. The reconciliation was effected by taking this doctrine to mean, not that God did not speak after the death of the last apostle, or that God did not say anything new after the death of the last apostle, but that since the death of the last apostle God has not revealed the existence of new salvific realities to mankind. This understanding was presented as having the advantage of solving the problem that the development of doctrine poses for anyone who wants to accept the teachings of the Church as divinely revealed. The problem is that historical evidence seems to show that many of these teachings did not exist before the death of the last apostle; so that demanding the assent of divine faith to these teachings seems to violate the doctrine, which the Church herself teaches, that revelation ceased with the death of the apostles.

The traditional answer to this problem was to assert that those teachings which were not actually asserted before the death of the apostles can be logically derived from teachings that were.[1] But historical investigation has made this answer rather suspect, and the further away Church teachings move from the time and mental world of the apostles, the more suspect it is. The idea that the doctrine of the completion of revelation refers to the salvific realities revealed, rather than to the propositions asserted by God, was presented as a superior answer to this problem. If we accept it we can say that the teachings of the Church that are first announced after the death of the apostles are not new revelation because they do not announce the existence of new salvific realities; they only tell us new things about the salvific realities whose existence was announced before the death of the apostles.

This understanding of the completion of revelation was supported by an appeal to Aquinas's claim (in *2a2ae* 1, 7) that all of Christian revelation is implicit in the belief that God exists and has a providential care for our salvation. It was claimed that this cannot be understood as asserting that all the propositions that must be accepted with divine faith are logically implicit in this belief, because they obviously are not. It is much more plausibly understood as asserting that all the salvific realities made known by Christian revelation are described in a general way by the statement that God exists and has a care for our salvation.

---

[1] For a classic exposition of this view, see Marín-Sola, 1924.

However, there are grounds for arguing that Aquinas really meant that all the teachings of the Christian faith were logically implied by this belief, and, what is more, that he had good reasons for thinking so. This appendix is meant to give the case that can be made for these conclusions, which, if true, would be of some importance for the development of doctrine.

What would make it possible for Aquinas to think that the whole Christian faith is logically implied by the assertion that God exists and rewards those who seek him is the fact that he had an externalist view of content. An externalist view of content holds that the content of propositions is not determined by what the people who think them can understand of them, but by the nature of the realities that the propositions are about. As Hilary Putnam put it, '"meanings" just ain't in the head'.[2] If this were so, the meaning of the proposition that God exists would be determined by the nature of God; it could thus be said to contain or imply the proposition that a trinitarian God exists, since it is God's nature to be three persons in one God. The proposition that God rewards those who seek him could be said to get its meaning from what God actually does to reward those who seek him; it could thus be said to contain or imply the doctrine of the Incarnation, and the whole economy of salvation. The fact that people who grasp these propositions need not understand that they imply these things is neither here nor there, because meaning isn't in the head.

Evidence of Aquinas's content externalism can be found in the following passage from *1a* 85 1, on whether the separated soul can understand anything. He writes:

> ... every intellectual substance possesses intellective power by the influence of the divine light. This light is one and simple in its first principle, and the farther off the intellectual creatures are from the first principle, so much more is the light diversified, as is the case with lines radiating from the centre of a circle. Hence it is that God by his essence understands all things, while the superior intellectual substances understand by means of a number of species, which nevertheless are fewer and more universal and bestow a deeper comprehension of things, because of the efficaciousness of the intellectual power of such natures; but inferior intellectual natures possess a greater number of species, which are also less universal, and bestow a lower degree of comprehension, in proportion as they recede from the intellectual power of the higher intellectual substances. If, therefore, inferior substances received species in the same degree of universality as the superior substances, since they are not so strong in understanding, the knowledge which they would derive through these species would be imperfect, and of a general and confused nature. We can see this to a certain extent in man, for those who are of weaker intellect fail to acquire perfect knowledge through the universal conceptions of those who have a better understanding, unless things are explained to them singly and in detail.[3]

---

[2] Hilary Putnam, 'The meaning of "meaning"', in *Mind, Language and Reality*, 1975, p. 227.
[3] *1a* 89, 1, in St. Thomas Aquinas, *Basic writings of St. Thomas Aquinas*, vol. 1, 1945, p. 853.

From this passage we can extract both an expression of content externalism and a simple but powerful argument for it. Aquinas states here that different people can have a different degree of understanding of the very same species, or form. But if this is true, it means that people can have different levels of understanding of the very same proposition. If this can happen, the content of a proposition cannot be determined by what is in the head, because what is in the heads of such people differs, but the proposition that they are thinking is one and the same. Meaning is therefore not in the head.[4]

Is Aquinas right in thinking that people can have different degrees of understanding of the very same proposition? It seems so. Take the proposition that honesty is morally obligatory. People can have different degrees of understanding of what honesty is. For example, some may realize that honesty excludes buying goods that you can reasonably believe to be stolen, while others do not. The former sort of people understand what honesty is better than the latter sort. Thus they will have a better understanding of the proposition that honesty is morally obligatory. But they do not understand a *different* proposition from the less morally sensitive people. The latter can understand what honesty is, even if they understand it less well than the former; hence they can understand what is said by 'honesty is morally obligatory'. If this were not so, people could not even disagree on whether buying goods that one reasonably believes to be stolen is dishonest, because the mere fact of their disagreement would mean that they understood different things by honesty. They would thus not be contradicting one another when one of them asserted that the buying of such goods is dishonest, and the other denied that it was. But obviously they can contradict one another.

Once we see that people can have different degrees of understanding of the same proposition, we can ask what it is that determines which person's understanding of a proposition is the right one, when these understandings happen to disagree. In the case given above, it is clear that what will determine who is right about the honesty of buying stolen goods will the nature of the virtue of honesty itself. But this virtue is a reality that exists outside people's thoughts about honesty. So, the content of the proposition that honesty is morally obligatory will be determined by the nature of the reality, the virtue of honesty, that it is about. (This conclusion leaves open the question of *how* the nature of things determines

---

[4] Further evidence for Aquinas's content externalism is found in his assertion that the proposition 'God exists' is self-evident in itself, but not to us (*1a* 2, 1). This can only be the case if the content of propositions is determined, not by what people can grasp of them, but by what they are about. Aquinas's content externalism may also be indicated by his contention that in some respects the intellect is incapable of erring (*1a* 85, 6; S.C.G. 1, 59, and 3, 108–10). We saw above that content externalism seems to imply that since content is determined by reality, then it is reality that must furnish content, and that since we get to reality through the exercise of intellectual virtues, all our grasp of content must therefore originate in knowledge. This may be part of what Aquinas has in mind when he asserts that the intellect cannot err.

the content of propositions. Aquinas has an interesting theory on this question, but examining it would take us too far from our subject.)[5]

It might be objected that this argument does not distinguish between different degrees of understanding of the content of a proposition, and different degrees of understanding of the implications of a proposition. In this case, it might be said, and in all other cases where people seem to have different understandings of the same proposition, what is in fact happening is not that the proposition itself is being understood differently, but that some people understand that the proposition implies certain other propositions, and other people do not.

This objection can seem plausible if we only consider those logical implications of a proposition that arise from its logical form. Grasp of these implications is separable from grasping the meaning of a proposition, since different propositions can have exactly the same logical form. But not all the logical implications of a proposition arise from its logical form. An example is the fact that the proposition expressed by 'This apple is red' implies the proposition expressed by 'This apple is not green'.[6] Implications of this sort result from the meaning of a proposition, rather than from a form it shares with other propositions. We cannot therefore separate understanding the meaning of a proposition from understanding those of its implications that result from its meaning rather than from its logical form, since it is understanding the meaning of a proposition that enables us to grasp these kinds of implications, and a greater degree of understanding of a proposition can enable us to grasp more of them. And it is clear that some of the differences between people's understanding of the same proposition are not a result of certain people's grasping implications that follow from the logical form of propositions, while other people do not grasp these implications. This appears from the example given above. There is no syntactical feature of the proposition 'honesty is morally obligatory' that will tell us whether or not it is morally obligatory to refrain from buying stolen goods, and there is no syntactical feature of the proposition 'buying stolen goods is dishonest' that can tell us that it is true. We can know that buying stolen goods is dishonest only through knowing what honesty is.

Aquinas's view that the meaning of a proposition is given by the realities it is about is not the only way of accounting for the fact that meaning is not in the head. An alternative explanation for why meaning is not in the head is that the content of propositions consists in the rules for the correct use of linguistic expressions. These rules are public rather than private, being established by the practices of a linguistic community; thus they are not in any particular individual's head. Differences in understanding of a proposition will on this view consist in differences in understanding of the rules of usage for a particular language, rather than differences in understanding of the natures of things.

---

[5] I have discussed this theory in John Lamont, 'Aquinas on divine simplicity', *The Monist*, 1997.

[6] Wittgenstein was influenced by examples of this sort in abandoning his previous view that all logical implications arise from the logical forms of propositions; see Ludwig Wittgenstein, 'Elementary propositions', in *Philosophical Grammar*, part 1, 1974, pp. 210–14.

Such a view is widely held among philosophers. It can be called the language-use view of content. It asserts that the grasp of a concept or a proposition just is the possession of an ability to use language; as John Skorupski puts it, 'Grasping a concept is understanding (the use of) an expression in a language. Grasping a proposition is understanding (the use of) a sentence in a language.'[7]

An immediate reaction to this view is that it is refuted by the example of disagreement given above. For if it were true, people who argue over whether the proposition that honesty is morally obligatory implies that buying stolen goods is morally forbidden would be arguing over the rules of English usage, or about the applications that people actually make of the word 'honesty'. But they are not; they are arguing over the nature of a reality, the virtue of honesty. A second reaction is to point out that a grasp of the rules for using language will itself involve a grasp of the meaning of propositions (this is certainly true of theories that explain understanding of a language in terms of a grasp of truth-conditions for utterances in the language, or in terms of a grasp of the circumstances in which such utterances are warrantably assertible), so that the language-use view runs into vicious circularity. A third reaction is to point out that the language-use view relies on a lack of clarity in its account of grasping the use of expressions in a language. Grasping the use of a linguistic expression can be understood as possessing the ability to say something by using a linguistic expression, or as possessing the ability to understand a linguistic expression when it is used by someone else. The language use view, if it is to be tenable, can only be understood as referring to the former ability. If it were understood as referring to the latter ability, it would fall victim to a similar kind of vicious circularity. For it would then be explaining content in terms of the grasp of language, while explicating the grasp of language in terms of the ability to understand the content of language. But this clarification of what the language use view must mean by the grasp of content enables us to see that the view is falsified by empirical evidence. There is a consensus among psychologists to the effect that children understand linguistic expressions before they are actually able to use them.[8] (This is hardly surprising; if it were not the case, how could children ever start to learn a language?) So the grasp of content cannot be explained as consisting in the ability to say things in language, since such children possess a grasp of content without being able to say anything. The language use view is thus no good, and it cannot be used as a basis for objecting to Aquinas's content externalism.

If we accept Aquinas's content externalism, and his view that all of the Christian faith is logically implied by the statement that God exists and rewards those who seek him, what will follow for our understanding of the development of doctrine? Some of the distinctions postulated in chapter 7 between different understandings of the completion of revelation will collapse. God's not telling us about the existence of any new salvific realities after the death of the last apostle,

---

[7] John Skorupski, 'Meaning, use, verification', in *Blackwell Companion to the Philosophy of Language*, 1997, p. 33.
[8] On this see for example Alan Slater and Michael Lewis, *Introduction to Infant Development*, 2002, pp. 258–60.

and his not communicating any new propositions after the death of the last apostle that are not logically implied by propositions he communicated before this death, will amount to the same thing. But not all these distinctions will collapse. There will still be a difference between God's not making any new information known after the death of the last apostle, and his not speaking after the death of the last apostle. This difference means that content externalism does not provide a way of salvaging the magisterial conception of revelation. It would be possible, if we accept some kind of content externalism, to argue that God does not make any new information known after the death of the last apostle, on the grounds that any doctrines taught by the Church after this death but not before it will be logically implied by what was taught before it, and hence will not be really new. But it will remain the case that there are doctrines taught after but not before the death of the last apostle for which the Church demands the assent of divine faith. As pointed out earlier, the mere fact that such doctrines are logically derivable from propositions that God has spoken does not mean that they can command the assent of divine faith, because such faith is only exercised when God actually speaks, not when we are presented with propositions that are only implied by what he says. The ecclesial conception of revelation remains the only way of justifying the assent of divine faith to such doctrines.

However, content externalism does permit one to accept a form of the logical theory of the development of doctrine. This is an advantage, since it enables us to accept without excessive distortion or pious interpretation the traditional view that all of revelation is contained in the Scriptures, and that study of the Scriptures is all that is needed to understand it. The resulting logical theory of development will be an improvement on previous ones, because it will give a satisfactory explanation of why sinners and unbelievers are not able to draw out the developments of doctrine as well as faithful and holy people; of why, in fact, holiness is necessary for theology. Since a grasp of the logical implications of revealed statements will depend in part on a grasp of the realities that they are about, and since such a grasp requires faith and holiness (and is increased by an increase in faith and holiness), those who are faithful and holy will, other things being equal, be better able (or solely able) to grasp these implications.[9] This vindicates the traditional emphasis on the necessity of holiness for theology, and justifies Aquinas's assertion that the devils, despite their superior intellectual capacities, are unable to draw the proper conclusions from revealed truth.

---

[9] This line of reasoning is put forward in St. Anselm in his *De Incarnatione Verbi* in *Anselm of Canterbury: The Major Works*, 1998, ch. 1.

Appendix II

Newman on the Development of Doctrine

In view of the importance of Cardinal Newman's views on the development of doctrine, and the extensive discussion that has been produced by them, it is worth while relating his views to the discussion of the development of doctrine in this book; particularly since this makes it possible to correct widespread misapprehensions about the purpose he had in mind in his ideas on development.

These misapprehensions arise from a failure to understand that Newman in his *Essay on the Development of Christian Doctrine* was not in fact interested in the problem of the development of doctrine as it has been stated here, that is, in the problem of explaining how it is that the Church can both teach that revelation ended with the apostles, and demand the assent of divine faith for teachings that were never stated until after apostolic times. He had a different goal in mind; that of showing how historic Christianity, that is, Christianity as it has existed from the century up to the present, is 'in its substance the very religion which Christ and his apostles taught in the first.'[1] Succeeding in this goal does not give a solution to the problem of the development of doctrine as defined above, because modern Catholic Christianity can be in substance the very religion taught by Christ and his disciples while having added teachings that were not explicitly uttered in apostolic times.

Newman builds his reasoning upon two assumptions. The first is that there is such a thing as Christian revelation, and the second is that Christian understanding of the revelation cannot have gone through fundamental changes over time, because such changes would negate the purpose for which revelation was given. Thus he says 'one [hypothesis] is that Christianity has even changed from the first and ever accommodates itself to the circumstances of times and seasons; but it is difficult to understand how such a view is compatible with the special idea of revealed truth, and in fact its advocates more or less abandon or tend to abandon the supernatural claims of Christianity; so it need not detain us here.'[2] These assumptions lead him to dismiss Chillingworth (whom he describes as a 'smart but superficial writer'[3]) at the outset. There are no traces of Chillingworth's Protestant positions, including 'his doctrine of the divine efficacy of the Scriptures as the one

---

[1] John Henry Newman, *An essay on the development of Christian doctrine*, 1989, p. 5.

[2] Newman, 1989, p. 9.

[3] Newman, 1989, p. 6.

appointed instrument of religious feeling'[4], during at least the first millennium of Christian history. Thus '... this one thing is certain; whatever history teaches, whatever it omits, whatever it exaggerates or extenuates, whatever it says or unsays, the Christianity of history is not Protestantism. If ever there were a safe truth, it is this.'[5] And since rejecting the Christianity of history means rejecting the idea of a Christian revelation, 'to be deep in history is to cease to be a Protestant.' So for Newman the scriptural view of revelation is demonstrably false, and does not even need to enter into his discussion of development. The need for this discussion arises from the fact that 'there are to be found, during the 1800 years through which [historical Christianity] has lasted, certain apparent inconsistencies and alterations in its doctrine and worship, such as irresistibly attract the attention of all who inquire into it.' Note that the problem is not the existence of apparent additions, but the existence of apparent inconsistencies and alterations. There are two available explanations for these inconsistencies. One is the Anglican explanation, which is that these apparent inconsistencies are due to the introduction of corruptions into Christianity, which should be removed by abandoning everything that does not have the sanction of primitive times. The other is the Roman Catholic explanation, which is that the changes that have occurred in historic Christianity are not inconsistencies or alterations at all, but rather the result of a deeper understanding of the revealed message. Newman's object in his *Essay* is to show that the Anglican explanation is wrong and that the Roman Catholic one is right. He tries to establish that the additions made to the apostolic message by the Church of Rome are not in reality a difficulty, but rather, when rightly understood, are the solution to his problem. They are the solution because Christianity, like all viable systems of ideas, requires to grow and thus change if it is to live, and the additions of the Church of Rome can in Newman's view be shown to be the manifestation of this growth; if they had not happened, Roman Catholic Christianity could not. be the Christianity taught by Christ and the Apostles.

Disregard of Newman's object in considering the development of doctrine fact has led to a fairly comprehensive misuse and misunderstanding of Newman's thought on development by Roman Catholic theologians during and after his time, who have stubbornly persisted in trying to use his theory of development as a solution to the problem of the development of doctrine.[6] It is not easy to say what

---

[4] Newman, 1989, p. 7.

[5] Newman, 1989, p. 7.

[6] This trend of thought is described in Walgrave, 1972. It also exists to some extent in Owen Chadwick, *From Bossuet to Newman*, 2nd edn, 1987). Chadwick speaks at times as if Newman was trying to *prove* that the teachings of Christ and the apostles still existed in historical Christianity in his *Essay*, rather than to find where exactly this historical Christianity now exists. Of course Newman was aware that succeeding in this task would serve an apologetic purpose, by providing an account of Christian history that would serve as an alternative to the picture given by unbelieving historians, but this was a secondary intention rather than his main goal. He explicitly set out to write theology rather than apologetics in his *Essay*, and, in consequence, explicitly assumed that the teachings of Christ and the apostles have been preserved up until the present day. The role that Chadwick

Newman thought of this problem, because he does not seem to have bothered about it as a problem. When the Jesuit theologian Perrone, presumably motivated by considerations connected with the problem of the development of doctrine, stated that he would not dare to deny that the Church had not always explicitly held all of the tenets that she has taught *de fide*, Newman replied by giving a list of doctrines (such as the validity of heretical baptism and the canon of scripture) of which this could not be true.[7] This reply rather missed the point of Perrone's difficulty. A similar failure to address the issue of the problem of the development of doctrine is found in a paper he wrote for the Irish priest John Stanislas Flanagan.[8] Flanagan had asserted the position that 'our Lord taught the Apostles explicitly all the truths of faith', 'these truths exclusively form or make up the depositum which the Apostles delivered to the Church', and 'the gift of infallibility [to the Church] secures (a) that not one of these divine truths should ever be lost, and (b) that no human addition whether of number or accretion should ever be made to them'.[9] This is exactly the position that has to be maintained by anyone who wants to hold the magisterial view of revelation. However, as Newman had pointed out, history shows that things did not happen that way. Newman's reply to Flanagan simply gave his own view of what had happened instead. Newman stated that:

> ... the Apostles had the *fullness* of revealed knowledge, a fullness which they could as little realize to themselves, as the human mind as such, can have all its thoughts present before it at once ... the Creed (i.e. the Deposit, I say the Creed as more intelligible since it consists of Articles) was delivered to the Church *with the gift of knowing its true and full meaning* ... there is nothing which the Church has defined or shall define but what an Apostle, if asked, would have been fully able to answer and would have answered, as the Church has answered, the one answering by inspiration, the other by its gift of infallibility ... the differences between them being that an Apostle could answer questions at once, but the Church answers them intermittently ... and secondly and on the other hand, that the Church does in fact make answers which the Apostle did not make, and in one sense did not know, though they would have known them, i.e. made present to their consciousness, and made those answers, had the question been asked.[10]

This answer simply makes perfectly clear the difficulty that arises in accepting developments of doctrine as teachings of the faith. Even if the Apostles would have

---

assigns to Newman in Catholic thought is also misleading, partly because of the point at which Chadwick starts his survey. By beginning with Bossuet he conceals the fact that Bossuet's view on doctrine and its development (which agreed with that of Flanagan given here) was actually an innovation that was not much more than a hundred years old, and that Newman, rather than departing from previous Catholic thought, was returning to the outlook held in the Middle Ages; a fact that emerges from the discussion of the ecclesial view of revelation in Chapter 7.

[7] See Chadwick, 1987, pp. 183–4.

[8] John Henry Newman, 'An Unpublished Paper by Cardinal Newman on the Development of Doctrine', *Journal of Theological Studies*, 1958.

[9] Newman, 1958, p. 327.

[10] Newman, 1958, p. 333. This account of development of doctrine agrees with the view I have presented (unsurprisingly since my view is based on Newman's).

given all the later teachings of the Church had they been asked about them, it remains the case and is plainly stated by Newman that in fact they were not asked about many of them, and did not say a single thing about them. If believing these teachings is an exercise of divine faith, and hence believing God, and God's speaking occurs only in the teachings of the prophets, of Christ, and of the apostles, how can we have divine faith in a teaching that was confessedly never actually uttered by any of these people? Newman does not say. (And he is clear that such faith is divine faith rather than simply Catholic faith.) Given Newman's deep patristic learning and his lack of understanding of scholastic thought, it may be that he had something like an ecclesial view of revelation in the back of his mind, which would prevent him from seeing why developments (as opposed to corruptions) of the apostolic teaching might be problematic. (The passage above is certainly suggestive of an ecclesial view of revelation, which is the only view upon which his theory of development can make sense.)

Seeing the problem of the development of doctrine as a problem would in any case have required him to turn his whole outlook backwards. Newman's coming to the conclusion that the Roman Catholic Church, and she alone, preserved the substance of Christ's teaching, was the crucial intellectual and personal step of his adult life. This conclusion was arrived at *on the basis of* the position that developments of doctrine – *real* developments, that involve more than simple logical deduction from what is already revealed – are not only legitimate but desirable and necessary, rather than problematic. This position just assumes that the problem of the development of doctrine is not a problem. I suspect that if he had been brought to face the problem of development clearly and squarely he would have thought that it was a theoretician's problem that was not of real interest. He held that we can know there is a Christian revelation originating in God, and hence that we can know that the substance of Christ's teaching must have been preserved in historic Christianity. When it can be shown that this substance is to be found in the teachings of the Roman Church, we then know that these teachings must be Christ's teachings. If these things can all be known, as he thought they could, difficulties about the completion of revelation do not pose a real problem for what it is that we should believe. We can just assume that they are open to a solution of some kind, even if we do not have a solution ready to be presented. I would agree that this problem does not pose a difficulty about what we should believe; I see the solution to it that has been proposed in this book as important chiefly for the logical defence and clarification it can provide for substantive accounts of development of Newman's sort.

One might ask how the account of the rational grounding of faith that is presented in this book is related to the account presented by Newman in his *University Sermons* and his *Grammar of Assent*. The answer I would offer is that Newman's account of the rational grounding of faith is a misconceived attempt to reconcile his spirituality and his philosophy. His spiritual perceptiveness and his deep knowledge of Christian tradition led him to hold that faith must exclude doubt: 'Faith is properly an assent, and an assent without doubt, or a certitude'.[11] His philosophy on the other hand led him to think that faith must be based on the motives of credibility. He therefore exerted himself to show that the motives of credibility, which he recognized as only giving probable evidence for the divinely revealed status of Christianity, could nonetheless justify a strength of assent as strong as that commanded by beliefs known beyond a shadow of a doubt. The mistake in this strategy, as can be seen from the discussion in this book, is its assumption that faith must be based on the motives of credibility. This mistake does not mean that Newman's work on the rational grounding of faith is valueless. I have argued[12] that Newman makes a powerful case for a moderately externalist understanding of knowledge. Such an understanding is necessary if we are to defend faith as excluding doubt; Newman in his discussion of knowledge thus provides strong weapons for the defence of his view that faith is certain.

---

[11] John Henry Newman, *Fifteen Sermons preached before the University of Oxford*, 3rd edn, 1900, p. xvi.
[12] John Lamont, 'Newman on faith and certainty', *International Journal for Philosophy of Religion*, 1996c.

Bibliography

(P.G. stands for Migne's *Patrologia Graeca*; P.L., for his *Patrologia Latina*.)

Primary sources

Peter Abelard (1987), *Theologia 'Scholarium'* (also known as *Introductio ad theologiam*), in *Petri Abaelardi Opera Theologica III, Corpus Christianorum, continuatio medievalis* Vol. XIII, ed. E.M. Buytaert, C.J. Mews, Brepols, Turnholt.

Alexander of Hales (1948), *Summa theologica*, ed. P. Perantoni, Quaracchi, Florence.

Alston, William (1993), *The Reliability of Sense Perception*, Cornell University Press, Ithaca.

St. Ambrose (1963), *Theological and dogmatic works*, tr. Roy J. de Ferrari, CUA Press, Washington.

Anscombe, G.E.M. (1979), 'What Is It to Believe Someone?', in C.F. Delaney ed., *Rationality and Religious Belief*, University of Notre Dame Press, Notre Dame.

Anscombe, G.E.M. (1981), 'Faith', in *The collected philosophical papers of G.E.M. Anscombe*, Vol. 3, Basil Blackwell, Oxford.

St. Anselm of Canterbury (1998), *De Incarnatione Verbi*, tr. by Richard Regan as *On the Incarnation of the Word*, in *Anselm of Canterbury: The Major Works*, ed. Brian Davies, Gillian Evans, OUP, Oxford.

Anselm of Laon (1895), *Sententiae*, ed. G. Lefèvre, Évreux.

St. Thomas Aquinas (1933), *Scriptum super sententiis Magistri Petri Lombardi*, ed. R. P. Mandonnet O.P., M.-F. Moos O.P., P. Lethielleux, Paris.

St. Thomas Aquinas (1945), *Basic writings of St. Thomas Aquinas*, Vol. 1, ed. Anton C. Pegis, Random House, New York.

St. Thomas Aquinas (1949), *In decem libros Ethicorum Aristotelis ad Nicomachum expositio*, ed. R. Spiazzi O.P., Marietti, Rome.

St. Thomas Aquinas (1950), *In librum Beati Dionysii de divinis nominibus expositio*, ed. Ceslaus Pera O.P., Marietti, Rome.

St. Thomas Aquinas (1952), *Super evangelium S. Ioannis lectura*, 5th revised edn, ed. Raphael Cai O.P., Marietti, Rome.

St. Thomas Aquinas (1953a), *Super epistolas S. Pauli lectura*, Vol. II, ed. Raphael Cai O.P., 8th revised edn, Marietti, Rome.

St. Thomas Aquinas (1953b), *Summa theologiae*, Commissio Piana, Ottawa.

St. Thomas Aquinas (1961), *Summa contra gentiles*, P. Lethielleux, Paris.

St. Thomas Aquinas (1963), *Summa Theologiae*, Vol. 1, Blackfriars edn, tr. Thomas Gilby O.P., Eyre & Spottiswoode, London.

St. Thomas Aquinas. (1964–5b), *De malo*, in *Quaestiones disputatae*, Vol. 2, ed. R. Spiazzi O.P., 10th edn, Marietti, Rome.

St. Thomas Aquinas (1967), *Summa contra gentiles*, ed. P. Caramelo, P. Marc, C. Pera, Marietti, Rome.

St. Thomas Aquinas (1972), *Quaestiones disputatae de veritate*, Vol. III, ed. A. Dondaine and others, Leonine edn, Vol. 22(2), Rome.

St. Thomas Aquinas (1974), *Summa theologiae*, Vol. 56, Blackfriars edn, tr. David Bourke, Eyre & Spottiswoode, London.

St. Thomas Aquinas (1992), *Super Boetium de trinitate*, ed. P.-M. J. Gils and others, in Leonine edn, Vol. 50, Rome.

St. Thomas Aquinas (1996), *Quaestiones quodlibetales*, ed. R.-A Gauthier and others, Leonine edn, Vol. 25, Rome.

ARCIC: The Final Report (1982), SPCK, London.

Aristotle (1958), *De sophisticiis elenchis*, in *Aristotelis Topica et Sophistici elenchi*, Clarendon Press, Oxford.

Ashcraft, Richard (1969), 'Faith and Knowledge in Locke's Philosophy', in *John Locke: Problems and Perspectives*, ed. John W. Yolton, CUP, Cambridge.

St. Athanasius (1978), *Third Discourse Against the Arians*, in *Library of the Nicene and Post-Nicene Fathers*, second series, Vol. IV, tr. J. H. Newman, A. Robertson, Eerdmans, Grand Rapids.

Aubert, Roger (1943), 'Le caractère raisonnable de l'acte de foi d'après les théologiens de la fin du 13e siècle', *Revue d'histoire ecclésiastique*.

Aubert, Roger (1950), *Le problème de l'acte de foi*, 2nd edn, Publications universitaires de Louvain, Louvain.

Aubrey, John (1958), *Brief Lives*, ed. Oliver Lawson Dick, Secker and Warburg, London.

St. Augustine (1895), *S. Augustini epistulae*, CSEL Vol. 34, ed. A. Goldbacher, Leipzig.

St. Augustine (1948), *De ordine*, in Bibliothèque Augustinienne, *Oeuvres de Saint Augustin*, Vol. 4, tr. R. Jolivet, Desclée de Brouwer, Paris.

St. Augustine (1951), *Contra Academicos*, tr. John J. O'Meara, Longmans, Green & Co., London.

St. Augustine (1956a), *The Harmony of the Gospels*, in *Library of the Nicene and Post-Nicene Fathers*, first series, Vol. VI, tr. S. D. F. Salmond, Grand Rapids, Eerdmans.

St. Augustine (1956b), *Enarrationes in Psalmos LI–C*, Corpus Christianorum Series Latina, Brepols, Turnhout.

St. Augustine (1956c), *Enarrationes in Psalmos CI–CL*, Corpus Christianorum Series Latina, Brepols, Turnhout.

St. Augustine (1962a), *De correptione et gratia*, in Bibliothèque Augustinienne, *Oeuvres de Saint Augustin*, Vol. 24, tr. Jean Chéné, Jacques Antard, Desclée de Brouwer, Paris.

St. Augustine (1962b), *De predestinatione sanctorum*, in Bibliothèque Augustinienne, *Oeuvres de Saint Augustin*, Vol. 24, tr. Jean Chéné, Jacques Antard, Desclée de Brouwer, Paris.

St. Augustine (1966a), *De gestis pelagii*, in Bibliothèque Augustinienne, *Oeuvres de Saint Augustin*, Vol. 21, tr. G. de Plinval, J. de la Tullaye, Desclée de Brouwer, Paris.

St. Augustine (1966b), *De natura et gratia*, in Bibliothèque Augustinienne, *Oeuvres de Saint Augustin*, Vol. 21, tr. G. de Plinval, J. de la Tullaye, Desclée de Brouwer, Paris.

St. Augustine (1975), *De gratia Christi*, in Bibliothèque Augustinienne, *Oeuvres de Saint Augustin*, Vol. 22, tr. J. Plagnieux, F.-J. Thonnard, Desclée de Brouwer, Paris.

St. Augustine (1991a), *Confessions*, tr. Henry Chadwick, OUP, Oxford.

St. Augustine (1991b), *De trinitate*, tr. Edmund Hill O.P., New City Press, New York.

St. Augustine (1993a), *De fide rerum quae non videntur*, in *Library of the Nicene and Post-Nicene Fathers*, first series, Vol. III, tr. P. Holmes, R. E. Wallis, rev. B. B. Warfield, T.&T. Clark, Edinburgh.

St. Augustine (1993b), *De spiritu et littera*, in *Library of the Nicene and Post-Nicene Fathers*, first series, Vol. V, tr. P. Holmes, R. E. Wallis, rev. B. B. Warfield, T.&T. Clark, Edinburgh

St. Augustine (1993c), *De gratia et libero arbitrio,* in *Library of the Nicene and Post-Nicene Fathers,* first series, Vol. V, tr. P. Holmes, R. E. Wallis, rev. B. B. Warfield, T.&T. Clark, Edinburgh.

St. Augustine *(*1993e), *Tractates on the Gospel of John,* in *Library of the Nicene and Post-Nicene Fathers,* first series, Vol. VII, tr. P. Holmes, R. E. Wallis, rev. B. B. Warfield, T.&T. Clark, Edinburgh.

St. Augustine (1993d), *On the Predestination of the Saints,* in *Library of the Nicene and Post-Nicene Fathers,* first series, Vol. V, tr. P. Holmes, R. E. Wallis, rev. B. B. Warfield, T.&T. Clark, Edinburgh.

Avramides, Anita (1989), *Meaning and mind,* MIT Press, Cambridge, Mass.

Baillie, John (1956), *The Idea of Revelation in Recent Thought,* Columbia University Press, New York.

Bardy, G. (1952), 'L'Inspiration des Pères de l'Église', in *Recherches de Science Religieuse,* 40.

Barr, James (1963), 'Revelation through History in the Old Testament and in Modern Theology', *Interpretation* 17.

Barr, James (1973), *The Bible in the Modern World,* SCM Press, London.

Barth, Karl (1936), *Church Dogmatics,* Vol. 1, T.&T. Clark, Edinburgh.

Baxter, Richard (1675), *Catholick Theologie,* London.

Baxter, Richard (1707), *The Reason of the Christian Religion,* in *The Practical Works of Richard Baxter,* Vol. II, London.

Billot, L. (1921), *De virtutibus infusis: commentarium in secundam partem S. Thomae,* Vol. 1, Rome.

Bonsirven, Joseph (1948), *Le divorce dans le Nouveau Testament,* Desclée, Paris.

Bouillard, Henri (1944), *Conversion et grace chez s. Thomas d'Aquin,* Aubier, Éditions Montaigne, Paris.

Boularand, Ephrem (1939), *La venue de l'homme à la foi d'après S. Jean Chrysostôme,* Analecta Gregoriana, Rome.

Bouyer, Louis (1954), *Du Protestantisme à l'Église,* Éditions du Cerf, Paris.

Bredvold, Louis I. (1959), *The Intellectual Milieu of John Dryden,* University of Michigan Press, Ann Arbor, Michigan.

de Broglie, Guy (1953), 'La vraie notion thomiste des "praeambula fidei"', *Gregorianum* xxiv.

Browne, Sir Thomas (1977), *Religio Medici,* in *Sir Thomas Browne: The Major Works,* ed. C. A. Patrides, Penguin, London.

Cartwright, Richard (1962), 'Propositions', in *Analytical Philosophy,* ed. R. J. Butler, Blackwell, Oxford.

Castellio, Sebastian (1554), *De haereticis, an sint persequendi,* repr. 1954, Geneva.

Castellio, Sebastian (1981), *De arte dubitandi et confidendi, ignorandi et sciendi,* (written 1563 but not published), ed. Elisabeth Feist Hirsch, Leiden.

de Castro, Alphonsus (1543), *Adversus omnes haereses,* Cologne.

Catechism of the Catholic Church (1994), Veritas, Dublin.

Chadwick, Owen (1987), *From Bossuet to Newman,* 2nd edn, CUP, Cambridge.

Chakrabarti, Arindam (1994), 'Telling and Letting Know', in Matilal, B. K. and Chakrabarti, A., eds, *Knowing from Words,* Kluwer, London.

Charron, Pierre (1986), *De la sagesse,* ed. Barbara Negroni, Fayard, Paris (orig. pub. Paris, 1604).

Charron, Pierre (1970), *Le petit traicté de la sagesse,* in *Oeuvres,* Slatkine, Geneva (orig. pub. Paris, 1635).

de Chateaubriand, François (1951), *Mémoires d'Outre-Tombe,* Vol. 1, Gallimard, Paris.

Chillingworth, William (1788), *Works,* London.

Cicero, Marcus Tullius (1928), *De republica, De legibus,* (Latin w. Eng tr. by C. W. Keyes) Heinemann, London.

Cicero, Marcus Tullius (1933), *De natura deorum; Academica,* (Latin w. Eng tr. by H. Rackham, Heinemann, London.

Cicero, Marcus Tullius (1969), *Academicorum reliquiae cum Lucullo,* recognovit O. Plasberg. Teubner, Stuttgart.

Cicero, Marcus Tullius (1994), *De officiis,* ed. M. Winterbottom, Oxford Classical Texts, Clarendon Press, Oxford.

Clement of Alexandria (1919), *Protreptikon,* tr. as *Exhortation to the Greeks* by G. W. Butterworth, in *Clement of Alexandria,* Heinemann, London.

Clement of Alexandria (1953), *Stromate II,* Sources Chrétiennes no. 38, intro. and notes by Th. Camelot O.P., tr. Cl. Mondésert S.J., Éditions du Cerf, Paris.

Clement of Alexandria (1981), *Stromate V* (2 vols.), Sources Chrétiennes nos. 278, 279, tr. and ed. Alain Le Boulluec, Éditions du Cerf, Paris.

Clement of Alexandria (1997), *Stromate VII,* Sources Chrétiennes no. 428, tr. and ed. Alain Le Boulluec, Éditions du Cerf, Paris.

Coady, C. A. J. (1992), *Testimony,* Clarendon Press, Oxford.

Collins, Raymond F. (1992), *Divorce in the New Testament,* Liturgical Press, Collegeville, Minn.

Congar, Yves, O.P. (1966), *Tradition and traditions,* trs. Michael Naseby and Thomas Rainborough, Burns & Oates, London.

Congar, Yves, O.P. (1983), *I Believe in the Holy Spirit,* Geoffrey Chapman, London.

Congar, Yves, O.P. and Dupuy, B-P., eds (1968), *Vatican II: La Révélation divine* (2 vols), Éditions du Cerf, Paris.

St. Cyril of Alexandria (1987), *St. Cyril of Alexandria: Letters 1–50,* tr. John McEnerney, CUA Press, Washington.

Denzinger, H. (1957), *The Sources of Catholic Dogma,* 30th edn, tr. Roy J. DeFerrari, Herder, St. Louis.

Des Maizeaux, Pierre (1725), *An Historical and Critical Account of the Life and Writings of William Chillingworth,* London.

The Divine Office (1974), 3 vols., Collins, London.

Dodd, C. H. (1928), *The Authority of the Bible,* Nisbet, London.

Dodd, C. H. (1952), *According to the Scriptures,* Nisbet, London.

Dulles, Avery, S.J (1964), 'The Theology of Revelation', *Theological Studies,* Vol. 25.

Dulles, Avery, S.J (1980), 'The Symbolic Structure of Revelation', *Theological Studies,* Vol. 41.

Dummett, Michael (1994), 'Testimony and Memory', in Matilal, B. K. and Chakrabarti, A., eds, *Knowing from Words,* Kluwer, London.

Duns Scotus, John (1639a), *Quaestiones in lib. III sententiarum,* in *Opera,* Vol. 7, Lyons.

Duns Scotus, John (1639b), *Reportata parisiense,* in *Opera,* Vol. 11, Lyons.

Duns Scotus, John (1639c), *Quaestiones quodlibetales,* in *Opera,* Vol. 12, Lyons.

Duroux, Benoît, O.P. (1963), *La psychologie de la foi chez St. Thomas d'Aquin,* Desclée, Tournai.

Erasmus, Desiderius (1979), *The Praise of Folly,* tr. Clarence H. Miller, Yale University Press, New Haven.

Ermel, J. (1963), *Les sources de la foi,* Desclée, Tournai.

Evans, Gareth (1982), *The varieties of reference,* Clarendon Press, Oxford.

Frede, Michael (1987), *Essays in Ancient Philosophy,* Clarendon Press, Oxford.

Frege, Gottlob (1988), 'Thoughts', in Nathan Salmon and Scott Soames, eds, *Propositions and Attitudes,* OUP, Oxford.

232 *Divine Faith*

Fricker, Elizabeth (1994), 'Against Gullibility', in Matilal, B. K. and Chakrabarti, A., eds, *Knowing from Words*, Kluwer, London.
Galen, *De pulsuum differentiis*.
Gardeil, Ambroise. O.P. 'Crédibilité', *Dictionnaire de théologie catholique*, Vol. 3.
Garrigou-Lagrange, Reginald, O.P. (1952), *Grace: Commentary on the Summa Theologiae of St. Thomas, 1a2ae, qq. 109–14*, tr. The Dominican Nuns, Corpus Christi Monastery, Herder, St. Louis.
Geach, Peter (1977), 'Faith', in *The Virtues*, CUP, Cambridge.
Geiselmann, J. R. (1958), 'Un malentendu éclairci. La relation Écriture–Tradition dans la théologie catholique', *Istina*, 5.
Geiselmann, J. R. (1962), *Die Heiliger Schrift und die Tradition*, Herder, Freiburg.
St. Gregory the Great, *Ep.* XXV, P.L. 78, 478.
St. Gregory the Great, *Hom.* 26, P.L. 76, 1197.
St. Gregory of Nyssa, *In Hexameron*, P.G. 44, 61.
Grice, Paul (1989), *Studies in the Way of Words*, Harvard University Press, Cambridge, Mass.
Grotius, Hugo (1859), *On the Truth of the Christian Religion*, tr. T. Sedger, London.
Hacking, Ian (1975), *The emergence of probability*, CUP, Cambridge.
Hanson, A. T. (1983), *The Living Utterances of God*, Darton, Longman & Todd, London.
Hanson, R. P. C. (1962), *Tradition in the Early Church*, SCM, London.
Hardwig, John (1985), 'Epistemic Dependence', *Journal of Philosophy*, July.
Harent, Stanislas, 'Foi', in *Dictionnaire de théologie catholique*, Vol. 6.
Helm, Paul (1972), 'Revealed Propositions and Timeless Truth', *Religious Studies*, 8.
Hooker, Richard (1990), 'A Learned and Comfortable Sermon of the Certaintie and Perpetuitie of Faith in the Elect', in *Folger Library Edition of the Works of Richard Hooker, Vol. 5: Tractates and Sermons*, Belknap Press, Cambridge, Mass.
Hugh of St. Victor, *Quaest. in epistolas Pauli*, P.L. 175, 438.
Hugh of St. Victor (1951), *On the sacraments*, tr. Roy J. DeFerrari, The Medieval Academy of America, Cambridge, Mass.
Hume, David (1911), *A Treatise of Human Nature*, 2 vols, J. M. Dent & Sons, London.
Hume, David (1975), *An Enquiry concerning Human Understanding*, 3rd edn, ed. P. H. Nidditch, Clarendon Press, Oxford.
Jenkins, John, C.S.C. (1997), *Knowledge and faith in Thomas Aquinas*, CUP, Cambridge.
St. Jerome, *Commentariorum in Epistolam ad Galatas*, P.L. 26, 307.
St. John of the Cross (1979), *The Ascent of Mount Carmel*, in *The Collected Works of St. John of the Cross*, trs. Kieran Kavanaugh O.C.D. and O. Rodriguez O.C.D., Institute of Catholic Studies, Washington.
St. John Damascene (1958), *De fide orthodoxa*, in *Writings*, tr. Frederic H. Chase jr., Fathers of the Church Inc., New York.
Justin Martyr (1948), *The first apology, The second apology, Dialogue with Trypho, Exhortation to the Greeks, Discourse to the Greeks, The monarchy*, tr. Thomas B. Falls, Christian Heritage, New York.
Lamont, John (1996a), 'Stump and Swinburne on revelation', *Religious Studies*.
Lamont, John (1996b), 'Believing that God exists because the Bible says so', *Faith and Philosophy*, January.
Lamont, John (1996c), 'Newman on faith and certainty', *International Journal for Philosophy of Religion*.
Lamont, John (1997), 'Aquinas on divine simplicity', *The Monist*, October.
Latourelle, René (1966), *Théologie de la révélation*, 2nd edn, Desclée de Brouwer, Bruges.
Latourelle, René, and Fisichella, Rino, eds. (2000), *Dictionary of Fundamental Theology*, Herder, New York.

Leeuwen, Henry G. van. (1963) *The Problem of Certainty in English Thought, 1630–1690*, Martinus Nijhoff, The Hague.

Leith, John H., ed. (1973), *Creeds of the Churches*, revised edn, John Knox Press, Richmond.

Lemmon, E. J. (1966) 'Sentences, statements and propositions', in *British Analytic Philosophy*, ed. Bernard Williams, Alan Montefiore, Routledge and Kegan Paul, London.

Leo XIII (1897), encyclical *Divinum illud munus*.

Leontius of Byzantium, *Contra Nestorianos et Eutychianos*, P.G. 86(1), 1257.

Lilla, Salvatore (1971), *Clement of Alexandria*, OUP, Oxford.

Locke, John (1751a), *A third letter concerning Toleration*, in *Works*, 5th edn, London.

Locke, John (1751b), *A second letter concerning Toleration*, in *Works*, 5th edn, London.

Locke, John (1751c), *The Reasonableness of Christianity as delivered in the Scriptures*, in *Works*, 5th edn, London.

Locke, John (1975), *An Essay concerning Human Understanding*, 4th edn with additions, ed. Peter H. Nidditch, Clarendon Press, Oxford.

Locke, John (1979), *The Correspondence of John Locke, Vol. V: Letters 1702–2198*, ed. E. S. de Beer, Clarendon Press, Oxford.

Peter Lombard (1971–81), *Magistri Petri Lombardi Parisiensis episcopi Sententiae in IV libris distinctae*, 3rd edn, Editiones Collegii S. Bonaventurae ad Claras Aquas, Grottaferrate.

de Lugo, John, S.J. (1891), *Tractatus de virtute fidei divina*, in *Disputationes scholasticae et morales*, Vol. 1, new edn, ed. J. B. Fournials, Vivès, Paris.

Luther, Martin (1964), *Lectures on Galatians, 1535*, in *Luther's Works*, Vol. 27, ed. Jaroslav Pelikan, Walter A. Hansen, tr. Jaroslav Pelikan, Concordia Publishing House, Saint Louis.

McDowell, John (1988), 'Criteria, Defeasibility and Knowledge', in Dancy, Jonathan, ed., *Perceptual Knowledge*, OUP, Oxford.

McDowell, John (1994), 'Knowledge by Hearsay', in Matilal, B. K., and Chakrabarti, A., eds, *Knowing from Words*, Kluwer, London.

Mackenzie, J. F. (1962), 'The Social Character of Inspiration', *Catholic Biblical Quarterly*, 24.

Mackenzie, R. A. F. (1958), 'Some Problems in the Field of Inspiration', *Catholic Biblical Quarterly*, 20.

Mackey, J. P. (1962), *The modern theology of tradition*, Darton, Longman and Todd, London.

Mackie, J. L. (1970), 'The Possibility of Innate Knowledge', *Proceedings of the Aristotelian Society*.

Macintyre, Alasdair (1990), *First principles, final ends, and contemporary philosophical issues*, Marquette University Press, Milwaukee.

Mandouze, André (1968), *Saint Augustin, l'aventure de la raison et de la grâce*, Études Augustiniennes, Paris.

Mangenot, E., 'Inspiration de l'Écriture', *Dictionnaire de théologie catholique*, 7(2).

Marín-Sola, F. (1924), *L'evolution homogène du dogme catholique*, 2nd edn, 2 vols., Librairie de l'oeuvre de Saint-Paul, Fribourg.

Marshall, John (1992), 'John Locke and Latitudinarianism', in *Philosophy, science and religion in England 1640–1700*, ed. Richard Knoll, Richard Ashcraft, Perez Zagorin, CUP, Cambridge.

Mascall, E. L. (1946), *Christ, the Christian and the Church*, Longmans, Green & Co., London.

Matilal, B. K. (1994), 'Understanding, Knowing, and Justification' in Matilal, B. K., and Chakrabarti, A., eds, *Knowing from Words*, Kluwer, London.

Matilal, B. K., and Chakrabarti, A., eds, (1994), *Knowing from Words*, Kluwer, London.

Mersch, Émile, S.J. (1938), *The Whole Christ*, tr. John R. Kelly S.J., Dennis Dobson, London.

de Montaigne, Michel (1992), '*Apologie de Raimond Sebond*', in *Les Essais*, Vol. II, ed. Pierre Villey, Quadrige/Presse Universitaires de France, Paris (orig. pub. 1580).

Newman, John Henry (1900), *Fifteen Sermons preached before the University of Oxford*, 3rd edn, Longmans, Green & Co., London.

Newman, John Henry (1958), 'An Unpublished Paper by Cardinal Newman on the Development of Doctrine', ed. C. Stephen Dessain, *Journal of Theological Studies*.

Newman, John Henry (1969), *Tract 85*, AMS Press Inc., New York (orig. pub. 1838).

Newman, John Henry (1989), *An essay on the development of Christian doctrine*, University of Notre Dame Press, Notre Dame.

O'Collins, Gerald, S.J. (1993), *Retrieving Fundamental Theology*, Geoffrey Chapman, London.

Origen (1965), *Contra Celsum*, tr. Henry Chadwick, CUP, Cambridge.

Origen (1981), *Homélies sur le Lévitique*, Vol. II (homélies VIII–XVI), Sources Chrétiennes no. 287, tr. Marcel Borret S.J., Éditions du Cerf, Paris.

Origen (1982), *Commentaire sur St. Jean, tome IV*, tr. Cécile Blanc, Éditions du Cerf, Paris.

Origen (1985), *Homélies sur la Génèse*, Sources Chrétiennes no. 7 bis, 2nd edn, tr. Louis Doutreleau, Éditions du Cerf, Paris.

Ott, Ludwig (1960), *Fundamentals of Catholic Theology*, 4th edn, tr. Patrick Lynch, The Mercier Press, Cork.

Owen, John (1826), *Of the Divine Original, Authority, Self-Evidencing Light and Power of the Scriptures*, (orig. pub. 1659), in *Works of John Owen D.D.*, Vol. IV, ed. Thomas A. Russell, London.

Owen, John (1852), *The Reason of Faith: or, the grounds whereon the Scripture is Believed to be the word of God with faith divine and supernatural*, (orig. pub. 1677), in *The Works of John Owen, D.D.*, Vol. IV, ed. Rev. William H. Goold, Johnstone and Hunter, Edinburgh.

Pannenberg, Wolfhart (1967), 'Response to the Discussion', in *New Frontiers in Theology*, Vol. III, ed. John B. Cobb Jr and James M. Robinson, Harper & Row, New York.

Pannenberg, Wolfhart (1991), *Systematic Theology* Vol. I, tr. Geoffrey W. Bromiley, T.&T. Clark, Edinburgh.

Philo of Alexandria (1974), *Quod omnis probus liber sit* (*Oeuvres de Philon d'Alexandrie* 28), tr. Madeleine Petit, Éditions du Cerf, Paris.

Pico della Mirandola, Giovanni (1520), *Examen vanitatis doctrinae gentium, et veritatis christianae disciplinae*.

Plantinga, Alvin (1993), *Warrant: The Current Debate*, OUP, Oxford.

Plantinga, Alvin (2000), *Warranted Christian Belief*, OUP, Oxford.

Popkin, Richard (1979), *The History of Scepticism from Erasmus to Spinoza*, University of California Press, Berkeley.

Putnam, Hilary (1975), 'The meaning of "meaning"', in *Mind, Language and Reality*, CUP.

Rahner, Karl (1961), *Inspiration in the Bible*, tr. Charles H. Henkey, Nelson, Edinburgh.

Reventlow, Henning Graf (1985), *Problems of Old Testament Theology in the 20th Century*, tr. John Bowden, SCM Press, London.

Richard of St. Victor (1958), *De Trinitate*, ed. Jean Ribailler, Vrin, Paris.

Rondet, Henri. (1948) *Gratia Christi*, Beauchesne, Paris.

Rondet, Henri. (1964) *Essais sur la théologie de la grace*, Beauchesne, Paris.

Rousselot, Pierre (1913), 'Remarques sur l'histoire de la notion de la foi naturelle', *Recherches de science religieuse.*

Du Roy, Olivier (1966), *L'intelligence de la foi en la Trinité selon S. Augustin,* Études Augustiniennes, Paris.

Sandbach, F. H. (1930), 'ΕΝΝΟΙΑ and ΠΡΟΛΗΨΙΣ in the Stoic Theory of Knowledge', *Classical Quarterly,* 24.

Santayana, George (1923), *Skepticism and Animal Faith,* Constable, London.

Schiffer, Stephen (1989), *Remnants of Meaning,* MIT Press, London.

Schillebeeckx, Edward (1967), *Revelation and Theology,* Vol. I, Sheed & Ward, London.

Schmitt, John J. (1992) 'Pre-Exilic Hebrew Prophecy', *Anchor Bible Dictionary,* Vol. 5, Doubleday, London.

Schofield, Malcolm (1980), 'Preconceptions, Argument and God', in *Doubt and Dogmatism,* ed. Myles Burnyeat, Jonathan Barnes, Clarendon Press, Oxford.

Searle, John (1969), *Speech Acts,* CUP, Cambridge.

Skorupski, John (1997), 'Meaning, use, verification', in *Blackwell Companion to the Philosophy of Language,* Blackwell, Oxford.

Slater, Alan, and Lewis, Michael (2002), *Introduction to Infant Development,* OUP, Oxford.

Smith, Richard F., S.J. (1968), 'Inspiration and Inerrancy', *Jerome Biblical Commentary,* Geoffrey Chapman, London.

Snowdon, Paul (1988), 'Perception, Vision and Causation', in Dancy, Jonathan, ed., *Perceptual Knowledge,* OUP, Oxford.

Sosa, Ernest (1991), *Knowledge in Perspective,* CUP, Cambridge.

Spanneut, Michel (1957), *Le Stoïcisme des pères de l'Église,* Seuil, Paris.

Stephen, Leslie (1876), *History of English Thought in the Eighteenth Century,* Vol. 1, Smith, Elder & Co., London.

Stump, Eleonore (1994), Review of Richard Swinburne's *Revelation,* in *The Philosophical Review,* October.

Swinburne, Richard (1992), *Revelation,* Clarendon Press, Oxford.

Tanner, Norman, and Alberigo, Giuseppe, eds (1990), *Decrees of the Ecumenical Councils,* 2 vols., Georgetown University Press, Washington.

Tavard, George (1959), *Holy Writ or Holy Church,* Burns & Oates, London.

Tavard, George (1978), *The Seventeenth-Century Tradition: A Study in Recusant Thought,* E. J. Brill, Leiden.

Temple, William (1934), *Nature, Man and God,* Macmillan, London.

Tertullian (1950), *Apologetical works,* tr.by Rudolph Arbesmann, Sr. Emily Joseph Daly [and] Edwin A. Quain, Catholic University of America Press, Washington, DC.

Thiemann, Ronald (1985). *Revelation and Theology,* University of Notre Dame Press, Notre Dame.

Tillotson, John (1707), *The Works of the Most Reverend Doctor John Tillotson...being all that were published by his Grace himself,* 5th edn, London.

Tillotson, John (1722), *Works,* 3nd edn, 2 vols., ed. Ralph Barker, London.

Turmel, J. (1936), *Histoire des Dogmes,* Vol. 5, Rieder, Paris.

Tyndale, William (1850), *An Answer to Sir Thomas More's Dialogue, The Supper of the Lord,* CUP, Cambridge (orig. pub. 1531).

van der Eynde, D. (1933), *Les normes de l'enseignement chrétien dans la littérature patristique des trois premières siècles,* Gembloux, Paris.

van Noort, G. (1961), *Dogmatic Theology, Vol. III: The Sources of Revelation* tr. and rev. John J. Castelot and William R. Murphy, The Newman Press, Westminster, Maryland.

Waldman, Theodore (1959), 'Origin of the Legal Doctrine of Reasonable Doubt', *Journal of the History of Ideas XX.*

Walgrave, Jan Hendrik (1972), *Unfolding Revelation,* Hutchinson & Co., London.

Walzer, Richard (1949), *Galen on Jews and Christians*, OUP, Oxford.
Webster, John (2000), 'Faith', in *The Blackwell Encyclopedia of Modern Christian Thought*, ed. Alister E. McGrath, Blackwell, Oxford.
Whitaker, William (1849), *A Disputation on Holy Scripture against the Papists, especially Bellarmine and Stapleton*, tr. William Fitzgerald, CUP, Cambridge (Latin original 1588).
William of Auxerre (also known as Guillelmus Altissidorensis) (1986), *Summa Aurea*, ed. Jean Ribailler, Spicilegium Bonaventurianum, Paris.
Williams, Bernard (1973), 'Deciding to Believe', in *Problems of the Self*, CUP, Cambridge.
Wittgenstein, Ludwig (1974), 'Elementary propositions', in *Philosophical Grammar*, part 1, ed. Rush Rhees, tr. A. Kenny, Blackwell, Oxford.
Zagzebski, Linda (1996), *Virtues of the Mind*, CUP, Cambridge.

Secondary sources

Abraham, W. J. (1982), *Divine Revelation and the limits of historical criticism*, OUP, Oxford.
Abraham, W. J. (1990), 'The Epistemological Significance of the Inner Witness of the Holy Spirit', *Faith and Philosophy*, October.
Alanus de Insulis, *Distinctiones dictionum theologicalium*, P.L. 210, 790.
Albert the Great (1894), *Commentarium in tertium librum sententiarum*, in *Opera omnia*, Vol. 28, ed. S. Borgnet, Vivès, Paris.
Anderson, B. (1957), *Understanding the Old Testament*, Prentice-Hall, Englewood Cliffs.
Annas, Julia (1990), 'Stoic epistemology', in *Companions to Ancient Thought: 1. Epistemology*, CUP, Cambridge.
St. Thomas Aquinas (1879), *In psalmos davidis*, in *Opera omnia*, Vol. 18, ed. E. Fretté, Vivès, Paris.
St. Thomas Aquinas. (1964–5a), *De caritate*, in *Quaestiones disputatae*, Vol. 2, ed. R. Spiazzi O.P., 10th edn, Marietti, Rome.
St. Thomas Aquinas (1964–5c), *De spe,* in *Quaestiones disputatae*, Vol. 2, ed. R. Spiazzi O.P., 10th edn, Marietti, Rome.
St. Thomas Aquinas (1968), *De rationibus fidei*, ed. H.-F. Dondaine, in Leonine edn, Vol. 40, Rome.
St. Augustine (1949), *De moribus ecclesiae catholicae*, in Bibliothèque Augustinienne, *Oeuvres de Saint Augustin*, Vol. 1, tr. B. Roland-Gosselin, Desclée de Brouwer, Paris.
St. Augustine (1950), *De magistro*, tr. Joseph M. Colleran, Longmans, Green & Co., London.
St. Augustine (1957), *De fide rerum quae non videntur*, in Bibliothèque Augustinienne, *Oeuvres de Saint Augustin*, Vol. 8, tr. J. Pegon, Desclée de Brouwer, Paris.
St. Augustine (1961), *Contra epistulam fundamenti*, in Bibliothèque Augustinienne, *Oeuvres de Saint Augustin*, Vol. 17, tr. R. Jolivet, M. Jourjon, Desclée de Brouwer, Paris.
St. Augustine. (1974), *Contra duas epistolas pelagianorum,* in Bibliothèque Augustinienne, *Oeuvres de Saint Augustin*, Vol. 23, ed. F.-J. Thonnard, E. Bleuzen, tr. A.C. de Beer, Desclée de Brouwer, Paris.
Austin, J. L. (1976) *How to Do Things With Words*, 2nd edn, OUP, Oxford.
Axtell, Guy (1997), 'Recent Work on Virtue Epistemology', *American Philosophical Quarterly*, January.

Ayers, Michael (1993), *Locke: epistemology and ontology*, Routledge, London.

Barr, James (1974), 'Trends and Prospects in Biblical Theology', *Journal of Theological Studies* XXV.

Barr, James (1982), *Old and New in Interpretation*, 2nd edn, SCM Press, London.

Baur, Chrysostomus, O.S.B. (1959), *John Chrysostom and his Time*, Sands & Co., London.

St. Bernard of Clairvaux (1963), *De consideratione*, in *Sancti Bernardi opera*, Vol. 3, ed. J. Leclercq O.S.B., H. M. Rochais O.S.B., Editiones Cisterciensis, Rome.

Bérubé, Camille (1983), *De l'homme à Dieu selon Duns Scot, Henri de Gand et Olivi*, Bibliotheca seraphico capuccina, Rome.

Blehl, Vincent Ferrer (2001), *Pilgrim Journey: John Henry Newman 1801–1845*, Burns & Oates, London.

Boethius, Anicius Manlius Severinus (1973), *The theological tractates*, (Latin text w. Eng. Tr. by H.F. Stewart and E.K. Rand and S.J. Tester), new edn, Loeb Classical Library 74, Heinemann, London.

St. Bonaventure (1941), *In III Sententiarum*, in *Opera Theologica Selecta*, Vol. 3, ed. L. Bello, Quaracchi, Florence.

St. Bonaventure (1938), *In II Sententiarum*, in *Opera Theologica Selecta*, Vol. 2, ed. L. Bello, Quaracchi, Florence

de Bovis, André (1962), 'Foi (doutes dans la vie de foi)' in *Dictionnaire de spiritualité*, Vol. 5.

Bultmann, Rudolf (1968) 'πιστεύω', in *Theological Dictionary of the New Testament*, Vol. 6, ed. Gerhard Friedrich, tr. Geoffrey W. Bromiley, Eerdmans, Grand Rapids.

Burtchaell, James (1969), *Catholic theories of biblical inspiration since 1810*, CUP, London.

Butler, Joseph (1896), *The Analogy of Religion*, Clarendon Press, Oxford.

Camelot, Th. O.P. (1945), *Foi et gnose*, Vrin, Paris.

Camelot, Th. O.P. (1967), 'Autorité de l'Écriture, autorité de l'Église; à propos d'un texte de Saint Augustin', in *Mélanges offertes à Marie-Dominique Chenu*, Vrin, Paris.

Campbell, Kenneth L. (1986), *The Intellectual Struggle of the English Papists in the Seventeenth Century*, The Edwin Mellen Press, Lewiston/Queenston.

Cano, Melchior (1890), *De locis theologis*, in *Melchioris Cani Opera*, Forzani, Rome.

Cessario, Romanus, O.P. (1996), *Christian Faith and the Theological Life*, CUA Press, Washington, D.C.

Cessario, Romanus, O.P. (1991), *The moral virtues and theological life*, University of Notre Dame Press, London.

Chadwick, Henry (1966), *Early Christian Thought and the Classical Tradition*, Clarendon Press, Oxford.

Chenu, Marie-Dominique, O.P. (1923), 'Contribution à l'histoire du traité sur la foi. Commentaire historique de II–II, 1, 2', in *Mélanges thomistes*, Kain, Le Saulchoir.

Chenu, Marie-Dominique, O.P. (1932a), *La psychologie de la foi dans la théologie du XIIIe s.*, in *Études d'histoire littéraire et doctrinale du XIIIe siècle, IIe sér.*, Paris/Ottawa.

Chenu, Marie-Dominique, O.P (1932b), 'Notes de travail', in *Bulletin thomiste*.

Chenu, Marie-Dominique, O.P. (1950), *Introduction à St. Thomas d'Aquin*, Vrin, Paris.

Childs, Brevard (1970), *Biblical Theology in Crisis*, Westminster Press, Philadelphia.

Crane, Tim, ed. (1992), *The contents of experience*, CUP, Cambridge.

Cressy, Serenus (Hugh Paulin de) (1647), *Exomologesis*, Paris.

Cullmann, Oscar (1967), *Salvation in History*, tr. Sidney G. Sowers, SCM Press, London.

Cushman, Robert E. (1955), 'Faith and Reason', in *A Companion to the Study of St. Augustine*, ed. Roy W. Battenhouse, OUP, New York.

Dancy, Jonathan, ed. (1988), *Perceptual Knowledge*, OUP, Oxford.

Dillon, John M. (1977), *The Middle Platonists*, Duckworth, London.

Dulles, Avery, S.J. (1994), *The Assurance of Things Hoped For*, OUP, Oxford.

Dummett, Michael (1987), 'Reply to McDowell', in Barry M. Taylor ed., *Michael Dummett: Contributions to Philosophy*, Martinus Nijhoff, Dordrecht.

Dummett, Michael (1991), *The Logical Basis of Metaphysics*, Duckworth, London.

Dummett, Michael (1993), 'Language and Communication', in *The Seas of Language*, Clarendon Press, Oxford.

Durandus of St. Pourçain (1964), *In Petri Lombardi Sententias Theologicas Commentariorum*, Gregg International Publishers Ltd., Farnborough (repr. of 1571 Venice edn).

Eichrodt, Walther (1961–67), *Theology of the Old Testament*, tr. John Baker, SCM Press, London.

Ellis, E. Earle (1957), *Paul's Use of the Old Testament*, Oliver & Boyd, Edinburgh/London.

Epictetus (1998), *Discourses, I*, Clarendon Press, Oxford.

Fricker, Elizabeth (1987), 'The Epistemology of Testimony', Proceedings of the Aristotelian Society, supp. vol.

Fricker, Elizabeth (1995), 'Telling and Trusting: Reductionism and Anti-Reductionism in the Epistemology of Testimony', critical notice of C. A. J. Coady's *Testimony*, in *Mind*, April.

Gardeil, Ambroise, O.P. (1928), *La crédibilité et l'apologetique*, 2nd edn, Gabalda, Paris.

Garrigou-Lagrange, Reginald, O.P. (1921), *De revelatione*, 2nd edn, Lecoffre, Paris.

Geiselmann, J. R. (1967), 'Das Konzil von Trient über das Verhältnis der Heiliger Schrift und der nicht geschriebenen Traditionen', in *Die mündliche Ueberlieferung*, ed. M. Schmaus, Munich.

Gilkey, Langdon (1961), 'Cosmology, Ontology and the Travail of Biblical Language', *Journal of Religion*, xli.

Gilson, Étienne (1943), *Introduction à l'étude de Saint Augustin*, 2nd edn, Vrin, Paris.

Griffin, Martin I. J. (1992), *Latitudinarianism in the Seventeenth-century Church of England*, New York, Brill.

Hanson, R. P. C. (1959), *Allegory and event: a study of the sources and significance of Origen's interpretation of Scripture*, SCM, London.

Heitz, Th. (1907), 'La philosophie et la foi dans l'oeuvre d'Abélard', in *Revue des sciences philosophiques et théologiques I*.

Helm, Paul (1973), *The Varieties of Belief*, George Allen & Unwin, London.

Holden, Henry (1658), *The Analysis of Divine Faith*, tr. by W.G., Paris.

Holte, Ragnar (1962), *Béatitude et Sagesse: Saint Augustin et le problème de la fin de l'homme dans la philosophie ancienne*, Études Augustiniennes, Paris.

Hooker, Richard (1977), *Laws of Ecclesiastical Polity*, in *Folger Library Edition of the Works of Richard Hooker*, Vol. 1, Medieval and Renaissance Texts & Studies, Binghamton, N.Y.

Hume, David (1976), *Dialogues concerning natural Religion*, ed. John V. Price, OUP, Oxford.

Isaac of Stella (1967–87), *Sermons, Sources Chrétiennes*, nos. 130, 207, 339, Éditions du Cerf, Paris.

John Capreolus (1904), *Defensiones theologiae Divi Thomae Aquinatis*, Vol. 5, ed. C. Paban, T. Pègues, Alfred Cattier, Turonibus.

John of St. Thomas (John Poinsot) (1884), *Tractatus de fide*, in *Cursus theologicus in summam theologicam D. Thomae*, Vol. 7, Vivès, Paris.

John of St. Thomas (John Poinsot) (1950), *The Gifts of the Holy Spirit*, tr. Dominic Hughes O.P., Sheed & Ward, New York.

Klein, P. (1971), 'A Proposed Definition of Propositional Knowledge', *Journal of Philosophy*, 68.

Lamont, John (1991), 'The nature of revelation', *New Blackfriars*, July/August.

Lamont, John (2001), 'Plantinga on Belief', *The Thomist*, October.

Leeming, Bernard (1960), *Principles of sacramental theology*, new edn, Newman Press, London.

Long, A. A., and Sedley, D. N. (1987), *The Hellenistic philosophers* (2 vols.), CUP, Cambridge.

de Lubac, Henri, S.J. (1946), *Surnaturel: Études historiques*, Aubier, Paris.

de Lubac, Henri, S.J. (1950), *Histoire et esprit*, Éditions Montaigne, Paris.

de Lubac, Henri, S.J. (1965), *Le Mystère du Surnaturel*, Aubier, Paris.

McCarthy, D. (1963), 'Personality, Society, and Inspiration', *Theological Studies*, 24.

McDonald, H. D. (1963), *Theories of Revelation*, George Allen & Unwin Ltd, London.

McDowell, John (1980), 'Meaning, Communication and Knowledge', in Zak van Straaten ed., *Philosophical Subjects*, Clarendon Press, Oxford.

McDowell, John (1994), *Mind and World,* Harvard University Press, London.

Macintyre, Alasdair (1985), *After virtue: a study in moral theory*, 2nd edn, Duckworth, London.

Macintyre, Alasdair (1990), *Three rival versions of moral enquiry*, London, Duckworth.

Madec, Goulven (1975), 'Christus scientia et sapientia nostra: Le principe de cohérence de la doctrine augustinienne', in *Recherches augustiniennes,* Vol. X.

Madec, Goulven (1971), 'Notes sur l'intelligence augustinienne de la foi', *Revue des études augustiniennes*.

Mersch, Émile, S.J. (1946), *La théologie du corps mystique*, Desclée de Brouwer, Paris.

Mondésert, Claude (1944), *Clément d'Alexandrie*, Aubier, Éditions Montaigne, Paris.

Mornay, Philippe du Plessis (1581), *De la vérité de la religion chrestienne*, Antwerp.

Newman, John Henry (1937), 'Cardinal Newman's Theses de Fide and His Proposed Introduction to the French Translation of the University Sermons', ed. Henry Tristram, *Gregorianum*, xviii.

Newman, John Henry (1979), *An essay in aid of a grammar of assent*, University of Notre Dame Press, Notre Dame (orig. pub. 1870).

Nichols, Aidan (1990), *From Newman to Congar*, T.&T. Clark, Edinburgh.

Nichols, Aidan (1991), *The Shape of Catholic Theology*, T&T. Clark, Edinburgh.

O'Daly, Gerard (1987), *Augustine's Philosophy of Mind*, Duckworth, London.

Oepke, Albrecht (1965), 'kalu,ptw', tr. Geoffrey W. Bromiley, in Gerhard Kittel ed., *Theological Dictionary of the New Testament* Vol. III (Θ – K), Eerdmans, Grand Rapids.

O'Meara, John J. (1997), *Understanding Augustine*, Four Courts Press, Dublin.

Orr, Robert (1967), *Reason and Authority: The Thought of William Chillingworth*, OUP, Oxford.

Osborn, E.F. (1957), *The Philosophy of Clement of Alexandria*, CUP, Cambridge.

Pannenberg, Wolfhart (1968), *Revelation as History*, tr. David Granskou, Macmillan, New York.

Pannenberg, Wolfhart (1971), *Basic Questions in Theology I and II*, tr. George H. Kelim, SCM Press, London.

Plantinga, Alvin. (1993) *Warrant and Proper Function*, OUP, Oxford.

de Poulpiquet, E. A. (1912), *L'objet integral de l'apologétique*, Bloud & Cie, Paris.

Prestige, G. L. (1940), *Fathers and Heretics*, SPCK, London.

Quine, W.V.O. (1953), 'Two Dogmas of Empiricism', in *From a Logical Point of View*, Harvard University Press, Cambridge, Mass.

Quine, W.V.O. (1960), *Word and Object*, MIT Press, New York.

Raitt, Jill, ed. (1981), *Shapers of Religious Traditions in Germany, Switzerland and Poland*, Yale University Press, London.

Raymond, P., 'Duns Scot'. *Dictionnaire de théologie catholique*, Vol. 4.

Reid, J. K. S. (1957), *The Authority of Scripture*, Methuen, London.

Reid, Thomas (1801), *An Inquiry into the Human Mind*, Bell & Bradfute, Edinburgh.

Reid, Thomas (1803), *Essays on the Intellectual Powers of Man*, Bell & Bradfute, Edinburgh.

Schillebeeckx, Edward (1963), *Christ the sacrament of the encounter with God*, Sheed & Ward, London.

Sergeant, John (1687), *The Second Catholic Letter*, London.

Sergeant, John (1688), *The Fifth Catholic Letter*, London.

Sommers, Fred (1982), *The Logic of Natural Language*, Clarendon Press, Oxford.

Stendahl, Krister (1962), 'Biblical Theology', in *The Interpreter's Dictionary of the Bible*, Vol. I, Abingdon Press, Nashville.

Stillingfleet, Edward (1700), *A Discourse concerning the Nature and Grounds of the Certainty of Faith*, in *Works*, Vol. VI, London.

Stillingfleet, Edward (1709), *Rational Account of the Grounds of the Protestant Religion*, in *Works*, Vol. IV, London.

Strawson, Peter (1971), 'Meaning and Truth', in *Logico-Linguistic Papers*, Methuen, London.

Suarez, Francis, S.J. (1856), *Tractatus de fide*, in *Opera omnia*, Vol. 12, ed. D. M. André, Vivès, Paris.

Todd, R. B. (1973), 'The Stoic Common Notions: a Re-examination and Reinterpretation', *Symbolae Osloenses*, xlviii.

Torrell, J.-P. (1996), *St. Thomas Aquinas, Vol. 1: The Person and his Work*, tr. Robert Royal, CUA Press, Washington.

Trethowan, Illtyd (1948), *Certainty philosophical and theological*, Dacre Press, Westminster.

Trevor-Roper, Hugh (1989), *Catholics, Anglicans and Puritans: Seventeenth-century Essays*, Fontana Press, London.

Tulloch, John (1966), *Rational Theology and Christian Philosophy in England in the Seventeenth Century*, 2nd edn, Georg Olms, Hildesheim (repr. of 1874 edn).

Vawter, Bruce (1972), *Biblical Inspiration*, Hutchinson and Co., London.

Veron, François (1660), *The Rule of Catholick Faith*, tr. Edward Sheldon, Paris.

von Rad, Gerhard (1962–65), *Old Testament Theology*, 2 vols., tr. D.M.G. Stalker, Oliver & Boyd, London.

Welbourne, Michael (1986), *The community of knowledge*, Aberdeen University Press, Aberdeen.

William of Auvergne (1963), *Opera Omnia*, Minerva, Frankfurt am Main (reprint of Paris 1674 edn)

William of St. Thierry (1959), *Deux traités sur la foi: Le Miroir de la foi, L'Enigme de la foi*, ed. and tr. M.-M. Davy, Vrin, Paris.

Williamson, Timothy (1995), 'Is Knowing a State of Mind?', *Mind*, July.

Wittgenstein, Ludwig (1967), *Philosophical Investigations*, 2nd edn, tr. G. E. M. Anscombe, Basil Blackwell, Oxford.

Wolterstorff, Nicholas (1995), *Divine Discourse*, CUP, Cambridge.

Wright, G. Ernest (1952), *God Who Acts*, Henry Regnery, Chicago.

Index